S0-BSE-047

# THE BIBLE AS BOOK
## THE FIRST PRINTED EDITIONS

# THE BIBLE AS BOOK
## THE FIRST PRINTED EDITIONS

*Edited by*

PAUL SAENGER AND KIMBERLY VAN KAMPEN

THE BRITISH LIBRARY
& OAK KNOLL PRESS
*in association with The Scriptorium:*
*Center for Christian Antiquities*
1999

FOR LEONARD E. BOYLE

First published 1999 by
The British Library
96 Euston Road
St Pancras
London NW1 2DB

Published exclusively in North and South America by
Oak Knoll Press
310 Delaware Street
New Castle
DE 19720

in association with
The Scriptorium: Center for Christian Antiquities
PO Box 770
Grand Haven
Michigan 49417-0770



British Library Cataloguing-in-Publication Data
A CIP record is available from The British Library

Library of Congress Cataloging-in-Publication Data

The Bible as book : the first printed editions /
edited by Paul Saenger and Kimberly Van Kampen.
p. cm
Includes bibliographical references and indexes.
ISBN 1-88471-892-2
1. Bible – Europe – History – Congresses. 2. Bible – Publication and distribution – Europe – History – 16th century – Congresses. 3. Bible – Publication and distribution – Europe – History – To 1500 – Congresses. 4. Incunabula. I. Saenger, Paul Henry, 1945- II. Van Kampen, Kimberly.
BS447.5.E85 B53 1999
220'.09'031 21 – dc21

99-042097

ISBN 1-88471-892-2 (Oak Knoll)
ISBN 0-7123-4601-5 (British Library)

Designed by John Trevitt
Typeset in England by Norman Tilley Graphics, Northampton
Printed in England by St Edmundsbury Press, Bury St Edmunds

# CONTENTS

# Contents

# CONTRIBUTORS

JULIÁN MARTÍN ABAD, *Biblioteca Nacional, Madrid*

GUY BEDOUELLE, *University of Fribourg*

KARLFRIED FROEHLICH, *Princeton Theological Seminary*

J. P. GUMBERT, *Rijks Universiteit Leiden, The Netherlands*

ANTHONY KENNY, *Oxford University*

PAUL NEEDHAM, *Scheide Library, Princeton University*

ADRIAN K. OFFENBERG, *Bibliotheca Rosenthaliana, Amsterdam University*

NIGEL F. PALMER, *Oxford University*

PAUL SAENGER, *The Newberry Library*

WILLIAM H. SHERMAN, *University of Maryland*

DAVID STEINMETZ, *Duke University*

KIMBERLY VAN KAMPEN, *Research Group on Manuscript Evidence*

MICHAEL WELTE, *Institut fur Neutestamentliche Textforschung*

# LIST OF ILLUSTRATIONS

(reproduced between pages 116 and 117)

## List of Illustrations



Photographs courtesy of: British Library; Huntington Library; Newberry Library; The Scriptorium; Biblioteca Palatina, Parma; Staatsbibliothek Preussischer Kulturbesitz, Berlin; Bibliotheek der Rijksuniversiteit, Leiden; Museum Catharijneconvent, Utrecht; John Rylands Library, Manchester; Bayerische Staatsbibliothek, Munich; Universitätsbibliothek, Heidelberg; Universtitätsbibliothek, Innsbruck.

# FOREWORD

*The Bible As Book: the First Printed Editions* is the second volume in a series based on the Hampton Court, Herefordshire, conferences sponsored by The Scriptorium: Center for Christian Antiquities in co-operation with the Van Kampen Foundation. The symposium was conducted in May 1996 and was dedicated to the investigation of Bibles printed prior to 1520. In keeping with the theme of the Bible as a book, an international programme of delegates made informative and provoking contributions to topics related to the first printed editions of the biblical text. Unlike the first volume in this series, which addressed the epoch of time during which the Bible was circulated and venerated in manuscript format, this collection of papers confines itself to a span of approximately sixty years – roughly from Gutenberg to Erasmus – and in so doing constitutes an intense examination of this period which produced well over 100 Latin editions, and numerous issues in Hebrew, German, and other vernacular languages.

As editors, we have hoped to present these findings less as contributions to the history of early printing, although indeed they are, but rather as a multi-faceted portrait of a text about which, all too often, errant generalizations are made. The Bible, as a text and as a physical object, is transformed in virtually every generation and in the hands of every user. Even in its role as the first printed text, its relevance and usage varied: for some a commodity, for others a tool for revolution; an innovation of technology, and at the same time a revival of lost medieval technique; a means of stabilization of an historically unstable text, yet also an instrument for scholarship that produced new versions of old texts. Within a topic often overshadowed by the name and accomplishments of the Bible's first printer, this volume is a first in its scope and approach to the other 'Bible Stories', if you will, of the cradle of printing.

One paper laments the lack of a comprehensive catalogue of incunable Bibles. We took this opportunity to furnish the scaffolding for such a work when we devised the Index of Incunables Cited as an appendix to the volume. This apparatus provides at a glance a list of all editions addressed in the volume, arranged by the reference numbers designated by Frederick R. Goff in *Incunabula in American Libraries*, Third Census, New York, Kraus International Publications, 1989. In the event that a Goff number is not available, alternative references are supplied in parentheses, including those for sixteenth-century books. Editions are listed in the order of their Goff numbers (by alphabetical designation and then by date); non-Goff references are listed by date within their various title headings.

We would like to extend our appreciation to those who participated in the 1996 conference, as contributors or organizers, and whose individual efforts have become part of the whole of this work. We also want to recognize those scholars who were unable to submit their papers, but who added their own richness of knowledge and personality to the forum: Eberhard Koenig; François Dupuigrenet-Desrousilles, J. B. Trapp, Elizabeth Eisenstein, David Daniell, Mervyn Jannetta and Lotte Hellinga. We express our thanks as well to David Way and John Trevitt at the British Library, and Robert Fleck of Oak Knoll Books, who have produced this series of beautiful books about beautiful books. In addition, a number of colleagues and Scriptorium and Van Kampen Foundation employees have assisted the editors in this project and we extend our appreciation to them: Dr Timothy Graham, Sidney Tibbetts, Lois Goossen, and Ellen Herron, who also prepared the Bibliography. And finally, we wish to dedicate this work to Leonard E. Boyle – model, mentor, and friend.

*21 June 1999*

PAUL SAENGER
The Newberry Library

KIMBERLY VAN KAMPEN
Research Group on
Manuscript Evidence

# INTRODUCTION

## *Anthony Kenny*

OUR WORD 'Bible' is the sawn-off Greek word for 'book', and during many centuries the history of the book is in large part the history of the Bible. The essays in this collection narrate elements of the two histories during a period when they were particularly closely interwoven: the century between 1450 and 1550. Our authors throw a fascinating light on many aspects of society, from mechanical innovation to devotional meditation; and they document the origins of many features of both Bibles and books that we so take for granted as to credit them with immemorial antiquity.

In the Middle Ages in western Europe the Bible used for church reading, for private study, or for theological research in the universities, was the Latin version, deriving from the fourth-century translation made from the Hebrew Old Testament and the Greek New Testament bearing the name of St Jerome. The Vulgate text, as it was called, circulated with many variants of structure and detail. Though it never attained the scrupulous uniformity maintained by manuscripts of the Hebrew Bible, it was moulded to a degree of standardization by the University of Paris in the thirteenth century. As Nigel Palmer observes, the Bible in the later Middle Ages was as much a concept as a tangible tome; Bibles existed and were reproduced as partial collections of biblical books as well as in their entirety. Complete Vulgate Bibles, varying somewhat in their context, fell into two classes: the rich formal texts on vellum individually commissioned for liturgical use by churches and monasteries, and small parchment texts in tiny Gothic hands mass-produced by university stationers.

Many manuscript Bibles were glossed, that is to say they were accompanied by a commentary, written between the lines of the Vulgate text or surrounding it in the margins. One such version, the *Glossa Ordinaria*, was a standard tool for teachers and preachers, containing quotations and summaries of the writings of revered interpreters of the text, the Church Fathers. After the invention of printing with movable types, plain-text and glossed Bibles were among the first books to appear in print, and the *Glossa Ordinaria* presented the new technology, right at its outset, with mechanical problems of formidable complexity.

The fourteenth and early fifteenth centuries were not periods of great Bible production; the manuscripts of the thirteenth century, which survive in substantial numbers to this day, seem to have sufficed for the readership in the reduced population of 1450. The invention of printing created a whole new demand. The Latin Bible was the first major book to be created with movable types, and it was an immediate commercial success. When Aeneas Sylvius (later Pope Pius II) admired the newly printed sheets of Gutenberg's Bible in early 1455 the first printing of 180 copies had already sold out. Paul Needham in this volume documents the success of Gutenberg's Bible; and after it, before 1500, eighty further plain-text editions of the Vulgate were printed, all but two of them derived from it.

The first printed Bibles were not for private use but were meant to duplicate the big chained manuscript Bibles: as Paul Saenger shows, there is little sign of the earliest Bibles having been much read; rather than working copies they were sacred status symbols. But Gutenberg's work affected the text and structure of Vulgate editions that were read and studied for a long time to come, such as the more portable later editions produced in Venice, or the first pocket bible of Froben in 1491. Even the Sixtine-Clementine Vulgate, the official Bible of the counter-reformation, can be shown to derive many readings from Gutenberg.

Almost as important as the printing of Gutenberg's plain text was the production in 1480 of the first printed version of the *Glossa Ordinaria* by the Alsatian printer Adolph Rusch, whose typographical skill is celebrated in this volume by Karlfried Froehlich. Rusch's edition was followed in 1495 by the Venetian edition of Bernadino Gadolo, which added to the glosses the commentary of Nicholas of Lyra, that great stand-by of popular preachers.

We have long been accustomed to Bibles whose books are divided into numbered chapters with numbered verses on numbered pages. Paul Saenger tells the story of how the printed Bible came to take on its now familiar aspect. In the ancient world, it seems, the book of Psalms was the first to be broken into numbered chapters; but by the thirteenth century chapter divisions of all books had been incorporated into the Parisian standardization of the Vulgate. Later, Dominican scholars in their writings would refer to sections of chapters by early letters of the alphabet: a citation of Mark 11b, for instance, would refer the reader to the second quarter of that chapter; but the text itself would not contain any corresponding mark. In the fifteenth century scribes began to number the folios of scholastic texts, but this was uncommon in biblical manuscripts, and the early printed Bibles, unlike other printed volumes, were not foliated. The numbering of pages, as opposed to folios, began with Erasmus in 1516. But in 1477 Bernhard Richel of Basle began to print the Dominican letters in the margins of chapters. This greatly facilitated the use of concordances and tables of parallel texts. As the Psalms had been the first text to be numbered by chapters, so, in Bibles at the end of the fifteenth century, they were the first book to have their text broken into numbered verses.

The latter part of the fifteenth century saw the printing not only of the Latin Vulgate but also, in many parts of Europe, of vernacular Bibles. The precursors of these were partial biblical texts, often accompanying series of pictures, such as the German *Biblia Pauperum* and the story of Antichrist and the Fifteen Signs of Doomsday (described in this volume by Nigel Palmer). Other examples were the biblical stories which accompanied Caxton's edition of the *Golden Legend* of Jacobus Voragine, or the English Franciscan text *Dives et Pauper*. By the end of the century there were complete editions of the Bible in Dutch and German and extensive paraphrases in French. England, as Kimberly Van Kampen emphasizes in this work, lagged far behind in the work of biblical translation. No complete English Bible appeared before Coverdale's in 1535. Even the Psalms, which had been translated into English by Richard Rolle of Harpole in the 1330s, did not find a printer until in 1508 a few of them were attached to a volume of sermons by Bishop Fisher. The dearth of Scripture in English was an abiding effect of the censorship imposed under Archibishop Arundel, during the Wycliffite crisis, in the Oxford Constitutions of 1409. But suspicion of the vernacular survived the breach with Rome. In 1543 Henry VIII forbade women, husbandmen, and labourers to read the Bible.

Simultaneously with the development of Bibles in the vernacular, printers began not only to move forward from the Vulgate into contemporary tongues, but also to reach behind it to the Hebrew and Greek originals of which it was a translation. In 1477 a Hebrew psalter appeared, in 1488 a complete Hebrew bible. The first printed Greek New Testament was produced in 1514 as part of the multilingual edition of the Bible supervised by the Spanish Cardinal Ximenes, known, from the Latin name of the town of Alcalá where it was printed, as the Complutensian Polyglot. This edition contained Hebrew and Aramaic texts in addition to the Vulgate and the Greek. It was a magnificent achievement of typography but it was not completed until 1522 and it was never a commercial success on the scale of the Gutenberg Bible. As Julián Martín Abad relates in his piece here on the Alcalá printing press, the six glorious volumes of the Polygot Bible could be purchased, a few years after its publication, at a 55 per cent discount to its marked price of six and a half gold ducats.

The Complutensian Polyglot was dedicated to the Medici pope Leo X, who had sent manuscripts from the Vatican to be used in its compilation. To this day, however, as Michael Welte shows in his essay here, no one knows exactly which Greek manuscripts lay behind the Complutensian text. But like Gutenberg, Ximenes affected the structure of New Testament editions for centuries to come. Most Greek manuscripts of the New Testament set out the Epistles of St Paul after, and not before, the Catholic Epistles; and Erasmus, in his edition of 1516, follows this manuscript tradition. But the Complutensian edition puts St Paul immediately after the Acts of the Apostles; and so do all the editions, in any language, with which we are nowadays familiar.

The decade which saw the publication of the Complutensian Polyglot and Erasmus' New Testament ended with Luther's publication of his anti-Papal theses and with Leo X's condemnation of Luther's teaching in his bull *Exsurge Domine*. Henceforth the editions of the Bible would become weapons in the politico-religious battle between two conceptions of the Church, Protestant and Catholic.

Condemned by the highest authorities in the universal church, Luther and his followers appealed, as to a higher court, to the authentic text of the Bible. While the Catholics of the Counter-Reformation at the Council of Trent canonized the Latin Vulgate as the definitive text, the Protestants sought to undercut its authority on two fronts. On the one hand, like the Renaissance humanists that many of the early reformers were, they demanded, in the case of the Bible as of Plato and Aristotle, that interpretation should be based not on translations but on the original texts. On the other hand, reforming translators such as Tyndale insisted with democratic fervour that the Bible, in the vernacular, should be placed in the hand of every ploughboy. The plain believer, guided by the inner voice of the Spirit, could interpret the Bible as well as any crabbed scholastic theologian.

David Steinmetz, in his essay here, enters sympathetically into all sides of the Reformation debate. The Catholics and Protestants of the first generation after Luther's breach had been brought up together and neither side could disown the humanist ambition, in which they had been educated, to return to the original sources of learning. Protestants believed that this return to the original texts of the Bible would show up Catholic innovation and error. But the Catholics could argue that as the Holy Spirit had inspired the authors of the original texts, so he could have assisted those who later translated them. (Ironically, this is the argument nowadays used by fundamentalists in the United States who swear by the *ipsissima verba* of the King James Bible.) Moreover, as Steinmetz puts it, 'The [Latin-speaking] Catholic Church believed it had been led into all truth by the Holy Spirit. If the gates of hell could not prevail against such a Church, it seemed unlikely it could be overturned by an aorist verb or a waw-consecutive.' Each side in the debate, initially, believed that a study of ancient Christian writers would show its own party to be in the right, that is to say, to be more in accord with ancient truth. Each side was, in the end, disappointed in this hope: but in the meantime the needs of controversy had led to scholarly printed editions of the Fathers to match the plain-text bibles and to replace the gutted anthologies of quotations which had made up the *Glossa Ordinaria*.

William Sherman in his essay here on the readership of English printed Bibles, as exhibited in their markings and marginalia, has this to say: 'This set of papers sets out to explore how the Bible emerges from the manuscript tradition and, under the inference of the twin forces of printing and protestantism, becomes a layman's book.' The positive and negative aspects of this transformation were wittily summed up by John Dryden in a passage of his poem *Religio Laici* to which Sherman alludes.

> The book thus put in every vulgar hand
> Which each presumed he best could understand,
> The common rule was made the common prey,
> And at the mercy of the rabble lay.
> The tender page with horny fists was galled,
> And he was gifted most that loudest bawled:
> The Spirit gave the doctoral degree;
> And every member of a Company
> Was of his trade and of the Bible free …
> While crowds unlearned, with rude devotion warm,
> About the sacred viands buzz and swarm,
> The fly-blown text creates a crawling brood,
> And turns to maggots that was meant for food.
> A thousand daily sects rise up and die;
> A thousand more the perished race supply.

The tension between the scholarly and the fundamentalist approach to the Bible is as strong at the end of the twentieth century as it was at the beginning of the sixteenth.

One final word. It is a commonplace that the invention of the digital computer in our day is as significant a revolution in the presentation of information as the invention of movable type in the fifteenth century. Detailed parallels between the two transformations are to be found everywhere in this volume. For instance, the tags and daggers of the first printed *Glossa Ordinaria* have as their purpose to create hypertext links between different corpora; and the same purpose is served by the illustrations of Old Testament types which flank the New Testament antitypes in the fifteenth-century wood-printed blockbooks. In the twentieth, as in the fifteenth century, we have learnt how information is to be made to migrate from one medium to another; and just as in the fifteenth century the first printed books imitated manuscripts, so in the twentieth century books generated electronically do their best to resemble those produced by movable type.

When I was invited to introduce the symposium which generated the essays in this volume, the invitation was a privilege conferred on me because I was then chairman of the board of The British Library. A duty which frequently fell to me in that capacity was to respond to those who said – in triumph or in sorrow – that the computer had rendered the printed book obsolete. My first response was to point to the fact that the computer – because of the possibility of desk-top publishing – had increased, rather than diminished, the number of titles which year by year reached The British Library under the legal requirement for the deposit of printed works. My second and more fundamental response was to embrace the analogy between the printing revolution and the computing revolution, but to point out that five and a half centuries after Gutenberg every child in school still learns to read and write manuscript text. Just as the Bible, as a source of edification and inspiration, has shown that it can survive the secularization of the West, so the book, as a source of information and entertainment, will prove that it can outlive the digitization of the planet.

# THE LAYOUT OF THE BIBLE GLOSS IN MANUSCRIPT AND EARLY PRINT

J. P. Gumbert

THERE IS NOTHING REMARKABLE in that an early printed book looks like a manuscript – it would have been more remarkable if it had not done so. Prior to Gutenberg there were no 'manuscripts' but only *books*; what Gutenberg invented was not a new thing, but a new way of making the same thing: *books*, which, of course, looked like all books did; and although, after Gutenberg, one could distinguish (if necessary) between 'books written by hand' and 'books printed', both were still *books*. The substantive 'manuscript', denoting an antique curiosity, only came into use at the end of the sixteenth century, when handwritten books had disappeared from most people's bookshelves for some sixty years at least.[1]

However, to say that a printed book is 'merely' a book made by a new technique would not be quite true. There are important differences, right from the start. The printed book, being an industrial product, is cheaper; but industrial production requires capital, machinery and marketing techniques. The scribe's craft is, in contrast, notable for its lightness and flexibility; production can be adapted very precisely to the circumstances and requirements of the market, and even of the individual client. The technical processes of making a manuscript book are also more flexible. For instance, an infinity of 'scalable fonts' is at the scribe's fingertips; for a printer, even one extra font implies a heavy outlay. For a scribe, colour means an extra ink pot and an extra quill; for a printer, a very laborious extra process.

These examples – the use of several sizes of script, or of distinct scripts, and of colour – belong to the realm of printer's devices often called 'typographical means'; but in fact these and many similar techniques had been in use for centuries before print, and it may be shown that manuscript technology offered particular scope for such devices, far beyond the possibilities of print, certainly of early print.[2]

In the following I wish to comment on the use of these and other devices in the layout of the glossed Bible: books containing a part of the Bible with a rather extensive commentary.[3] The layout is governed by three main problems: how to *fit* an amount of text on a page together with the commentary pertaining to it; how to make clear which part of the commentary *refers* to which part of text; and how to *distinguish* visibly the text from the commentary.

This type of problem is already familiar in Antiquity, and the basic solution was soon found: the comments are placed in the margins which surround any text, or perhaps, if short, are squeezed between the lines; in both cases one naturally writes in smaller letters. The problem of fit does not occur, provided the comments are not too extensive; reference is assured by the placing of the comments; and distinction is by size.[4]

The earliest manuscripts of the *Glossa Ordinaria*[5] show a standardized form of this same principle: a column of text, with generous line spacing to accomodate interlinear glosses, and sufficiently wide margins at either side for the marginal gloss (Pl. 1). All glosses begin with paragraph signs (¶), those for the interlinear gloss being smaller than those for marginal glosses. Marginal glosses often open with the first words of the text passage they refer to (a lemma or 'handle'); other means for reference appear to occur more rarely. Fit is seldom a problem: if there is less gloss, there is simply more unused margin (Pl. 2). Distinction is by size; gradually three sizes rather than two begin to be employed, the interlinear gloss being written even smaller than the marginal gloss.

In this type of layout, the text itself is a rigid feature: its width and line spacing, and its number of lines per page, are constant throughout the book.[6] But the resultant presence of much blank space – which to our eyes is clear and restful – was to 'Gothic' eyes unclear and wasteful. To achieve a closer fit, flexibility per page was introduced (in the middle of the twelfth century, according to de Hamel): the width of the columns could be modified in accordance with the amount of gloss expected on that page.[7] Another development is a gradual change in line ruling. Originally the text was written on generously spaced lines, which extended only between the bounding lines of the text column; for marginal glosses some (much narrower) ruling was added as required.[8] Later the gloss ruling tends to become harmonized with the text ruling, one text line corresponding to two gloss lines. The text is now written in the space between two such lines, in large letters which more or less 'fill' that space; and the next space is left empty, or it contains a line of interlinear gloss in small script, as the case may be. If the interlinear gloss is long, one can leave more line spaces between the text lines.[9]

In the end full local flexibility was achieved, with both line width and line spacing fluctuating according to the demands of the moment. This was possible on the basis of an underlying, invariable page-wide all-over grid of ruled lines (in plummet) for text and gloss together. Horizontally this was ruled for the gloss; the text was written, as mentioned, in larger script, in principle between every second pair of lines; if there was one line of interlinear gloss, this could go in the other space, but if more lines of interlinear gloss were necessary, the text left more line spaces free. Vertically there was now no longer a central text column flanked by gloss columns, but rather one page divided into three 'lanes', with the text occupying one, two or three lanes as the amount of gloss permitted (Pl. 3). A text, which begins in the middle lane and continues on the left+middle, may then continue in only the left lane, then perhaps on all three at once, eventually to end up in the right-hand lane. (There are also four-lane solutions (Pl. 4) and various other possibilities.)[10]

Writing such an elastic layout is a job requiring much attention from the scribe. First he must finish any glosses left 'open' from the preceding page; then put in a bit of text, having judged how much gloss this carries, and select the text width accordingly; then put in the gloss, and see how much space this leaves for the next bit of text.[11] Reference is not felt to be a problem (reference signs are rare, except for 'read-on' marks on glosses carried over to the next page); the distinction into three script sizes is standard; for the problem of fit this elastic layout is really the ultimate solution.

While the 'elastic' layout for the *Glossa Ordinaria* was being perfected – or, according to de Hamel, even before that happened[12] – Peter the Lombard (d. 1160) composed a very different type of gloss, on the Psalms and the Pauline Epistles.[13] This gloss posed different problems. Instead of providing separate pieces of comment, of varying lengths, referring to precise words or to short stretches of text, he gave a more or less continuous commentary. Since this closely followed the text, sentence by sentence, reference problems should be easy to avoid. On the other hand his gloss incorporates Bible words, skilfully woven into his own sentences; these must, of course, be clearly distinguished, and that was a new feature, for which the *Ordinaria* suggested no solution. The method chosen for this distinction within the gloss was, almost universally, that of underlining, generally in red.[14]

The principal problems concerning the Lombard gloss are fit, and distinction of text from gloss. Probably the oldest solution is to give the text in one continuous column, the gloss in another continuous column – a good example of this is New York, Pierpont Morgan Library M. 939 (Lombard on Epistles, Spain 1181). The drawbacks are evident: in de Hamel's plate it can be seen that the comment already on the first page substantially outruns the text.[15]

A better solution to ensure fit is to break up the text into chunks, which were written first and then were followed by the relevant chunk of gloss; so the page was well filled and still each piece of gloss was close to its text. But how best to distinguish text and gloss? Various permutations of technical means were experimented with:

– The distinction may be by *size* (text big, gloss small), and the text placed *column-wide* (on a two-column page). Here everything is perfectly clear, and the writing of such a book is very easy; and yet this solution found no lasting favour (at least for this text).[16]

– Another possibility is to distinguish the text not by size, but by *colour* (red, of course); but, although this looks fine and is easier for a scribe than it would be for a printer, it still is a laborious process.[17]

– The use of colour, not size, can also be combined with placing the text in a *half-column* (a sort of 'two-lane' layout within the column); the gloss will then first fill the half-column adjacent to the text, and then continue column-wide for as far as is needed.[18]

– The final permutation is half-column layout with size (not colour) as a distinction. This became the standard layout for the Lombard gloss[19] (Pl. 5). It is a very good layout: fit, reference and distinction are all most satisfactory and perfect; and it is very easy to execute.

In a way these Lombard pages look rather like the 'elastic' *Ordinaria* pages; de Hamel even pointed out that the elastic layout was developed only *after* the Lombard gloss had found its characteristic shape, and especially after the ruled grid, which regularized the 2:1 ratio of text to gloss lines, had been invented. However, the two layouts are in other ways fundamentally different:

– For the *Ordinaria*, the grid is (in almost all cases) page-wide, and allows for the use of (normally) three or four 'lanes'. For the Lombard, it is column-wide, and allows for only two lanes in each column.

– In the *Ordinaria*, the text is continuous, even if it may appear in sinuous shapes. In the Lombard, it is broken up into chunks.

– In the *Ordinaria*, text and two grades of gloss are distinguished by size and placing.

In the Lombard, text and gloss are distinguished by size, and the gloss is subdistinguished by underlining.
– In the *Ordinaria*, the problem of reference is treated as non-existent (it is left to placing). In the Lombard, it really does not exist (as a consequence of 'chunking').
– In the *Ordinaria*, the problem of fit (how to fill the page with what really belongs together) is solved by an interesting, but exacting, way of executing. In the Lombard, it does not exist.

After the middle of the thirteenth century the making of glossed bibles – both *Ordinaria* and Lombard – stops. Apparently the market was saturated; the gloss was indispensable for serious Bible reading, but everyone could, if he wanted to, reach a copy to consult. It was not until late in the fifteenth century that printers began to think that the gloss might sell.

There is a magnificent edition of the *Glossa Ordinaria*, by Rusch 1480 (four vols, 1211 leaves in all, a Royal folio measuring 50×35 cm, B-607;[20] Pl. 6). The remarkable fact is that this edition (contrary to what has been said) does *not* follow the layout of its model (neither the 'rigid' nor the 'elastic' type), but instead is modelled on a very different example: that of the Law gloss (which had already been amply tested in print), with only the interlinear gloss added to that pattern. The Law gloss has its own development through several centuries of scribal work, and its own answers to what are, obviously, the same problems. (The text is arranged in two columns of large script; the gloss is around it, in small script, in two columns of a characteristic bracket shape, see Pl. 7. The pattern of widths, and the height of the gloss above the text, is (normally) fixed; fit is assured by modulating the length of the text columns. Reference is by marks – normally letters of the alphabet.)[21] In manuscripts, Law and Bible gloss can be distinguished at a glance by their characteristic layouts. It is a noteworthy fact that, when Koberger wanted to print the *Ordinaria*, he never thought of following the layout of his model, but instead fell back on a trusted and familiar, but totally different layout.[22]

As for the Lombard gloss, the only printed edition I have seen is a copy of the Psalm gloss, Nuremberg: Sensenschmidt 1478, also a Royal folio (P-477).[23] This has the first of the four possible layouts discussed above: text chunks in large type, column-wide, followed by gloss in smaller type. The biblical text incorporated into the gloss is, however, not underlined – that was a feat beyond the possibilities of early print.

## NOTES

1 The adjective 'manuscript' is older; but one would always speak carefully of a *liber manu scriptus* or a *codex manuscriptus*, never of 'a manuscript', without an accompanying substantive meaning 'book'. The history of these terms deserves to be traced more fully.

2 J. P. Gumbert, '"Typography" in the Manuscript Book', *Journal of the Printing Historical Society*, 22 (London: Printing Historical Society, 1993), 5-28.

3 The most important book on this subject is C. F. R. de Hamel, *Glossed Books of the Bible and the Origins of the Paris Booktrade* (Woodbridge, Suffolk, & Wolfeboro, New Hampshire: D. S. Brewer, 1987), which I have used gratefully. My own experience is not (like de Hamel's) based on study of numerous originals, but mainly on reproductions, of which there seem to be fewer than one would wish – and so often only a fine initial is reproduced, not the

whole page, which is what is needed for research on layout; but even a whole page may be misleading, because leafing through the entire volume might surprise one by revealing differences within the book not apparent from inspection of a single page.

4 See for instance C. H. Roberts, *Greek Literary Hands 350 B.C.-A.D. 400* (Oxford: Clarendon Press, 1955), pl. 14: Pindar, s.ii; E. G. Turner, *Greek Manuscripts of the Ancient World* (Oxford: Clarendon Press, 1971), pl. 47: Callimachus, s.vi or s.vii. For reference placing was often not sufficient; a good possibility was to use reference marks (letters, or other signs) in the text, corresponding to identical marks at the beginning of sections of comment; see for instance the Bembine Terentius of s.iv, often reproduced (for instance in M. P. Brown, *A Guide to Western Historical Scripts from Antiquity to 1600* (London: The British Library, 1990), pl. 7). This system had a great future; it was used for Greek *catena* commentaries (see for instance J. Irigoin 'Le Livre de Job commenté' in *Mise en page et mise en texte du livre manuscrit*, ed. by H.-J. Martin & J. Vezin ([Paris]: Editions du Cercle de la Librairie-Promodis, *c.* 1990), pp. 66-71), and another branch of this tradition survives as our footnote references. But for the theme of this paper this method is not relevant.

5 I cannot go into the question of what precisely is 'the' Ordinary Gloss, where and when (early twelfth century) and in what way it originated, and how it differs in its numerous manuscripts.

6 For such manuscripts, see for instance de Hamel, *Glossed Books*, pls 1, 3, and de Hamel, *A History of Illuminated Manuscripts*, 2nd edn (London: Phaidon Press, 1994), pl. 86 (the same page also in M. T. Gibson, *The Bible in the Latin West* (Notre Dame: University of Notre Dame, 1993), pl. 14). Another specimen in C. Sauer, *Studium Lektüre Andacht, Zur Handschriftenproduktion im 13. Jahrhundert* (Stuttgart: Württembergische Landesbibliothek, 1996), p. 10; another in *Glanz alter Buchkunst, Mittelalterliche Handschriften der Staatsbibliothek Preußischer Kulturbesitz Berlin* (Wiesbaden: L. Reichert, 1988), pl. 28.

7 De Hamel, *Glossed Books*, p. 16.

8 This implies that while the text ruling could be executed in advance, the gloss ruling could be added only as the scribe progressed (and so, presumably, by the scribe himself).

9 A page showing variably used line spacing, with interlinear gloss taking up one, two, three or four lines (as measured against the marginal gloss): Sauer, *Studium* (as n. 6) p. 13. Other specimens: de Hamel, *Glossed Books*, frontispiece and pl. 15.

10 Three lanes: the Berlin *Glanz* (as n. 6), pls 42, 43; D. Debes, *Leipziger Zimelien, Bücherschätze der Universitätsbibliothek* (Weinheim: VCH, 1989), pl. 42 (with rich secondary glosses in the wide margins); *Mise en page* (as n. 4), pl. 111 (with even richer secondary annotations!). Three unequal lanes: de Hamel, *Glossed Books*, pls 13, 20, and de Hamel, *History*, pl. 93. Four lanes on one page, three on the next: de Hamel, *History*, pl. 120. Two columns, each in three lanes: H. Köllner, *Die illuminierten Handschriften der Hessischen Landesbibliothek Fulda* I (Stuttgart: Hiersemann, 1976), fig. 762 (MS Fulda Aa 63). The grid (though not the whole layout) is particularly well seen in de Hamel, *History*, pl. 101.

11 It would be a worthwhile exercise to study this process in detail for one or two manuscripts.

12 De Hamel, *Glossed Books*, p. 24.

13 I leave out of consideration the gloss of Gilbert de la Porrée, on which see de Hamel, *Glossed Books*, pp. 18-21; I do not know it from my own inspection, and it does not fundamentally influence the point of my observations.

14 Red lines are not drawn during the process of (black) writing, but subsequently in a separate stage of work. The rubricator, who did this, needed guidance; this was provided by the scribe, who put black dots at the points where underlining was to begin and end; the rubricator merely needed to put his red lines from dot to dot (the dots function like 'paired codes'). In Brown, *Guide* (as n. 4), pl. 32, one can see one of the rare cases where the rubricator failed to do his job: the dots are present but the red lines are not!

15 Pl. 19 in de Hamel, *Glossed Books*. Evidently, on this page, the initials were laid out first (but not yet executed); then the text was written, in a narrow column but bulging around the end knob sketched in for the great initial; then the gloss was added as a continuous mass (reference being assured by the versals which mark the beginning of each Pauline sentence). Note that the underlining has no dots, and therefore, presumably, was executed during the copying (making a neat detour around the tails of all *p*s and *q*s). Similarly, in Gibson, *Bible* (as n. 6), pl. 17, the commentary lags behind the text, even although the latter has only an almost ridiculously narrow column (see also Gibson's remarks on the layout) – in Gilbert's gloss, the problem of fit seems to have been solved by writing the gloss first and the text afterwards, see de Hamel, *Glossed Books*, p. 20 and pls 6, 7.

16 De Hamel, *Glossed Books*, p. 22: not used after 1200: see his Pl. 9. Also Köllner, *Fulda* (above, n. 10), fig. 734 (MS Aa 115).

17 An example in Sauer, *Studium* (above, n. 6), p. 15; see also p. 46. See also de Hamel, *Glossed Books*, p. 22.

18 De Hamel, *History*, pl. 98.

19 See for instance de Hamel, *Glossed Books*, pl. 21, and the Berlin *Glanz* (above, n. 6), pl. 41. Untypical: de Hamel, *Glossed Books*, pls 10, 11, and de Hamel, *History*, pl. 97.

20 See the facsimile edition: *Biblia Latina cum Glossa Ordinaria: Facsimile Reprint of the Editio Princeps, Adolph Rusch of Strassburg 1480/81*, by Karlfried Froehlich & Margaret T. Gibson, 4 vols (Turnhout: Brepols, 1992).

21 Other examples of Law gloss layout: for instance de Hamel, *History*, pls 116, 119.

22 See B-613. B-608 is an edition with the same layout, this time for the *Ordinaria* plus Nicolaus de Lyra (Venice: 1495): Gibson, *Bible* (above, n. 6), pl. 16.

23 The copy I examined is The Hague, Royal Library 169 A 13, with rich North Holland penwork decoration (ownership entry: Weesp, Tertiary Sisters of St Mary, 'for the use of the confessor').

## EXTENDED CAPTIONS TO PLATES

*Plate 1:* Bruges, SB 379, fol. 94$^{v}$. Jesaia. A complicated specimen. Most marginal glosses begin with a lemma, which is underlined. Note the use of signs for reference where there is no lemma ('dash over two dots' over the second gloss at left, referring to *capud* in line 10 of the text); also the 'read-on' signs to link the end of the last block of gloss at left with its continuation top right, and the end of the last gloss right with its continuation on the next page. Note also that there is a problem of fit; the last gloss right, with the lemma *Ecce virgo etc.*, belongs to text which is on line 6 of the next page! Owned in the thirteenth century by Magister Walterus de Haltre (=Aalter, near Ghent), later by the Cistercian abbey of Ter Duinen, also in Flanders.

*Plate 2:* Laon, BM 108, fol. 165$^{r}$: Epistles of Paul. A very simple (although beautiful) specimen of the basic layout. Note the two sizes of ¶ sign. Owned by the Cistercian abbey of Vaucler (northern France).

*Plate 3:* Berlin, Staatsbibl. Preussischer Kulturbesitz, Theol. lat. fol. 222, fol. 110$^{r}$: Deuteronomium. Note the underlying grid ruling; the text leaving one or two lines free for interlinear gloss; and the text, which is at first confined to the middle lane, extending into the left lane in the penultimate line, only to shrink again in the last line.

*Plate 4:* Leiden, Univ. Library, Voss. lat. fol. 43, fol. 56$^{r}$: Job. The text width is two lanes at first, then one, then three, and two again in the last line. At one point in the middle, the interlinear gloss needs two lines (which means that at the end the text does not fit the grid; there, to avoid waste of space, the marginal gloss extends under the text). Note 'read-on' signs for one gloss at the top, two at the end.

*Plate 5:* Utrecht, Museum Catharijneconvent, BMH h 4, fol. 1$^{r}$: Lombard on Psalms. A fine specimen of the 'standard' Lombard layout. The gloss normally hugs the text closely – if the last line of the chunk of text is short (as in the first and third chunks), the gloss will profit to occupy that space; and the gloss to the next chunk will not start on a fresh line but join up with the preceding gloss (see *Et erit*, col. 2 line 10 of gloss). But in the penultimate line of the second column the scribe wrote the end of the gloss on the right half-column only, because otherwise he would not have had enough space to put the first line of the new text chunk, and on the other hand would not have been able to fill the column with the gloss in hand. In the margin, in red, references to the source authorities, AU(gustinus), CA(ssiodorus), almost hidden by the annotations of later readers.

*Plate 6:* Utrecht, Museum Catharijneconvent, BMH Warmond i 1263 H 2, fol. 483$^{v}$: Psalms [Strasbourg, Rusch 1480]. On this page, the amount of interlinear gloss is extraordinarily great: it takes from one to five lines of small print. (A new feature is reference signs linking this interlinear gloss to single text words.) The marginal glosses are arranged in the bracket shapes typical of Law layout; they open with lemmas and authors' names. The ¶ signs have been put in by hand, as has the fine initial (which must be from the northern Netherlands, although it still defies precise localization).

*Plate 7:* Leiden, Univ. Library, BPL 6 C, fol. 156$^{v}$: Digestum Vetus, *c.*1200. Two narrow columns of text, of equal length. The gloss is written, in two 'columns' of characteristic bracket shape, by another scribe. (The problem of fit in this layout deserves a thorough study on its own.) Note the reference marks (signs) along the left-hand margins of the gloss (the corresponding marks placed in the text are very tiny). The manuscript was used in Orléans early in the thirteenth century; later it was in Oxford.

# AN EXTRAORDINARY ACHIEVEMENT

## THE *GLOSSA ORDINARIA* IN PRINT

Karlfried Froehlich

THE LATIN BIBLE of the Middle Ages came in many sizes, shapes, and forms – full and partial, plain and decorated, large and small. One of the most important formats was that of the 'glossed' or annotated Bible, *Biblia cum Glossa*, which was the Bible of school and study, the standard tool of masters, students and preachers. The epithet *Ordinaria* (standard) does not appear until the end of the thirteenth century[1] and refers to a particular textual form as well as a specific layout on the page: a window of Vulgate text is surrounded by interpretative glosses which are written between the lines and in the two margins, often filling the space above and below the text window as well. The annotations may be direct quotations from the glossator of interpretation of the text, but often they are condensed versions or summaries of patristic and medieval exegetical material. Many of the annotations feature an abbreviated reference to their original, e.g. Aug (for Augustine), Ier (for Jerome), Or (for Origen) and so on. They were not just meant to identify a source but also encouraged readers to consult the full exposition of a particular church father as part of their endeavour to understand the meaning of the biblical text in its proper context.[2] Thus the glossed Bible was more than just a convenient exegetical tool, an encyclopedia which one would consult from time to time. Its parts were read and studied coherently because they presented everywhere the combined theological authority of Scripture and Tradition in an easily accessible form.

It was once believed that a ninth-century scholar, Walahfrid Strabo, was the compiler of the *Glossa Ordinaria*: if not of the whole, then at least of the marginal part. I have shown elsewhere that this myth can be traced to Johannes Trithemius, abbot of the small monastery of Sponheim in the Rheingau, one of the great figures of late medieval bibliography.[3] In his celebrated handbook *De scriptoribus ecclesiasticis*, first printed in 1494 (T-452), Trithemius revived the venerable genre of the treatise *De viris illustribus* and applied it to the literature of the Christian Church. His notices on scores of authors preserve extremely valuable information, but Trithemius was also 'improving' and even inventing sources to serve his specific agenda. His attribution of the *Glossa Ordinaria* to Walahfrid Strabo belongs in the context of the effort of German humanists such as Jacob Wimpheling and Conrad Celtis to demonstrate the early existence of a respectable German national literature against the scepticism of French and Italian detractors who scorned the 'barbarity' of the Germanic past. Trithemius was a member of this circle of friends and lent his help by glorifying the achievements of German literary heroes wherever he saw a chance. The fiction of Walahfrid Strabo as the compiler of the famous anonymous gloss simply created one more such hero.

In reality, the compilation of the *Glossa Ordinaria* must be dated three hundred years later, during the early decades of that exciting century which we call the twelfth.[4] The gloss originated in the French cathedral schools in the service of a new academic style, the teaching of the Bible as a textbook to a much wider audience outside the monastery. Laon, Chartres and finally Paris were the centres of its early development and distribution. It took several decades for all the books of the Bible to become available in this peculiar format which was clearly tailored to the needs of the new university community, teachers and students alike. Normally, a glossed manuscript would contain no more than one or two biblical books, or sometimes a group such as the Pentateuch, the four Gospels, the major or minor Prophets, or the Epistles of St Paul. Old catalogues and present library holdings suggest that there were medieval libraries, especially those of cathedral chapters, which possessed a complete or nearly complete set comprising up to twenty-one volumes: Paris, Monza, Messina, Toledo, Canterbury. I found that a substantial twelfth-century set now in the Stadtbibliothek, Nuremberg, was acquired as late as 1404-5 by the Nürnberg Dominicans through an agent in Strasbourg with the help of a generous donation by a citizen of that town.[5] Most libraries, however, especially those of smaller religious houses where copies of glossed biblical books were soon very much at home, had to be content with just a few volumes, but they often tried to augment their holdings, sometimes by having glossed biblical parts copied in their own scriptorium, sometimes by soliciting gifts or purchasing additional volumes.

It seems that around the middle of the twelfth century the text of the *Glossa Ordinaria* for many biblical books had achieved a considerable stability, partly due to of the efforts of influential teachers, such as Gilbert of Poitiers, who used the gloss as the basis for their exgetical lectures.[6] Also, there was a logistical difficulty when it came to copying gloss manuscripts; a scribe would have to re-calculate the layout of his page if he had changed the text of the previous page, for example, by adding new or different glosses. Few scribes were interested in making such changes. Rather, assuming a defined content for each page as they found it in their exemplars, scribes of the thirteenth century enjoyed the aesthetic challenge of quilting the material in ever-new artificial patterns, allowing the Vulgate text at one point to extend to the inner marginal column, and then again to the outer, and nesting marginal glosses one within another. This entire culture of the glossed Bible, the artful, individualized production of this indispensable tool by highly skilled scribes, the collecting, acquiring, exchanging and selling of individual or combined volumes from multi-volume sets, was changed overnight when the *Glossa Ordinaria* appeared in print.

Like the earliest history of the Gloss, the appearance of the *editio princeps* is shrouded in mystery (B-607).[7] The edition, mostly bound in four, sometimes three volumes, was published anonymously. There is no title-page, no colophon, no printer's or editor's preface, no indication of place, date or provenance. What we have is just the text. At the present time, I am aware of three sets carrying notes of acquisition which establish 1480 as the date of purchase (extendable to March 1481 if annunciation style applies): two are in Britain (London, Sion College, and Cambridge University Library), one in Austria (Abbey of Zwettl). Documented dates of rubrication in other sets confirm 1481 as the year when the processing of their raw sheets, which must have been printed a little earlier, was finished. Strasbourg as the place of printing is mentioned in the treasurer's account book of the Cathedral at Basle for 1480-1 and in notes written in at least two further sets (Strasbourg, Grand Séminaire; Freiburg i.Br., Universitätsbibliothek). A panegyric poem on the creation of the printed gloss, published in 1486 by the humanist Rudolf Lange who had celebrated the achievements of Johann Mentelin, Strasbourg's first printer, with a similar artifice, finally gives us the printer's name: Adolph Rusch of Ingweiler in Alsace.[8]

Rusch must be regarded as one of the truly important figures in the annals of early printing.[9] Having worked for Mentelin in Strassburg for some time, he married Salome, one of the master's daughters, and took over the printing shop after Mentelin's death. Wimpheling suggests that the shop passed into the hands of Martin Flach when Rusch himself died, relatively young, in May, 1489. One of Rusch's characteristics was that he did not sign his editions. They came out in a steady stream from 1473 on and included a number of classical texts as well as a fine Bible (B-534). The correspondence of Hans Amerbach, scholar and printer in Basle, includes several original letters from Rusch to Amerbach which give us an impression of his personality, his professional activities, his interests, and the circle of his acquaintances.[10] He was apparently fairly well educated, wrote a passable Latin, and seemed sympathetic to the cause of the new humanist learning. He had, however, no scholarly pretensions. Rather, as a passage in one of the letters indicates, he regarded himself as a merchant dealing in paper supplies, distributing books and perhaps manuscripts as a sideline.[11] Through his diversified business activities he accumulated a moderate fortune which allowed him to build an impressive villa near Ingweiler, and he apparently had a taste for good food and fine wines.

There are references in the Rusch-Amerbach correspondence to the *Glossa Ordinaria* project. Rusch borrowed the type he needed from Amerbach and printed under a contract with Anton Koberger of Nuremberg. Unfortunately, we do not learn anything about the planning stage or the early phases of production. After his initial experience with the market for printed goods, Rusch must have had a vision of the enormous potential of the new *ars impressoria* for the distribution of a large composite work such as the standard glossed Bible. By carefully calculating and controlling in advance the arrangement of the various components on each page – an activity which was, after all, the printer's professional job – the bulky manuscript pandect could be drastically reduced in size and reproduced in hundreds of identical copies which would truly standardize the text of the *Ordinaria*, the biblical gloss for all. Both Rusch and his distributor Koberger must have envisioned a reading public whose willingness to buy this convenient tool they judged optimistically enough to warrant the investment.

It remains astonishing that Rusch was not deterred by the enormity of the task. What he set out to print was what modern computer experts call a 'hypertext'. Michael Sperberg-McQueen, one of the developers of SGML, the Standard General Markup Language of the electronic Text Encoding Initiative in the humanities (TEI), has been known to show a slide of a page from the Rusch edition when he wants to demonstrate to his audience the classical prototypes of the concept of hypertext. Each directory, one page at a time, contains three independent files which must be co-ordinated and linked to each other by appropriate tags. Rusch achieved this feat by figuring out the exact ratio of Vulgate text and marginal glosses appropriate to each page, linking the latter to the Vulgate by giving a lemma for each, and inventing a system of visual symbols to connect each interlinear gloss to its proper reference in the Vulgate text on the line below: dagger, two-point and three-point staff, hooked s-paraph. We do not know how long the preparatory phase lasted; it may have been years. The final product presented the entire glossed Bible on 1211 royal size folios, using four sizes of type on each page: the largest one was reserved for page titles and the first words of prologues and chapters; the second largest size was used for the Vulgate text, the text of prologues, and the lemmata in the marginal gloss; the third for the running text of marginal glosses and *prothemata*; the smallest for the interlinear material.

Rusch paid special attention to the page titles, which indicate the biblical book and the chapter number in roman numerals. They were intended as the main guide for the proper sequencing of folios and quires, which was an important consideration for the binders of the volumes. The printed signatures which one finds at the bottom of many folios cannot have this function because they do not reveal any sequence; they probably designate different workers or presses involved in the printing process. The system worked well, it seems, except when the beginning of a biblical book coincided with the beginning of a new quire. In those cases the binder was left to his own knowledge or intuition in establishing the order of the biblical books. The extant copies show numerous variations, especially with regard to the place of the books of Ezekiel, Daniel, the minor Prophets, Maccabees, and Acts. Close inspection also reveals that individual pages, even entire quires in the Old Testament volumes, were reset, sometimes even more than once, in order to 'mend defects' as the correspondence suggests. The task, it seems, was never really finished.

Did Rusch have the help of a scholarly editor for the demanding work of preparing the edition? He borrowed the type from Amerbach, who also may have assisted him in locating suitable manuscript exemplars for the various biblical books, probably borrowed from several libraries. There is no indication, however, that Amerbach or another scholar actively participated in the textual work. On the contrary, I have found at least two hints that Rusch relied on his own experience and common sense, not on any expert. At the end of the Psalter, he printed a short note: *Cantica in locis suis require* ('Look up the canticles in their own places').[12] Gloss manuscripts regularly included six Old Testament and four New Testament canticles with their Gloss at this point, such as the Songs of Moses, the Canticle of Habakkuk, the Magnificat, and the Benedictus. Referring the reader to 'their [canonical] place' was a space-saving device which avoided duplication and used the advantage of the reader having immediate access to all biblical books in one compact set. The other hint is even more telling: at the beginning of the Apocalypse, the printer added a two-sentence paragraph under the rubric, *Prologus alius Hieronimi, ut habetur in quibusdam bibliis*.[13] It is true that this paragraph sometimes appears in Bibles as a prologue in this location, but only a lay person would be unaware that it is a quotation from Jerome's Epistle 53 *ad Paulinum* ('Frater Ambrosius') which was printed in full at the beginning of Volume One already. On the whole, the *editio princeps* is surprisingly free of errors and faulty expansions of manuscript abbreviations. Rusch must have had some good help in finalizing his text: he certainly had an excellent team of printers ('*societas mea*') as well as competent proof-readers which may have included the women of his household, especially Salome Mentelin. But at bottom the edition was his own work and achievement, and this is the essence of Rudolf Lange's extravagant poetic praise of the edition: 'You, beloved victor, lead the triumph, unstained by any blood that was spilled, and while declining to have the kings of the conquered peoples bound with chains, you liberated with your right hand the codices which were kept in harsh captivity so that they went out free'[14] – in plain prose: Rusch single-handedly conquered all odds in producing a masterpiece, the complete glossed Bible available to all.

If one is looking for unsung heroes of the Northern Renaissance, perhaps Adolph Rusch, the creator of the magnificent *Glossa Ordinaria* of 1480, should be a candidate. But in his world, not that of scholars but of craftsmen, not of the academy but of the market-place, there is rarely time to rest on one's laurels. Rusch's initiative seems to have been successful; the printed gloss sold well. Only four years later, however, we see the printer of this incomparable work pleading with Hans Amerbach not to ruin his livelihood by producing a competing edition of the gloss while so many copies of the *editio princeps* still remained unsold. Amerbach apparently obliged, but it did not take long for the competition to materialize. The second edition of the glossed Bible appeared in Venice in 1495, six years after Rusch's death (B-608).[15] This time, it did have a scholarly editor who was not shy to identify himself and to present his own person and contribution in a favourable light. His name was Bernardino Gadolo of Brescia; his dedicatory preface addressed to Cardinal Francesco Piccolomini, the future Pope Pius III, tells the genesis of the edition in a vivid account:

There are a number of dream plans, most reverend Father, which I most ardently desired: especially the one that the Bible with the ordinary and interlinear glosses be produced by that divine new art of printing together with Nicholas of Lyra. When during a visit with Your Highness on business of our order three years ago we were talking about literary endeavours, I explained this desire of mine in order to ask your kind advice whether I should pursue the project or abandon the idea. You lavished such praise on my desire and tried to persuade me to pursue it with so many reasons and arguments that they could have excited and motivated a person who would not even have thought about the matter. It so happened that a large number of persons in your noble and learned entourage of whom I did not know anyone who was not very well versed in literary culture (people try to emulate the life of their prince) even added spurs to my running, as the saying goes. And so, confirmed by your judgement and authority, I confidently asked many printers to undertake the task. To one man, they all approved such a wonderful plan, but, deterred by the magnitude of the labour and expense, they did not dare to lay hand on the project. Finally, with the help of God, I was able to persuade my compatriot and friend Paganinus de Paganino by many reasons that he should take on the task of most diligently printing this work.

It is clear that tangible business considerations were hiding behind the pious and devout rhetoric of the letter. Gadolo mentioned that a 'printed Bible with the ordinary gloss' was available, but he was obviously thinking ahead and had a marketing instinct which might be envied by many a business executive today. He knew how popular Lyra's *Postilla Litteralis* was among preachers, both mendicants and seculars. The presentation of Vulgate, *Glossa Ordinaria*, and Lyra together on the same page could provide a one-stop shopping tool for the preacher, a dream library for all practical purposes. Gadolo and his printer apparently were convinced of the cash value of the idea. They secured a marketing privilege from the Signoria and probably enjoyed good sales in Italy. On the strength of Gadolo's arguments, no printer after Paganinus could afford, or dared to print, the *Glossa Ordinaria* without Lyra any more. Instead, the tendency was toward further expansion. The Koberger correspondence reveals that, in 1502, a mega-project was under discussion between Koberger and the Basel gloss printers,

Froben and Petri, which would have combined Vulgate, *Glossa Ordinaria*, Lyra's two *Postills* with the Additions, plus Hugh of Saint-Cher's commentary on the whole Bible in one immense Bibelwerk.[16] The grandiose plan was not pursued. Even for early-sixteenth-century printers who were used to thinking big, there were limits.

The 1495 edition was produced in the finest Venetian tradition and, apart from the addition of the entire Lyra, included several new features which Gadolo touted with accomplished salesmanship: Two new prefaces ('Qui sunt multi' and 'Notandum quod translatores'); a continuous foliation in Arabic numerals; the subdivision of each page into sections from A to G for easier orientation; occasional references to biblical parallels in the margins. The letter fails to mention a most important fact, however: that the actual text of the interlinear and marginal gloss in the upper half of each page was in no way revised or changed; it was copied from Rusch line by line. All subsequent editions prior to the final major revision, undertaken by a team of Parisian theologians in 1590, and its successors, Douai 1617 and 1634, reproduced basically this same text. It is somewhat ironic to consider that in a very real sense Adolph Rusch of Ingweiler, an anonymous Alsatian printer, not a scholar, remains the one and only identifiable 'author' of one of the most important early bibles in print.

## NOTES

1 Beryl Smalley, 'Glossa Ordinaria', *Theologische Realenzyklopädie*, XIII (Berlin: de Gruyter, 3rd edn, 1983), p. 452; Smalley, *The Study of the Bible in the Middle Ages* (Oxford: Basil Blackwell, 1952), p. 56.

2 Smalley, *Study of the Bible*, pp. 226f, had suggested this purpose for a number of exegetes, especially Stephen Langton. Her opinion is supported for Gilbert of Poitiers by the findings of Theresa Gross-Diaz: *The Psalms Commentary of Gilbert of Poitiers: from Lectio Divina to the Lecture Room* (Leiden & New York: E. J. Brill, 1996), esp. pp. 149-55.

3 See 'The Printed Gloss', in *Biblia Latina cum Glossa Ordinaria: Facsimile Reprint of the Editio Princeps, Adolph Rusch of Strassburg, 1480/81*, ed. by Karlfried Froehlich & Margaret T. Gibson, 4 vols (Turnhout: Brepols, 1992), pp. xii-xxvi; here pp. xxiiif; Froehlich, 'Walafrid Strabo and the *Glossa Ordinaria*: The Making of a Myth', in *Studia Patristica*, vol. xxviii, ed. by Elizabeth A. Livingstone, *Papers Presented at the Eleventh International Conference on Patristic Studies held in Oxford 1991: Latin Authors (other than Augustine and his Opponents); Nachleben of the Fathers* (Leuven: Peeters, 1993), pp. 192-6.

4 It was the patient research of Beryl Smalley of St Hilda's College, Oxford, that established this fact once and for all; see her section on the Glossa ordinaria in *The Study of the Bible*, pp. 46-66. The more recent literature on the origin of the Gloss is listed in my article, 'Makers and Takers: the Shaping of the Biblical *Glossa Ordinaria*' (*Sacris Erudiri*, forthcoming).

5 For a description of the set, see Ingeborg Neske, 'Die lateinischen mittelalterlichen Handschriften 2. Bibelhandschriften und Liturgica einschließlich der griechischen Texte', in *Die Handschriften der Stadtbibliothek Nürnberg, Band II: Die lateinischen mittelalterlichen Handschriften, Teil 2: Bibelhandschriften und Liturgica einschliesslich der griechischen Texte* (Wiesbaden: Harrassowitz, 1987), pp. xiii, 33, 37ff.

6 On Gilbert's involvement in the shaping of the biblical gloss, see the recent contributions of Theresa Gross-Diaz, *The Psalms Commentary* (above, n. 2), pp. 122-48, and Patricia Stirnemann, 'Où ont été fabriqués les livres de la Glose ordinaire dans la première moitié du XIIe siècle?', in *Le XIIe siècle: Mutations et renouveau en France dans la première moitié du XIIe siècle*, ed. by Françoise Gasparri (Paris: Le Léopard d'Or, 1994), pp. 257-301.

7 For a description of the edition and its problems, see 'The Printed Gloss,' in the facsimile edition mentioned above in n. 3, pp. xii-xvi.

8 For the complete text, see C. Schmidt, *Zur Geschichte der ältesten Bibliotheken und der ersten Buchdrucker zu Strassburg* (Strasbourg: C. F. Schmidt's Universitätsbuchhandlung Friedrich Bull, 1882; repr. Graz: Akademische Druck- und Verlagsanstalt, 1971), pp. 160-2.

9 On him, see the brief sections in Schmidt, *Zur Geschichte*, pp. 100-4, and Ferdinand Geldner, *Die deutschen Inkunabeldrucker: ein Handbuch der deutschen Drucker des XV. Jahrhunderts nach Druckorten; Erster Band: Das deutsche Sprachgebiet* (Stuttgart: Anton Hiersemann, 1968), pp. 62f, to be supplemented by the same author's retraction concerning Rusch and the Glossa Ordinaria: Geldner, 'Johannes Amerbach und die Biblia cum glossa ordinaria Walafridi Strabonis aliorumque et interlineari Anselmi Laudunensis', part 3 of his 'Amerbachstudien', *Archiv für Geschichte des Buchwesens*, 23 (1982), col. 684-90.

10 See Letters no. 1, 2, 7, 10, 11, 12, 13, 14 in *Die Amerbachkorrespondenz*, ed. by Alfred Hartmann, *I. Band: Die Briefe aus der Zeit Johann Amerbachs, 1481-1513* (Basel: Verlag der Universitätsbibliothek, 1942). These letters are also printed as appendix v in C. Schmidt, *Zur Geschichte*, pp. 152-9.

11 'Scitis quod libros emere non audeo, bapiri autem commercium [h]abeo', *Die Amerbachkorrespondenz*, no. 10:28f, p.14.

12 *Biblia Latina cum Glossa Ordinaria* (see above, n. 3), vol. II, p. 651.

13 Ibid., vol. IV, p. 549.

14 'Ducis triumphum victor amabilis / Nullo rubentem sanguine gentium / Reges catenis stringere renuens / Duro ligatos carcere codices / Dextra resolvis, liberi ut exeant.' See C. Schmidt, *Zur Geschichte* (above, n. 8), p. 161.

15 On this edition, see 'The Printed Gloss', in *Biblia Latina cum Glossa Ordinaria* (above, n. 3), vol. I, pp. xvi-xvii.

16 See Oscar von Hase, *Die Koberger: Eine Darstellung des buchhändlerischen Geschäftsbetriebes in der Zeit des Überganges vom Mittelalter zur Neuzeit*, 3rd edn (Amsterdam: Gérard Th. van Heusden, & Wiesbaden: Breitkopf & Härtel, 1967), nos 56-7 and 59, pp. lxvii-lxx.

# BIBLICAL BLOCKBOOKS

Nigel F. Palmer

THE BIBLE is not just 'the Book of Books', but also a book of books, that is, a book made up of books. In the Middle Ages the Bible may have been more important as a concept than as a book. Certainly there are individual manifestations in which the whole canon of the Scriptures is made up as a book, in a single volume, or in a pair or set of volumes. There are the Tours bibles, the giant bibles, the Paris bibles, the Gutenberg Bible, and more. But complete bibles were rather special books, and the Bible can only be said to have been omnipresent during the Middle Ages in its more abstract form, as a concept. Individual parts of the Bible were often made up as individual books, and were used for particular purposes: with or without commentary and apparatus, sometimes in response to a liturgical function; or of the monastic *lectio continua* of the Bible in church and refectory; sometimes to meet the needs of individual readers; or to complement what had already been brought together in a library. Manuscripts which contained only part of the Bible were almost always used with an awareness of the text belonging to a larger conceptual whole.

It is clear, given these general observations, that a number of factors combine to make the Gutenberg Bible a major landmark in the history of western book production. The first major book to be created with movable type was a text of the complete Latin Bible with its canonical structure and prologues, indeed one of the most perfect manifestations of the concept. The choice of such an object for Gutenberg's project was in harmony with the special importance which the written word (and then the printed word) came to acquire in the later Middle Ages, a phenomenon that also manifested itself in the spread of paper production, the invention of typography, and the rebuilding and reconstitution of institutional libraries. (That Gutenberg's choice was timely is clear from the large number of reprints, and from the appearance a decade later of a German printed Bible to match the Latin.) The Gutenberg Bible provided a new orientation for the production of the Bible as a book, which pointed the way to the future, in particular to Luther's translation project and the other vernacular bibles.

Roughly contemporary with the Gutenberg Bible in origin, and to be seen as a minor parallel phenomenon to the development of printing with movable type during the first quarter-century of the new medium, are the blockbooks, which were printed by a xylographic rather than a typographic process. The blockbooks are mostly slim volumes of fewer than fifty leaves, printed from woodblocks without the use of movable type, occasionally containing handwritten text, and characteristically printed on one side of the paper and arranged so that each double spread is a single sheet of chancery paper folded as a bifolium. By virtue of this arrangement of the leaves, the blockbooks constitute a distinctive and rare codicological type which stands quite apart from the quire structure of the traditional manuscript codex, which in turn gave rise to the regular form of the typographic book. It was obviously not possible to print the Bible as a blockbook, but it is my purpose in this paper to show how, during the period when the first great printed bibles were made, biblical subject matter also came to be privileged by the xylographic printers.[1]

The first biblical blockbook was the Latin *Apocalypse*, the earliest impression of which was made in the early 1450s in the Low Countries (Pl. 8).[2] This is a picture cycle with short texts consisting of forty-eight or fifty pages, and deriving directly from the manuscript tradition of the Anglo-Norman illustrated Apocalypses.[3] It is therefore to be seen as a printed version of an ensemble of texts and pictures from the thirteenth century.

At about the same time, in Bavaria, the earliest blockbook *Antichrist und die fünfzehn Zeichen vor dem Jüngsten Gericht* was printed (Pl. 9), twenty-one pages with woodcut illustrations and handwritten text, printed on both sides of the paper in a small hand-press and arranged in a single quire.[4] This work, which describes the life of Antichrist and the Fifteen Signs before Doomsday, is a German-language text together with a picture cycle, and like the *Apocalypse* it derives directly from a tradition of illustrated manuscripts. It is extracted from the extended version of a German picture chronicle, the *Konstanzer Weltchronik*,[5] of which this section has its origin in a Latin illustrated life of Antichrist.[6] The eschatological subject-matter of the Life of Antichrist and the Fifteen Signs before Doomsday, which constitutes the final chapter of salvation history and is anticipated in Jesus' words to the disciples on the Mount of Olives, makes it appropriate to place this work alongside the 'biblical' blockbooks in the strict sense.

The Heidelberg *Biblia pauperum* (Pl. 10), which is preserved in a unique copy, can be dated some seven or eight years after the *Antichrist*.[7] Here the Latin text is handwritten, whereas the pictures are printed from woodblocks. Here too an illustrated manuscript exemplar was imitated directly in the new medium of the blockbook, in this case a typological text-and-picture ensemble that had been created in the mid- or later thirteenth century and circulated in the monasteries of Austria and Bavaria.[8] Within a year or two this process was repeated. The Netherlandish *Biblia pauperum* (Pl. 11), with Latin printed text and printed pictures, the earliest edition of which is thought to date from about 1460, derives independently from a different branch of the manuscript tradition of the *Biblia pauperum*.[9] This was to be the most frequently printed blockbook of all. Ten years later, in 1470, the third stage of the blockbook *Biblia pauperum* tradition begins, with the publication of a German-language *Biblia pauperum*, which is again derived independently from the manuscript tradition.[10] Meanwhile there had already been a Latin typographical edition printed in the early 1460s by Pfister in Bamberg (Hain-3177).[11]

There are three biblical blockbooks, the *Cantica Canticorum*, the *Historia David* and the *Ars memorandi quattuor evangelia*, all from the mid-1460s. The *Canticum canticorum* (Pl. 12) was originally printed in the Netherlands and then a little later, in a second edition, in Germany.[12] This is a cycle of thirty-two pictures on sixteen pages, based on the Song of Songs, and presenting the Bride as a model for the devout soul in accordance with a widespread devotional practice among nuns. There is a close parallel to the blockbook in a cycle of partly identical wall-paintings dating from about 1350 in a Polish nunnery, at Chelmno (or Culm) on the Vistula, which makes it certain that the two versions have a common model from the fourteenth century.[13] So the *Apocalypse*, the *Antichrist*, the *biblia pauperum*, and the *Canticum canticorum* all represent the more-or-less direct transposition of manuscript models into the new medium.

This does not appear to have been the case with the *Historia David* (Pl. 13), for which no manuscript parallels of any kind are known.[14] This book consists of a summary of biblical history from the Book of Kings, beginning with the birth of Solomon and concluding with the death of David, following the numbered chapters of the bible one by one, and accompanied by a cycle of forty pictures. There is evidence that this book was conceived from within the blockbook tradition, because several of the illustrations appear to be indebted to the Netherlandish *Biblia pauperum*.[15] The choice of this subject matter for a blockbook may relate to the tradition of monastic readings from the Books of Kings at matins and in the refectory during the period after Pentecost.[16]

Finally there is the *Ars memorandi quattuor evangelia*, a handbook for memorizing the content of the four Gospels – John, Matthew, Mark and Luke – chapter by chapter (Pl. 14).[17] There are fifteen text pages and fifteen picture pages facing each other. Each picture page is dominated by the symbol of the appropriate evangelist, upon which are superimposed up to nine numbered pictorial symbols, placed in a regular sequence of positions, to remind the reader of the content of the appropriate chapter in the Gospels. The text pages contain headings or one-sentence summaries of the chapters presented on the facing picture page. Towards the end of the fifteenth century similar books were produced, but in small format, for memorizing the content of the whole of the Bible, also using a system based on mnemonic images. These 'mnemotechnic picture bibles' exist not only as manuscripts, from the early 1490s, but also in a printed edition, said to be printed from copper engravings, and of the same date.[18]

It is striking just how disparate the various biblical works are in both content and audience, which came to be united by the common medium of block printing: the *Apocalypse*, an illustrated eschatological text prized by the Anglo-Norman lay nobility; the German *Antichrist*, comparable in appeal, but a product of the boom in book production in fifteenth-century Germany; the *Biblia pauperum*, invented to facilitate the practice of a particular mode of Bible interpretation in the Austrian and Bavarian monasteries; the *Canticum canticorum*, which bears the hall-marks of nuns' devotions, and is otherwise known only from fourteenth-century Poland; the *Historia David*, a piece of straight Bible paraphrase, paralleled only in the monastic practice of *lectio continua*; and the *Ars memorandi*, a late-medieval experiment in the art of mnemonics designed to facilitate learning the Gospels by heart.

The next step in the argument to be presented here is to show how the biblical blockbooks were sold and collected in *Sammelbände*. The later state has not simply arisen fortuitously, as the result of that understandable inclination of librarians to get similar books in the same format bound up together, but was originally planned by the printers and collectors.[19] This argument involves a reversal of the trend of the last two hundred years of collecting which has prioritized the concept of the printed book as a discrete bibliographical item to be separated either physically or conceptually (in a library catalogue) from any items with which it might originally have been bound up. Blockbooks, on account of their scarcity and desirability as collectors' items, were often provided with fine bindings in the late eighteenth or early nineteenth century, so that considerable detective work is required to reconstruct their original context. An important criterion for associating blockbook copies with one another is the paper they are printed on. Sometimes it can be observed that the blockbooks united in a *Sammelband* are printed on the same paper (or on stocks of paper from the same source), suggesting that editions of several different blockbooks were printed at one and the same time in a single workshop with a view to being sold together as a collection. Another piece of evidence that may be employed to identify an 'original *Sammelband*' is the use of scrap from the printing of blockbooks in the binding process, or as a pastedown. It seems unlikely that scrap paper from the printing of blockbooks would have been available in any context other than that of the workshop where such books were printed (and bound). A third, but less good, criterion for establishing that a set of books originally belonged together in a single binding is the use of the same range of colours and the same style of colouring. In general it can be supposed that the individual parts of a volume were coloured before they were bound together.

Examples of collections of blockbooks that can be identified as original *Sammelbände* in this sense are the following: former *Sammelband*, Oxford, Bodleian Library, Arch. G c.14 and Auct. M 3. 12 (*Biblia pauperum* and *Canticum canticorum*);[20] the Malaspina *Sammelband* in the Museo Civico di Pavia (Castello Visconteo), comprising the *Biblia pauperum* (inv. 4780), the *Canticum canticorum* (inv. 4897) the *Apocalypse* (inv. 4819) and the *Ars memorandi* (inv. 4867), with the leaves of a secular text as pastedown (inv. 4912);[21] the Pertusati *Sammelband* in the Bibliothèque Nationale in Paris, identified by Ursula Baurmeister, with *Apocalypse* (Rés. Xylo. 9), *Ars memorandi* (Rés. Xylo. 17), *Ars moriendi* (Rés. Xylo. 25), *Biblia pauperum* (Rés Xylo. 1), *Canticum canticorum* (Rés. Xylo. 28) and *Antichrist* (Rés. Xylo. 30);[22] the former *Sammelband* in the Kupferstichkabinett in Berlin (Staatliche Museen zu Berlin – Preußischer Kulturbesitz), which was stolen from the Jagiellonian Library in Cracow shortly after 1800, containing *Calendarium* (Cim. 10), *Planetenbuch* (Cim. 10), *Ars moriendi* (Cim. 2), *Biblia pauperum* (Cim. 5), *Historia David* (Cim. 12), *Ars memorandi* (verschollen), *Apocalypse* (Cim. 1), *Antichrist* (Cim. 7), and the *Fabel vom kranken Löwen* (Cim. 9)[23] The Malaspina *Sammelband* still preserves its original binding, whereas the others have fine morocco bindings of a later date. There are numerous further *Sammelbände* of blockbooks for which, with varying degrees of confidence, the claim of 'originality' can be made, but the four listed here are the best authenticated.

The four *Sammelbände* all contain the *Biblia pauperum*, and indeed if we were to extend the list this same observation would hold for virtually all of them. Of all the biblical blockbooks in the strict sense, the *Biblia pauperum* is the only one which is not simply a reworking of one individual part of the Bible: it contains a life of Christ, extended beyond the Ascension and Pentecost into the eschatological domain, together with a wide range of Old Testament texts and pictures. It presents one particular way of looking at biblical history, which provided a framework into which the biblical themes of other blockbooks could be conceptually integrated. In such a context the plan of the *Biblia pauperum* can be seen to acquire a function quite different from that originally envisaged.

The original manuscript version of the *Biblia pauperum* seems to have consisted of a cycle of thirty-four New Testament pictures presenting the life of Christ from his Annunciation to the Ascension and Pentecost, and concluding with the Coronation of the Virgin. This is the one picture in the New Testament cycle that goes beyond the Bible text. Each New Testament event is understood as an antitype of two events in the Old Testament, which are treated as prophecies now coming to fulfillment and which, in the blockbooks, are placed on either side of the New Testament picture.[24] The Old Testament types each consist of a picture and a text, the latter being a quotation or paraphrase form the Old Testament, often with a few words of interpretation. Twenty-one of the sixty-eight Old Testament events are selected from Genesis, twenty-four from the Books of Kings, giving these narrative sections of the Old Testament and the stories of Abraham, Solomon and David special prominence in the *Biblia pauperum*. There are also four texts on each page spoken by Old Testament prophets, verses from the Bible, and three metrical verses, which sum up the meaning of the three pictures. This is the version that was reproduced as a blockbook in the slightly earlier Heidelberg *Biblia pauperum*, of which only a single copy survives.

In the Netherlandish version of the *Biblia pauperum* from about 1460, a different recension of the manuscript tradition was chosen, in which the cycle of New Testament pictures had been extended from thirty-four to forty. It is therefore known as the 'forty-page blockbook *Biblia pauperum*'. There is some variation and elaboration of the events between the Last Supper and the Mocking of Christ, but most importantly the story of salvation history is extended to the Last Judgement, the Dragging of the Damned to Hell, the Saving of the Blessed in Abraham's bosom, and the Coronation of the Blessed in Heaven, including the Coronation of the Virgin. The Coronation of the Blessed in Heaven is striking in that it echoes directly, in its pictorial design, the last page of the original version, which also portrays the Coronation of the Virgin in heaven. The meaning of the last page is a matter of interpretation, as the accompanying texts fail to make the direction intended absolutely clear. The Mariological conclusion to the *Biblia pauperum* might be said to match its Mariological opening, the Annunciation, but given the lack of any consistent Mariological tendency throughout the work, it is surely better to understand the Coronation of the Virgin as signifying the establishment of the Church, in which there is a place for the bestowing of eternal life on the individual soul. This idea is then repeated, or made explicit, in the last page of the forty-page blockbook. That scene marks out a devotional perspective, mediating between the events of the Bible and the beholder, which is an important key to the devotional use of which the *Biblia pauperum* blockbook was most probably intended.

We have seen that the *Biblia pauperum* begins as a work that sets out structures within the canonical text of the Bible, relating Old Testament events, especially from Genesis and the Books of Kings, to a life of Christ distilled from the Gospels, and that in the forty-page blockbook this narrative is continued into eschatological time, with the Last Judgement and the damnation and salvation of the souls. This is a conception of biblical narrative that can frequently be found in the Middle Ages: the Bible is understood to contain the revelation of salvation history from the creation of the world through to the time of Christ and prophetically, through revelations inscribed in the Scriptures, beyond this to the end of the world.

Furthermore, the *Biblia pauperum* provides the conceptual framework within which the other biblical blockbooks are positioned when they are found together in a *Sammelband*. The *Historia David* presents a section of the Bible in consecutive form, chapter by chapter, following a text which is of particular importance for the typologies of the *Biblia pauperum* and some of whose pictures, as suggested above, seem to be directly derived from the *Biblia pauperum*. Its presence in the *Sammelbände* underpins the biblical content of the *Biblia pauperum*. Likewise, the *Canticum canticorum* presents an elaborate devotion corresponding to the final picture of the *Biblia pauperum*, an elaboration of the relationship between the blessed souls and God, as a model for the devout reader. If the blockbook is compared with the fresco in Chelmno, one of its most striking features, which is also a difference between the two versions, can be seen to be the first and last pictures, which in the blockbook have been given a Mariological interpretation. The last picture of the blockbook is the coronation of the devout soul in Paradise, but portrayed as the Virgin Mary, and thus relating directly to the last pictures of the *Biblia pauperum*.

Within the conception of biblical history attested by the forty-page *Biblia pauperum* the eschatological blockbooks can now easily be placed. The *Antichrist und die fünfzehn Zeichen vor dem Letzten Gericht* is held in place by its final picture, of the Last Judgement, which is an iconographical match to plate 37 of the forty-page *Biblia pauperum*, and it gives an account of events predicted to take place immediately before that time. There is also a thematic association between the representations of destruction in the Fifteen Signs and the pictures of Dathan and Abiron and Sodom and Gomorra in plate 38 of the forty-page *Biblia pauperum*. This is also the conceptual position to which we can assign the *Apocalypse*. Finally, the *Ars memorandi quattuour evangelias* takes its place in the framework of these 'collective xylographic bibles' which may be seen as comparable to that of the *Historia David*. The *Ars memorandi* is designed to impress on the reader the canonical structure of the Gospels which is replaced, in the *Biblia pauperum*, by a life of Christ conceived in terms of salvation history.

Thus it can be shown that some of the surviving collections, or groupings, of blockbooks themselves made up a 'Book of Books', in which the parts constitute a meaningful whole when related to the distinctive structure of biblical thought documented in the *Biblia pauperum*. The relationships described undoubtedly exist between the individual picture books that were printed by the xylographic method, taken at a certain level of abstraction. That argument may, however, be taken a step further on the basis of the study of the actual surviving copies, and it is possible to transfer the generic association that can be established between the biblical blockbooks as a group to the make-up of individual *Sammelbände*.

## NOTES

1 For a good introduction to xylographic printing in English see Arthur M. Hind, *An Introduction to the History of the Woodcut*, 2 vols (London: Constable, 1935; repr. New York: Dover, 1963). The standard handbook is Wilhelm Ludwig Schreiber, *Manuel de l'amateur de la gravure sur bois et sur métal au Xve siècle. Tome quatrième contenant un catalogue des livres xylographiques et xylochirographiques, indiquant les différences de toutes les éditions existantes* (Leipzig: Otto Harrassowitz, 1902; repr. as id., *Handbuch der Holz- und Metallschnitte des XV. Jahrhunderts*, 3rd edn, vol. IX <Manuel IV> (Nendeln & Stuttgart: Kraus Reprint; Otto Harrassowitz, 1969). The subject is brought up to date in the exhibition catalogue *Blockbücher des Mittelalters: Bilderfolgen als Lektüre*, ed. by the Gutenberg-Gesellschaft and Gutenberg-Museum (Mainz: Gutenberg-Gesellschaft, 1991).

## Biblical Blockbooks

2 Manchester, John Rylands University Library, 9403-1. Facsimile: *Die Apokalypse: Älteste Blockbuchausgabe in Lichtdrucknachbildung*, ed. by Paul Kristeller (Berlin: Bruno Cassirer, 1916).

3 Gertrud Bing, 'The Apocalypse Block-Books and their Manuscript Models', *Journal of the Warburg and Courtauld Institutes*, 5 (1942), 143-58; Elke Purpus, 'Die Vorläufer der Blockbücher der Apokalypse', in *Blockbücher des Mittelalters: Bilderfolgen als Lektüre*, pp. 99-118.

4 Schweinfurt, Bibliothek Otto Schäfer, Xylo-A. Facsimile: *Der Antichrist und die fünfzehn Zeichen: Faksimile-Ausgabe des einzigen erhaltenen chiroxylographischen Blockbuches*, ed. by Theodor Heinrich Musper (Munich: Prestel-Verlag, 1970).

5 For the *Konstanzer Weltchronik* see Rudolf Gamper, *Die Zürcher Stadtchroniken und ihre Ausbreitung in die Ostschweiz: Forschungsgeschichte, Überlieferung, Analyse der Chroniktexte* (Zurich: H. Rohr, 1984), with reference to Munich, Bayerische Staatsbibliothek, Cgm 426, and Zurich, Zentralbibliothek, MS. A 172 (pp. 181-3). The blockbook version is dependent in its readings on the text as found in these manuscripts.

6 London, Wellcome Institute for the History of Medicine, MS> 49, fol. $10^{v}$-$13^{r}$. Microfiche facsimile: *Apokalypse – Ars moriendi – Medizinische Traktate – Tugendund Lasterlehren: Die erbaulich-didaktische Sammelhandschrift London, Wellcome Institute for the History of Medicine, Ms. 49: Farbmikrofiche-Edition*, ed. by Almuth Seebohn (Munich: Edition Helga Lengenfelder, 1995). For a detailed analysis of the text (which is printed in the footnotes) see Jessie Jean Poesch, *Antichrist imagery in Anglo-French Apocalypse manuscripts* (unpublished doctoral dissertation, University of Pennsylvania, 1966), pp. 291-342.

7 Heidelberg, Universitätsbibliothek, cod. Pal. germ. 438. Facsimiles: *Biblia pauperum: Unicum der Heidelberger Universitätsbibliothek*, ed. by Paul Kristeller, Graphische Gesellschaft: Veröffentlichung 2 (Berlin: Bruno Cassirer, 1906); *Die Zehn Gebote – Beicht – und Sündenspiegel – Biblia pauperum – Totentanz – Symbolum apostolicum – Septimania poenalis – Planetenbuch – Fabel vom Kranken Löwen – Dekalog: Farbmikrofiche – Edition der Handschrift und der Blockbücher in dem Cod.Pal.Germ.438 der Universitätsbibliothek Heidelberg*, ed. by Wilfred Werner (Munich, 1994).

8 Henrik Cornell, *Biblia pauperum* (Stockholm: Thule-tryck, 1925); Gerhard Schmidt, *Die Armenbibeln des XIV. Jahrhunderts* (Graz & Cologne: Böhlau, 1959); Karl-August Wirth, 'Biblia pauperum', in *Die deutsche Literatur des Mittelalters: Verfasserlexikon*, ed. by Kurt Ruh et al. (Berlin & New York, 1978), vol. 1, cols 843-52.

9 Facsimile: *Biblia Pauperum: a Facsimile and Edition*, ed. by Avril Henry (Aldershot: Scolar Press, 1987).

10 Facsimile: *Biblia pauperum: Deutsche Ausgabe um 1471*, ed by Rudolf Ehwald (Weimar: Gesellschaft der Bibliophilen, 1906). Cf. August Christian Adolph Zestermann, *Die Unabhängigkeit der deutschen Biblia pauperum von der lateinischen xylographischen Biblia pauperum* (Leipzig: T. O. Weigel, 1866).

11 Bamberg: A. Pfister, *c.* 1462/3; GK 4325. Facsimile: Louis Gillet, *La Cathédrale vivante* (Paris: Flammarion, 1964), pp. 190-229. There is also an extended version from the same printing house: GK 4327.

12 Facsimiles: *Canticum Canticorum: Holztafeldruck von c. 1465, mit einer Einleitung*, ed. by Otto Clemen (Zwickau: Ullmann, 1910); *Canticum Canticorum: Editio archetypum anni circiter 1465 imitans*, ed. by Julius Meier-Graefe (Munich: Officina 'Ganymedes', 1922); *Le Cantique des cantiques: Canticum canticorum. Historia seu providentia Beatae Mariae Virginis ex Cantico canticorum*, ed. by Francis Bouvet (Paris: Éditions de Minuit, 1961).

13 Nigel F. Palmer, 'Junius's blockbooks: Copies of the *Biblia pauperum* and *Canticum canticorum* in the Bodleian Library and their place in the history of printing', *Renaissance Studies*, 9 (1995), 137-59 (p. 147). The Chelmno frescoes are discussed and illustrated by

Jeffrey F. Hamburger, *The Rothschild Canticles: Art and Mysticism in Flanders and the Rhineland circa 1300* (New Haven, Conn., & London: Yale University Press, 1990), pp. 85-7 and ills. 154-63.

14 Facsimiles: *Liber Regum. Nach dem in der k.k. Universitätsbibliothek zu Innsbruck befindlichen Exemplar*, ed. by Rudolf Hochegger (Leipzig: Otto Harrassowitz, 1892); *Riproduzione del codice palatino latino 143: Canticum Canticorum – Biblia pauperum – Dis ist ein baum indem man lichtlicht des biblisthen hystorien geschicht in gedencken mag – Historia Davidis*, ed. by Lamberto Donati & Luigi Michelini Tocci (Città del Vaticana: Biblioteca Apostolica Vaticana, 1979). Cf. Rudolf Hochegger, *Ueber die Entstehung und Bedeutung der Blockbücher mit besonderer Rücksicht auf den Liber Regum seu Historia Davidis* (Leipzig: Otto Harrassowitz, 1891; repr. Nendeln and Wiesbaden: Kraus Reprint Ltd; Otto Harrassowitz, 1968).

15 See in particular *Historia David*, pl. 9, and *Biblia pauperum* (ed. Henry), pl. g.

16 For the monastic tradition of *Lectura continua* see Hilaire Marot, 'La Place des lectures bibliques et patristiques dans l'office latin', in *La Prière des heures*, ed. by Monseigneur Cassien [Serge Bezobrazov] and Dom Bernard Botte, Lex orandi 35 (Paris: Les éditions du Cerf, 1963), pp. 149-6 (??). Cf. the lists of readings contained in Michel Andrieu, *Les Ordines romani du haut moyen âge*, 5 vols (Louvain: Université catholique de Louvain, 1931-61), II, 481-8 (Ordo XIIIA and III), 39-41 (Ordo XIV).

17 Facsimiles: *Ars memorandi reproduit en fac-similé sur l'exemplaire de la Bibliothèque Nationale*, ed. by Adam Pilinski & Gustave Pawlowski (Paris: Pilinski et fils, 1883); *Ars memorativa: Aus der Offizin von Anton Sorg in Augsburg zirka 1490 [...] getreu dem Original neu gedruckt*, ed. by Ernst Weil (Augsburg: B. Filser, 1922). Cf. Jean Michel Massing, 'From manuscript to engravings: Late medieval mnemonic bibles', in *Ars memorativa: Zur kulturgeschichtlichen Bedeutung der Gedächtniskunst 1400-1750*, ed. by Jörg Jochen Berns & Wolfgang Neuber (Tübingen: Max Niemeyer Verlag, 1993), pp. 101-15 (pp. 104f).

18 Cf. Massing, 'From manuscript to engravings'; Susanne Rischpler, '*Biblia Sacra figuris expressa*': *Mnemotechnische Bilderbibeln des 15. Jahrhunderts* (unpublished doctoral dissertation, University of Würzburg, 1995).

19 For a detailed discussion see Palmer, 'Junius's blockbooks' (above, n. 13).

20 Palmer, 'Junius's blockbooks', pp. 142-52.

21 Palmer, 'Junius's blockbooks', p. 152.

22 See Ursula Baurmeister, *Livrets xylographiques et collectionneurs* (Paris: Bibliothèque nationale, 1991), pp. 11-13; Ursula Baurmeister, *Catalogue des incunables (CIBN)* (Paris: Bibliothèque nationale, 1992), vol. 1, fasc. 1, nos AA-4 (2nd copy), AA-5, AA-13, BB-7, CC-2 (1st copy), VV-2; Palmer, 'Junius's blockbooks', pp. 151-2.

23 Microfiche facsimile: *Apokalypse – Ars moriendi – Biblia pauperum – Antichrist – Fabel vom kranken Löwen – Kalendarium und Planetenbücher – Historia David: Die lateinisch-deutschen Blockbücher des Berlin-Breslauer Sammelbandes. Farbmikrofiche-Edition*, ed. by Nigel F. Palmer (Munich: Edition Helga Lengenfelder, 1992).

24 For an introduction to biblical typology and the organisations principles of the *Biblia pauperum* see Henry, *Biblia pauperum* (above, n. 9), pp. 8-18.

# THE IMPACT OF THE EARLY PRINTED PAGE ON THE READING OF THE BIBLE

*Paul Saenger*

SCHOLARS have often speculated in global terms about the impact of printing on the history of reading, intellectual history and the history of literacy and social change. While printing has had far-reaching effects on literacy in western culture, it is easy to exaggerate both the rapidity and the dimensions of printing's impact on reading in general and reading of the Bible in particular. Historical syntheses are best developed – that is they are most apt to be valid – when they are closely tied to the study of individual examples. It is a commonplace of critics of fiction to state that an author who seeks to populate a novel with types frequently creates stereotypes, while the novelist who bases characters on real individuals will succeed in describing believable characters, that is, those who constitute truly representative types. This analogy is useful for narrating the history of the reading of the Bible, a book which by good fortune survives in so very many specific artifacts – manuscript and printed.

The Bible presents a somewhat special case for illustrating the limited but significant impact that printing had on text format and consequently on the history of reading. Throughout the Middle Ages bibles, like books of hours, breviaries and other liturgical books, were usually copied on vellum in the most formal of book scripts. In this respect they stand in contrast to ordinary scholastic textbooks. In the fifteenth century, when the pecia system had fallen into decline and textbooks were in short supply in the new universities of eastern France, the Low Countries and Germany, new copies of the standard texts were privately copied on paper in hastily written cursive script. These university books were frequently produced not visually (i.e. from an exemplar placed before the eyes of the scribe), as bibles and pecia books had been, but in officially sanctioned dictation sessions.[1] In the period 1460-1500 printed substitutes for such rapidly copied university books were often dramatically more legible than their manuscript antecedents.

Bibles represented a distinctly alternative situation to ordinary school texts precisely because they had almost always been copied in formal scripts. In the thirteenth century hundreds, perhaps several thousand, highly standardized and generally extremely legible portable bibles in formal scripts had been produced by professional scribes, mostly at the universities of Paris and Oxford. In 1450, even after a century of destructive wars between England and France, an ample number of bibles survived to meet the needs of readers, and even today these volumes are still regularly available through the antiquarian book trade, often at relatively reasonable prices. In the mid-fifteenth century, the supply of university bibles was especially copious in Paris where the student population, due to plagues and wars, was but a fraction of what it had been in the early fourteenth century.[2] For this reason, and because of the reverence given to the Word of God, Latin bibles were infrequently copied on paper in gothic cursive script in the decades preceding the introduction of printing.[3] Although seldom used for copying complete bibles, Gothic cursive writing on paper was employed for extracts from Scripture. Little booklets containing such *auctoritates* could be used in the composition of lectures and sermons (Pl. 15).

Although early printers drew their texts from the scholastic bibles of the University of Paris, the first printed bibles that appeared in Mainz, Bamberg and Strasbourg were not intended to replace thirteenth-century portable manuscript bibles as the ordinary reference tools of scholars, for an abundant supply of the latter still survived. Rather the size, script and decoration of the first printed bibles were intended to duplicate the appearance of the large bibles that were often chained on public display in the fifteenth century in monastic churches and cathedrals. Such chained bibles typically constituted de luxe products of the late medieval scriptorium. The new typographic bibles, often produced on parchment support (the earliest of which can surely be linked to reform movements within the Benedictine order), are difficult to distinguish from the manuscripts that served a similar display function. Of the surviving copies of the Mainz 42-line Bible, the first printed Bible, only a few (the copies now at Eton College,[4] Aschaffenburg,[5] the University of Göttingen,[6] the Public Library in Burgos,[7] the University of Texas,[8] Yale University,[9] and a fragment on display in the King's Library of the British Library[10]) evince signs of use, either for liturgical reading proper or for the quasi-liturgical *lectio divina*, the programmed oral reading of Scripture and the Fathers that in Benedictine, Cistercian and Carthusian refectories traditionally accompanied meals served otherwise in silence. None of the earliest printed bibles show signs of significant private use by scholars. In general, the 42-line Bible and its immediate successors are remarkable for the absence of signs of any contemporary use whatsoever, and there is every reason to believe that, although highly legible, they were in fact infrequently read.

Rather than bearing the annotations of scholars, the large, cumbersome printed volumes produced in the first two decades of the incunable period were frequently luxuriously illuminated by hand, to enhance their primary function as palpable icons of God's revealed word.[11] The same large size that made them laborious to consult and awkward to read rendered them all the more impressive as manifestations of the divine authority. In this function they resembled the monumental manuscript bibles that had appeared in the western tradition in England in the late seventh century and that thereafter formed an intrinsic aspect of Christian monastic book culture.[12] The largest of all surviving medieval manuscript bibles, the thirteenth-century *Gigas librorum* (Stockholm, Royal Library A. 148) copied at the Benedictine abbey of Podlazic in Bohemia, was clearly not intended for normal reading. Rather, contemporaries regarded it as one of the seven wonders of the world.[13]

The first large-format printed bibles, like their monumental large-format manuscript antecedents, entirely lacked the apparatus of marginal notes and complementary tables that in the course of subsequent decades would become common in printed bibles. The first printed bibles also lacked the glossary of Hebrew names and mnemonic resumés, usually written in rhythmical verse, which had regularly been appended to thirteenth-century portable manuscript bibles, the books that medieval theologians regularly used; and late-fifteenth-century cataloguers of monastic libraries noted this absence.[14] Both the new and traditional aids were particularly valuable to late-fifteenth-century preachers for the composition of sermons. In contrast to the portable thirteenth-century tomes, the almost pristine copy of the 42-line Bible now housed in the Houghton Library at Harvard contained a deed of gift written on a flyleaf, explaining that it had been given by one Johannes Vlieghen to be chained in the Brigittine monastery at Soest near Amerfoort with the hope that monks would pray for the soul of its donor.[15] As symbols of divine authority, large and often grandly illuminated printed volumes resembled the comparable lavishly-decorated fifteenth-century manuscripts. Nicolao degli Albergati, Cardinal of Santa Cruce (1395-1453), donated one such Bible to the Charterhouse of San Lorenzo in Florence to encourage the monks there to pray for his soul; a contemporary described it as a *Biblia pulcherrima*.[16] Paris, BN lat. 25, the calligraphically written and expensively illuminated bible prepared for King Louis XI of France, is another example of a large-format fifteenth-century manuscript bible with dimensions equivalent to those of a Gutenberg Bible.[17]

In manuscripts, the changes that distinguish the biblical reading habits of the decades immediately preceding the introduction of printing from those of the early thirteenth century are subtle indeed and relate directly neither to cursive script, nor to paper support, and not even to the monumental illuminated manuscript bibles described above. Evidence of an evolving new page format for manuscript bibles during the fifteenth century occurs not in new books, but in modest late-medieval reworkings or emendations of thirteenth-century bibles. To appreciate these modest annotations, it must be remembered that in the year 1450 most readers still found their way through the dense pages of thirteenth-century copies of the Vulgate either by simply scanning the standard division of its numbered chapters or by using the Dominican index system of mental distinctions invented by Hugh of Saint-Cher (1263). In this system each chapter was divided mentally either *a* to *d* for short chapters or *a* to *g* for longer chapters.[18] However, in the fifteenth century this mental system was beginning to be supplanted by the innovation of foliation, a new mode of establishing arbitrary, visually defined locus points for reference. Although in the thirteenth century perhaps ten per cent of scholastic books at the universities of Paris and Oxford had been foliated, portable bibles used by university scholars seem generally not to have been among them.[19] During the thirteenth and fourteenth centuries the combination of the University of Paris's system of standardized chapter divisions and the Dominican system of mental alphabetical distinctions within the chapter had evidently sufficed, for contemporary leaf numbering of these volumes had not been deemed warranted. However, in the mid-fifteenth century scribe-emendators were frequently foliating thirteenth-century bibles to facilitate their use.

In the light of the generally growing practice of foliation in the fifteenth century, evinced in the manuscript emendation of thirteenth-century portable bibles, it is particularly instructive to note that copies of the early large-format printed bibles of Johannes Gutenberg, Peter Schoeffer and Johannes Fust, Johannes Mentelin and Heinrich Eggestein were neither foliated in print, nor generally by manuscript emendation. Indeed, to my knowledge, no copy of the 42-line or the 36-line Bible (the second printed Bible) bears contemporary manuscript foliation (B-526, B-527),[20] and I know of but one copy of the Fust and Schoeffer 1462 Bible foliated contemporaneously (B-529), in this case with mid-leaf printed marginal arabic numbers resembling the earliest printed foliation at Cologne.[21] Among the early large-format bibles in two volumes, Eggestein's second Vulgate Bible of *c.* 1468 appears to be a rare exception, for a number of the surviving copies were foliated in red by contemporary rubricators, perhaps acting in a co-ordinated manner close to the print shop.[22] The pervasive absence of foliation in early printed Vulgate bibles stands in contrast to the numerous foliated copies (whether in manuscript or in print) of other large-format reference texts such as the *Postilla Literalis* of Nicolaus de Lyra, Thomas Aquinas's *Summa Theologica*, and Jerome's very extensive (and bibliographically highly complex) *Corpus epistolarum*, all of which were published on paper of dimensions equivalent to that of the earliest bibles in Rome, Strasbourg and Mainz. Indeed, the first edition of de Lyra's *Postilla* (N-131) was printed in Rome in 1472 with tables indicating a foliation to be added by an emendating rubricator, and Peter Schoeffer's prologue to his 1470 edition of Jerome's *Epistolae* (H-165) implied that the reader would use a hybrid system of foliation and alphabetical distinctions.[23] Many early editions of Jerome's letters also contain tables explicitly indicating that foliation was to be added by hand, and many individual copies of this work bear early manuscript foliation in anticipation of intensive reference consultation.[24]

Reference in print to leaf numbering appeared in Latin bibles a decade after it had penetrated the printed text tradition of Jerome's epistolary corpus. Bernhard Richel's 1477 Basle Bible (B-553) contained an enumerative table of biblical books indicating, in addition to the number of chapters contained in each biblical book, the number of the opening where each book began. The printer anticipated that an emendating rubricator would add the requisite numbering of the leaves by hand (Pl. 16).[25] However, the first printed bibles to have manuscript foliation provided by contemporary rubricators were not editions of the Vulgate, but rather copies of the earliest German language Bibles. The first printed bible in any language to appear with printed foliation was the German translation produced by Gunther Zainer no later than 1476 (B-627). The precocious shift to foliation in German-language bibles doubtlessly reflected the fact that lay readers of vernacular texts would have been less capable of using the mental alphabetical distinctions on which university-trained scholars of the Latin Vulgate relied.

The first Latin bibles with printed foliation corresponding to a printed table of the order of the biblical books referring to folio numbers were produced by Anton Koberger and Conrad Winters, in Nuremberg and Cologne in 1478 and 1479 respectively (B-557, B-565). These volumes continued a tendency, already evident in Richel's 1475 Bible (see below), of combining a smaller and more condensed text format than that of the earlier monumental printed bibles with short supplementary texts that served as study aids. In the incunable period most non-biblical printed text traditions were marked by either printed or manuscript leaf numbering and either printed or manuscript analytical tables referring to leaf numbers. For Bibles, however, the innovations of foliation and analytical tables (i.e. tables analysing a volume's subject content as opposed to an enumerative table of books and chapters) referring to foliation played only a peripheral role. To date I have identified but a single instance of an incunable bible accompanied by an analytical table referring to leaf numbers, which were in the event printed quire and leaf numbers.[26] The common incunable phenomenon of printed analytical tables prepared explicitly for subsequent scribal emendators to add leaf numbers was generally absent from the text tradition of incunable Latin bibles. Only in 1516 did the fastidious Erasmus, the father of Latin pagination, renew emphasis on the leaf as a locus point by introducing page numbers to the textual tradition of the Latin New Testament in the course of retranslating it from the Greek original. His use of pagination rather than foliation reflected a concern with precision in text location as an indispensable aid in the painstaking task of textual comparison.[27]

Despite the fact that foliation was relatively infrequent and tardy in printed bibles, and that pagination was never present in any printed bible of the incunable period, printing nevertheless had an important impact on the biblical page that may be analysed as a series of discrete phenomena. The first of these relates directly to the imaginary alphabets that Hugh of Saint-Cher (1263) and three successive generations of Parisian Dominicans of the convent of Saint Jacques had employed. During the thirteenth and fourteenth centuries the Dominican letter system had been used not only in Hugh's Concordance and two other closely related Parisian Dominican verbal concordances, but similarly in more modest analytical subject indexes to the Vulgate, also referred to as concordances, which theologians continued to produce into the early years of the fifteenth century.[28] Indeed, a liturgical table for the lessons of the Mass that was appended to Newberry MS-19, a very small Franciscan portable bible of the thirteenth century, also employed the Dominican system. However, even in this book, where the Dominican letters were intended for liturgical use (perhaps to aid a friar to follow silently the readings of the Mass when they were pronounced aloud), letters corresponding to those written in the tables were not actually written into the margins.[29] Marginal letters *a* to *h*, combined with abbreviations for *prima*, *secunda* and *tertia*, do appear in some manuscript bibles of monastic provenance, with the earliest examples apparently dating from the twelfth century.[30] These letters, however, transcend chapter divisions and direct the reader to the appropriate passage of the continual sequence of the *lectura divina* of the refectory. They apparently relate to the liturgical octave and the *litterae dominicales* used in certain liturgical calendars and almanacs. Periodically, some scholars have confused such monastic alphabets with those of the Dominicans, which guided reference readers to specific passages within each chapter, to which, however, the Dominican letters are only remotely related.[31]

A visible, graphic system of subdividing the chapters of the Gospels had in fact existed in late antiquity and survived in the Middle Ages until the early years of the thirteenth century. Marginal demarcation of short sections with references to parallel passages in the other Gospels was invented by Ammonius (third century) and then perfected by Eusebius (*c.* 260-340). These marginal notations were accompanied by canon tables in Greek, Syriac and Latin Gospel books of late antiquity and the early Middle Ages, and were even used to provide references to commentaries on the Gospels.[32] Hugh of Saint-Cher's Dominican system of mental chapter divisions was clearly of greater general utility because it was not exclusively limited to the Gospels, but rather extended to the entire New and Old Testaments. Nevertheless, because the Dominican system lacked all marginal graphic signs, it was inherently cumbersome and time-consuming to employ, especially for a reader of Latin not specifically trained in scholastic theology. A reader seeking to retrieve a specific citation was first obliged to gauge whether a given chapter was a short or long one, and then was obliged to divide it mentally into the requisite four or seven segments. Since the boundaries of the segments were imaginary, they necessarily remained approximative, even in the mind of a trained university theologian. Indeed, only a theologian possessing a memory carefully trained in the relative length of the Vulgate Bible's chapters could use such a mental system with a modicum of speed. At Oxford, Robert Grosseteste, a Franciscan, strove to create a concordance to the Bible based on a system of encoded marginal, graphic signs, but no Bible with a full set of these signs has yet been discovered.[33] Grosseteste's concordance itself survived only in a single copy.

As late as 1476 the first German and French printers of small portable bibles in Venice aspired simply to replicate the page format of the thirteenth-century manuscripts with which the three Dominican concordances had originally been employed. They were so successful in imitating northern thirteenth-century bibles that the average modern reader (ignoring the fact that the Psalms in these printed tomes are invariably numbered) would have difficulty in distinguishing the printed books from their thirteenth-century handwritten models.

In 1475 Bernhard Richel in Basle began a dramatic reformatting of the Vulgate text as it had been transmitted by thirteenth-century university manuscripts (B-540). To appreciate his originality, one must remember that the canons of Eusebius had disappeared from western biblical manuscripts by the mid-thirteenth century. For three centuries their essence had survived only in the chapter headings of Zacharias of Besançon's *Harmony of the Gospels* (Z-13)[34] In most manuscripts of the *Harmony*, the canon tables themselves were not copied, but only described verbally. The prefatory material contained in one such thirteenth-century codex would indicate that the reader without access to an ancient Bible containing Eusebius's numbered sections (contemporary Bibles would have had only the standard university chapter divisions) was expected to treat the numerical references in the chapter headings as mental distinctions.[35]

Having viewed the Eusebian canons in their ancient form (probably in a Carolingian codex in one of Switzerland's ancient Benedictine libraries), Richel replicated them along with their related marginal concordance typographically in his first Bible printed in Basle (B-537; Pl. 17). This constituted an eccentric humanistic impulse with scant parallel in fifteenth-century manuscripts.[36] Concomitantly, Richel emulated the Carolingian practice of numbering the psalms with roman numerals, a practice that, while it had never entirely disappeared, had waned after the ninth century.[37] Richel's typographic replication of ninth-century graphic reference systems constituted a spark that kindled further and more radical visual experimentation. In Nuremberg in July 1477, Anton Koberger used intra-textual alphabetical letters, similar to those that he employed to mark distinctions in sermon books, as tie marks (or *signes de renvoi*) to link the Eusebian references in the margins to specific phrases in the text (B-552).[38] Tie marks had not been used with Eusebian references in Carolingian times.

Printing the Eusebian canons was but a prologue to Richel's second major innovation in 1477: the representation in print of the sequential Dominican letters in the margins of biblical chapters (B-553). Introduced by Richel, the new system greatly diminished the ambiguity inherent in the use of the Dominican verbal concordances. Readily visible printed marginal letters permitted even the inexperienced reader to find rapidly a specific reference in the otherwise undivided chapters of the Vulgate. To appreciate this peculiar system, we must understand that early printed books were marked by a variety of marginal as well as intra-textual graphic-alphabetical indexing systems. These were particularly utilized in the large sermon collections that constituted, after the Bible, the most intensively used preachers' reference tool. In incunables, alphabetical systems for denoting locus points within a text rivalled foliation.

The genius of fifteenth-century printers was that they were wont to adopt a highly useful graphic device, such as marginal and intra-textual alphabets, which was employed only very rarely in manuscripts (and then only in the restricted context of a specific community or genre), and to apply it in contexts where it previously had not occurred. Marginal alphabets in sermon books came to print from the manuscript traditions of central Europe. In the early years of the century, analogous alphabets had been present in Ulrich von Pottenstein's German language *summa* on the catechism.[39] In Latin sermon books, graphic alphabets occur in a variant intra-textual form in certain fifteenth-century manuscripts of Germanic origin, notably those containing the Franciscan friar Johannes Grütsch's *Quadragesimale* or collection of sermons for Lent, copied in the upper Rhine valley just prior to 1450. Grütsch's sermons were divided into twenty-two sequences of alphabetical letters arbitrarily placed within the text. Such letters, especially when touched with red or yellow by a rubricator, constituted clear indicators for sections of text. The text format of these handwritten codices was precisely replicated by all the incunable editions of a work that became truly popular for the first time in print.[40]

Marginal biblical alphabets had their own peculiar tradition, linked to England and central Europe. It is crucial to stress that the manuscript codices that inspired Richel's second Bible, published in Basle in 1477, were entirely different from those that he had employed in 1475. Indeed, within the textual tradition of the Latin Vulgate they were true anomalies. Alphabets resembling those that later became common in the margins of printed bibles first occurred in the English vernacular New Testaments produced by the Lollards at the end of the fourteenth and in the first decades of the fifteenth century (Pl. 18). For their Latin compositions, the Wycliffite heretics had employed the same mental alphabetical indexing systems akin to those employed in the Dominican verbal concordances.[41] However, when the Lollard scribes copied New Testaments in English primarily for lay use, they placed graphic letters in the margins. These were normally selected from the customary 'Dominican' range *a* to *g* with the sequence beginning anew within each chapter.[42] Each letter was assigned on an *ad hoc* basis according to the relative position within the chapter of the designated incipit of the requisite Gospel or Epistle reading of the day, as assigned by missals of the Use of Salisbury. It is important to understand that these Lollard books did not contain continuous alphabetical sequences as did later printed bibles, but only selective alphabetical characters that were designated according to the Dominican principles for mental spatial division. Calendrical liturgical tables that were often appended to the Wycliffite New Testament manuscripts referred the reader to these markers. The scribes also employed a special intra-textual double slash mark, placed marginally or intra-textually to designate the end of the reading, a sign that in slightly variant form occurs again in Richel's 1477 Bible (Pl. 19).[43] Some of the Lollard bibles containing these tables and alphabets were very small volumes and thus easily carried to Mass.[44] A layman using such a volume could discreetly locate and then read silently with full comprehension a vernacular version of a Latin text which he was unable to fully understand when pronounced orally by the priest.[45]

It is doubtful that Swiss printers would have had direct access to this peculiarly Insular late medieval text format, but it has long been known that the Lollards had contact with Jan Hus in Prague, and that numerous Wycliffite manuscripts and at least one English vernacular bible made their way to central Europe.[46] In the 1420s two Bohemian scribes, Mathias of Raudnitz and Blasius of Domazlice, copied two Latin Vulgate codices that in the margins of each chapter contained in red the letters either *b* to *d* or *b* to *g* (the letter *a* remaining mental). The same scribes provided a marginal concordance, also in red, that referred to book, to chapter and, usually, to letter (Pl. 20).[47] In the former codex, the passages to which the concordance references pertained were denoted by red tie notes formed by a point and a slash, marks similar in form to those used in England in Lollard bibles. Concomitantly, the Psalms in these two manuscripts were numbered and divided into alphabetical distinctions. A Latin New Testament, copied in Bohemia *c.* 1400 and containing many vernacular interlinear glosses (formerly in the library of the Counts of Stolberg and now in the Van Kampen collection in Grand Haven, Michigan), contains a marginal concordance referring to book chapter and alphabetical distinction *a* to *g*, although the distinctions themselves were unmarked by marginal letters (Pl. 21).[48] The concordance references in all three of these biblical codices of Bohemian origin constitute direct antecedents to those that first appeared in printed bibles beginning in Basle in the summer of 1477.

Richel's entirely reformatted Bible of 1477, apparently drawing inspiration from Bohemian Vulgate manuscripts similar to those described above, omitted the *Canons of Eusebius*, and in their stead substituted a marginal alphabetical concordance that extended throughout the New Testament and referred to regularly spaced marginal printed letters *B* to *D* and *B* to *G* within each chapter (the letter *A*, as in the Bohemian manuscripts, remaining mental (Pl. 19)).[49] The concordance throughout the New Testament was identical in form and function to the marginal concordances found in the Bohemian bibles. Furthermore Richel used an intra-textual slash mark to tie concordance references to the text that was remarkably similar to that which Lollard scribes had used to delimit the passages referred to by the marginal alphabets.

In 1479, this new marginal concordance system was adopted by Johannes Amerbach who perfected it by making the letter *A* graphic as well (B-561).[50] In 1482 the format spread from Basle to Lyon via two German printers, Marcus Reinhard of Strasbourg (a relative and associate of Johannes Grünninger) and Nicolaus Philippi of Bensheim. Their Bible placed equally-spaced marginal typographic capital letters *A* to *D* and *A* to *G* in the New Testament of their complete Bible, expanded the marginal concordance, and used intra-textual double slash marks virtually identical to those in the Lollard bibles (B-574).[51] In Venice in 1484 and in Speyer in 1489, Johannes Herbort of Seligenstadt and Peter Drach respectively placed marginal printed alphabets and concordances in the New Testament portions of their portable bibles (B-580, B-587). The positioning of the letters in all these editions was still entirely consistent with the references provided by the Dominican concordances, with each letter denoting the beginning of an alphabetical *distinctio* within the chapter.

In October 1487 Nikolaus Kessler, who had begun his career as an associate of Bernhard Richel, printed a compact-format folio bible in which he, like earlier Bohemian scribes, extended the marginal locus letters and concordance to the Old Testament, with the exception of the Book of Psalms (B-585).[52] In effect, Kessler thereby completed the conversion of the Dominican mental system into a fully graphic one that was easy for any inexperienced person literate in Latin to manipulate.[53] The practice of placing typographical alphabets throughout the entire Bible spread quickly, first among the printers of Basle and then to cities in Italy, Germany and France.[54] In June 1491 Johannes Froben, having placed marginal letters in both the Old and New Testaments, vaunted the fact on the title-page of his small octavo bible (B-592). Cataloguers of fifteenth-century monastic libraries carefully noted the presence of this new study aid.[55]

The new graphic system had an impact on the new short auxiliary texts that served as biblical access aids. Gabriel Bruni, a conventual Franciscan friar who flourished in the second half of the fifteenth century, was the author of an alphabetical table of contents referring to book and chapter that, beginning in 1492, was frequently printed among the prefatory materials in small-format portable bibles (B-594). In 1495 he, or his printer Froben, added references in the table to the new marginal alphabets (B-598). While during the Middle Ages a Dominican concordance had scarcely been a rare book (overall, approximately one hundred thirteenth- and fourteenth-century manuscript copies of different versions of the Dominican verbal concordance survive), in the age of print it became a bestseller, for it could be much more easily used with the new printed bibles that contained marginal alphabets. Between 1485 and 1496 in Nuremberg, Speyer and Basle a standard form of the Dominican concordance was printed in press runs that were remarkably large for the incunable period. The total output was reasonably several thousand copies (C-849-853).

In about 1497, inspired by the reformatting of portable bibles, German printers began to place evenly spaced marginal letters in the folio-sized bibles printed for scholars. These volumes contained the Vulgate text accompanied by either the *Postilla Literalis* of the Franciscan Nicolaus de Lyra or the *Postilla* of the Dominican Hugh of Saint-Cher, the two standard medieval guides to the historical exposition of Scripture (B-609, B-610). The letters also provided the reference points for the Franciscan Peter Mollenbecke of Cologne's *Tabula Directoria*, a self-contained index of Nicolaus de Lyra's commentary that a reader could use as a subject index to any small portable printed bible with marginal alphabets (M-807).

The second principal change which printing effected in biblical text format was the introduction and eventual perfection of graphic techniques for the designation of specific verses within biblical chapters, a phenomenon that was also directly related to the use of alphabetical characters. The ultimate product of the varied systems that fifteenth-century printers pioneered for the unambiguous citation by chapter and verse of specific words within the text, an essential aspect of modern exegesis and evangelical discourse, was the modern system of numbered verses. Among the immediate manuscript antecedents for this graphic innovation of early printing was the intra-textual letters used in sermon collections, discussed above. As has been noted, Anton Koberger and Johannes Zainer divided sermon collections in this manner and in 1477 used the same intra-textual letters as tie-notes in bibles for the Eusebian marginal concordance.

In July 1481, very soon after intra-textual letters had first been used as tie-notes for marginal concordances, Johannes Herbort, a German printer working in Venice for Nicolaus Jenson and Johannes of Cologne, perfected superscript letters as tie-notes to link Nicolaus de Lyra's *Postilla Literalis* to the text of the Old and New Testaments (B-611). This was the same Herbort who some three years later would print the first Venetian bibles with marginal Dominican alphabets (B-580). His tie-note reference system was directly modelled on the page format of the fourteenth-century civil and canon law codices that had been produced at Bologna by the pecia system. Herbort's tie-notes complemented the lemmata that in the manuscript tradition of de Lyra's *Postilla Literalis* and in the previous editions had provided the sole link between text and commentary. Ironically, the text format of de Lyra in print thus came to resemble quite closely that of the thirteenth-century Hebrew codices that had contained his principal source, Rashi's commentary on the Hebrew Bible.[56] Within the Latin manuscript tradition, Petrarch in the late fourteenth century had experimented with the use of juristic page format for glossing classical texts, but his innovation had not been emulated. A century later early printing successfully served to transfer the textual format that had until then been limited in manuscripts to juristic texts produced in northern Italy to the new and highly fertile contexts of classical texts and the Bible. Within Bibles, alphabetical tie-notes spread throughout central and western Europe.

The new superscript printed letters in bibles allowed for indicating reference loci even more precisely than with modern numbered verses. In the Froben and Petri 1498 edition containing the *Glossa Ordinaria* and the *Postilla Literalis* of de Lyra, equally-spaced capital letters marked the Dominican system of chapter divisions, and lower-case alphabetic letters marked the printed line in the text within which superscript letters denoted each *glossa* or *postillum* (B-609). Johannes Amerbach's 1498-1502 folio edition of the Bible with Hugh of Saint-Cher's *Postilla* used marginal lower-case letters to mark the line and lower-case superscript letters to denote the exact words within the line to which each of Hugh's *postilla* was attached (B-610).[57]

In the wake of these typographical innovations, the first true biblical verse numbering appeared in the Book of Psalms. Prior to the thirteenth century, the Psalter had had its own peculiar text format of numbered *capitula*. In antiquity it appears to have been the first biblical book of either Testament and, indeed, one of the first major ancient literary texts to have had numerical subdistinctions (the chapter divisions in classical pagan texts being generally unnumbered).[58] In Hebrew, the Psalms as transmitted by the Dead Sea Scrolls were unnumbered; marginal Psalm numbers were said to have been introduced by the translators of the Septuagint, and they are indeed present in the *Codex Sinaiticus* and *Codex Alexandrinus*.[59] In the seventh century, Syriac scribes in the East and Irish scribes in the West continued the practice of numbering the Psalms, and in the ninth century the practice was normal within the confines of the Carolingian Empire.[60] However, the practice of numbering the Psalms waned in the tenth century, and the Psalms in thirteenth-century portable bibles were, more often than not, unnumbered –

presumably because university-trained clerics were expected to retain the entire Psalter by heart. Indeed, the usual text format for the Book of Psalms in university bibles had no space for psalm numbers comparable to the space allotted to chapter numbers in other books.[61] A significant number of thirteenth-century bibles did not even include a Psalter.[62] In this context, Mary Carruthers's notion of the book incorporated into memory rings particularly true.[63]

The evolution of the text format of the Psalter toward unnumbered psalms thus ran contrary to the general late-medieval tendency to develop graphic numbered sub-distinctions that could serve as an efficacious substitute for rote memorization. From the eleventh to the fourteenth century, the usual mode for citing a psalm was to identify it by its incipit rather than by its number. In his letters Peter the Venerable, abbot of Cluny (1156), never cited psalms by their number, and in ordinals, breviaries and books of hours readings from the Psalms were identified by verse incipit, which served as a cue when the full text to be recited was not written out.[64] While the verbal concordance prepared by Hugh of Saint-Cher referred to psalms by number and alphabetical distinction,[65] like all other biblical books, at least one abridged concordance (dating from *c.* 1400) and subsequently the incunable editions of the Dominican concordance referred to psalms by number only (B-540). Indeed, the tables of the temporale and sanctorale of the mass in Newberry MS-19, cited above, provide only the incipit of the psalm verses for references in contrast to the chapter and letter provided for all other biblical books.[66] All these special modes of referring to the Psalter clearly implied greater reliance on rote memory than for the rest of the Bible. It is also uncertain how references to psalm numbers would have been used with the many university Bibles that were without numbered psalms. Some readers may have annotated their copies;[67] others may have mentally provided numbers by relying on the large illuminated initials that frequently identified the eight psalms beginning key liturgical divisions.[68]

Although the practice of numbering psalms had waned in the tenth century, scribes continued to write the Book of Psalms in lines of sense (i.e. *per cola et commata*), long after the rest of the Old and New Testament was regularly written out as prose.[69] In thirteenth-century university bibles copied in Paris and Oxford, where the Book of Psalms, like the other books, was written out as prose, scribes evolved a unique text format in which the incipit of each psalm was marked by a major initial and the incipit of each verse within the psalm was highlighted by a minor alternating red or blue initial. In essence, this special 'Psalter' format preserved the ancient distinctions of the *cola* and *commata*. The same text format occurred in the Psalters of portable breviaries from the thirteenth to the fifteenth century. However, scribes of this period did not completely avoid the provision of additional aids, notably in vernacular versions. A German-language Psalter copied in 1378, probably in Erfurt, used a complex dual system of alpha-numerical leaf numbering to aid the reader.[70] It was, however, the unnumbered format characteristic of most university bibles and Roman breviaries that was replicated by the early large-format monumental printed bibles.[71]

While the tradition of psalm numbering in the waning centuries of the Middle Ages was weak, it had not perished. Indeed, as already noted, the scribes of the two early fifteenth-century Bohemian manuscripts discussed above numbered the Psalms and even provided tabular concordances for matching psalm numbers to titles and incipits. By the mid-fifteenth century, an increasing number of scribes were returning to the ancient Carolingian practice of numbering psalms, the practice that Richel, as explained above, restored typographically in 1475.[72] The marginal notes that identified sources – a common printers' reader's aid in the incunable period – virtually always after 1475 referred to psalms by their number.

It is thus somewhat ironic that the Psalter, the biblical book so often retained by rote memory and that had been graphically retrograde in the late Middle Ages, provided the venue for the introduction of verse numbering. However, the foundations for numbering the verses of the Psalter date back to late antiquity. Jerome, probably following the Hebrew original and Greek Septuagint models that are now lost, introduced the practice of writing the entire Latin Bible in lines of sense (*per cola et commata*), and thus created the possibility of establishing verse numbers for biblical books.[73] Whereas the psalms in the Dead Sea Scrolls were written out as prose, they were written as verse in the oldest surviving Greek papyri and parchment codices.[74] In the Eastern Empire in the mid-fourth century, the corpus of biblical aids attributed to Euthalius made abundant use of numerical verse references to the New Testament, and among Jews the practice of denoting verses, which began in the Talmudic period, was rendered canonical by the Masoretic Hebrew text prepared between *c.* 600 and *c.* 1000.[75] The earliest surviving manuscripts with verses denoted by a special, colon-like sign (called a *silluk*) date from the ninth century.[77]

In contrast in the West, the verse distinctions introduced to the Latin Vulgate by Jerome were never standardized, and since these varied from codex to codex, a verse reference system like that employed by Euthalius in Greek and the Masoretes in Hebrew was impracticable. Nevertheless, reference to the total number of verses of biblical books in the Greek and Hebrew manner occur in a fourth-century index to the Bible's content that is preserved in two monastic codices dating from the ninth and tenth century;[77] another rare instance of the notation of total verses occurs at the end of I Corinthians in three early medieval Latin codices and in one dating from the thirteenth century.[78] While no Latin bibles contain marginal verse numbers, Jewish scribes in the Middle East and western Europe, who maintained a tradition of consistent verse distinctions, noted running totals of verses in the margins and at the ends of books.[79] Rabbi Isaac Nathan in about 1440 could therefore use verse numbers as locus points for the first verbal concordance of the Hebrew Bible, a reference tool printed by Daniel Bomberg in Venice in 1524 and translated into Latin in 1556.[80]

For the Latin Bible, the hybridization of numbered psalms and numbered verses occurred first in print. As has been noted, from 1475 onward the Psalms were regularly numbered in printed bibles, although not always in printed breviaries. In Würzburg, Georg Ryser in the mid-1490s combined printed Psalm numbers with a return to the *cola et commata* format in order to facilitate the reader's consultation of Bishop Bruno of Würzburg's eleventh-century verse-by-verse commentary printed in the margins of his edition of the Psalter (P-1046). In Anton Koberger's 1494 edition of the same text alphabetical tie-notes, similar to those of the de Lyra editions, linked each verse to its commentary (P-1050). The verse divisions used in Bruno's work differed greatly from those generally present in scholastic bibles. In his 1494 bilingual Psalter, the Augsburg printer Erhardt Ratdolt denoted the usual verses of the numbered psalms with capitals and then used sequential alphabetical tie-notes to link, verse by verse, the Latin Vulgate Psalms to a German translation printed in the margins.[82] Consequently, each letter of the alphabet denoted a discrete verse within each numbered psalm. The progression from alphabetical superscript tie-notes to the modern inter-text numbering of verses was a logical one in light of the long medieval tradition dating back to Bede that had viewed alphabetical characters as an attractive alternative to clumsy roman numerals.[83]

Marcus Reinhard and Nicolaus Philippi in their 1482 Bible (probably following the model of the initial *Fontibus ex graecis* edition of 1479), in a revival of ancient practice, had prefaced each of the Gospels with a register of *capitula* or list of titles for each chapter that did not occur in the body of the Gospel text itself (B-574). The printers had denoted each *capitulum* with an arabic number in the margin, thus introducing a peculiar sort of marginal verse number into the Bible's page format. In Venice in 1484, Johannes Herbort in his second Bible had included the same registers (B-580). In 1496 in Venice, in the first edition of Hugh of Saint-Cher's *Postilla* on the Psalms, Johannes and Gregorius de Gregoriis printed the Psalter with marginal Arabic numbers to denote the biblical verses, and these same numbers appear in modern editions of the Vulgate. The numbers, which complemented marginal alphabets, were clearly useful because the lengthy commentary that followed each verse made it difficult for the reader to orient himself in regard to the basic biblical text.[84] However, it is also relevant that Venice housed one of western Europe's largest and most intellectually active Jewish communities, and it is indeed probable that the de Gregoriis, who actively participated in the humanist program of recovering ancient literature, were inspired by the Jewish practice of noting running totals of verses in the margins.[85]

Without doubt after 1500 the movement towards verse numbering was driven by the characteristically humanistic passion for accuracy in translating the rediscovered languages of the East. In 1509 and again in 1513, Henri Estienne employed verse numbers in the *Psalterium quincuplex* (Schreiber 8, DM6095), the text of which was prepared by Jacques Lefèvre d'Etaples on the basis of his retranslation of the Hebrew.[86] Verse numbers occurred yet again in the new Latin translation of the Hebrew Psalms prepared by the converted Jew and Augustinian friar Felice da Prato, a volume that Pope Leo X commissioned and Daniel Bomberg printed in Venice in 1515 (DM6095 bis).[87] Verses numbered uniquely for the Psalms occurred again in the Ethiopic column of Johann Potkin's Cologne 1518 Polyglot Psalter. In 1528, the Dominican friar and noted Hebraist Santes Pagnini expanded marginal enumeration of verses to the entire Bible in his new translation of both the Old and New Testament printed in Lyon (Pl. 22).[88] In 1534 when Sebastian Münster published the first Protestant retranslation of the Hebrew Bible, he provided in Latin the traditional Masoretic sum totals for the number of *versus* or *sententiae* at the end of Genesis and Exodus (DM5087). His printers also emulated Daniel Bomberg's use of space to enhance the visibility of the traditional Jewish punctuation marks for the distinction of verses.[89] In mid-century Robert Estienne, appreciating the convenience of verse numbers, commenced their popularization by using marginal numbers throughout his 1551 New Testament, and in April 1555 he printed a complete Latin Bible with intra-textual rather than marginal numbers (DM6132, DM6135). The 1555 Bible also had marginal concordance references to verse numbers in addition to alphabetical distinctions (Pl. 23). Estienne vaunted the advantages of using this tome in conjunction with his biblical concordance that he had printed three months earlier.[90]

Finally, printing's new page format encouraged silent reference consultation of the Bible as well as other books by rendering the text less ambiguous. This new intense usage had three tangible consequences on bindings, each of which was designed to facilitate rapid consultation. One was the presence of finger tabs that enabled rapid entry into the biblical text. Although tabs in printed books had antecedents dating back to at least the fourteenth century, they became ubiquitous for the first time in the era of print. In bibles with marginal alphabets, tabs guided the reader's fingers rapidly to the beginning of each chapter as well as the glossary of Hebrew names (Pl. 24).[91]

Another great innovation in fifteenth-century bookbinding design was the emergence of 'projecting squares' or *chasses*, the rectangular, square cornered areas of a book's cover that protruded beyond the edges of the pages (Pl. 25). Before 1450 the leaves of manuscript codices had been crudely cut with a chisel after the boards had been attached so that the roughly cut edges and boards were generally flush, with a few leaves often protruding slightly beyond the edge, a style that posed no problem as long as books were shelved flat. In the mid-fifteenth century, however, *chasses* or projecting corners were introduced to facilitate steeply angled and vertical shelving without damage to the leaves, which increasingly were made of paper. They were particularly useful when the books were placed on the innovative bookshelves and tiered *pupîtres* that characterized the late gothic library.[92] In combination, *chasses* and the new furnishings permitted the creation of reference libraries that were more compactly stored and far larger than those that had existed previously in the Middle Ages.[93] Bevelled finger grips, spine titles, alphabetical shelf-marks written either on the spine or cover, and colour-stained edges facilitated the removal of closely shelved volumes, helping the reader to consult them rapidly in the new and radically larger institutional libraries of the late fifteenth century.[94]

For these new 'Gothic' libraries that first emerged in Germany, Austria, Switzerland, the Netherlands and eastern France, new catalogues referring to the alpha-numerical shelf-marks placed on either cover, spine or fore-edges were prepared. These catalogues – all of which were manuscript but at least one of which was explicitly referred to as a *catalogus typographicus*[95] – typically contained alphabetical characters and arabic numbers in their margins and were written in a format clearly linked to that of the pages of incunable Bibles that bore marginal, printed Dominican letters. The earliest dated example, prepared in 1474 (Pl. 26), comes from the monastery of Saint Ulrich and Saint Afra in Augsburg, an abbey whose printing press produced texts divided into alphabetical distinctions.[96] Thus around the year 1500, the macrocosm of the catalogue of the *bibliotheca* had become graphically conjoined to the microcosm of the printed Bible.

## NOTES

1 P. Saenger, 'The Impact of the Early Printed Page on the History of Reading', *Bulletin du Bibliophile* II (1996), p. 248.

2 Carla Bozzolo & Ezio Ornato, *Pour une histoire du livre manuscrit au Moyen Age: Trois essais de codicologie quantitative* (Paris, Éditions du Centre National de la Recherche Scientifique, 1983), pp. 89-121.

3 A rare example of an incomplete Bible written in gothic cursive script is Newberry Library

MS f58.1; see P. Saenger, *A Catalogue of the Pre-1500 Manuscript Books at the Newberry Library* (Chicago: University of Chicago Press, 1989), p. 110.

4 Paul Schwenke, *Johannes Gutenbergs zweiundvierzigzeilige Bibel: Ergänzungsband zur Faksimile-Ausgabe* (Leipzig, 1923), p. 14 (no. 28); Don Cleveland Norman, *The 500th Anniversary Pictorial Census of the Gutenberg Bible* (Chicago, Coverdale Press, 1961), p. 101.

5 Schwenke, *Johannes Gutenbergs zweiundvierzigzeilige Bibel*, p. 7 (no. 1); Norman, *500th Anniversary Pictorial Census*, p. 61.

6 Eberhard König, 'A Leaf from a Gutenberg Bible Illuminated in England', *British Library Journal*, 9 (1983), 48, n. 15; Schwenke, *Johannes Gutenbergs zweiundvierzigzeilige Bibel*, p. 8 (no. 5).

7 Norman, *500th Anniversary Pictorial Census*, p. 24.

8 William B. Todd, 'The Texas Gutenberg Bible: Procedures Determining the Selection', *Journal of Library History*, 15 (1980), 288-90 with two plates; Karen Gould, 'The Gutenberg Bible at Texas: an Educational Resource', *The Library Chronicle of the University of Texas at Austin*, ns 22 (1983), 93 and pl. of fol. 49; Norman, *500th Anniversary Pictorial Census*, p. 134.

9 Norman, *500th Anniversary Pictorial Census*, pp. 139-41.

10 König, 'A Leaf from a Gutenberg Bible Illuminated in England', pp. 33-4 (pl. of recto and verso) and 35-6.

11 For some examples, see Eberhard König, 'New Perspectives on the History of Mainz Printing: a Fresh Look at Illuminated Imprints', in *Printing the Written Word*, ed. by Sandra Hindman (Ithaca, N.Y.: Cornell University Press, 1991), pp. 143-73; *Die illuminierten Seiten der Gutenberg-Bibel* (Dortmund, 1983).

12 Armando Petrucci, *Writers and Readers in Medieval Italy: Studies in the History of Written Culture* (New Haven & London: Yale University Press, 1995), pp. ix and 59. For analogous symbolic properties of large-format books in the early modern period, see Henri-Jean Martin, *The French Book: Religion, Absolutism and Readership* (Baltimore, Johns Hopkins University Press, 1996), pp. 57-9.

13 Samuel Berger, 'Un ancien texte latin des Actes des Apôtres retrouvé dans un manuscrit provenant de Perpignan', *Notices et extraits des manuscrits de la Bibliothèque Nationale et autres bibliothèques*, 35, pt 1 (1895), 177; *Vetus Latina*, 25, pt 1 (1975-82), 15-16. The manuscript measures 893×490 mm.

14 This lack was explicitly noted in the *c.* 1500 catalogue of the Carthusian monastery at Erfurt, Paul Lehmann, *Mittelalterliche Bibliothekskatologe Deutschlands und der Schweiz* 2 (1928), 273.

15 James E. Walsh, *A Catalogue of the Fifteenth-Century Printed Books in the Harvard University Library*, 1 (Binghamton, N.Y., 1991), pp. 4-5.

16 Newberry Library MS 75, see Saenger, *Catalogue of the Pre-1500 Manuscript Books at the Newberry Library* (above, n. 3), p. 137. Vespasiano mentions this book in his life of the Cardinal in his *Memoirs*.

17 *Bibliothèque Nationale: Catalogue des manuscrits latins* 1 (1939), pp, 36-7; Léopold Delisle, *Le Cabinet des manuscrits de la Bibliothèque Nationale* (Paris: Imprimerie Nationale, 1868-81), I, 75; Delisle, *Mélanges de paléographie et de bibliographie* (Paris: Champion, 1880), p. 355.

18 Richard H. Rouse & Mary A. Rouse, *Preachers, Florilegia and Sermons: Studies on the Manipulus Florum of Thomas of Ireland* (Toronto: Pontifical Institute of Mediaeval Studies, 1979), pp. 9-13; *idem*. 'The Verbal Concordance to the Scriptures', *Archivum fratrum praedicatorum*, 44 (1974), 5-30.

19 Saenger, 'The Impact of the Early Printed Page' (above, n. 1), p. 255.

20 Two copies, those in the Biblioteca Pública del Estado in Burgos and at Yale University, have added manuscript marginal alphabets (about which see below), Eberhard König, *Zur Situation der Gutenberg-Forschung: ein Supplement* (Münster: Verlag Bibliotheca Rara, 1995), frontispiece; Norman, *500th Anniversary Pictorial Census* (above, n. 4), pp. 24 and 139.

21 British Library, Grenville 12,231.

22 These include the fragment at the Newberry Library and copies at the British Library. It is not clear whether this pattern might have anything to do with the table of rubrics for this volume, which I have not seen; cf. Paul Needham, 'A Gutenberg Bible Used as Printer's Copy by Heinrich Eggestein in Strasbourg, *ca.* 1469', *Transactions of the Cambridge Bibliographical Society*, 9 (1986), 71. The copy of the Eggestein German vernacular Bible in the Van Kampen collection, VK Inc. 802, has similar red foliation.

23 Goff N-131 and H-165. For the *Summa Theologica*, see the Newberry copies of Goff T-208 and T-209.

24 Saenger, 'The Impact of the Early Printed Page', p. 261.

25 Numbers were added in black ink in the upper right hand corner of the Van Kampen copy, VK Inc. 765.

26 B-612. In its margins this bible contains the *Postilla literalis* of De Lyra accompanied by the additions of Paul of Burgos.

27 Saenger, 'The Impact of the Early Printed Page', pp. 275-8.

28 For the earlier ones, see Rouse & Rouse, *Preachers, Florilegia and Sermons*, pp. 9-13.

29 See Saenger, *Catalogue of the Pre-1500 Manuscript Books at the Newberry Library* (above, n. 3), pp. 35-6. Curiously, the table itself was divided by marginal graphic alphabets. A similar table is recorded by N. R. Ker, *Medieval Manuscripts in British Libraries* 1 (Oxford: Clarendon Press, 1969), 97.

30 For an example see Newberry Library MS 22, illustrated in *Convivencia: Jews, Muslims and Christians in Medieval Spain*, ed. by Vivian B. Mann, Thomas F. Glick & Jerrilynn D. Dodds (New York: Braziller, 1992), pp. 178-9; see also Saenger, *Catalogue of the Pre-1500 Manuscript Books at the Newberry Library*, p. 38.

31 See Todd, 'The Texas Gutenberg Bible' (above, n. 8), pl. 2. These letters are often late medieval emendations but in a thirteenth-century manuscript recently acquired by The Scriptorium: Center for Christian Antiquities, VK MS 805, they have been written in lead, along with chapter numbers, as indications for the rubricator. The eventual rubricator, however, ignored the former while copying the latter. A late and derivative use of these letters occurs in Thomas More's private prayer book, cf. Louis L. Martz & Richard S. Sylvester, *Thomas More's Private Prayer Book* (New Haven & London: Yale University Press, 1969), pp. xxxi-xxxiv and plates of fols v verso-vi verso.

32 H. Leclercq, 'Canons d'Eusèbe', *Dictionnaire d'archéologie chrétienne et de liturgie* 2 (Paris: Letouzez & Ané, 1910); Carl Nordenfalk, *Die spätantiken Kanontafeln: Kunstgeschichtlichen Studien über die eusebianische Evangelien-Konkordanz in den vier ersten Jahrhunderten ihrer Geschichte* (Göteborg: Isacsons, 1938).

33 The only Biblical manuscript with any Grosseteste note is a Greek Gospel. On Grosseteste see: S. Harrison Thomson, 'Grosseteste's Topical Concordance of the Bible and the Fathers', *Speculum*, 9 (1934), 139-44; Thompson, *The Writings of Robert Grosseteste Bishop of Lincoln 1235-1253* (Cambridge: University Press, 1940), pp. 122-4; R. W. Hunt, 'Manuscripts Containing the Indexing Symbols of Robert Grosseteste', *Bodleian Library Record*, 4 (1953), 241-55; Hunt, 'The Library of Robert Grosseteste', in *Robert Grosseteste Scholar and Bishop*, ed. by D. A. Callus (Oxford: Clarendon Press, 1955), pp. 131-45, especially 132-5. A Hebrew Psalter thought to be from Grosseteste appears to have none of his notes, see A. G. Little, *Franciscan Papers, Lists, and Documents* (Manchester: University Press,

1943), p. 140; cf. M. R. James, *The Western Manuscripts in the Library of Trinity College, Cambridge* 2 (Cambridge: University Press, 1901), 244-5.

34 See Bernard Ardura, *Dictionnaire de Spiritualité*, 16 (1994), cols 1581-83. This work has been reprinted by Migne, *PL* 186: 10-619; it was widely copied and was printed in Strasbourg in 1473.

35 A note on the Eusebian canons beginning *Ex ordine librorum quatuor*, not printed by Migne, is reproduced by George F. Warner & Julius P. Gilson, *Catalogue of Western Manuscripts in the Old Royal and King's Collections* (London: British Museum, 1921), IV, pl. 38, cf. I, 91.

36 A rare example of a fifteenth-century manuscript containing marginal concordance references is Newberry Library MS 161, a *Harmony of the Gospels* copied *c.* 1450 at the Groenendaal monastery of the Devotio Moderna. This book was written in parallel columns in a format anticipating the polyglot Bibles of the sixteenth century. The concordance references referred not to the Eusebian sections but to the standard university chapter divisions. Since these were far longer, the references were relatively ambiguous and cumbersome to use.

37 The instructions for the rubricator that accompanied the Gutenberg and other monumental Bibles did not call for the Psalms to be numbered.

38 In the first printed Bible produced in Ulm in 1480, Johannes Zainer used intra-textual letters for the same purpose that appear to be identical to those he used to divide the sermon collections that he also printed B-567 (*GW* 4232); they are also comparable to the letters he used to divide his edition of Ps. Jerome's *Vitae patrum* into sections.

39 See Gabriele Baptist-Hlawatsch, *Der katechetische Werk Ulrich von Pottenstein* (Tübingen: Niemeyer, 1980). I am indebted to Professor Nigel Palmer for this reference.

40 Saenger, 'The Impact of the Early Printed Page' (above, n. 1), pp. 294-5.

41 Rouse & Rouse, *Preachers, Florilegia and Sermons* (above, n. 18), pp. 202-3; Anne Hudson, *Lollards and their Books* (London: Hambleton Press, 1985), pp. 4-5.

42 The letter *h* occurs rarely.

43 A special // sign was used to denote the explicit; see the rubric for the table of lessons edited by J. Forshall & F Madden, *The Holy Bible Made from the Latin Vulgate by John Wyclife and his Followers* (Oxford: University Press, 1850), IV, p. 683*.

44 Four of these very small vernacular New Testament manuscripts with marginal letters in the Gospels and the Epistles and a vernacular lectionary that refers to marginal letters in the Gospels are in the collection of The Scriptorium: Center for Christian Antiquities. These books are very different from the de luxe volumes described by Bernard Louis Manning, *The People's Faith in the Time of Wyclif* (2nd edn; Sussex, 1975), pp. 10-11. See Anne Hudson, *The Premature Reformation: Wycliffite Texts and Lollard History* (Oxford: Clarendon Press, 1988), pp. 198-9; Hudson, 'Lollard Book Production', in *Book Production and Publishing in Britain 1375-1475*, ed. by Jeremy Griffiths & Derek Pearsall (Cambridge: University Press, 1989), pp. 131-2 and pls 13-14.

45 Manning, *The People's Faith*, pp. 6-7. In England the reading of the Bible had a peculiar importance for the laity, see Margaret Aston, *Lollards and Reformers: Images and Literacy in Late Medieval Religion* (London: Hambleton Press, 1984), pp. 199-200 and 205-6. For a description of the comparable reading of vernacular devotional texts during the Mass on the Continent see Paul Saenger, 'Books of Hours and the Reading Habits of the Later Middle Ages', in *The Culture of Print: Power and Uses of Print in Early Modern Europe*, ed. by Roger Chartier (Princeton, N.J., 1987); cf. Thomas Frederick Simmons, *The Lay Folks Mass Book or the Manner of Hearing Mass with Rubrics and Devotions for the People* (EETS, o.s., no. 71; London, 1879), pp. xxxv-xxxvii.

46 See Hudson, *Lollards and Their Books*, p. 7, n. 34, reprinted from *Notes and Queries*, 21 (1973), 443-53.

47 The former was copied in 1421. For it see Sir George Warner, *Descriptive Catalogue of the Library of C. W. Dyson Perrins* (London: Oxford University Press, 1920), pp. 294-5, and Sam Fogg Catalogue no. 14, pp. 65-73. The latter, copied in 1429 (not 1419), is now at the The Scriptorium: Center for Christian Antiquities. It was formerly in Manhattan College and sold at Christie's in New York, 1 June 1991, lot no. 5. I am indebted to Sidney Tibbetts for bringing this codex to my attention and providing me with the salient details of its marginal annotation.

48 The passages to which the marginal concordance pertains are denoted by tie notes in black ink.

49 On reading this paper, Sidney Tibbetts has reported to me that some of the marginal references are to the Old Testament; in these instances the alphabetical distinctions referred to are mental.

50 This was the earliest of the editions designated as the *Fontibus ex graecis* (so named from the opening line of a Latin distich found in them), which regularly contained marginal alphabets (*GW*, vol. 4 (1930), col. 68); see T. H. Darlow & H. F. Moule, *Historical Catalogue of the Holy Scripture in the Library of the British and Foreign Bible Society* (London: The Bible House, 1903), II, 911 and Henri Quentin, *Mémoire sur l'établissement du texte de la Vulgate* (Rome & Paris: Desclée, 1922), pp. 79-80.

51 Saenger, 'The Impact of the Early Printed Page', p. 282 (pl.).

52 In complete incunable Bibles, the Psalms seem never to have been divided by marginal letters.

53 See also *GW* 4262, cf. 4268. Kessler also reformatted the *Book of Sentences* of Peter Lombard along similar lines. The typographical humanist Bernhard Richel had already restored the marginal identification of *auctoritates* found in twelfth-century manuscripts, a graphic element that university scribes had discarded in the thirteenth century. Richel at the same time also introduced to Lombard's text format tables refering to mental alphabetical *subdistinctiones* within the questions, a reference system clearly related to that of his marginal concordance to the Bible. Within two years of his 1487 Bible, Kessler introduced this system to the page format of Peter Lombard's *Sententiae*.

54 In 1491 another Basel printer, Johannes Amerbach, placed marginal alphabets throughout his Bible and indicated the passages that were referred to with the double slash mark; B-590; BMC, III, 694.

55 See above, n. 14.

56 See Malachi Beit-Arié, *Hebrew Manuscripts of East and West: Towards a Comparative Codicology* (London: The British Library, 1992), pp. 88-95.

57 See Stanley Morison, *German Incunabula in the British Museum* (London: Gollancz, 1928), pl. 63. A precursor of this complex apparatus exists in the form of early manuscript annotations to a copy of the second Eggestein Bible, now in the British Library, IC 702.

58 Nigel Palmer, 'Kapital und Buch', *Frühmittelalterliche Studien* 23 (1989), 43-56. Scribonius Largus's book of medical recipes, the *Compositiones*, ed. by Sergio Sconocchia (Leipzig: Teubner, 1983) demonstrates that the practical advantages of numerical subdivisions of text were not unknown in Rome in the first century A.D., at least within a utilitarian genre of text. See also Diana Albino, 'La Divisione in capitoli nelle opere degli antichi', *Annali della Facoltà di lettere e filosofia Università di Napoli*, 10 (1962-3), 219-34. On the importance of *capitula* to Christian readers of the patristic age, see Brian Stock, *Augustine the Reader: Meditation, Self Knowledge, and the Ethics of Interpretation* (Cambridge, Mass.: Harvard University Press, 1996), p. 97.

59 See the prologue *Omnem psalmorum*, Donatien de Bruyne, *Préfaces de la Bible Latine* (Namur: Godenne, 1920), pp. 73-4.

60 For examples of ninth-century manuscripts with numbered Psalms, see the Utrecht Psalter and the facsimiles of the Palaeographical Society, series I, nos 69. Ninth-century Tironian

Psalters also had numbered Psalms, e.g. Franz Steffens, *Lateinische Paläographie* (Trier, 1909), pl. 56.

61 See for example Newberry Library Ruggles MS 26. In Newberry Library MS-19 the Psalms were numbered in the margins by a rubricator who did not participate in the initial confection of the book. In Newberry MS-18 they were numbered in small red Roman numerals in the margins, also in a *post factum* manner.

62 See for example N. R. Ker, *Medieval Manuscripts in British Libraries* I (1969), p. 267 and Newberry Library MS 22 (above, n. 30).

63 Mary Carruthers, *The Book of Memory: a Study of Memory in Medieval Culture* (Cambridge: University Press, 1990).

64 Stephen J. P. Van Dijk, *Sources of the Modern Roman Liturgy: the Ordinals by Haymo of Faversham and Related Documents*, 2 vols (Leiden: Brill, 1963); Van Dijk, *The Ordinal of the Papal Court from Innocent III to Boniface VIII and Related Documents* (Freiburg, Switz.: University Press, 1975).

65 See Rouse & Rouse, 'The Verbal Concordance to the Scriptures' (above, n. 18), pls I and II.

66 See above, n. 31.

67 Newberry Library MS 16 was thus annotated with Arabic numbers in the fifteenth century.

68 These were Psalm numbers 1, 26, 38, 52, 68, 80, 96 and 109.

69 For late examples of the Book of Psalms writen in lines of sense, see L. Delisle, *Notice de douze manuscrits royaux du XIIIe et XIVe siècle* (Paris: Imprimerie Nationale, 1902).

70 Sold at Christie's, 26 June 1991, lot 26; Van Kampen collection VK MS 776. I am grateful to Sidney Tibbetts for bringing this codex to my attention.

71 See above, n. 40.

72 For example the Psalms were numbered in red in Newberry MS 81, a liturgical Psalter dating from after 1461 and in the Psalter contained in a Camaldolese Breviary copied *c.* 1463, Newberry Library MS 77.

73 Charles Graux, 'Nouvelles recherches sur la stichométrie', *Revue de philologie, de littérature et d'histoire anciennes*, n.s. 2 (1878), 97-143, see especially p. 138. The Old Latin translation antedating Jerome had been copied in a *scriptura continua* text format similar to that customary for the pagan classics, see *Palaeographical Society Facsimiles*, series I, no. 54. In the thirteenth century, Hugh of Saint-Cher believed that Jerome had adopted the *cola et commata* format from the original Hebrew, a logical inference given the carefully marked Hebrew codices of the day: see his *Postilla* to the phrase *Novo scribendi genere distinximus* in Jerome's prologue to Isaiah, reprinted by M. Hubert in *Archivum latinitatis Medii Aevi*, 37 (1970), 152.

74 J. W. B. Barns & G. D. Kilpatrick, 'A New Psalm Fragment', *Proceedings of the British Academy*, 43 (1957), 229-32; H. J. M. Milne & T. C. Skeat, *Scribes and Correctors of the Codex Sinaiticus* (London: British Museum, 1938).

75 G. Bardy in *Dictionnaire de la Bible: Supplément* 2 (1934), cols 1215-18; Christian D. Ginsburg, *Introduction to the Massoretico-Critical Edition of the Hebrew Bible* (London: Trinitarian Bible Society, 1897), pp. 99-100; Ernst Würthwein, *The Text of the Old Testament: an Introduction to Kittel-Kahle's Biblia Hebraica* (Oxford: Blackwell, 1957), p. 17; Artur Weiser, *The Old Testament: Its Formation and Development* (New York: Association Press, 1961), p. 366.

76 Ginsburg, *Introduction to the Massoretico-Critical Edition of the Hebrew Bible*, p. 68.

77 Quentin, *Mémoire* (above, n. 54), p. 505; Theodor Mommsen, 'Zur lateinischen Stichometrie', *Hermes*, 21 (1885), 142-56 and 25 (1890), 636-8.

78 Berger, 'Un ancien texte latin des Actes des Apôtres retrouvé' (above, n. 13), p. 171.

79 Ginsburg, *Introduction to the Massoretico-Critical Edition of the Hebrew Bible*, pp. 67 and 68-108.

80 *The Jewish Encyclopedia* 6 (1916), 628. See the remarks of E. Mangenot, 'Concordances de la Bible', *Dictionnaire de la Bible* 2 (1910), cols 899-1900 and Walter F. Specht, 'Chapter and Verse Divisions', in *The Oxford Companion to the Bible*, ed. by Bruce M. Metzger & Michael D. Coogan (Oxford: University Press, 1993), pp. 105-6. In Antonius Reuchlin's Latin translation of Nathan's concordance printed by Heinrich Petit in Basel in 1556, the chapter and verse numbers used were those of the Latin text.

81 Margaret M. Smith has recently published an excellently illustrated study of the early editions of this text: 'The Typography of Complex Texts: How an Early Printed Eliminated the Scribes' Red', *Typography Papers*, 1 (1996), 75-92.

82 See Morison, *German Incunabula* (above, n. 68), pl. 57.

83 See Paul Saenger, *Space Between Words: The Origin of Silent Reading* (Stanford: University Press, 1997).

84 Goff H-530; Hain 8972*; Saenger, 'The Impact of the Early Printed Page' (above, n. 1), p. 292 (pl.). Marginal letters were absent in the Book of Psalms in incunable Bibles which had them elsewhere in the Old Testament. Their presence here is indicative of the reader's perceived need of assistance in determining textual locus. See above, n. 56. Thomas Walleys, as printed in *Expositiones super Psalterium* (London, 1481; Oates 4174), in the headings repeatedly refers to verse numbers as reference points, but a full text of the Psalter with actual verse numbers is not present.

85 Gianvittorio Dillon, 'Sul libro illustrato del Quattrocento: Venezia e Verona', in *La stampa degli Incunaboli nel Veneto*, 2nd edn (Vicenza: Pozza, 1984), pp. 94-5.

86 Fred Schreiber, *The Estiennes* (New York: E. K. Schreiber, 1982), pp. 18-20.

87 In passing, we should also note that in this volume textual variants recorded by the editor and printed in the margin were attached not by sequential letters but by arabic numbers, an innovation that moved tie-notes one step closer to the modern footnote.

88 Printed by Antoine du Ry; see F. Vigouroux, *Dictionnaire de la Bible* 4 (1910), 1948; N. Smith, *NCE* 10 (1967), 862; *Encyclopaedia Judaica* 13 (1971), cols 13-14.

89 This use of space is apparent both in the 1516 *Biblia rabbinica* and in the 1525 *Biblia hebraica* (DM5079, DM5085), both produced in Venice, see Würthwein, *The Text of the Old Testament*, pp. 126-7 (pl.).

90 A. A. Renouard, *Annales de l'imprimerie des Estienne* (Paris: J. Renouard, 1843), p. 86 (no. 2).

91 Newberry Library Inc. 7755a (Goff B-593) is an example of a small-format bible with tabs.

92 Léon Gilissen, *La Reliure occidentale antérieure à 1400* (Bibliologia, 1; Turnhout: Brepols, 1983), p. 27; Graham Pollard, 'Describing Medieval Bookbindings', in *Medieval Learning and Literature: Essays Presented to Richard William Hunt*, ed. by J. J. G. Alexander & M. T. Gibson (Oxford: Clarendon Press, 1976), p. 61; Jacques Lemaire, *Introduction à la codicologie* (Louvain: Université Catholique, 1989), p. 201; Jean Vezin in Elisabeth Baras, Jean Irigoin & Jean Vezin, *La Reliure Médiévale: Trois conférences d'initiation* (Paris: Presses de l'Ecole Normale Supérieure, 1978), p. 41.

93 See P. Saenger, 'The Implications of Incunable Description for the History of Reading Revisited', *Papers of the Bibliographical Society of America*, 91 (1997), 499-501.

94 See the introduction to the late fifteenth-century catalogue of the library of the Dominicans in Vienna, *Mittelalterliche Bibliothekskatologe Österreichs* 1 (Akademie der Wissenschaft in Wien, 1915), 294.

95 Gilbert Ouy, *Le Catalogue de la bibliothèque de Saint-Victor de Paris de Claude de Grandrue* (Paris: Editions du Centre de la Recherche Scientifique, 1983), p. xxxxiv.

96 Antonius de Rampegollis' *Compendium morale*, not after 1473 (Goff R-22) was divided into alpha-numerical subsections and included a printed table referring to them. Johannes Nider's *Praeceptorium* printed by Anton Sorg, who was closely associated with Saints Ulrich and

Afra's press, was also divided into alphabetical *distinctiones* (N-199). Newberry Library Inc. 1643 (Goff C-292), an incunable codex printed by Sorg and confected at the Augustinian convent of Rebdorf in nearby Eichstätt, was annotated with marginal alphabets during this period.

# THE CHANGING SHAPE OF THE VULGATE BIBLE IN FIFTEENTH-CENTURY PRINTING SHOPS

*Paul Needham*

THE ERUDITE AND TRENCHANT Ernst Schulz once wrote that the incunable period was of peculiar significance for book history, for within that half-century span there appeared in printed versions a sort of résumé of essentially all the written culture alive in Europe, from the ancient world to the present.[1] With minor but noteworthy exceptions of a few special programmes, especially some humanistic ventures, the motivation of printers and publishers at this time was not to resurrect forgotten writings, but to supply readers with familiar texts that were actually in wide enough use to define a market. The number of printed editions – each representing a substantial though usually unspecified set of copies – can provide, if carefully analysed, a more accurate gauge of the relative popularity and use of texts than do censuses of surviving manuscripts – each unique, representing only itself. Viewed under Schulz's standpoint it is hardly surprising that there were numerous printed editions of the Latin Bible in the fifteenth century – specifically, eighty-one plain-text editions, and thirteen with surrounds of various commentary. The Bible is a text that in Christian society has self-evidently been in continual use from the Roman Empire onwards. It is not news that it still played significant roles in late medieval society, and that full-text copies of the Latin Bible found usership and readership then. And yet, perhaps there is, on closer look, some lesser element of surprise in the appearance of tens of thousands of new copies of the Latin Bible within a span of fifty years. In the thirteenth century, following the consolidation of the Paris Vulgate, there was a tremendous quantity of Bible-making. Manuscript bibles of the fourteenth and fifteenth centuries are considerably rarer. If someone were to tell you today, with no further information given, that he or she owned a medieval Latin Bibles, you could presume that it belonged to the thirteenth century, and almost always be right.

To put this minor paradox in sharp terms: the fifteenth century, before the advent of printing, was an age when a great many Latin manuscripts in general were written – but it was not an age when a particularly substantial number of Latin Bibles were made. And yet, once printed bibles became available, 1455 and after, there was strong and steady demand for them. Perhaps we may visualize the situation as this: the flood of thirteenth-century Bible was so great that for another two hundred years there was no shortage of Vulgate manuscripts. The thirteenth-century stock continued to be nearly adequate, changing hands as the generations passed, for the needs of most of the individuals and religious foundations that used the Bible, and the constituents of this stock continued to have active, useful lives.[2] But once, or soon after, printed Bibles became available, the existing stock of older manuscript bibles came to look antiquated and makeshift. There was a change of fashion, and users soon actively desired their bibles to be new, printed ones. A signal of the role of fashion in this change is the luxury (or more precisely: receptive-to-luxury) aspect of many of the earliest printed editions of the Bible. The first four printed Bibles were all in large, Royal folio format; three of them (Gutenberg Bible (B-526), 36-line Bible (B-527), and 1462 Bible (B-529)) were published both in paper and in vellum issues. The vellum issues in particular invited correspondingly expensive hand illumination, and a substantial proportion of the surviving copies of these editions were so illuminated, in shops widely spread over Europe.[3]

I would like to propose an addendum to Schulz's characterization of the incunable age. This period is also of intrinsic interest because it was a time of unusually rapid change and experimentation not just in printing technology, but also in the design and presentation of texts. When we study a frequently printed text in its early editions, we should want to be able to visualize and quantify its changing appearance from one edition to another, for it is certain that the same text will look very different in an edition of the 1460s, say, from what it will in the 1480s, and again in the 1490s. The changes, of course, do not float on to the pages of a new edition by the power of mental projection. They result from physical processes of book-making, which must be closely understood. I suspect that these changes in appearance are more striking than what we find in any five decades of the twentieth century. It is true, of course, that our own generation has witnessed more rapid and radical changes in printing technology than in any period since the Invention, but the look of the end result has hardly, from the viewpoint of the ordinary reader, changed at all. It is commonplace to say that the earliest European typographic printing 'imitated' manuscripts. But we can say with even fewer necessary qualifications that today's books successfully imitate typography.

The following pages attempt to provide a preliminary, very concise survey of the Latin Bible as a published text in the first fifty years of printing, taking into account aspects both of physical production, and of selection and arrangement of texts. Underlying this is the presumption that every conscious change resulted from the calculation of printers, publishers and other financial supporters that buyers would be attracted to these changes. In essence, for every printed Latin Bible subsequent to the Gutenberg Bible, we may usefully ask: 'Why do you look different from, or work differently than, the Gutenberg Bible?' For the sake of providing clear discussion points, we present our overview 'scholastically,' arranged in two quasi-opposing theses or themes: the success of the Gutenberg Bible, and the insufficiencies of the Gutenberg Bible.

## I. THE SUCCESS OF THE GUTENBERG BIBLE

From the earliest eyewitness response of Aeneas Silvius (the future Pius II) in early 1455 down to the present, the Gutenberg Bible has made a continuing impact as a work of great dignity and beauty.[4] But let us ignore this aspect which, however salient, has been so often expatiated on that it has become banal. Let us ask rather: was the Gutenberg Bible a successful publication? We may answer that, by several measures, it was notably successful. With regard to sale, we have from Aeneas Silvius the further statement that by the late winter of 1455 – very possibly before the final quires had gone through the press – the entire edition of 180 copies or so both on paper and vellum had perhaps already been sold.[5] And, by a textual yardstick, one may argue that the Gutenberg Bible has been the most lastingly influential of all incunable editions.

To gauge this, we must review very sketchily the history of the Bible in Latin. Only one of several early Latin versions of the Bible concerns us: the Vulgate, which, as its name implies, was the most widely circulated version in western Christianity.[6] This version was chiefly put together and consolidated, in the late fourth to early fifth centuries, by St Jerome: partly from his original translations from the Hebrew, partly from his and others' revisions of existing Old Latin versions of the New Testament books, and of the Old Testament Apocrypha. The earliest complete physical witness to the Vulgate Bible as so defined is the late-seventh-century Northumbrian Codex Amiatinus, in the Biblioteca Laurenziana, Florence.[7]

Throughout much of the Middle Ages, there was no unified Vulgate Bible to the degree that there was (and is) a unified Hebrew Bible. To paraphrase Jerome's letter to Pope Damasus on the Old Latin versions, one might say, with the liberty of only a little exaggeration, that there are almost as many different Vulgates as there are manuscripts: *tot paene quot codices*. The differences may reside not just in strikingly variant readings, but also in varying 'shapes': that is, in the inclusion or exclusion of particular books (especially as to Old Testament Apocrypha), in the sequence of books, in the divisions of books into chapters, in the selection of prefatory prologues, and in the varying rubric titles, identifying the prologues and books.

An important movement toward uniformity occurred, without explicit documentation, in the first decades of the thirteenth century, in and around the university of Paris.[8] Within this milieu some form of quasi-standardized Vulgate became defined. Apart from coalescence of the text proper, the selection and sequence of books, selection of prologues (out of many dozens of possible alternative choices) and chapter divisions, all became much more rigid than they had been. This Paris Vulgate, as it may conveniently be called, spread very widely during the later decades of the thirteenth century, especially through the agency of the Dominicans and Franciscans. Some of the Paris Vulgate exemplars are large-format, high-luxury copies, but the most characteristic format was much smaller and more portable: what have been called octavo codices, written in two columns in strikingly small Gothic hands, on very thin, usually very high quality parchment.[9] It must be emphasized that what we call the textual uniformity of this class of Bible is relative. By the standard of scroll-form copies of the Hebrew Pentateuch (Torah), the hundreds of surviving exemplars of the Paris Vulgate would all be seen as so variable, so labile, that they might as well be thrown away as unusable.

There is a gap of something over two hundred years between this 'crystallization' of the Paris Vulgate and the printing of the Gutenberg Bible. Those intervening generations are something of a black hole in our knowledge of the Latin Bible. For the thirteenth century, we have at least a sensible picture of the steady production of many hundreds of closely similar small-format, thin-vellum bibles, much resembling one another in layout and text. For the fourteenth and first half of the fifteenth century, we have no very clear picture at all. How many Bible manuscripts were written, by whom and for whom; what did these bibles look like? What proportion were written on vellum, and what on paper? In what hands were they written? Except for mostly art-historical studies of a small group of mid-fifteenth century high-luxury 'giant' bibles, little has been published.[10]

When the Gutenberg Bible came to be printed in the early 1450s there were in principle many different kinds of Bible manuscripts that might have been chosen as setting copy for its compositors. There is no reason to think that particular care was devoted within the 'Bible Shop' to the selection of this exemplar.[11] As I've suggested elsewhere, the most unusual aspect of the Gutenberg Bible is its inclusion of the so-called 4th book of Esdras or Ezra, a Christian-era Latin apocryphal work decidedly rare in the Vulgate tradition. There are distinct bibliographical reasons to suppose that this text was supplied from a separate exemplar.[12] Certain typographic errors in the Gutenberg Bible suggest that its chief exemplar was a rather small-format (i.e. small-script) and highly abbreviated manuscript.[13] The order of the books, chapter divisions, and prologue selection show that the lost exemplar was a representative of the Paris Vulgate family, though with a number of variant and corrupt readings not found in the early representatives of the family.

The 'randomness' of the Gutenberg Bible's exemplar emerges when we compare the Gutenberg Bible with the Butzbach Bible, a paper Royal folio manuscript which was made for the Augustinian chapter in Butzbach. The two bibles, one single and one miraculously multiple, were created concurrently and as near neighbours. Annotations on the lower pastedown of the Butzbach Bible record that it was written, illuminated and bound in Mainz during the years 1452 to 1454. It was completed on 19 September of the latter year.[14] This was just a few weeks before our earliest solid evidence for the existence of the Mainz 31-line Cyprus Indulgence (a copy of which was issued in Erfurt on 22 October 1454), and likewise before the session of the Imperial Diet in Frankfurt am Main, where Aeneas Silvius saw complete quires of the Gutenberg Bible (15-28 October 1454). A striking physical feature of the Butzbach Bible, which has not been remarked on by its students, is that it is written on the same supply of paper as that on which the earliest quires of the Gutenberg Bible were printed. The two bibles, very possibly created in workshops within hailing distance of each other, are 'paper twins'.[15] The exemplar for the Butzbach Bible was yet another representative of the Paris Vulgate, but the differences of text and structure between the two bibles are considerable. In the Butzbach Bible, 4 Esdras was not present; each of the twelve minor Prophets had a prologue, or argumentum, whereas the Gutenberg Bible's exemplar had none; and so on. Within the same town, in the same years, the Vulgate Bible clearly did not have a stable definition and a standard shape.

However, the Gutenberg Bible's exemplar, because of its transmutation in the printing shop into multiple typographic copies, has had an influence incomparably beyond any intrinsic merits. The reason is that it had children: subsequent editions that used various copies of the Gutenberg Bible as exemplar or copy text. Then some of these children themselves had children – yet other printed editions were set from copies of these – and so on. Of the 81 plain-text editions of the Latin Bible (without surrounding gloss), only two, a very rare 1475 edition printed in Piacenza (B-542), and a 1476 edition printed in Vicenza (B-549), are outside the Gutenberg clan, having been set from independent manuscripts. All remaining editions – although in some cases they embody scattered emendations and corrections derived from manuscripts – descend by strict family lines from the Gutenberg Bible; I hope some day to publish a full genealogy of them.[16]

The topic of emendations in incunable editions of the Vulgate text is still amorphous. We know well that in certain editions, from the Fust and Schoeffer 1462 Bible (B-529) onward, variant readings were introduced from sources other than the primary printed exemplar. But we have as yet no useful picture of the general character of this editing. Why was it done; under what auspices; did readers even notice that certain readings had been changed? The questions await exploration. The most extensive body of evidence for the editing of the Vulgate text in this period is that found in Eggestein's third edition, printed in Strasbourg not after 8 March 1470 (B-533). Some years ago I had the remarkable good luck to discover that the copy of the Gutenberg Bible now in Cambridge University Library had served as printer's copy for this edition.[17] Various compositorial and other editorial markings on the pages of that Gutenberg Bible enable us to follow the setting of Eggestein's Bible closely, through the eyes of the compositors. Alternate readings written lightly in the margin of the Cambridge Gutenberg Bible lead us to more than 180 textual variants, clustered within a few books of the Bible, which were introduced into Eggestein's Bible. Because no subsequent Vulgate used Eggestein's edition as exemplar, the variants remained a dead end. I wrote by way of summary that 'the majority of the emendations represent a further corruption'[18] of Gutenberg's text. But this does not answer all questions. A detailed study of these variants from other standpoints awaits a quiet time of opportunity.

One scholar has made the interesting suggestion that such instances of textual revision of the Vulgate in the early printing shops should be understood 'in the light of monastic orders and their reform movements'.[19] But appropriate arguments for this view have not yet emerged, and I am personally doubtful that this will prove to be a profitable direction of study. To begin with, there is little evidence that the fifteenth-century monastic reform movements were generally much concerned with uniformity of text of the Latin Bible. There is, of course, one well-known (but surprisingly understudied) exception, the Windesheim congregation of the Augustinian order. The provost of Windesheim, Johannes Busch (*c.* 1400-*c.* 1479), describes the process of Bible revision in fascinating detail. A copy of the Vulgate now at Darmstadt, written by Thomas à Kempis in the 1420s and 1430s, has been taken to exemplify the revision.[20] Several more manuscript Vulgates of later decades have been found to contain characteristic 'Windesheim' readings, but so far I have found none of these readings in any incunable edition.[21]

These remarks are intended not to undervalue but rather to re-balance our picture of the significance of monastic reform movements in the third quarter of the fifteenth century in encouraging and supporting the printed-Bible trade. In particular, I suspect that too great an emphasis has been placed in recent years on the participation of the Bursfeld and Melk congregations of the Benedictine order.[22] When we look beyond the Gutenberg Bible to the distribution patterns of all the early large-format printed Vulgates, we should consider that too narrow an emphasis on the role of monastic reform movements as customers runs the risk of overlooking the market, very possibly equally large, of the secular clergy.[23] But it is premature to generalize at all on this question until we have a larger body of evidence from early provenances.

Our best evidence for the direct involvement of a religious house in the production of printed incunable Bibles centres, rather later, on the convent of the Franciscans in Venice. Their members supplied both an alphabetical table of subjects and proof-reading corrections in the Paganini octavo Vulgate, Venice, 7 September 1492 (B-594).[24] And yet, even here, there is no evidence that the Franciscans played a larger role than an editorial one. To summarize, I suggest we hold to the following picture until empirical reasons to modify it are gathered and digested. To the best of our knowledge, campaigns of Vulgate emendation in the fifteenth-century printing shops seem to have been sporadic and secular, carried through by the editorial apparatus of publishers who contemplated selling Vulgates to a general readership, irrespective of specific religious orders, and indeed to readers not necessarily in religious orders at all.

The Gutenberg Bible's influence did not end in the fifteenth century. The sixteenth century was of course an era of tremendous changes in Bible history. The great Protestant vernacular translations appeared, as well as new, humanistic Latin versions and revisions by Erasmus, Santi Pagnini, Sebastian Castellio and others. During this same century, there were a number of campaigns of correction of the Vulgate Bible text, particularly centred in the university of Louvain. However, none of these attempts at correction was so thoroughgoing as to build from the foundations of the ancient manuscript tradition. The underlying copy text was always a direct descendent of the Gutenberg Bible. This holds true even for the Sixtine-Clementine revision of the late 1580s to early 1590s, which dogmatically 'fixed' the Vulgate text for centuries to come. The result is that a number of variant readings in the text of the Clementine Vulgate, unattested in the manuscript tradition, can be shown on closer scrutiny to descend directly from the Gutenberg Bible; indeed, a small number of these can even be shown to be nothing more than errors made by the compositors of the Gutenberg Bible. In a real sense, then, the textual influence of the Gutenberg Bible has extended until well into the twentieth century. Offhand, I can bring to mind no other incunable edition for which a similar claim can be made.

To summarize, we may say that in the Gutenberg Bible we encounter the second major crystallization of the Vulgate text, after that of the Paris movement of the early thirteenth century. This crystallization did not, by the way, affect the Rusch glossed Bible (B-607). The text of Rusch's edition, presumably assembled from a number of manuscript exemplars for different books of the Bible, reflects twelfth-century, pre-Paris Vulgate sources.[25] But the Gutenberg Bible crystallization did affect the nine incunable editions of the Vulgate with Nicolas de Lyra's *Postills* set as surrounding commentary. The first of these editions, Venice 1481 (B-611), drew its text for the Bible proper from one of the Venetian Vulgate editions of Francis Renner, 1475 and after (B-540), that is, from a grandchild or great-grandchild of the Gutenberg Bible; and all later editions of Vulgate + Lyra descend from it. This is appropriate, of course, for both Lyra's *Postills* and their common companion, William Brito's commentary on the prologues were specifically based on the Paris Vulgate tradition.

What is the history of the Latin Bible in the decades after the Gutenberg Bible appeared? At first glance into the literature it may appear that the early editions are adequately and even amply recorded and described. In fact, there remains a tremendous amount still to be learned about this specialized, but clearly thriving, corner of the larger printed-book market of the time. The printing and selling of bibles very rapidly became consolidated to a few major printing towns. This general process of consolidation of the early printing trade has not been as thoroughly studied as it might be: it is one of the major themes in that history of early printing which remains unwritten. In all, something over 250 European cities and towns (including Constantinople) had printing shops in the fifteenth century – but a good many of these qualify only as brief, though fascinating, experiments. Among these roughly 250 towns, twelve major printing centres were responsible for fully two-thirds of all surviving output. Among these twelve centres, six greatly dominated the market for printed Bibles from the 1470s onward: in Germany, the chief 'bible cities' were Basle, Nuremberg, Strasbourg and Cologne; in Italy, Venice (the greatest early printing town of all); in France, Lyon. Of the 94 fifteenth-century editions of Latin bibles, these half-dozen towns produced fully 79. Three more editions were printed in Mainz (but the last in 1472), two in Speyer, and two in Freiburg im Breisgau. Eight other towns produced one edition apiece (all but one of which are no later than 1480).

It would be profitable to investigate and speculate, though there is no space for the question here, on how these six towns became dominant in this market. To cite only one quasi-paradox: Paris was a much more active early centre of printing than Lyon, producing twice as many incunable editions or more. And it was, of course, the home of Europe's greatest theology faculty. This situation would seem to provide the ingredients for a major position in the production of printed Vulgate bibles, yet only one edition was printed in Paris (B-550), against nine in Lyon. Similarly, only one Vulgate Bible – the striking 1471 Sweynheym and Pannartz edition (B-535) – was published from Rome, as against twenty-two from Venice. Of the dozen major early printing towns, four – Leipzig, Augsburg, Milan and Florence – produced no Vulgate editions at all, although Augsburg was a major centre for printed High German Bibles.

In fact, early Vulgate Bible printing was even more consolidated than these raw figures suggest. Cologne is on the 'top' list, with seven Vulgate bibles, but these editions all fall within the brief span from 1475 to 1480. Curiously, though perhaps coincidentally, this period almost exactly fills a sort of lacuna in the production of Strasbourg bibles. Five editions were printed there from 1460 to 1473. There then ensued a gap until the appearance of Rusch's great glossed Bible of 1480. In 1483 and after, 'plain-text' Bible printing resumed in Strasbourg, with four more editions before the end of the century.[26]

## II. THE INADEQUACY OF THE GUTENBERG BIBLE

The central point to be made about early printed bibles is that there are many differences among the various editions. It would be very misleading to treat the statement that there were ninety-four incunable editions of the Latin Bible as an operable statistic for analysis, for these editions are not a single known quantity. But the existing descriptions of bibles in incunable catalogues fall so short of giving us the information we need to know, that the differences between one edition and another are effectively hidden. Even where catalogues provide transcriptions of text, the unstated presumption is that one simply gives the first words of Jerome's general prologues, the beginning of Genesis, the last words of the Apocalypse, and any ensuing printer's colophon – and that what falls in the middle is so obvious that it doesn't need describing. This is by no means the case. Our chief secondary sources for the contents of Vulgate Bibles are, comprehensively, *Gesamtkatalog der Wiegendrucke*;[27] and selectively, *Catalogue of Books Printed in the XVth Century now in the British Museum*,[28] and *Catalogue des Livres Imprimées au XVme Siècle des Bibliothèques de Belgique*, edited by M. Louis Polain.[29] Polain's descriptions are the fullest, but all three sources omit entirely, or indicate only by implication, a great body of relevant information, most of which could be very concisely recorded. The emphasis in incunable cataloguing, from Hain onwards, on apparently full but actually highly selective and arbitrary 'quasi-diplomatic' transcription, has tended to obscure or eclipse the cataloguer's duty of adequately recording the contents of incunables. Such records of contents are often better communicated outside the strictures of transcriptional rules and protocols.[30]

It should especially be emphasized that the Gutenberg Bible itself truly belongs to the earliest stage of printing. Within a relatively short period it began to look archaic to contemporary eyes, and printers of Vulgate bibles developed, over the next decades, many 'modernizations'. Already by the late 1460s no printer would have thought of producing a Bible that in every way looked like the Gutenberg Bible. It may be useful to attempt to sketch out rapidly, without giving complete details, some – far from all – of the ways in which one incunable Vulgate edition may differ significantly from another. We may think of the process of organizing these editions as one of putting them into various boxes, insofar as they meet one specification or another. As we fill these notional boxes of formally similar bibles, we begin to see the variety of ways in which, within a few years, the kind of book represented by the Gutenberg Bible came to be seen as needing modification.

For instance, we may make a *textualis formata* box: bibles printed with types based on this, the most formal Gothic script. That box has only two members, the Gutenberg Bible and its 'daughter' the 36-line Bible, which was printed, in apparently a quite small edition, in Bamberg, not after 1461 (B-526, B-527). The 'antiqua' box, of course, is even smaller, having a single member, the 1471 Vulgate of Sweynheym and Pannartz (B-535). That Bible is likewise the only member of the 'single-column' box: all other incunable Bibles are printed in double columns. To our eyes, the Swenyheym and Pannartz Bible is a spacious, beautiful production. But we may say with some confidence that to fifteenth-century readers' eyes an antiqua-type single-column Bible, such as was produced by Sweynheym and Pannartz, was an unnecessary object: one that had no advantage. In 1475, Johann Sensenschmidt in Nuremberg used a copy of the Sweynheym and Pannartz Vulgate as setting copy for a new edition (9 December 1475; B-544), but the text was put back into a more acceptable format: Gothic type, set in double columns.

Here are some other boxes we may notionally fill: Royal folio bibles; small-format bibles; ready-to-use bibles (vs. bibles needing rubrication to be usable); bibles with the same prologue sets; bibles omitting 4 Esdras; bibles accompanied by the Interpretations of Hebrew Names; bibles with the Eusebian canon tables; bibles with lection tables (the *Capitulare lectionum et evangeliorum*); bibles equipped with the still somewhat mysterious *casus summarii*; bibles with marginal cross-references; bibles with chapter sub-divisions. Each of these categories represents a class of bible whose history has been, until now, only incompletely studied, if studied at all. As seemingly self-evident a class as that of bibles of which there were vellum (besides paper) issues has been, until now, entirely invisible. There appear to have been twelve editions with vellum issues.

Each of these represents somewhat different marketing or patronage intents from those of the paper-only editions. The more closely we look, the more such boxes we may find.[31] One that particularly interests me, and that seems to have attracted hitherto no notice whatever, is that of printed Vulgate bibles with christianizing psalm-*tituli*.[32]

*Royal folio bibles:* A significant area of change in early printed bibles that is invisible in catalogue descriptions, but immediately apparent in the physical volumes, is differences in size. The Gutenberg Bible is a Royal folio; that is, made of Royal-size sheets of paper, the resulting volume being, when not heavily trimmed, about 40 cm (just under 16 inches) tall. This was the standard size and format of all the earliest printed bibles up to 1475, when Venetian bible printing began. The Venetian bibles, though also folio format, were printed on the smaller sheet which may be called Chancery paper, producing a leaf height of about 30 cm (12 inches) or a little less if the trim is not too severe. Unfortunately, incunable catalogues treat all folios as identical, without distinguishing paper sizes.[33] But if one stands a Royal folio next to a Chancery folio, the difference between the two is immediately apparent. The Royal folio is distinctly a lectern book, not easily handled for rapid consultation as opposed to connected reading. The Chancery folio is a much handier book. These Venetian Vulgate editions were intrinsically less expensive books, aimed at a different market from the Royal folio series.

With regard to physical size, there were three distinct periods of Vulgate printing: before 1475, when all editions were Royal folios; an interim period of 1475 to about 1480, when Royal folios for lectern use were produced alongside smaller Chancery folios (printed especially in Venice and Cologne), with at least the potential for private ownership and use; and the period after 1480, when virtually all editions were the smaller, Chancery folios; and some, as we shall immediately note, were smaller still. What is perhaps most striking is that the Royal folio Latin bibles belonged so strictly to a single generation of marketing. For at least the last two decades of the fifteenth-century, Royal folios were no longer needed, so to speak. What I don't know – for with regard to paper sizes, sixteenth-century books lie even more in terra incognita than fifteenth-century books do – is whether any other Royal folio Vulgates were printed before Robert Estienne's famous and ambitious 1528 production. It must be noted parenthetically that Rusch's glossed Bible was of even larger format, Imperial folio. This edition, containing over six hundred sheets per copy, was the lengthiest Imperial folio printed in the fifteenth century (B-607). Here too a step down the ladder of paper sizes can be seen in later editions. The Paganinus edition (Venice, 18 April 1495; B-608), which included both the *Glossa Ordinaria* and Lyra's *Postilla*, moved down in size to Royal folio; and Johann Froben's reprint of the latter (Basel, 1 December 1498; B-609) moved down to Chancery folio.

*Small-format bibles:* It is a commonplace that in 1491 Johann Froben of Basle produced the first 'pocket Bible' – specifically, an octavo Bible, and even more specifically, a Median octavo Bible (27 June 1491: B-592). Froben advertised its handy format as an innovation – it might, he wrote in a preface, better be called a 'Bibliola' than a 'Biblia'.[34] In a sense, of course, this was not an innovation, but rather a revival of the thirteenth-century manuscript tradition of the portable Bible. It should also be said that within the incunable period it was not absolutely an innovation; several forerunners are well worth our attention. The most interesting of these is the 1475 Piacenza Vulgate (B-542), already briefly mentioned as one of two Vulgate incunables with a text tradition outside that established by the Gutenberg Bible. This was the first Bible printed in (Chancery) quarto format, and was clearly likewise intended to be, sixteen years before Froben, a portable Bible. In particular, it was set with a specially cut miniature type, roughly the size of eighteenth-century nonpareil, and almost exactly the size of Froben's later octavo Bible-type. The Piacenza Bible was, besides its smaller format, set to more lines per page than any preceding printed edition, and so took up fewer leaves than any predecessor. In the early sixteenth century, octavo Bibles became common, but here we enter unmapped territory. To the best of my knowledge, true miniature Vulgates, of 16mo format or under, were first produced in Paris in the early 1520s, in publishing ventures by Simon de Colines, Jean Petit and Pierre Vidoue.[35] These Paris miniatures are not, however, 'pocket pandects' in the same sense as the single-volume octavos. They were issued in parts, so that eight or nine volumes were needed to make up the full Bible.

*Ready-to-use bibles:* The Gutenberg Bible, as has often been remarked, was '*halbfertig Ware*', half-ready goods. When you bought the Gutenberg Bible, in sheets, you did not have a book ready to use. The characteristic palette of the medieval manuscript book was that of black (or dark brown) and red (or red and blue) writing on cream parchment or paper. The black was the text proper, the red (or red and blue) rubrication provided visual and thematic structure. Additional colours and gilt were primarily signals of luxury. In the Gutenberg Bible, as it left the printing shop, you got only the black text of the books and of their traditional prologues, with spaces reserved for filling in the names of the books and prologues (these rubric headings having their own traditional phraseology), chapter numbers and headlines to help you find your way through the volumes. In the earliest stages of printing the Gutenberg Bible, there was a brief experiment with printing the rubric titles in red, by a second run of the sheets through the press; but this was soon abandoned. Thus, once the sheets of the Gutenberg Bible were acquired, there was a considerable amount of professional work remaining to be done by hand, by rubricators (literally, those who add red) and (if wanted) by decorators of initials. But the Gutenberg Bible shop did provide one useful help toward this: it came with a printed table of rubrics, giving the exact suggested wording for the spaces provided at the heads of the prologues and books, and before each of the Psalms.

Most of the earliest printed bibles were likewise 'half-ready goods,' in need of the rubricator's hand before the copies could be put to effective use. A number of these editions, in Bamberg, Strasbourg and Basle, similarly provided printed rubric tables. The elegant 1462 Bible printed in Mainz by Fust and Schoeffer (B-529) marked the first attempt to provide an *almost* ready-to-use Vulgate, with red and blue printing providing rubric headings, chapter initials and chapter numbers (though these elements were not printed with absolute consistency, so some had to be supplied by hand). Most significantly, the 1462 Bible had neither major initials nor headlines; and without headline identification of the various books, a Bible is essentially unusable. The process of applying these 'finishing touches' in red and blue typographically was a complex, slow and expensive one: no subsequent printer went to the effort that Fust and Schoeffer did. Sweynheym and Pannartz's 1471 Bible (B-535), although set from a copy of the 1462 Fust and Schoeffer Bible, did not attempt to follow it in supplying printed initials and printed rubrics. Chapter numbers were printed – but in black. Fust and Schoeffer's 1472 (B-536) reprint likewise represented a retreat from the ambition of

1462: rubric headings were printed in red, but instead of red- and blue-printed chapter initials, spaces were left for initials to be supplied by hand.

A number of printers in the mid-1470s continued the experiment of providing rubrics, etc., in red-printing, by a second run-through of the sheets. By the standard just now defined, the first printed Vulgate to be fully ready-to-use was a Royal folio produced in Basle by Bernhard Richel in 1475 (B-540), which included, besides red-printed rubrics and black-printed initials, printed headlines (with the further elegance that the first headline for a book or prologue was printed in red). This edition is a somewhat overlooked monument. But the major step toward producing 'ready-to-read' bibles (as of several other complex texts) was one of changing expectations: by the 1480s readers became fully used to encountering in black the rubrics which had traditionally been supplied in red. This change in expectations was especially encouraged or catered to – for the chain of causality may run back and forth – by the first Venetian bibles of 1475 and after. They were certainly cheaper than the northern Royal folios of Strasbourg, Basle and Nuremberg. A particular sign of their relative cheapness is that they had headlines, rubric titles and chapter numbers printed in black. The only decorative work that needed to be supplied were the initial letters of books, for which blank spaces were left.

*Bibles with the same prologue sets:* There are many changes and variations in Vulgate Bible printing with regard to the absence or presence of a wide variety of extra-biblical apparatuses, designed to make reading and consultation of the text easier. Some of these apparatuses go back to a very early period, most notably the prologues or prefaces attached to a number of the books, some of which were written by St Jerome himself. In the manuscript bibles of the Middle Ages, hundreds of various and varying prologues are to be found. The prologues in the Gutenberg Bible are a common set, such as occurs (though with numerous smaller variations) in virtually all manuscripts of the Paris Vulgate. These prologues continued to be included with all later Vulgate editions, but with two distinct later supplementary stages, when editors must have felt that (simply) more prefaces made a better Bible.

The first stage came in the Sweynheym and Pannartz 1471 Bible (B-535), when 20 prefaces were added, the majority of which provide brief *argumenta* or summaries of the twelve minor Prophets. The second stage came with the first Venice Bible of 1475 (B-541), which took over the Gutenberg Bible + Sweynheym and Pannartz sets, and added some 25 additional prologues, with the result that many books of the Bible have duplicate, triplicate, even quadruplicate prefatory material. Ideally, one would like to have an outline of the varying prologue sets of all early printed bibles, for they provide a major clue, perhaps the easiest single clue, to textual affiliations. No published catalogues give this information.

Many other extra-biblical supplements occur, in varying combinations, in the early printed bibles, and help to classify them into distinct groups. This process of adding supplementary material began in the 1470s; the history of the process again marks out distinct periods in the production of Latin bibles. Most of the Royal folio bibles of the first period provide a bare text appropriate for refectory reading, with only the traditional prologues included.

*Bibles accompanied by the Interpretations of Hebrew Names:* The first distinct supplement to be added, in the Sweynheym and Pannartz Bible, 1471, was the dictionary known as *Interpretationes nominum hebraicorum* – on the (literal) meanings of Hebrew names. This text goes back to the early thirteenth century, and is closely associated with the formation then of the Paris Vulgate. There must have been many readers who thought of the Interpretations as automatically belonging to the Latin Bible. The copy of the Gutenberg Bible now at Eton College came originally from Erfurt, and (I think it can be shown) originally belonged to the Carthusian house in Erfurt. These Carthusians produced a wonderfully detailed manuscript catalogue of their great library in the third quarter of the fifteenth century, and this Gutenberg Bible can be identified in the catalogue, where it is described as (in translation), 'a complete printed Mainz Bible, rubricated and corrected according to the Carthusian system but without the Interpretations of Hebrew Names.' The reference here to Carthusian corrections must refer specifically to a distinctive Carthusian system of chapter division, where the marginal letters P-S-T-Q (*pars prima, secunda, tertia, quarta*) were written to break chapters into smaller units for easier consultation.[36]

*Bibles with chapter sub-divisions:* A related system of marginal sub-division breaks chapters into up to seven subsections, marked by the letters A to D or for lengthier chapters, A to G. These first appear in Bernhard Richel's Royal folio edition dated 8 September 1477, where they were printed only in the New Testament (and were omitted from the Epistle to the Romans; B-553). Amerbach's Chancery folio Bible, Basle 1479, applied these marginal chapter divisions to the entire New Testament (B-561). The Amerbach model spread widely in the 1480s, in his own and other Basle reprints, and in reprints from Lyon, Speyer, and Venice.[37] Froben's octavo Bible of 1491, already mentioned, extended the system to the Old Testament; and the tradition continued until eventually in the 1520s fully numbered verses were invented. Like so many other of the *supplementa* to the early printed Vulgates, this handy A to G system, which considerably facilitated cross-referring and the construction of name and subject concordances, was by no means a modern printing shop invention. The Rouses have shown that the system belongs to the thirteenth century, and was developed by the Dominicans of Paris as a necessary complement to the Bible concordances that they constructed.[38]

As already indicated, many more supplements and helps made their ways into the early printed Bibles. Each addendum has a distinct history, waiting to be written. Thus, one may identify, for example, the first Bible to include a printing of the Eusebian canon tables (Richel's Royal folio, not after 1474; B-537); the first to include marginal cross-references or concordances (again Richel's, not after 1474, the marginalia being constructed from the canon tables); the first to include tables of lections and gospel readings (Amerbach's of 1479 (B-561), already mentioned for its marginal chapter divisions in the New Testament); the first to contain the chapter-summaries known as *casus summarii* (Johann Zainer's Royal folio, Ulm, 29 January 1480 (B-567): one of the most beautiful incunable Bibles).

Of course, our goal should not be simply identifying 'firsts', but rather contexts. We want to know the history, fates and interrelationships of all these supplements, many of which, as remarks already made have indicated, represent not innovations, but a gradual bringing into type of the standard bible helps of the thirteenth century. We are very much in need of a catalogue of early bibles formed on an entirely different descriptive basis from what is now found in the standard bibliographical sources. The printed bibles of the 1490s look very different and work quite differently from those of the 1450s and 1460s. These later editions are less handsome, to most eyes, than the Gutenberg Bible or the 1462 Bible, but as objects of use they are far superior. With such a book as Froben's 1491 octavo Vulgate you can, with very little practice, find your way about, cross-refer, track down Gospel story parallels, learn a quick mnemonic to keep in your mind all the books of the Bible and their sequence, and so on. In short, you can use it just about as easily as a modern-day Bible. By the standard of form following function, these 'late' (to an incunabulist) bibles are conspicuous successes.

We may conclude with a quick look at one of the briefest and most conspicuously extra-biblical of the many addenda found in early printed bibles. In 1483, Johann Herbort, in Venice, printed a Chancery folio Vulgate Bible (B-579) which included, at the end of the Interpretations of Hebrew Names, three Latin couplets by Quintius Aemilianus Cymbriacus – the learned name of a minor humanist, Giovanni Stefano of Vicenza (*c.* 1445-50?–1499).[39] These verses, never hitherto commented on, make a contribution to a still insufficiently explored theme: the humanist response to the invention of printing. I've suggested elsewhere that the early praises of the invention of printing far outweigh the dispraises and reservations. Almost all the praises fall into four categories of comment and amaze: the speed of printing, the cheapness of copies, the textual identity of copies, and finally surprise that the 'humane' activity of book-making now incorporates a mechanical, and specifically a metalworking technique.[40] Aemilianus's verses, clearly referring implicitly to Gutenberg, and appearing only in this 1483 Vulgate, exemplify this last response:

*Qui primus latias effinxit in aere lituras*
*Et docuit sacros aere notare libros*
*Non ne putas dicti coelum superasse myronis?*
*Phidiacas veneres? parrhasiosve ioves?*
*Hunc ego daedaleos etiam vicisse labores.*
*Hunc ego palladias credo habuisse manus.*

(He who first created Latin letters in bronze
And taught how with bronze can be made all the sacred books –
Surely he surpassed the skill of Myro's chisel,
The Venuses of Phidias, the Joves of Parrhasius?
He, I should say, excelled even the works of Daedalus
He, I should say, possessed true 'Palladian hands.')

Today's theorists of *le livre* would do well to learn Cymbriacus's respect for the mechanical processes embodied in the books they study. A knowledge of the processes and materials of book-making, of copy handling and copy correction as type is set and formes are made up – all that is subsumed under the mysterious word 'bibliography' – allows discoveries to be made that could arise from no other channel of thinking. It safeguards against the danger of attempting to launch physically impossible hypotheses, and frees one from the shackles of trying to draw valid conclusions from reliance only on published catalogues and other secondary sources of information. It brings books to life.

## NOTES

1 Ernst Schulz, *Inkunabelsammlungen und ihr wissenschaftlicher Wert: Bemerkungen zur Sammlung Vollbehr* (Munich: Privatdruck, 1927), pp. 6-7: 'mehr als die gedruckte Literatur irgendeiner späteren Periode sind die Frühdrucke Ausdruck und Spiegel des gesamten geistigen Lebens und der Kultur ihrer Zeit. Als nämlich der Buchdruck technisch soweit leistungfähig geworden war dass er die bisher von Schreiberhand besorgte Bücherherstellung übernehmen und bewältigen konnte da mussten die gelehrten Kreise den Wunsch haben, möglichst alle Literatur, deren sie bedurften, in dieser modernen und angenehmeren Form zu besitzen. Ihr Wunsch ging dahin, möglichst bald nicht nur ihre eigenen literarischen Arbeiten, sondern auch die gesamte ältere Literatur, soweit sie ihnen noch irgendwie lesenswert und brauchbar erschien, in die neue Form des Druckbuches übertragen zu lassen.' The name of the private scholar Schulz (1897-1944) is not widely prominent, but his influence on the quality of text identifications in the *Gesamtkatalog der Wiegendrucke* – first by the spur of a critical review, then by active consultation – makes him in fact one of the most influential incunabulists of this century. For a brief account of his difficult life, see Hans Koch, 'Ernst Schulz 8. Okt. 1897-19. Dez. 1944', in *Das werck der Bucher, eine Festschrift für Horst Kliemann zu seinem 60. Geburtstag*, ed. by Fritz Hodeige (Freiburg/Br: Rombach 1956).

2 This suggested picture should, of course, be carefully criticized. A chief field of evidence will be the signs of continuing use (or their absence) in surviving thirteenth-century Vulgates. Consider as an example London, Lambeth MS. 1361, a small-size thirteenth-century Vulgate containing a note of bequest by John Mone (d. 8 June 1474), vicar of Bredgar, Kent: he gave 'this goode bybill to the chyrch of bradgare that his bredren of this forsayd chyrche schuld rede upon hit when it plese hem,' with added instructions that succeeding vicars should see that this and other chained books of the church should be safeguarded. See N. R. Ker, *Medieval Manuscripts in British Libraries,* 4 vols (Oxford: Clarendon Press, 1969-92), vol. I, pp. 95-6. It seems clear that this small Bible was thought of, more than two centuries after its making, as a work of continuing reference. By the end of 1473, by the way, ten or eleven printed editions of the Vulgate had been published on the continent, and copies of some of these editions had already been sold to English customers.

3 This field of investigation has been revolutionized in the past two decades by Eberhard König; among his important and heavily documented studies on the Gutenberg Bible are: 'Die Illuminierung der Gutenbergbibel', in *Johannes Gutenbergs zweiundvierzigzeilige Bibel ... Kommentarband*, ed. by Wieland Schmidt & F. A. Schmidt-Künsemüller (Munich: Idion, 1979); 'Möglichkeiten kunstgeschichtlicher Beiträge zur Gutenberg-Forschung ...', *Gutenberg-Jahrbuch* (Mainz: Gutenberg-Gesellschaft, 1984); 'The History of Art and the History of the Book at the Time of the Transition from Manuscript to Print', in *Bibliography and the Study of 15th-Century Civilisation*, ed. by Lotte Hellinga & John Goldfinch (London: The British Library; Wolfeboro, N.H., 1987); and on the 1462 Bible: *The 1462 Fust and Schoeffer Bible: an Essay ... with an Original Leaf from the 1462 Bible* (Akron, Oh.: Bruce Ferrini; Evanston, Ill.: Hamill & Barker, 1993).

4 Aeneas Silvius to Card. Juan de Carvajal, Wiener Neustadt, 12 March 1455: 'I saw [in Frankfurt] quires of different books [of the Bible], exceedingly clean and correct in their script, and without error, which your Excellency could read effortlessly without glasses.' *Non vidi [apud Frankfordiam] biblias integras sed quinterniones aliquot diversorum librorum, mundissimae ac correctissimae litterae, nulla in parte mendaces, quos tua dignatio sine labore et absque berillo legeret.* See Needham, 'The Paper Supply of the Gutenberg Bible', *Papers of the Bibliographical Society of America*, 79 no. 3 (1985), 309 (resuming earlier literature); see also Martin Davies, 'Juan de Carvajal and Early Printing: the 42-line Bible and the Sweynheym and Pannartz Aquinas', *The Library*, 6th ser. XVIII: 3 (September, 1996), with

significant new information and commentary, including the discovery that this letter, hitherto known only from manuscript copies, was also printed in an incunable edition: Aeneas Silvius, *Epistolae saeculares* (Cologne: Arnold ther Hoernen, *c.* 1480), C4°, HC 159, VK 967.

5 Needham, 'The Paper Supply of the Gutenberg Bible', p. 309: 'If I had known of your wish, I should certainly have bought a copy I shall try, if possible, to get a copy for sale here [at Wiener Neustatt]. But I fear it won't be possible, both because of the distance and because they say that ready buyers had all been found before the volumes were finished.' *Si scivissem desiderium tuum, emissem unum procul dubio volumen Conabor, si fieri poterit, aliquam huc bibliam venalem afferri Quod timeo, ne fieri possit: et propter distantiam itineris, et quia, antequam perficerentur volumina, paratos emptores fuisse tradant.*

6 For a highly abbreviated survey with notes, Needham, 'The Text of the Gutenberg Bible', in *Trasmissione dei Testi a Stampa nel Periodo Moderno* II, ed. by Giovanni Crapulli (Rome: Edizioni dell'Ateno, 1987); and see also Light and McGurk, cited below, for more detailed surveys with extensive references.

7 For a conspectus of pre-Carolingian Latin Bibles, see Patrick McGurk, 'The Oldest Manuscripts of the Latin Bible', in *The Early Medieval Bible*, ed. by Richard Gameson (Cambridge: University Press, 1994).

8 Laura Light, 'Versions et revisions du texte biblique', in *Le Moyen Age et la Bible*, ed. by Pierre Riché & Guy Lobrichon (Paris: Beauchesne, 1984) and 'French Bibles *c.* 1200-30: a New Look at the Origin of the Paris Bible', in *The Early Medieval Bible*, ed. by Gameson (Cambridge: University Press, 1994): both important studies.

9 Light, 'French Bibles *c.* 1200-30', pp. 156-7, is entirely right to emphasize that 'Paris Vulgate' means something quite different from 'small-format thirteenth-century Vulgate', but the great majority of copies in this latter class do embody, textually, the Paris Vulgate.

10 e.g., Elgin Vaassen, 'Die Werkstatt der Mainzer Riesenbibel in Würzburg und ihr Umkreis', *Archiv für Geschichte des Buchwesens*, XIII 5-6 (March 1973).

11 The classic study is Heinrich Schneider, *Der Text der Gutenbergbibel zu ihrem 500jährigen Jubiläum untersucht* (Bonn: Bonner Biblische Beiträge 1954): a compressed but important textual survey of a substantial group of Vulgate manuscripts of middle-Rhine provenance or origin, which provide the closest identifiable context for the lost exemplar(s) of the Gutenberg Bible. This group includes a number written in the fourteenth and first half of the fifteenth centuries.

12 Needham, 'The Compositor's Hand in the Gutenberg Bible: a Review of the Todd Thesis', *Papers of the Bibliographical Society of America*, 77 no. 3 (3rd quarter 1983), 348ff; Needham, 'Division of Copy in the Gutenberg Bible: Three Glosses on the Ink Evidence'. *Papers of the Bibliographical Society of America*, 79 no. 3 (3rd quarter 1985), 417ff; Needham, 'The Text of the Gutenberg Bible' (above, n. 7).

13 Needham, 'The Compositor's Hand in the Gutenberg Bible', 351ff. The four-part division of copy among compositors, with subsequent subdivisions, could conceivably indicate that several Vulgate copies were put to use in the Bible Shop, but no direct evidence of that has been brought forward.

14 Giessen UB, Hs. 653; Wolfgang G. Bayerer, *Die Handschriften des ehem. Fraterherrenstift Sankt Markus zu Butzbach* (Wiesbaden: Otto Harrassowitz, 1980), pp. 33-4; Schneider, *Der Text der Gutenbergbibel*, 34ff; Vaassen, 'Die Werkstatt der Mainzer Riesenbibel in Würzburg und ihr Umkreis', pp. 1149-50; Hellmut Lehmann-Haupt, *The Göttingen Model Book: a Facsimile Edition and Translations of a Fifteenth-Century Illuminators' Manual* (Columbia, Mo.: University of Missouri Press, 1972), 83ff, figs 11-12.

15 Other manuscripts written in Mainz for the Butzbach Augustinians likewise draw on this stock: Giessen UB Hs. 697, 699, 700, 753 (dated 1449, 1451); and thus we see that the paper stock used to produce the earliest quires of the Gutenberg Bible was available in Mainz as

early as 1449. A more detailed paper examination of this group of manuscripts is much to be desired.

16 Needham, 'The Text of the Gutenberg Bible', is a first trial, based on the nine earliest editions. Readers should be warned that, because of international problems of proof correction, its tables of indicative variant readings contain more than a reasonable share of typographical errors.

17 Needham, 'A Gutenberg Bible used as Printer's Copy by Heinrich Eggestein in Strassburg, ca. 1469', *Transactions of the Cambridge Bibliographical Society* IX: 1 (1986).

18 ibid., p. 57.

19 Lotte Hellinga, 'Three Notes on Printer's Copy: Strassburg, Oxford, Subiaco', *Transactions of the Cambridge Bibliographical Society* IX: 2 (1987), p. 196: 'It is in the light of monastic orders and their reform movements that we should try to understand emendation (of the Bible) when we encounter it in the fifteenth century. The B42 copy (used by Eggestein) may well have belonged to a monastic house, partly emended before it was entrusted to the printers. Such contact (between religious house and printing shop) assumes a longer tradition in the fifteenth century, and is even more interesting.'

20 Busch, Johannes, *Chronicon Windeshemense und Liber de Reformatione monasteriorum*, ed. by K. Grube (Halle i. Sachsen: Hendel, 1886), 310ff; N. Greitemann, *De Windesheimsche Vulgatarevisie in de vijftiende eeuw* (Hilversum: N. v. P. Brand's Uitgeversbedrijf, 1937).

21 Hellinga, 'Three Notes on Printer's Copy', pp. 194-6, hinted that the revisions in Eggestein's third Vulgate may have been connected with this 'Windesheim Vulgate', but I considered and rejected this possibility before publishing. Four points are relevant. First, none of the new readings in Eggestein's edition correspond to the sample of 'Windesheim' readings given by Greiteman. The books where he found characteristic Windesheim readings are, in fact, unrevised in Eggestein's edition. Second, Eggestein's broadside advertisement for this edition refers to the work of *viros elegantissimos artium humanarum imbutos*. These are not terms we should expect for indicating monastic participation; the phrase surely is meant rather to indicate, simply, university graduates (contrast this with the colophon of the 1475 Piacenza Bible (B-542), stating that the text was *a religiosis uiris ac prudentissimis correctum*). Third, the distribution of copies of Eggestein's edition was clearly heaviest in Swabia, Bavaria and Austria, well outside the centre of gravity of the Windesheim movement. By 1470, the only significant Augustinian house in this region under Windesheim reform was that of Rebdorf, near Eichstätt. Fourth, as I noted explicitly in my original study, the copy of the Gutenberg Bible used in Eggestein's shop was unrubricated and unbound, and was completed and sold only after it had served its time as printer's copy. We cannot easily think that it came to Eggestein, with existing marginal emendations, on loan from a monastic library, as has been suggested (Hellinga, 'Three Notes on Printer's Copy', p. 196: 'The B42 copy used in Eggestein's workshop may well have belonged to a monastic house, partly emended before it was trusted to the printers. It is not difficult to imagine that some intermittent proof reading and further emendations to the text in proof took place in a contact between a monastic house and a printer's shop').

22 Cf. Hellinga, 'Three Notes on Printer's Copy', p. 196: 'Dr E. König has observed that the B42 may well have been primarily intended for, and therefore initiated by, the Benedictine houses that had joined the Bursfeld and Melk reform movement.' I believe this pushes König's observations (e.g. 1987: 169ff) beyond their natural bounds. The chief result of König's indispensable researches has been to emphasize the breadth of distribution of the Gutenberg Bible, well outside the regions of these two congregations into other cultural and political regions. Original ownerships of several copies of the Gutenberg Bible do go back to a few houses within these congregations: the Benedictines of Mainz, Melk, Tegernsee and, very probably, Erfurt. But they also go to Benedictine houses outside the congregations; and

to Cistercian, Carthusian, Carmelite, Brigittine, Dominican, Franciscan and Augustinian houses; to a collegiate church; and to a parish church (see Gerhard Powitz, *Der Frankfurter Gutenberg-Bibel: ein Beitrag zum Buchwesen des 15. Jahrhunderts*, Frankfurt: Frankfurter Bibliothekschriften, 1990, 121ff).

23 One may note that Johann Zainer's Royal folio Vulgate, Ulm, 29 January 1480 (Goff B-567), advertised itself and its various apparatus as being designed for the use of simple priests: *ad simplicium sacerdotum vtilitatem*.

24 B-594. The compiler of the subject index was Gabriele Bruno, OFM, 1508; see (DBI): *Dizionario biografico degli Italiani* (Rome: Instituto della Enciclopedia Italiana, 1960), 14, pp. 651-2. Existing literature, including DBI, has gotten itself quite confused in distinguishing between what Bruno contributed to the Paganini's 7 September 1492 edition (viz., the alphabetical subject guide), and what the Paganinis copied from Froben's 27 June 1491 edition. To complete the circle of confusion, it has even been said, quite erroneously, that Bruno's subject index first appeared in Froben's 1491 edition. The fullest account of the contents of Froben's 1491 octavo edition is found in (Felix De Marez Oyens & Paul Needham) *The Estelle Doheny Collection: Part I: Fifteenth-Century Books* (Christie's New York, 22 October 1987), lot 64.

25 See Karlfried Froehlich & Margaret T. Gibson, *Biblia latina cum glossa ordinaria. Introduction to the Facsimile Reprint of the Editio Princeps ...*, vol. I (Turnhout: Brepols, 1992).

26 I should emphasize that this is an example only of the type of question that could be investigated with regard to the production and distribution of printed Vulgate Bibles. The study of publishing and distribution of incunables is in its infancy. I suggest that further studies, much to be desired, can never usefully be based on raw counts of editions, but must take into account the separate markets of distinct texts and classes of text.

27 *Gesamtkatalog der Wiegendrucke* (Leipzig: Hiersemann, 1925-40, repr. Stuttgart & New York 1978; Stuttgart: Hiersemann; Berlin: Akademie-Verlag; New York: Kraus, 1978- ).

28 *Catalogue of Books Printed in the XVth Century now in the British Museum* (London: British Museum, 1908- ).

29 Brussels, Société des Bibliophiles et Iconophiles de Belgique, 1932.

30 Several English and American auction catalogues in the past decade have experimented in giving fuller accounts of the contents of incunables than are found in published incunable catalogues. The first of these was (De Marez Oyens & Needham) *The Estelle Doheny Collection, part I*, Christie's New York, 22 October 1987; see also, for a slightly variant system (Paul Needham), *The George Abrams Collection*, Sotheby's London, 16 November 1989. The principle of the contents notes in both catalogues is that the texts within an edition are not only listed, but specified as to both the pages they occupy and their position within the structural collation.

31 The boxes might equally well be called sets, and it is certain that the intersections of two or more sets will produce interesting subsets of familiarly related Bibles.

32 See Pierre Salmon, OSB, *Les 'Tituli Psalmorum' des Manuscrits Latins* (Rome: Cittá del Vaticano: Abbaye Saint-Jérome: Libreria Vaticana, 1959). Christianizing psalm-*tituli* have a tradition going back at least to the sixth century, originating in Psalters proper rather than full Bibles. I am unaware of any study of their appearances in Vulgate Bibles. Scattered christianizing tituli appear, sometimes as appendages to the traditional Hebrew *tituli*, in, for example, the 1475 Piacenza Vulgate (B-542), and the 14 April 1478 Nuremberg Vulgate of Anton Koberger (B-557).

33 For a general account of varying paper sizes in incunables, see Needham, 'Aldus Manutius's Paper Stocks: the Evidence of two Uncut Books', *Princeton University Library Chronicle*, 55 no. 2 (Winter 1994); issued also as: *The Same Purposeful Instinct: Essays in Honor of William H. Scheide*, ed. by William P. Stoneman (Princeton, N.J.: Princeton University

Library, 1994), and 'Res papirea: Sizes and Formats of the Late Medieval Book', in *Rationalisierung der Buchherstellung im Mittelalter und in der frühen Neuzeit*, ed. by Peter Rück (Marburg an der Lahn: Institut für Historische Hilfswissenschaften, 1994).

34 It is worth considering whether the octavo Hebrew Bible (Pentateuch and Scrolls with Haftarot) completed by Gershom Soncino in Brescia, 24 November 1493 (OffCensus 22), was influenced by Froben's example. The full octavo Hebrew Bible finished by Soncino in late May 1494 (Offenberg 12) comprises the original sheets of the November 1493 edition's Pentateuch and Scrolls, with new setting and printing to supply the Prophets and Hagiographa.

35 See Brigitte Moreau, *Inventaire chronologique des Éditions Parisiennes du XVIe siècle*, III (Paris: Service des travaux historiques de la ville de Paris, 1985), 1522.265ff. Reliable bibliographical descriptions of early-sixteenth-century books are so scarce that there may well be Vulgate miniatures before the 1520s. It will be a pleasure to be corrected.

36 For the later history of the Eton copy see Claudine Lemaire, 'La Bible du Gutenberg d'Eton Library, propriété de la comtesse Anne d'Yve de 1811 à 1814', *Gutenberg-Jahrbuch* (Mainz: Gutenberg-Gesellschaft, 1993). The copy of the Gutenberg Bible at the University of Texas, Humanities Research Center, besides being marked for refectory reading, contains similar but tripartite marginal chapter divisions: P-S-T.

37 See Paul Saenger, 'The Impact of the Early Printed Page on the History of Reading', *Bulletin du Bibliophile*, II (Paris: Techener, 1996), 279ff, for further interesting information. Saenger 281 n. 1 expresses some uncertainty on whether the Amerbach editions of 1479 and after (the *Fontibus ex graecis* editions, so-called after commendatory verse they contain) include marginal chapter divisions. They do, for the entire New Testament, as was noted by Dom. Henri Quentin, *Mémoire sur l'établissement du texte de la Vulgate* (Rome & Paris: Desclée, 1922), pp. 80-1 (see also Paul Needham, *Incunables from the Schøyen Collection*, Sotheby's New York, 12 December 1991, lot 9, illustrated (B-571).

38 Mary A. Rouse & Richard H. Rouse, 'La concordance verbale des … écritures', in *Le Moyen Age et la Bible*, ed. by Pierre Riché & Guy Lobrichon (Paris: Beauchesne, 1984), pp. 115-22. Saenger makes the important observation that in the manuscript Vulgate tradition these four- or seven-part chapter divisions were notional, rather than being marked marginally.

39 DBI 42, 613-15, with extensive references.

40 Needham, 'Haec sancta ars: Gutenberg's Invention as a Divine Gift', *Grolier Club Gazette*, 42 (New York: Grolier Club, 1990).

# HEBREW PRINTING OF THE BIBLE IN THE XVTH CENTURY

*Adrian K. Offenberg*

DURING THE LAST HUNDRED YEARS a number of important studies on early printed Hebrew biblical editions have appeared.[1] In 1897 Christian D. Ginsburg's introduction to the masoretic text of the Hebrew Bible appeared in London, a turning point in the study of the subject.[2] Half a century later, in 1950, Lazarus Goldschmidt's bibliophile publication on the earliest editions of the Hebrew Bible summarized the results of further research in an almost cynical tone.[3] In 1982 the Chief-Librarian of the Hebrew Union College Library at Cincinnati, Ohio, Herbert C. Zafren, published his concise but revealing article on early Hebrew Bible editions, adding analytical-bibliographic and sociological viewpoints to the topic.[4] He made a clear distinction between Bible texts only, texts with commentary and/or translation (mainly in Aramaic) and commentaries and/or translations with incidental text.

One of the often returning questions is: Why did the Hebrew Bible text appear relatively so late in comparison to Gutenberg's Latin Bible? The first complete Hebrew Bible appeared only on 22 April 1488 at Soncino (Heb-8),[5] while most bibliographers are considering a north Italian Hebrew Psalter with commentary, dated 29 August 1477, as the first separately printed Hebrew biblical text (Heb-28).[6] According to Goldschmidt, 'it might have been regarded as profanation to reproduce the Holy Text by mechanical means by which it was robbed of its dignity, stripped of every vestige of individuality and reduced to the degrading status of a mass-produced article'.[7] Zafren on the other hand is of the opinion that 'if one may assume that the profit motive was a primary concern of early printers, we might conclude that they chose to print commentaries first, and in a large number of editions, because there was a far greater demand for them than for text alone. This suggests,' he continues, 'that, at least relatively speaking, there were enough manuscript copies of Pentateuch (and/or Bible) texts around to satisfy the demand.'[8]

These opinions need some adjustment. First, the 1477 Psalter is not the earliest printed Hebrew biblical text – I shall return to this subject presently – and second, it was not religious reluctance in the first place but a technical problem which delayed a rapid development of the production of Hebrew Bibles, that is, the addition of vowel points to the unvocalized Hebrew text.[9] The fact that relatively so many Hebrew biblical editions appeared and were out of print quickly, once the technical problem was solved, contradicts, third, Zafren's assumption that there were enough manuscript texts around to satisfy the demand.

However, it may be useful to start with a very short introduction to the spread of Hebrew printing in the fifteenth century.[10] Hebrew incunabula appeared in Italy, Spain, Portugal and one edition in the Ottoman Empire, in Constantinople. According to modern research about 140 editions, printed on about forty presses, were printed before 1501. Many of these editions are very rare now – in all about two thousand copies are still preserved in public collections dispersed throughout the world. The first Hebrew printed books appeared in Italy only a few years after the introduction of printing in Subiaco and Rome by Sweynheym and Pannartz. As early as about 1469-73 a group of six undated books printed in square Hebrew types were printed in Rome, among which were three biblical commentaries (Heb-86, 92, 71). In 1475 the first *dated* Hebrew book was finished in southern Italy, in Reggio di Calabria, Solomon ben Isaac's (Rashi's) *Perush al hatorah* (Commentary on the Pentateuch (Heb-93)) and in the same year in northern Italy, in Piove di Sacco near Padua, a large and beautifully printed edition of Jacob Ben Asher's *Arba'ah Turim* (The Four Orders of the Code of Law (Heb-47)) appeared. Between 1474 and 1477 the press of Abraham Conat was active in Mantua and published seven attractive books in Italian semi-cursive Hebrew types, among which is another commentary on the Pentateuch (Heb-69). Conat's work was continued in Ferrara by Abraham ben Hayyim of Pesaro; he printed the first vocalized *Humash* (Hebrew Pentateuch) with Aramaic translation and Rashi's commentary at Bologna in 1482 (Heb-18).

After 1483 members of the Soncino family, originating from Speyer in Germany, became the leading printers of Hebrew books in Italy. Joshua Solomon ben Israel Nathan began to publish separate treatises from the Talmud at Soncino (halfway between Milan and Mantua) sometimes using decorative woodcut initials, panels and a frame. (Incidentally, this decorative frame had been used earlier by the Christian printer Francesco del Tuppo in Naples.) Joshua published the *Nevi'im* (Prophets) with commentary in 1485 and the first complete vocalized Hebrew Bible in 1488 (Heb-22, Heb-24, Heb-8). The master printer was Abraham ben Hayyim of Pesaro. Also working at Soncino were Joshua Solomon's nephews Gershom ben Moses and Solomon ben Moses. Presumably under pressure from the Church, Joshua Solomon ultimately had to flee to Naples; Gershom became an itinerant printer who established presses at Brescia, Barco and later, in the sixteenth century, at Fano, Pesaro, Rimini, Ancona and Cesena, and finally at Salonika and Constantinople.

In Naples there was another Hebrew press besides Joshua Solomon's: that of Joseph ben Jacob Ashkenazi Gunzenhauser and his son Azriel. Joseph Gunzenhauser published the *Ketuvim* (Hagiographa) with commentaries and vowelpoints in 1487 and Joshua Soncino published a splendid second edition of the complete Hebrew Bible (Heb-9, Heb-34, Heb-26). An attractive decorative frame, used by Azriel Gunzenhauser and possibly cut in wood by his brother-in-law Moses ben Isaac, also appears in a Christian edition in Naples, printed by Aiolfo de Cantono. Probably as a result of the war between France and the Kingdom of Naples the production of Hebrew books there came to an end in about 1492, after twenty works had been published.

Our knowledge of the history of Hebrew book production in the Iberian peninsula during the fifteenth century is much more fragmentary. Historical evidence was destroyed on a large scale with the expulsion of the Jews from Spain in 1492 and the subsequent events in Portugal in 1496. Apart from a group of Iberian Hebrew books which have come down to us in fragments only, Rashi's Commentary on the Pentateuch from the press of Solomon ben Moses Alkabiz Halevi at Guadalajara, probably dating from 1476, seems the oldest known Spanish Hebrew book (Heb-94). Ten years later Eliezer Alantansi was active in Híjar. His books display a high degree of aesthetic perfection. He used a decorative frame cut in metal by the silversmith/printer Alfonso Fernández de Córdoba, which is universally regarded as a masterpiece. This frame had also been used in a Christian book of earlier date, *Manuale Caesaraugustanum* (Híjar: Alfonso Fernández de Córdoba, *c.* 1486; 2°; M-212), and decorates a splendid Hebrew Pentateuch with scrolls of about 1487-8 (Heb-14). The first Hebrew book to be printed in Portugal was an edition of the Pentateuch, issued at Faro in 1487 from the press of Samuel Giacon. This was also the very first book to be printed in Portugal (Proctor 9832). The press was subsequently carried on by Samuel Porteiro. In Lisbon Eliezer Toledano published a number of very fine printed books, using the same decorative frame as used a few years before in Híjar in Spain by Alfonso Fernández de Córdoba and Eliezer Alantansi. In Leiria Samuel Dortas owned a printing shop together with his sons. He published not only Hebrew books but Latin and Spanish as well. The Lisbon and Leiría presses also published separate parts of the Hebrew Bible, but no complete bibles, as far as we know (Heb-20, 23, 33, 35).

The first Hebrew press in the Ottoman empire was founded as early as 1493. The brothers Samuel and David Ibn Nahmias, who had escaped fom Spain, published the popular *Turim* by Jacob Ben Asher on 13 December 1493 in Constantinople (Heb-49). Their typographical material had originally been used in Naples and Lisbon.

In all, about seventy different Hebrew texts were published in the fifteenth century, including biblical texts, commentaries, rabbinics, and linguistic, philosophical, historical and literary works. Most popular, it seems, were the editions of the Pentateuch and the *Turim* by Jacob Ben Asher, both of which were published at least thirteen times. To summarize, I count thirty-six different Hebrew biblical editions in the fifteenth century. Twenty-four appeared in Italy, twelve survive from the Iberian Peninsula. Two-thirds of these editions are biblical texts alone, one-third has been printed with an added commentary. Here I shall restrict myself to what I consider the earliest edition of a Hebrew biblical text.

There exists an undated north Italian edition of *Tehillim* (the Hebrew Psalter), which is very rare indeed (Hain 13446/7).[11] Two copies are in the Biblioteca Palatina at Parma (Pl. 27); one on parchment. One is in the Badische Landesbibliothek, Karlsruhe, and two in the United Kingdom – in the British Library and the Bodleian. The descriptions of these copies in bibliographical literature are rather vague and contradictory; from them one might conclude that the edition had a small, unidentified format. Furthermore, an eighteenth-century description noted significant differences between some of the copies.[12] The first question to be addressed, then, was whether there existed two different editions or states of this rare small book.

Both the copy in the British Library in London[13] and that in the Bodleian Library in Oxford[14] apparently belong to the same (second) state of the edition, which is contrary to some information[15] (see Pl. 28). This edition was printed in a *sextodecimo* format (or 'in sixteens') on divided sheets, each sheet cut into eight small sections, mainly in quires of ten leaves (five sheets).[16] The book has seven quires. In this edition for the first time in a Hebrew printed book marginal notes (the numbering of the Psalms) are to be found. This technical innovation led to a number of errors, resulting in irregular beginnings of lines on the verso pages and irregular line endings on the recto pages, together with mistakes and omissions in the numbering itself. In Italy, marginal notes in non-Hebrew books appeared first in Venice in 1474 (G-363)[17] and books in sixteens first appeared in Rome in 1473, in Venice in 1474, and in Naples in 1478.[18]

The London copy has been severely cut by the binder's knife, measuring only 126×95 mm, and consequently the remnants of the watermarks in the upper and lower outer margins have completely disappeared. In the Oxford copy, on the other hand, the original size has been preserved much better; it measures 183×105 mm, showing clearly the two halves of its watermark, which appears to be a nice dragon[19] (or more precisely, a pair of dragons, since watermarks are twins[20]). The original sheets of paper used for this small book must have measured somewhat over 420×572 mm, which means that Royal-size paper was used. Royal paper with a dragon as watermark (old-fashioned paper historians used to call this harmless monster a basilisk) was mainly used in Parma and environs, like Mantua and Ferrara, in Hebrew and non-Hebrew books, printed around 1474-7.[21]

It seems appropriate to compare these technical data with that of the book which is generally considered the earliest printed Hebrew biblical text,[22] a north Italian Psalter, place of printing unknown, this time in folio format, and dated 29 August 1477 (Pl. 29; Heb-28). This book was printed on sheets of Chancery paper, measuring about 275×390 mm, in quires of eight leaves (four sheets). This provides us with an interesting case of transition from one-pull press to two-pull press, which took place in some Italian towns in the middle of the 1470s and which is also demonstrable in the Hebrew printing shops in Italy.

The key words are 'imposition' and 'casting off'. Imposition is the arrangement in formes of the typeset pages in such an order that after the printing and folding of the sheets the pages follow each other in proper sequence. Casting-off is the notation of the estimate of copy text by the compositor or the master of the printing office, to ensure that the amount of paper will be used economically and that the pages which have to be set will fit with those which have already been set. Originally, at least in the case of a folio edition, every page had to go separately through the press. But thanks to the invention of the two-pull press this procedure could be accelerated considerably: the inner forme and the outer forme, set in type according to the new rules of imposition, had to be placed on the bed of the press only once.[23] This also implied that much more type was required. Almost simultaneously we can observe a transition from five sheets to four sheets per quire and a transition from large Royal paper to the smaller dimensions of Median and Chancery paper for most categories of books. I have no full explanation for this phenomenon, but possibly the new dimensions of the two-pull press had something to do with it – and maybe there were economic reasons to produce books of a somewhat smaller size too. However, in most cases it is very difficult or even impossible to decide whether a folio book was printed page by page or forme by forme. Only when the book was never in a binder's press or when errors or irregularities can be detected might there be a clue. I am of the opinion that there are such clues to be found in both Psalters.

As mentioned before, the Psalter in sixteens was printed on previously divided sheets. This can be concluded easily from the Bodleian copy in which remnants of the watermarks are still visible. In the first quire, for example, three heads but no tail of a dragon can be distinguished. This means that the first quire was not produced from one single large sheet, folded four times – in that case only one head and one tail would be expected. Due to its small format it is still possible, however, that the text was set and printed in small formes of two pages, in which for instance page 1 and page 20 (the first and last page of the first quire) were printed in one pull, to be followed by page 2 and 19 on the other side. There are indications within the pages of the book that support this possibility. In the fourth quire a leaf was cut out from the middle in both copies I have seen, without loss of text. So probably there was originally a blank leaf in the middle of the book. This strongly suggests that printing was done by small formes from the outer side to the inner side of the quire, and that an error was made in the casting off. Yet the fact that the sheets were divided into eights may prove that the small Psalter was printed on a one-pull press.

On the other hand, there are several indications that the folio Psalter was printed on a two-pull press. Not only the Chancery paper and the quires of eight leaves point in that direction, but also the fact that the vocalization of the text in the first quire is missing from the sixth leaf only, to be continued on the next leaves of the quire. This most probably signifies that the sixth leaf, which with its conjugate, the fifth leaf, is in the middle of the quire, was set and printed after the ninth, eighth and seventh leaves and their conjugates in the first half of the quire. Apparently it was decided after the typesetting of the verso of leaf 5 to abandon the difficult and time-consuming inclusion of the vowel points. (The case is somewhat obscured by the fact that in this quire an odd, disjunct leaf is at its front, making it a nine-leaf quire. The first Psalm begins on the second leaf. One has to assume, too, that before imposition the four pages of leaves 5 and 6 were set *seriatim* – in their proper textual sequence – which seems a reasonable procedure in this case.) Thus we must conclude that the book was most probably set and printed by formes, which for a folio edition is only possible on a two-pull press. In any case, book-historical evidence suggests that of these two early editions of the Psalms, both printed at an unknown place somewhere in northern Italy, the pocket-sized 16mo just pipped the larger one at the post.

Ginsburg's discussion of the 1477 folio edition of the Psalms occupies fourteen pages of his 1897 *Introduction*, mentioned above.[24] In contrast, he allocated only one paragraph to a description of the small-sized edition, in which he stated that it exhibits the same orthographical and textual features as the Psalter of 1477, and which he dated between 1478 and 1480. This dating seems rather arbitrary to me. Actually I suspect Ginsburg of not having inspected a copy carefully, although in general he intensively perused the early printed Hebrew biblical editions in the library of the British Museum where this rare small book was kept since 1868. In his analysis of the 1477 folio Psalter, Ginsburg states that as a result of their inability to overcome the difficulty in connection with the vocalization of the text the editors tried to help the readers to pronounce the words correctly by a profuse insertion of additional letters. None of those changes, however, are to be found in the 16mo Psalter, neither is there any resemblance between the two editions as far as manifest errors and omissions are concerned. In the folio Psalter Ginsburg established the omission of no fewer than 108 whole verses. The Psalter in sixteens has them all. From the list of errors indicated by Ginsburg in the folio edition I compared twenty-one with the text of the 16mo Psalter and found only four correspondences, which may possibly be explained by a textual tradition, varying from the later *textus receptus*.

My conclusion will be obvious. There is no reason at all to follow Ginsburg in his opinion that the small Psalter exhibits the same orthographical and textual features as the folio edition, and in consequence it is not necessary to date it after August 1477. On the contrary, based on the bibliographical evidence it seems highly probable that the pocket-sized Psalter is the real first Hebrew printed biblical text.

## NOTES

1 There are a few interesting eighteenth- and nineteenth-century studies too, but these are, generally speaking, obsolete.

2 Christian David Ginsburg, *Introduction to the Massoretico-Critical Edition of the Hebrew Bible* (London: Trinitarian Bible Society, 1897; repr. with a Prolegomenon by H. M. Orlinsky, New York: Ktav, 1966).

3 Lazarus Goldschmidt, *The Earliest Editions of the Hebrew Bible: with a Treatise on the Oldest Manuscripts of the Bible by Paul Kahle* (New York: Aldus Book Co., 1950). Limited edition of 330 copies only.

4 Herbert C. Zafren, 'Bible Editions, Bible Study and the Early History of Hebrew Printing', in *Eretz-Israel. Archaeological, Historical and Geographical Studies*, 16, *H. M. Orlinsky Volume* (Jerusalem: Israel Exploration Society, 1982), pp. 240-51.

5 Ludwig Hain, *Repertorium bibliographicum in quo libri omnes ab arte typographica inventa usque ad annum MD. typis expressi ordine alphabetico ... enumerantur* etc. (Paris & Stuttgart, 1826-38; repr. Milan: Görlich 1948) (abbreviated here: Hain), no. 3029; Robert Proctor, *An Index to the Early Printed Books in the British Museum from the Invention of Printing to the Year 1500, with Notes of Those in the Bodleian Library* (London: Kegan Paul, Trench, Trübner,1898; repr. London: Holland Press, 1960) (Proctor), no. 7305; *Gesamtkatalog der Wiegendrucke* (Leipzig: Hiersemann, 1925-40; repr. 1978, Stuttgart: Hiersemann; Berlin: Akademie-Verlag; New York: Kraus, 1978- ) (GW), no. 4198; Frederick R. Goff, *Incunabula in American Libraries: a Third Census of Fifteenth-Century Books Recorded in North American Collections*, annotated repr. (Millwood, N.Y.: Kraus, 1973); A. K. Offenberg in collaboration with C. Moed-Van Walraven, *Hebrew Incunabula in Public Collections: a First International Census* (Nieuwkoop: De Graaf, 1990) (OffCensus), no. 10.

6 Hain 13451; Proctor 7330; OffCensus 34.

7 Goldschmidt, pp. 12-13.

8 Zafren, p. 241.

9 This is a complicated procedure which I cannot discuss now but which aided the correct pronunciation of the sacred text.

10 Source: A. K. Offenberg, 'Hebräischer Buchdruck', in *Lexikon des gesamten Buchwesens (LGB²)*, ed. by Severin Corsten, Günther Pflug & Friedrich Adolf Schmidt-Künsemüller (Stuttgart: Anton Hiersemann, 1991), III, pp. 408-10, and OffCensus, 'Introduction', pp. viii-xxix.

11 Proctor 7436; OffCensus, 36, 37.

12 Johannes Bernardus De-Rossi, *Annales Hebraeo-typographici seculi XV* (Parma: Ex Regio Typographeo, 1795; repr. 1969), pp. 128-30.

13 Pressmark C.50.e.22. Samuel Van Straalen, *Catalogue of Hebrew Books in the British Museum, Acquired During the Years 1868-1892* (London: The British Museum, 1894), p. 37.

14 Pressmark Opp. add. 12°. 81. Arthur Ernest Cowley, *A Concise Catalogue of the Hebrew*

*Printed Books in the Bodleian Library* (Oxford: Clarendon Press, 1929; repr. Oxford: Clarendon Press, 1971), p. 74.

15 David Goldstein, *Hebrew Incunables in the British Isles: a Preliminary Census* (London: The British Library, *c.* 1985), nos 22, 23.

16 For more information on analytical bibliography, cf. Philip Gaskell, *A New Introduction to Bibliography* (first published 1972, repr. with corrections, Oxford: Clarendon Press, 1985); Ronald B. McKerrow, *An Introduction to Bibliography for Literary Students* (first published 1927, repr. with introduction by David McKitterick, Winchester/New Castle, Del. 1994); Paul Needham, 'ISTC as a Tool for Analytical Bibliography', in *Bibliography and the Study of 15th-Century Civilisation, 1984*, ed. by Lotte Hellinga & John Goldfinch (London: The British Library, 1987), pp. 39-54.

17 *Catalogue of Books Printed in the XVth Century now in the British Museum* (London: British Museum, 1908- ), V: Venice (first published 1924; Lithographic repr. London: British Museum, 1963), p. 174: IC. 19678.

18 *Indice generale degli incunaboli delle biblioteche d'Italia*, III: *G-L*, ed. by T. M. Guarnaschelli e E. Valenziani in collaboration with E. Cerulli (Rome: La Libreria dello Stato, 1954), p. 100: 4813, 4814, 4817.

19 For this type of watermark cf. Gerhard Piccard, 'Wasserzeichen Fabeltiere: Greif-Drache-Einhorn', *Findbuch 10 der Wasserzeichenkartei Piccard im Hauptstaatsarchiv Stuttgart. Veröffentlichungen der Staatlichen Archivverwaltung Baden-Württenberg, Sonderreihe* (Stuttgart: Kohlhammer, 1980).

20 Allan Stevenson, 'Watermarks are Twins', in *Studies in Bibliography*, 4 (1951-2), pp. 57-91, 235.

21 Giorgio Montecchi, *Il libro nel Rinascimento: Saggi di bibliologia* (Milan: Editrice La Storia, 1994), pp. 136-40.

22 See above, n. 6.

23 For more information on the fifteenth-century printing press, cf. Michael Pollak, 'The Performance of the Wooden Printing Press', *The Library Quarterly*, 42 (1972), 218-64; Leonhard Hoffmann, 'Druckleistungen in der Inkunabeloffizin', in *Zur Arbeit mit dem Gesamtkatalog der Wiegendrucke: Vorträge der internationalen Fachtagung vom 26. bis 30. November 1979 in Berlin*, ed. by Dieter Schidmaier (Berlin: Deutsche Staatsbibliothek, 1989), pp. 119-26; and especially Lotte Hellinga, 'The Codex in the Fifteenth Century: Manuscript and Print', in *A Potencie of Life: Books in Society*, ed. by Nicolas Barker (London: The British Library, 1993), pp. 63-88 (pp. 70-3).

24 Ginsburg (above, n. 2), pp. 780-94.

# BIBLICAL BOOKS AND THE CIRCULATION OF THE PSALMS IN LATE-MEDIEVAL ENGLAND

*Kimberly Van Kampen*

THE STUDY OF INCUNABULA is, among other things, an investigation of the intellectual development of a society. The mechanical mass replication of texts was a catalyst in one way or another of social and cultural change.[1] Even the most cursory examination of a catalogue of early printed books for a given country displays a pattern of gradual progression – more vernacular books, more secular, classical and literary books, and a relatively higher percentage of contemporary texts (as opposed to those which had circulated for generations in manuscript). Printing nourished the popularization of literacy and education, and was essential to the propagation of Renaissance values and the success of the Reformation.

Historians of early English printing are faced with a difficult task when they look for parallels between Britain and the Continent in the late part of the fifteenth and early sixteenth centuries. Printing came to England from Bruges in the early part of the 1470s with the work of William Caxton, but English printing never developed into an industry similar to that which flourished by the end of the century on the Continent. It may be said in general that England's output of printed books at this time constituted just over one per cent of the total output of printed texts in Europe.[2] In addition to its low productivity, the English print industry lagged behind its counterparts on several other levels – the types of texts produced, the level of technological sophistication, the quality of materials and the numbers of issues and editions, not to mention the rarity of the English print-shop in itself.[3] These disparities, however, should not diminish the accomplishments of the first printers in England. The imprints of Caxton, de Worde and Pynson, like the works of the Continental printers, are monuments inasmuch as they are valid representations of the cultural climate in which they were produced. At issue is not the importance of the work of England's first printers; it is the relative scarcity and simplicity of such accomplishments that is striking when compared to the quantity and sophistication of Continental book production.

The state of printing in fifteenth-century England has yet to be included in the current discussions of the larger social and religious context of the period. In the last twenty years revisionist historians have challenged the traditional view of the nature of the Church in late medieval England and the effects of the Reformation on that society.[4] In the words of one, 'The determinist progression from a corrupt and spiritually bankrupt church, by way of mystics and early heretical movements like the Lollards and the Hussites, to a cataclysm which tore apart the old Catholic order to give religion a new life, is now coming to be recognized for the Protestant propaganda that it always was.'[5]

Proponents of this view argue that documentary evidence, such as wills and chantry records, portray a healthy fifteenth-century Church and strong orthodox sentiments among the lay people. From this perspective, the Reformation is an enigmatic phenomemon. Christine Carpenter concludes, 'The upshot of all this is that not only does the Reformation become a less obvious conclusion to late-medieval religious history, it begins to be positively inexplicable.'[6]

Scholars who argue for the traditional view also have done so on the basis of documentary and textual evidence. Nicholas Watson, in 1995, conducted an investigation of the effects of censorship on the English society of the fifteenth century, based on a comparison between fourteenth- and fifteenth-century vernacular composition.[7] He argued that the legacy of the Oxford Constitutions of 1409 (sometimes called the Constitutions of Arundel after the bishop who was their strongest proponent) was a subsequent climate of stunted English intellectual development. Expanding his investigation beyond the texts of the Lollards, Watson concludes that the Constitutions as a whole embodied 'one of the most draconian pieces of censorship in English history, going far beyond its ostensible aim of destroying the Lollard heresy and effectively attempting to curtail all sorts of theological thinking and writing in the vernacular that did not fit within the pragmatic bounds set by earlier legislation like Peckham's Syllabus of 1281'.[8] The articles of the Constitutions prohibited, among other things, the unauthorized translation of the Bible into English and the writing of theological works in English. This prominent legislation effectively governed the activities of the intellectual centres, primarily the universities and the book trade, well into the sixteenth century, and in so doing severely damaged the cultural and academic fabric of England. The Constitutions were an unnatural interruption of a vernacular movement which had had vigorous and early success. The result of this movement's demise was to set cultural progress back by one hundred years.

In addition to religious works, this gap in English cultural development is apprent in a lack of secular works printed at the time. The silence of the English presses on the subjects which were most popular on the Continent is too great to be attributed simply to a developmental delay. Henri-Jean Martin noted thirty years ago that 'the Latin classics which were the greatest successes for publishers undoubtedly continued to be those which had been most popular in the Middle Ages, those which had most frequently been adapted and translated into the vernacular'.[9] Ten of the fifteen most often printed Latin classical authors in the fifteenth century – Ovid, Seneca, Caesar, Vegetius, Livy, Sallust, Plautus, Lucian, Persius and Juvenal – were never printed in England prior to the sixteenth century. Virgil was produced in only one edition (V-199), Cicero in two, both in English (C-627, STC 5312). Cato, Aesop and Terence, however, were published and reissued at least four times each during this period, Cato and Aesop in translation only (see C-313, A-118, T-111, respectively). Furthermore, publications of classical Latin scientific texts were also absent. No editions of Pliny, Ptolemy, Euclid or Avicenna were printed in England, when they were regularly issued by Continental presses. On the other hand, twenty-one editions of late medieval scientific works were printed in England in the fifteenth century, primarily translations of Continental works. Martin indicated that this was a topic of growing popularity on the Continent as well (although much of medieval scientific writing has been found to be more fabulous than factual).[10] This dearth of significant publications in England reflects a general state of intellectual mediocrity in the area of orginal composition, evident in the manifest void in the canon of English vernacular composition between Chaucer and the Elizabethan poets (with the possible exception of Malory),[11] and the noticable silence of original thought in English universities after Wyclif.[12]

Overall, there is a pressing need for a comparative re-evaluation of early printing in England which would examine the nature of the first English presses in the light of current understanding of the cultural, social, and political issues of the period, both in England and on the Continent. This article seeks to address only one aspect of that understanding, that is, the relationship of the state of the fifteenth-century printed biblical text in England (in both Latin and English) to the implications of enforced vernacular censorship. My investigation is divided into two parts: first a general summary of the forms of printed Scripture in England, both in Latin and the vernacular up to 1500; then an examination of the cultural decline under the impetus of censorship, focusing on the textual history of the Psalter, the most widely-circulated religious text in the late Middle Ages.

## THE BIBLE IN PRINT IN ENGLAND IN THE FIFTEENTH CENTURY

In the 1877 catalogue of the Caxton Celebration, Henry Stevens contributed a brief review of all printed bibles, beginning in 1450.[13] In the section titled Class C, Holy Scriptures, he listed 133 incunable bibles, but included only two 'bibles' of English origin – Caxton's several editions of Voragine's *Golden Legend*, beginning in 1483 (beginning with J-148), and the *Sermons on the Psalms* by John Fisher, printed by Wynkyn de Worde in 1508 (STC 10902) – because nothing close to a Bible had been printed in England prior to the sixteenth century. Although A. S. Herbert in 1968 listed a number of other texts that contained various amounts of translated Scripture in his revision of Darlow & Moule's *Historical Catalogue of Printed Editions of the English Bible*, he, like subsequent bibliographers, settled for the *Golden Legend* as the stand-in for an English incunable Bible.[14] Indeed, modern scholars tend to view the situation as does John King, historian of English Reformation literature, who found that 'the only vernacular form in which English laymen could approach the Bible prior to Edward IV's reign was Caxton's translation of Jacobus de Voragine's *The Golden Legend*'.[15] This is a slight over-simplification of the state of things. A century after their enactment, the influence of the Constitutions was strong enough to discourage printers from overt attempts to reproduce a Lollard or equivalent text.[16] And yet biblical matter constituted a significant percentage, even the majority in some years, of publications in England. For lack of a printed Bible in England in the late fifteenth century, English readers could glean the Holy Scriptures from three possible sources: in Latin, in domestically produced standardized liturgical texts and orthodox writings of the Church; in English, embedded in texts of popular piety, whether versified, paraphrased, or loosely translated from the Vulgate; and in imported Continental, mostly Latin, books.[17]

A cursory examination of the output of the earliest English print-shops reveals the greater part of the earliest Latin publications in England to be for the use of the Church.[18] Indulgences, liturgies, Latin rites, breviaries, books of hours, primers and

Psalters were consistent products of the new invention from its earliest recorded use. These texts, although the rarest extant examples of early English printing, with many surviving only as a single fragment, were nonetheless by far the most plenteous of early English publications.

The tools of the mass and office were complex and varied, representing many forms and uses, and are omnipresent in the early history of the English press. Their high production rate suggests a close relationship between the Church and the press in fifteenth-century England. Claire Bolton, in her discussion of Caxton's indulgence of 1476, suggests that from the very start the Abbot of Abingdon Abbey recognized the 'advantage of quick multiple copies' of an item which brought revenue to the Abbey.[19] The possibilities of monetary motivation notwithstanding, the early press in England was undoubtedly an oft-used pedagogical tool in the hands of the Church.

This detail surprises those who are accustomed to the rhetoric of the reformers who claimed, as John Foxe proudly did, that printing signalled the demise of the false church. He wrote in the *Acts and Monuments* (first published in 1563 (STC 11222)) about the fear on the part of the Orthodox Church of the presses of the reformers: 'Accordingly, the Vicar of Croydon in Surrey is said to have expressed himself to the following purpose in a sermon which he preached at Paul's Cross about this time: *We must root out printing or printing will root out us.*'[20]

Certainly the English press was well and effectively utilized by the established Church long before it became useful to the proponents of the Reformation. In addition to liturgical books, the Latin Vulgate was transmitted by way of treatises, sermons, prayers and occasional books such as Mirk's *Liber Festivalis* (M-620).[21] The writings of the Fathers and contemporary theologians such as Nicolaus de Harapis, Thomas of Waleys, Traversanus, Bonaventura, Bernard, Richard Fitzjames and others enjoyed popularity in Latin, with most appearing in several editions during the incunable period.[22] Some dealt directly with portions of Scripture, such as Thomas of Waley's exposition of the Psalms in 1481 (STC 19627) and the many editions of the *Meditationes Vitae Christi* (B-903), a sort of harmony of the Gospels attributed (falsely) to Cardinal Bonaventura. De Worde's 1499 *Contemplation* (C-869), endorsed by the Bishop of Durham, contained Latin prose selections from the Bible with English verse meditations on the Latin passages. Augustine was printed severally in Latin and in English translation, beginning in 1483 (STC 922 and forward). Nicholas Hanapus's testament containing selections of Scripture is listed in the *Short Title Catalogue* under the heading 'Bible' for the year 1481 (N-107).

It is necessary to note parenthetically that the success of the Reformation and the production of predominantly vernacular Protestant texts did not diminish the rate of Latin publications of the Church throughout the formidable sixteenth century. Sixteenth-century printers continued the production of large runs of Latin breviaries, Psalters, missals, graduals and indulgences as well as a fair share of orthodox polemical writings. The sixteenth-century press served the Counter-Reformation in much the same way as it had the orthodox establishment in the previous century.[23]

If there is a distinguishing characteristic of the fifteenth-century English press, it is the ratio of vernacular publications to those in Latin. English titles equalled or slightly exceeded those in Latin.[24] This is remarkable when compared to the Continent where the ratio of Latin publications to those in the vernacular was approximately five to one.[25] Much of the credit for this goes to William Caxton for his English translations of French and Latin bestsellers, which were continuously reprinted by his successors, de Worde and Pynson. The high production of translations of Continental works suggests important insights into the first patrons of printed books in England, but I shall not embark on that topic here. For our purposes, the fact that England during the incunable period produced a relatively higher number of vernacular imprints than anywhere else raises the question all the more of why it did not produce a vernacular Bible. Although England did produce a number of pseudo-biblical books in which portions of the Bible were printed in the vernacular, English texts that contained biblical quotations were far outnumbered by similar Latin publications.

Caxton claimed personally to have translated from French many of his English hagiographical and romantic texts. His *Golden Legend* exemplifies the treatment of the Scriptures in the first publications in English. The collections of saints' lives were an immensely popular genre of late medieval piety, and the *Legenda Aurea* of Jacobus Voragine was a universal favourite. Voragine's text, however, served as only the starting point for Caxton's version. 'Englished' by Caxton himself (according to the prologue) from both the Latin and French versions, the *Golden Legend* contains much more than its ancestor. For instance, his edition includes many of his personal experiences and observations, and a separate chapter entitled 'Bible Stories' (which was responsible for its place in the Sacred Scriptures section of the Caxton Celebration catalogue). The passages chosen for the stories are accompanied by directions for their liturgical use, indicating that the *Golden Legend* was intended for use in services, an Insular practice for which other evidence exists.[26] The specific stories are primarily from the Old Testament – concerning Adam, Noah, Abraham, Isaac, Jacob, Joseph, Moses, the Ten Commandments, Joshua, Samuel, Saul, David, Solomon, Rehoboam, Job – with apocryphal material included, such as Tobit and Judith. The section containing the saints' lives includes a glossary of their names. The biblical portions (in paraphrase) have been ordered according to the liturgical calendar, the usual structure of hagiographical compilations.

*The Golden Legend* was not the only text of this type. A number of fifteenth-century vernacular publications in England may be said to have contained biblical material in one of three ways: paraphrases of Bible stories resembling the *Golden Legend* (such as Nicholas Love's translation of Bonaventure's *Mirror of the Life of Christ* (B-903));[27] meditations on the names and person of Christ or the shedding of his blood (such as de Worde's *Meditations of St Bernard* (B-411) and various untitled prayer books);[28] and treatises that contain instruction of a biblical nature.

*Dives and Pauper* (P-117; Pl. 30) is the most notable of this last category in that it contains more than seven hundred biblical citations which are loose translations of the Vulgate into English. It is also significant in that it is a native fourteenth-century Franciscan vernacular composition.[29] A treatise on holy living, it was written in prose and structured into ten precepts, one for each of the ten commandments. It is presented in the form of a dialogue between Dives (from *divitae*, riches or wealth) and Pauper, a poor mendicant, with Dives functioning as a device, posing questions which outline Pauper's responses. In spite of the unusually high incidence of biblical quotations, *Dives and Pauper* was not censored by the ecclesiastical authorities, because it promoted traditional orthodoxy. As a text it represented the period prior to the rise of the Lollard heresy, the era of Richard Rolle and other non-heretical efforts towards vernacular religion.

Far more than their value as purveyors of vernacular biblical text, these early publications are exceptional in their role in the evolution and development of English as a literary language. It has been said that a language comes of age when it is first used to translate the Bible.[30] Beginning in the late fifteenth century, and certainly throughout the sixteenth, English grew in its respectability and capability as a vehicle of transmission of intellectual matters. Within two hundred years a process begun by Chaucer and perfected by Spenser took English from the simple to the profound. These early publications were instrumental in establishing confidence in the versatility of our native tongue among writers, translators, scholars, printers and readers.

Despite the great number of vernacular publications and their effect on the development of the language, England clearly suffered from the lack of a national vernacular Bible in the fifteenth century. To infer, as some do, that as a Christian society it could thrive without one when substitutes were available in the form of pseudo-biblical literature, is to ignore the pattern of the rest of the Christian west.[31] Nigel Palmer observes of the period when such literature circulated as much as, if not more than, the biblical text itself; in the Middle Ages the Bible may have been more important as a concept than as a book.[32] Yet the impression of the Bible as a cohesive and independent text (what Palmer refers to as 'the larger conceptual whole') was never abandoned. In all places but England, pseudo-biblical texts enjoyed popularity in places where the Bible itself was readily available in manuscript and print, in both Latin and the common tongue.

## THE CIRCULATION OF THE PSALMS IN FIFTEENTH-CENTURY ENGLAND

The Book of Psalms was the portion of the Bible which existed most commonly in the Middle Ages both as an independent text and as part of the whole, and until the fifteenth century the Psalter enjoyed a rich tradition of vernacular transmission in England.[33] Contrary to the current theory that the cultural environment in fifteenth-century England was progressive and beneficial for the lay practice of Christianity, the following survey of the history of the English Psalter provides a paradigm for the premise that intellectual culture in England was neither developing in a manner consistent with its own past, nor in a mode similar to other western nations. Rather, England was arrested in its cultural progress, even while the Continent was enjoying the fruits of the late-medieval and Renaissance enthusiasm for vernacular letters. This phenomenon can be credited to the censorship of vernacular biblical and theological texts.

Paradoxically, England has the distinction of being both one of the first western cultures to have had vernacular Scriptures and one of the last. The biblical translations of the Anglo-Saxons were among the earliest in the western world, and the eighth-century Vespasian Psalter is arguably the earliest biblical translation in English.[34] The Psalter was translated in Anglo-Saxon England as both an interlinear gloss and as a complete translation,[35] but most commonly as the former. Possibly hundreds of glossed psalters circulated prior to the twelfth century,[36] serving the education of monks not yet literate in Latin.

Following the Norman Conquest, the tradition of the 'English' Psalter continued, that is, the Psalms were readily available in the languages of the people of England, be it Norman French or later Middle English. Perhaps the earliest post-Conquest Psalter is the Eadwine Psalter, a twelfth-century polyglot which contains Anglo-Norman French, Old English and Latin versions.[37] The Oxford Psalter,[38] from approximately the same time, represents the earliest witness for the most common Anglo-Norman French version, which found its audience amongst the educated French-speaking upper-class of the fourteenth century. There is also at least one manuscript witness to a Middle English translation of a French commentary on the seven penitential psalms from the same period.[39]

A number of translations of the Psalms into Middle English existed in the fourteenth and fifteenth centuries. The Sarum primer and the prayer book, both of which had circulated for several centuries in Latin, began to appear in translation in the fourteenth century.[40] Both texts, although far from standardized, could contain up to fifty-two psalms. The entire corpus was translated both in the text of the West Midland Psalter and that of the hermit Richard Rolle of Hampole.[41] The former, a translation from the Norman French, was, according to Margaret Deanesly, the 'best-known biblical book in the vernacular' before Wyclif.[42] However, the first biblical translation from the Latin into English since the Anglo-Saxon period was Rolle's Psalter and commentary of the mid-1330s (Pl. 31). By the time of the establishment of the Constitutions of Oxford, Rolle's Psalter had become the prominent English version.[43] Sanctioned by the Church, it was one of the few pre-Wyclif vernacular texts to be permitted after the ban on vernacular theology, and it continued to be copied at least until 1415.[44] It remained the only approved version of the vernacular Psalms in England for two hundred years and it is extant in over twenty manuscripts.[45] The Wycliffite scholar and translator, John Purvey, cited Rolle's Psalter in his prologue to the English Bible as an historical precedent for the activities of the Lollards, who later adapted Rolle's commentary to make it conform with their own theological tenets.[46]

The Psalms were especially relevant to Rolle's acute sense of the personal experience of worship. Rolle was a mystic who rejected the conventional clerical programme of Oxford for a life of solitude and individual revelation. His writings, the majority of which were written in the vernacular, were filled with the peculiar language of mystical union with God. The Latin sources for his translation were the Gallican Psalter and the preceding Old Latin version.[47] His commentary initially follows that of Peter Lombard, but becomes progressively more personalized. He prefixed a prologue to the Psalms in which he provided an exposition on the three types of psalms and a methodology for interpretation. In it he defined the purpose of the translation. Following in the tradition of every English biblical translator before him, Rolle regarded the English Scriptures as a tool by which one might learn Latin.[48] He stated:

> In this work I shall not be using learned expression but the easiest and commonest words in English which approximate most closely to the Latin, so that those who do not know Latin can acquire many Latin words from the English.

Of his own method of translating he explains:

I follow the letter as much as I am able to, and where I cannot find an exactly equivalent English word, I follow the sense, so that those who are going to read it need have no fear of not understanding. In the explanation I follow the holy doctors of the church since it could be that it will come into the hands of someone malicious who has no idea how he ought to interpret the work ... and in this way cause grave harm to himself and to others by despising a work which is beneficial both to himself and for others.[49]

Rolle's text format intermingled the Latin and Middle English texts, in keeping with his expressed purpose of using English to teach Latin. Each verse is written first in Latin, followed by an English translation with an explanation, which provides the translated portions of the glossators, as well as Rolle's interpolation. He does not indicate where the Fathers fall away and he himself carries on.

In the history of the Psalms in English, Rolle's Psalter is followed by the Wycliffite version. The followers of John Wyclif, who came to be known as the Lollards, borrowed from Rolle's Psalter in both text and format.[50] Rolle's translation of the biblical text was accepted by the Lollard translators, probably owing to the preference of both parties for word-for-word translation. Unlike the full Wycliffite Bible, the Lollard Psalter provided the Latin text along with the English and the commentary, in keeping with its translators' critical concerns with the text.[51] In essence, Rolle's commentary was amended and expanded by the Lollards to reflect their own theological views. Anne Hudson describes the textual format of the Lollard Psalter commentary:

The material is presented in a continuous flow, not constantly interrupted by the intrusion of a source's name and by the repetition or backtracking that occurs through the citations of a second commentator whose views go over the same ground as the first. This continuity of writing extends in sense, despite the visual differentiation of biblical text from commentary, over the verse and even over the psalm boundary; a discussion of one verse often ends 'wherefore the Psalmist David says' and the next verse or the next psalm follows.[52]

The Constitutions of 1409 were unsuccessful initially in quelling the production and circulation of vernacular manuscripts, but by the later part of the fifteenth century the Lollard movement, battered by persecution, had dwindled, and came to survive only in underground pockets in outlying communities. From all indications, illicit copying of Lollard texts ceased after 1450.

It was almost a century after the instatement of the Constitutions before an authorized printed vernacular Psalter appeared. The first printed English edition of the Psalms in 1508 was a poor descendant of earlier manuscript compendia of texts and commentaries. In fact, it included only fragments of seven psalms. This material had originally been preached as part of a series of sermons given by Bishop John Fisher, who was ardently anti-Lutheran but at the same time favourable towards controlled distribution of portions of Scripture in the language of the lay person. His slim volume of sermons on the Psalms became one of the bestsellers of the sixteenth century, presumably because of the limited availability of both the illegal Wyclif manuscripts and the licit but even scarcer manuscripts of Rolle or the West Midland Psalter. If one had wanted to read and meditate on the Psalms in English, the only approved and readily available text would have been these sermons. To meet the demand, three editions were published and one reissued by two printers in two years.[53]

The format of Fisher's *Sermons on the Psalms* looks like that of the manuscript predecessors, most likely by design (Pl. 32). A verse is provided in Latin with the translation and commentary following. The Latin words of Scripture are set apart from the verse by type size and font. Although his format evokes former English traditions, Fisher's version falls short on several counts. Only some of the verses are cited in either language, never the entire psalm. At times, the Latin portions are left untranslated. Furthermore, the author takes liberties in his translations,[54] and although he occasionally cites other portions of Scripture throughout his commentary, he does so without providing reference or context. His commentary, which follows the translation of each verse, does not draw on traditional sources and appears to be entirely original. Presented in the tone of a sermon, the text is more instructional and less devotional than its forebears. In contrast to Rolle's commentary, which was the meditation of one man, and the Lollard Psalter, which was the reflection of a theological system, Fisher's commentary was an orthodox homily. Unlike its predecessors, which were rich in the fullness of the complete psalms, the first printed English Psalter, the *Sermons on the Psalms* of John Fisher, constituted only a sampler of the text.

The Constitutions of Oxford thus effectively ended 'a nascent vernacular religious culture with a depth and range of interest in matters of theology that was not equalled again for well over a hundred years'.[55] In a wider sense, this legislation may be viewed as the primary cause of England's general exclusion from the blossoming of vernacular learning on the Continent. In Europe, multiple editions of whole bibles in modern languages, as well as separate editions of the Psalms, were produced, the equivalent of which never emerged in the British Isles.

A cursory examination of Continental vernacular bibles emphasizes the relative paucity of the English effort. In Germany, the eventual heartland of the Reformation, the Scriptures had been translated from the Vulgate since the eleventh century.[56] The rich manuscript tradition of the German Bible, in both High and Low German, was followed by eighteen printed editions of the complete Bible in German prior to Martin Luther's *Septembertestament* of 1522. (Unlike William Tyndale in England, Luther enjoyed an environment of vernacular liberty in which his translation, not to mention his Protestant views, could survive.) Two Psalters in High German appeared in Strasbourg some time before 1475, one printed by Eggestein (P-1074), the other by the printer of Henricus Ariminensis (P-1066). The Eggestein edition was produced in both quarto and octavo for portability, and contained a short preface and a forty-page apparatus for the titles and subjects of the Psalms – tools which had been customary in manuscript psalters. At least six subsequent editions of the Psalms were printed in High German prior to 1525.[57] At least two German Psalters appeared with glosses,[58] and no fewer than eight editions of the Psalter were in German and Latin.[59] The first Low German Psalter was printed in 1475, revised in 1493, and reprinted with the Latin text in 1509.[60]

Similarly in the Netherlands, a vernacular manuscript tradition preceded the sanctioned printing of the vernacular biblical text. The fourteenth-century proto-Reformation movement, the *Devotio Moderna*,[61] and in particular the Windesheim community, was responsible for the dissemination of the translations of the Scriptures into Dutch by Geerte Groote and Johan Scutken. Several proponents of the New Learning were influenced by its principles, including Erasmus and Luther. The movement evinced a concern for the integrity of the Scriptures and new translations in both Latin and Dutch were produced and copied. The first Dutch Bible was printed in 1477 (B-648), and the first Dutch Psalter at Delft in 1480, in octavo format (P-1070).[62] Three subsequent editions of the Dutch Psalter were printed before the turn of the century.[63]

In France the vernacular Scriptures in one form or another were translated and circulated as early as the fourteenth-century.[64] The primary vernacular biblical text of the fifteenth century was Guiars des Moulins' translation of Peter Comestor's Latin paraphrase, the *Biblia Historiale*, which was continually revised and expanded to include greater Scriptural content. This text began to appear in print as early as the mid-1470s under titles such as *Le Viel Testament de la Bible*, *La vraye exposicion de la Bible* and *La Table du nouveau testament*.[65] In the early 1480s the first illustrated psalter in French was printed (a *c.* 1480 edition by Huss and Siber (P-1073) in Lyons). The first Latin Bible was printed in Paris in 1476/77 by Gering, Kranz and Friburger (B-550), in addition to several Latin publications of portions of Scripture.[66]

The record in England is startling in contrast. Not only was no vernacular Bible printed in England until Nycolson's Coverdale Bible of *c.* 1535 (STC 2064), but, in fact, no complete Bible in any language was issued from an English press for the first sixty years of printing in England. In 1535 Thomas Berthelet produced the first printed Vulgate Bible (STC 2055), an edition that compared poorly to Continental equivalents – being both technologically inferior and textually incomplete (for it contained only portions of the Old Testament with the complete New Testament).[67]

It is difficult with our present sensibilities to accept the notion that English fifteenth-century lay society was better for not possessing religious texts in its native tongue. The modern mind, sympathetic to democratized learning, may find it problematic that some have applauded the ecclesiastical program of 'controlled instruction' which had the purpose of maintaining the stability of an English society with no need of reform. Carpenter states: 'Like Judaism and Islam, the church knew what is was doing when it undertook to teach its members the rudiments of the faith. If it controlled the means of instruction, then it controlled the belief of the laity, and by replacing ignorance with knowledge it controlled the spread of heresy.'[68] Control here is a euphemism for censorship and persecution, the primary rationale behind the enactment of *de Heretico Comburendo* that prescribed the death penalty for heresy in 1401.[69] The burning of heretics continued unabated until the middle of the sixteenth century, and those who owned vernacular Bibles did so at risk of their lives.

In this light, the transmission of the Psalter is a most helpful model in an examination of the effects of vernacular censorship on fifteenth-century English society. In spite of its historical prominence and availability on the Continent, the vernacular Psalter was reintroduced to England in an inferior state after one hundred years of silence. And yet Latin psalters were plentiful, with numerous editions produced each year. Like other liturgical tools that were the mainstay of the printing industry, these were commissioned for the virtually exclusive use of the Church. Because of the Constitutions of Oxford, a seven-centuries-long tradition of the Psalms in both English and Latin – a tradition, indeed, of lay education in both languages – had been abruptly interrupted.

The study of incunabula thus has much to offer the various disciplines which address the cultural issues of the fifteenth century. The analysis of early printed texts is a regular preoccupation of the historians of those countries where the innovation of the new technology produced remarkable numbers of texts, but it is one which receives relatively little attention from historians of fifteenth-century England where the advent of printing was less auspicious. Nevertheless, the record of the production and dissemination of printed texts is another factor to be considered in the assessment of the cultural condition of England overall, and has implications in the current discussion of the cause and value of the Reformation of the English Church. Although the Bible (or portions of it) was a relatively popular text in late-fifteenth-century England, the lack of production of a printed edition of the Scriptures in their entirety (in either Latin or English) suggests that intellectual and religious culture there suffered under the imposed state of censorship. English historians stand to benefit from the testimony of the first books that came to be printed in that country, as well as from the silence of those that did not.[70]

## NOTES

1 The nature of cultural change, and the time in which such changes occurred, are matters of debate. The initial presumption that the onset of printing marked a radical end to the medieval world as defined by the types of readers and their practices, and the birth of the Modern, culminates in the work of Henri-Jean Martin & Lucien Febvre, *The Coming of the Book* (London: Verso, 1990; first published as *L'Apparition du Livre*, Paris: Michel, 1958), as well as that of Marshall McLuhan, *The Gutenberg Galaxy: the Making of Typographic Man* (Toronto: University of Toronto Press, 1962), and Elizabeth Eisenstein, *The Printing Press as an Agent of Change* (Cambridge: University Press, 1979). Subsequent opinions have challenged the initial premises of these early works. Sandra Hindman's introduction to *Printing the Written Word: the Social History of Books, circa 1450-1520* (Ithaca, N.Y.: Cornell University Press, 1991), is a helpful summary of the dissenting view. See also Paul Saenger's article, 'The Impact of the Early Printed Page on the History of Reading', *Bulletin du Bibliophile* II (1996): 237-301, and his contribution to this volume.

2 Modern bibliographers have estimated that between 400 and 450 editions of books were produced by English presses in the fifteenth century. This may be compared to 30,000 to 35,000, the estimate of the total number of printed editions in the fifteenth century arrived at by Febvre & Martin. See Gordon Duff, *Fifteenth Century English Books* (Oxford: University Press, 1917), and C. E. Sayle, *Early English Printed Books in the University Library Cambridge* (Cambridge: University Press, 1900). See also the *Short-Title Catalogue of English Books Printed in England, Scotland, and Ireland* (STC), 3 vols, ed. by A. W. Pollard & G. R. Redgrave, 2nd edn, rev. by Katharine F. Pantzer & Philip R. Rider (London: The Bibliographical Society, 1976-91), and Febvre & Martin, p. 248.

3 H. S. Bennett, in *English Books and Readers: 1475-1557* (Cambridge: University Press, 1952), presents a generally rosy, if not patriotic, picture of early English printing. He does, however, contextualize the disparity between Continental and Insular printing as beneficial to the market: 'The real challenge, however, which de Worde and Pynson had to face arose from the greater superiority of the work of their Continental rivals to their own. England lacked the skill and technical resources, together with the funds, that made possible the work of the printers of Paris, Rouen, Venice, and a half dozen other centres ... Other liturgical and devotional works also came from overseas, and set a standard altogether beyond anything usually achieved by printers in England, and no doubt formed a healthy incentive at a time when competition within the country was so limited' (p. 185). For information on Continental books in England during the fifteenth century, see n. 17.

4 Scholars began to apply revisionist historical criticism to late medieval England in the late

1970s, publishing several defining works in the mid-eighties, several of which are cited here. See Christopher Haigh, 'Some Aspects of the Recent Historiography of the English Reformation', in *The Urban Classes, the Nobility and the Reformation,* ed. by Wolfgang J. Mommsen with Peter Alter, Publications of the German Historical Institute, London, 5 (1980), pp. 88-106 and *Historical Journal* 25 (1982), pp. 995-1007. See also Duffy (below, n. 37) and Carpenter (below, n. 5). Other revisionist works include those of J. Bossy and J. J. Scarisbrick.

5 Christine Carpenter, 'The Religion of the Gentry in Fifteenth-Century England', in *England in the Fifteenth Century*, ed. by Daniel Williams (Woodbridge, Suffolk; Wolfeboro, N.H.: Boydell Press, 1987), p. 53.

6 ibid., p. 54.

7 Nicholas Watson, 'Censorship and Cultural Change in Late Medieval England: Vernacular Theology, the Oxford Translation Debate, and Arundel's Constitutions of 1409', *Speculum*, 70 (1995), 822-64. See also below, n. 16.

8 ibid., 826.

9 Febvre & Martin (above, n. 1), p. 253.

10 ibid., p. 239.

11 See Watson, pp. 834-5. According to Watson's findings, not only does vernacular theological writing all but cease in the fifteenth century, but so does vernacular writing of any kind. Furthermore, the English culture's aesthetic development appears to decline significantly in what Watson calls 'the process of narrowing that in the fifteenth century is often said to have befallen the Chaucerian tradition' (p. 858). John King, in his *English Reformation Literature: the Tudor Origins of the Protestant Tradition* (Princeton: University Press, 1982), comments on the literary climate of the fifteenth century as it relates to early Protestant writing, noting that 'literary taste had undergone little change from the time of Chaucer to the beginning of the Tudor age ...', p. 35.

12 For an explanation of the origins and influence of Wyclif's philosophical thought, see Anthony Kenny, *Wyclif* (Oxford: University Press, 1985).

13 'The History of Printing Illustrated by the Printed Bible, 1450-1877' and 'Class C-Holy Scriptures' by Henry Stevens, in *Caxton Celebration, 1877: Catalogue of the Loan Collection of Antiquities, Curiosities, and Appliances connected with the Art of Printing*, ed. by George Bullen (London: Elzevir Press, Trübner and Co., 1877), pp. 77-192.

14 *Historical Catalogue of Printed Editions of the English Bible, 1525-1961, revised and expanded from the edition of T. H. Darlow and H. F. Moule, 1903*, ed. by A. S. Herbert (London: The British and Foreign Bible Society; New York: The American Bible Society, 1968). See especially pp. xxvi -xxxi, 'Scripture Translations and Scripture Printing before 1525'. A revision of this catalogue is currently being undertaken at Cambridge University by the British and Foreign Bible Society.

15 King, pp. 38-42.

16 The text of the Constitutions is published in *Concilia Magnae Britanniae et Hiberniae*, ed. David Wilkins, 4 vols (London: 1737). Watson (above, n. 7) provides a helpful summary of the content of the Constitutions in his above cited work (n. 7), along with a partial transcription, pp. 825-30.

17 The availability of Continental bibles in England in the late fifteenth and early sixteenth century is relevant to the present issues, especially since studies have shown that the majority of books in England at this time were imports. More research is needed. Lotte Hellinga has prepared a pilot study on the topic in general entitled 'Importation of Books Printed on the Continent into England and Scotland before c.1520', in Hindman, *Printing the Written Word* (above, n. 1). This study was prepared for inclusion in vol. 3 of *The Cambridge History of the Book in Britain*, ed. by Hellinga & J. B. Trapp (Cambridge: University Press, forth-

coming). Preliminary studies on this subject are cited in Hellinga's article. Christine Ferdinand also remarks upon imported books purchased by Magdalen College, Oxford, during the late fifteenth century in 'Magdalen College and the book trade: the provision of books in Oxford, 1450-1550' in *The Book Trade and its Customers: 1450-1900*, ed. by Arnold Hunt, Giles Mandlebrote & Alison Shell (Winchester, Hampshire: St Paul's Bibliographies; New Castle, Delaware: Oak Knoll Press, 1997).

18 See the Chronological Index to the STC (above, n. 2), vol. 3, p. 331.

19 A resetting and reprinting of Caxton's 1476 indulgence was done in 1995 by the Alembic Press, Marcham, with an introduction by Claire Bolton. A survey of early printing in any country is incomplete without a consideration of the job printing function of the first presses, that is, the production of single-sheet imprints and special editions. The indulgence was the most copious job imprint of the fifteenth-century. For a discussion of the printed indulgence in England, see Paul Needham, *The Printer and the Pardoner* (Washington, D.C.: Library of Congress, 1986) and K. Van Kampen, 'The Bible in Print in England Before Tyndale', *Reformation*, II (1997), pp. 111-26.

20 *The Acts and Monuments of John Foxe*, ed. by S. R. Cattley & C. Townsend, 8 vols (London: R. B. Selley & W. Burnside, 1837-41; repr. New York: AMS Press, 1965), p. 927.

21 STC 17957-17975.

22 In 1481 a compendium of scriptural exempla derived from Hanapus was printed at St Albans (STC 2993). This Latin treatise was translated into English in 1560 (STC 12742).

23 See Martin's chapter, 'The Book and the Reformation', in *The Coming of the Book* (above, n. 1), pp. 287-319.

24 I have based this ratio on a tally of the titles in Duff's *Fifteenth Century English Books* (above, n. 2), excluding the entries for indulgences and single sheet publications. The rough percentages are: 49% English, 44% Latin and 6% French.

25 Febvre & Martin, p. 256.

26 See N. S. Aurner, *Caxton: Mirror of Fifteenth-Century Letters* (New York: Russell, 1965), p. 117, who cites Aspland & Butler in *Golden Legend*, from the Holbein Society, 1878, p. 35. Indeed, the devout, educated layperson was encouraged to read from such texts (in either Latin or English) during the Mass itself. For the English practice of bringing books to the Mass see M. Pantin's 'Instructions for a Devout and Literate Layman' in *Medieval Learning and Literature: Essays Presented to Richard William Hunt*, ed. by J. J. G. Alexander and M. T. Gibson (Oxford: Clarendon Press, 1976): pp. 398-422, and Paul Saenger's contribution to this volume, above, p. 000.

27 Fifteen editions were published in English during the years 1486-1525. See also STC 3259 and forward.

28 De Worde began to publish the meditations of St Bernard in 1496; see also STC 1916-1923. Deathbed prayers were also published in the fifteenth century in the form of broadsides, as they were throughout the sixteenth century. A fifteenth-century example is STC 14554. See also untitled books of prayers by de Worde and Caxton, STC 14546 and 20195.

29 See Anne Hudson & H. L. Spencer, 'Old Author, New Work: The Sermons of MS Longleat 4', *Medium Aevum*, 53 (1984): 219-38.

30 See Richard Marsden, 'Cain's Face, and Other Problems: the Legacy of the Earliest Bible Translations', *Reformation*, I (1996), 35-6. He elaborates: 'In being brought face to face with the ineffable texts, couched as they are in the imagery and syntax of alien cultures and transmitting profound and often difficult concepts, the vernacular language is stretched to the limit.'

31 Eamon Duffy says of the early part of the sixteenth century, 'The ban on English versions of the New Testament had to a large extent been ameliorated by the production of Nicholas Love's translation of the *Meditationes Vitae Christi*, for that work was essentially an

expanded Gospel harmony, and went a long way towards satisfying lay eagerness for knowledge of the Gospels.' This, in essence, is the sum total of Duffy's treatment of the subject of vernacular censorship in the fifteenth-century in his *The Stripping of the Altars: Traditional Religion in England, 1400-1580* (New Haven & London: Yale University Press); the Constitutions of Oxford are not mentioned. See also David Daniell's answer to Duffy's statement, in *William Tyndale: a Biography* (New Haven & London: Yale University Press, 1994), pp. 96-101.

32 See p. 23 above.

33 The textual format of the Psalter evolved througout the Middle Ages in both the East and West, Latin and vernacular traditions. In its earliest forms, the Psalms appeared either alone or with commentary. For example, London, British Library Papyrus CCXXX is a fragment of an independent Greek Psalter. The only evident addition to the text in this case is a series of markings made to facilitate oral reading. Eventually, it became common to add ancillary texts such as canticles, prayers, creeds, and calendars. The nature of the additional texts depended on the Psalter's intended use, whether for personal study or use in the Divine Office. The earliest extant example with collects from England is the Galba Psalter of the first third of the tenth century (London, British Library, Cotton MS Galba A.XVIII). In the fourteenth century, the West Midland Psalter contained the text in both Latin and English, along with the Canticles, and occasionally additional texts such as the religious poems of William of Shoreham in London: British Library Add. Ms. 17376. Rolle's Psalter, however, contained only the biblical text, in Latin and English, and commentary, as did the Lollard Psalter and ultimately Fisher's. I have used the term 'Psalter' in the most general sense to describe the various manifestations of the Book of Psalms, whether as separate or as part of the Bible, in keeping with V. Leroquais, *Les psautiers: manuscrits latins des bibliothèques publiques de France* (Macon: Protat Frères, 1940), and more recently, Michelle Brown's definition in her *Understanding Illuminated Manuscripts: Guide to Technical Terms* (London: The J. Paul Getty Museum & The British Library, 1994).

34 BL Cotton Vespasian A.i. See Marsden, 'Cain's Face', pp. 31-2.

35 The whole Bible was never translated into Old English. Marsden estimates that the total of all the various scriptural passages in Anglo-Saxon translation would come close to a quarter of a complete Bible. See 'Cain's Face', p. 31.

36 See Marsden, p. 32. For a study of the text families of English and Irish Psalters of the period, see Martin McNamara's article, 'The Psalms in the Irish Church: the Most Recent Research on Text, Commentary, and Decoration – with Emphasis on the So-Called Psalter of Charlemagne', in *The Bible as Book: the Manuscript Tradition*, ed. by John Sharpe & Kimberly Van Kampen (London: The British Library, 1998).

37 Cambridge, Trinity College R.17.1. See *The Eadwine Psalter: Text, Image, and Monastic Culture in Twelfth-Century Canterbury*, ed. by M. Gibson, T. A. Heslop & R. W. Pfaff (London: Modern Humanities Research Association and University Park, Pa.: Pennsylvania State University Press, 1992).

38 Laud. Misc. 91

39 Cambridge University Library Kk. I. 6, ff. 2-147. *The Seven Psalms* was translated by Dame Eleanor Hull, thought to be the earliest woman translator known by name in England. The commentary is edited by Alexandra Barratt for The Early English Text Society (Oxford & New York: Oxford University Press, 1995). Margaret Deanesly mentioned a similar tradition in *The Lollard Bible and Other Medieval Biblical Versions* (Cambridge: University Press, 1920; repr. 1966), p. 143, although it is unclear whether she referred to the same manuscript.

40 See *The Primer or the Lay Folks' Prayer Book*, parts I & II, ed. by Henry Littlehales, Early English Text Society Series 105 and 109 (1895, 1897), reprinted as one volume in 1981 by

Kraus Reprint, New York. This volume contains a facsimile of Cambridge University Library Ms. Dd. 11. 82.

41 See n. 39 above

42 Deanesly, p. 143.

43 ibid., p. 144.

44 ibid., p. 145.

45 *Richard Rolle: the English Writings*, ed. by Rosamund S. Allen (New York: Paulist Press, 1988), p. 66.

46 Anne Hudson, *The Premature Reformation* (Oxford: Clarendon Press, 1988), p. 27.

47 Allen, p. 66.

48 Jerome's preference for word-for-word translation is respected by all the early translators of the Latin Bible within the English tradition of Bible translation. See 'Aelfric as Translator: the Old English Prose *Genesis*' by Richard Marsden in *Anglia*, 1991 (pp. 319-58).

49 Allen, pp. 68, 69

50 See Hudson, *Premature Reformation*, and D. Everett, 'The Middle English Prose Psalter of Richard Rolle of Hampole', *Modern Language Review* 17 (1922): pp. 217-27, 337-50; 18 (1923): 381-93.

51 Vulgate textual criticism was foreseen and rudimentarily practiced by Wycliffite scholars in the fourteenth century. Hudson, *Premature Reformation*, pp. 243-4, identified four steps in the Wycliffite process of translation (she gleans this from the General Prologue to the Later Version of their Bible). She says, 'There was evidently an acute consciousness of the variation between different copies of the Vulgate: the reader *no doute ... shal fynde ful manye biblis in Latyn ful false, if he loke [examine] manie, nameli [especially] newe* ... (FM i.58/1)'.

52 Hudson, pp. 260-1.

53 Two editions and a reissue in 1509 by W. de Worde (STC 10903, 10903a, 10904); one in 1510 by R. Pynson (STC 10905). Subsequent editions appeared in 1525 and 1529, both by de Worde (STC 10906, 10907), and by T. Marshe in 1555 (10908); all are quartos with the exception of the latest, an octavo.

54 At Psalm 129, the Latin text, *Et ipse redimet Israel ex omnibus iniquitatibus eius*, is rendered, 'He shall make euery penytent persone parte taker of his redempcyon. ...' My thanks to Sydney Tibbetts for this observation.

55 Watson (above, n. 7), p. 859

56 Werner Kohlschmidt and Wolfgang Mohr provide a summary of the first vernacular German biblical translations in *Reallexikon de Deutschen Literaturgeschichte* (Berlin: de Gruyter, 1958), vol. 1, pp. 145-8.

57 Darlowe & Moule identified four: 1489/90 Zainer?: Ulm or ?: Strasbourg; 1492, Dinckmut: Ulm; 1492, Sorg: Augsburg; 1498, Schönsberger: Augsburg (Hain 13513, 13517, 13516, 13518). Copinger identified two earlier editions, an edition from Strasbourg in 1477 (HC 4958) and Augsburg imprint, 1490 (HC 4959).

58 P-1074 (see above) and 1504, Drach: Speyer (DM4178).

59 1494, 1499, Ratdolt: Augsburg (P-1067, P-1068); 1502, 1503 Furter: Basel; 1506, Hüpfuff: Strasbourg; 1508, Knoblouch: Strasbourg; 1513, Hochfedder: Metz; 1518, ?: Venice. (See Wilhelm Walther, *Die deutsche Bibelübersetzung des Mittelalters* (Brunswick: 1889-92).)

60 1475, Brandis: Lübeck (Hain 13520); 1493, Brandis?: Lübeck (Hain 13519); 1509, Bungart: Cologne (Adams L1252), respectively.

61 An English translation of certain writings of the Modern Devotion was printed in 1988, *Devotio Moderna: Basic Writings* (New York: Paulist Press), trans. by John Van Engen, prefaced by Heiko A. Oberman, with a bibliography provided in the notes.

62 1477, Jacobszoen and Yemantszoen: Delft (DM 3271);1480, Jacobszoen and Yemantszoen (DM 3273; HC 13521).

63 Darlow & Moule list three other fifteenth-century editions of the Dutch Psalter, nos 550-2 in M. F. A. G. Campbell, *Annales de la typographie néerlandaise au xv^e^ siecle* (The Hague: Nijhoff, 1874-84). Wouter Nijhoff, in *L'Art Typographique 1500-1540* (The Hague: Nijhoff, 1935), does not include any of the psalters.

64 An early-fifteenth-century lectionary in French at the Scriptorium specifies in its colophon the date of the translation as having been completed on 13 May 1326, by Jean de Vignay (VK MS 644). The two fundamental sources for the history of the biblical text in France are Samuel Berger, *La Bible française au XVI^e^ siècle: Etude sur les origines de la critique biblique* (Paris, 1879), and Jean Bonnard, *Les Traductions de la Bible en vers français du moyen âge* (Paris: Imprimerie Nationale, 1884). See also W. J. Van Eys *Bibliographie des Bibles et des Nouveaux Testaments en langue française* (Geneva: H. Kündig, 1901), parts 1 and 2, whose list of early printed French biblical books is more comprehensive than mine.

65 The earliest editions of the *Biblia Historiale* and related works were undated. Darlowe & Moule estimated the first to have appeared sometime between 1474 and 1478 (DM 3699-3701); The British Museum Catalogue gives a date of 1478 for the Lyons edition by Barthélemy Buyer (BMC VIII, 235, 41509-10). Goff dates the first edition to *c.* 1476 (B-651); Hain-Copinger is more conservative, giving the range 1477-80 (HC 1041). The earliest French work listed in the *Gesamtkatalog der Wiegendrucke* under 'Biblia, franz' is Comestor's *Historia Scholastica*, printed in Paris in 1498 by Antoine Vérard (GW 4310; B-623).

66 *Exempla Sacre Scripture* was published by Gering in Paris in 1478 (N-105). A quarto edition of Gregory's Commentary on the *Cantica canticorum* was published with the full Latin text by Gering and Rembolt in Paris in 1498 (G-396). Similarly, Augustine's commentary on the Pauline epistles, with the Latin text, appeared in Paris in 1499 by the same publishers (A-1277). De Lyra's *Postilla* was included in at least three Latin biblical publications – the Psalms in 1483 (Gering in Paris (N-123)) and 1490 (Le Rouge in Paris (P-1064)), and the Epistles and Gospels in 1497 (Morin in Rouen (BMC VIII, 397, IA 43971) – but was not printed with a whole Bible in this period. Several editions of the liturgical Epistles and Gosples were published in Latin between 1478 and 1497, and portions of the Gospel of John in Latin were printed in Paris by G. Mittelhus in *c.* 1495 (BMC VIII, 129, IA 40085), and at least four other editions in Paris, Rouen and Poitiers.

67 The first English Bible printed on English soil was an edition of the Coverdale Bible, printed in Southwark for J. Nycolson in *c.* 1535 (STC 2063.3). The *editio princeps* of the Coverdale had been printed on the Continent in 1535 (STC 2063).

68 Carpenter (below, n. 5), p. 64.

69 For the text of this legislation, see *Rotuli Parliamentorum* (7 vols, London, 1832), iii.467; *The Statutes of the Realm*, 10 vols (London: G. Eyre & A. Strahan, 1810-28), 125-8.

70 I wish to thank Paul Saenger, Sidney Tibbetts and Richard Marsden for their contributions to this article.

# THE BIBLE, PRINTING AND THE EDUCATIONAL GOALS OF THE HUMANISTS

*Guy Bedouelle*

*(Translated by Dr Barbara Beaumont)*

IN ANY EDUCATIONAL ESTABLISHMENT, a major subject for debate has always been the establishment of a curriculum of studies that will be the most suited to the needs of those who are to learn. In classical historiography, it has been thought that a revolution in education took hold in the second half of the fifteenth century and throughout the sixteenth. It was due above all to the rediscovery of ancient languages, which were vaunted and taught by professors of *studia humanitatis*, and this later formed a current of thoughts, known by historians as 'humanism'. In some sense there was a shift 'from the Humanities to Humanism'.[1]

I shall consider the relationship established at the time of the spread of printing between, on the one hand, the educational goals of the humanists and, on the other hand, the presentation of biblical texts. In other words, I should like to point out some of the ways in which printing, at a particular stage in its development, and especially in the hands of a humanist like Lefèvre d'Etaples, brought a renewed educational approach to Bible reading.

## THE BIBLE AT THE CENTRE OF THE RETURN *AD FONTES*

The return to sources that became axiomatic for the humanist was first applied to the Bible. Scripture occupied the highest rank in the lists for the ideal library or in theoretical *curricula* such as were compiled by those who believed themselves entrusted with the guidance of minds or who enjoyed a certain reputation in the domain of *bonae litterae*. The Word of God should constitute the pinnacle of learning.

There is nothing new in this. Letter 53 from Jerome to Paulinus of Nola clearly points to the supremacy of the Bible over all knowledge. Hugh of Saint Victor (d. 1141), in the final section of his 'Art of Reading', *Didascalicon*, which is at one and the same time a hierarchy of the branches of learning and an annotated list of the canonical and apocryphal books, presents the Bible with detail. These explanations concern its threefold meaning, the four degrees of reading appropriate to it and the threefold categories of readers.

The humanists no longer presented the Bible in terms of this symbolic arithmetic. Nevertheless, the place occupied by the Word of God remained the same: in the first or the highest rank. In the *Enchiridion*, prescribing for his 'Christian soldier' 'a programme for life more than for learning', Erasmus proposed the study of philosophy and the poets but 'in moderation and for a season' ... then 'you should hasten with greatest speed towards that manna of celestial Wisdom which shall nourish and vivify you amply'.[2] In his *De artium scientiarumque divisione* of 1500, republished in 1506, Josse Clichtove, doctor of theology of Paris, commented on the hierarchy of sciences extending to 'knowledge of the celestial sciences ... starting with the holy scriptures, the oracles of the prophets, and the authority of the divine words handed on through the writings of the holy apostles and the prophets'.[3]

In 1506 Lefèvre d'Etaples, in an aside to a commentary on a passage from Aristotle's *Politics*, proposed a *ratio studiorum* which makes a direct transition from the *Metaphysics* of Aristotle and its 'otherworldly philosophy' (*supramundana*) to 'the sacred books which are to be studied with veneration'. Lefèvre subsequently relied on the authority of Jerome (Letter 107 to Laeta) in establishing a pedagogical order in the approach to the various books of the Bible. Our attention is alerted, however, by a remark of Lefèvre in which he demanded what amounts to a reworking of the presentation of 'books by good authors'. Lefèvre advises that these works should not be approached without having first removed those somewhat chilling glosses and wild imaginings from the writer's authentic text (*rejectis absque certa authoris alicujus littera glossematis et frigidiusculis phantasiolis)*.[4] The recommendation applies even more stringently to the inspired authors.

It becomes possible to undertake this eradication and simplification of superfluous glosses (as far as the Bible is concerned) as progressively more and more works became entrusted to the printing press, the servant of educational ideals.

## THE BIBLE *SINE GLOSSA*: TOWARDS CLARITY OF TEXT

Glosses and wild imaginings! How can one avoid thinking that Lefèvre must have had in mind, among other examples, the complicated presentations of the Bible and commentaries that he had encountered in both manuscript and in printed form which, in his view, shed precious little light on the primary text. As we know, the Bible at that time was presented in such a way that the sacred text almost completely disappeared to the benefit of the glosses (both interlinear and marginal) of the *Postilla* of Nicholas of Lyra, accompanied by the *Additiones* of Paul of Burgos, which were themselves refuted by the *Replicae* of Mathias Döring, who defended the literal interpretations of Nicholas of Lyra. Cardinal de Lubac showed that this confrontation between two schools of theology had catastrophic consequences for the pedagogical approach to the Bible.[5] This is why, around 1510, editions of the Bible began to set aside the commentary in order to publish a text purified of its appendages, making room, visually as well as verbally, for the Word of God to stand alone.

It should be noted that the same pedagogical effort was being made as far as the teaching of Aristotle was concerned. It had become the custom to print Aristotle's texts accompanied by commentaries. As late as 1503 an *Interpretatio in Summulas Petri Hispani cum Bricot quaestionibus* was published in Paris consisting of Johannes Buridan's *Commentaries* on Aristotle's *Logic* as abridged by Peter of Spain.

The task that amounted to a rediscovery of the real Aristotle was undertaken by Lefèvre d'Etaples at the time when he was teaching at the Collège du Cardinal Lemoine, near the Sorbonne. In his preface to the *Physics* (F-12) of 1492, his second work published by Jean Higman in Paris, Lefèvre clearly points out that his own annotations are very few. Clichtove, in a subsequent edition (1501), explains that this is the case so that the reader might enjoy more direct access to the text.[6]

Indeed, as his work progressed, Lefèvre, who was described at the time as 'the restorer of the true Aristotle' and whose work is to be compared to that of Ficino for Plato, and Reuchlin for Pythagoras, was to publish and comment on the whole of the Aristotelean corpus. For this purpose he was to bring into use an ingenious method of presentation. First he favoured the setting out in columns, or more exactly, synoptically, of the various Latin translations: thus in 1497 for the *Nicomachean Ethics* (A-991), he set the text in three columns, and then in two for the *Metaphysics* printed in 1515. Then, with a method that he inaugurated with the *Logic* in 1503, he divided the Aristotelean text into verses. *Notae* explain the text word for word, followed by *Paraphrases* which correspond to the various verses. These commentaries are illustrated by charts and tables.

The reader is thus continuously guided throughout his reading, deciphering each word in turn to determine its meaning until he comes to the sentence where the teacher – for this is indeed a pedagogical exercise – provides the meaning. In this way the reader is not offered first and foremost an interpretation, but care is taken that the text, which has once more become the centre of interest, might be truly understood. Aristotle's text unambiguously occupies the middle of the page, and is moreover printed in bolder type than the notes that follow. The aim is to understand it, to expound it before commenting on it or providing a gloss.

This is the paradigm that Lefèvre d'Etaples was to adapt for use with the text of the Bible, thanks to a printer of talent or even of genius, Henri Estienne, who published his *Quincuplex Psalterium* in 1509 (Schreiber 8; Pl. 33) as well as the revised second edition of 1513. One notices the splendour of this two-colour work (black with red for titles and important words such as the various names of God). The synoptical arrangement was obviously inspired by Origen's *Hexapla*. There are the three versions attributed to Jerome, the Augustinian Psalter and a Psalter called *Conciliatum*, a work by Lefèvre himself, whose exegetical options overlay Jerome's translation made from the Hebrew. For greater ease the Psalms are divided into verses, permitting an ingenious system of references, prefiguring the numbering that we have inherited from Robert Estienne in 1551 for the Greek and Latin New Testament and in 1553 for his French Bible. This practical improvement was as significant as Stephen Langton's division into chapters in the thirteenth century.

The Psalms may be read in successive stages, according to the method perfected for the Aristotelean texts: first, a very brief explanation in a *Titulus*, then verse by verse in the *Expositio continua*, and finally difficulty by difficulty in an *Adverte*. There are summary charts and tables, especially concerning the Hebrew characters and the divine Names, which make the work close to those of the Christian cabalists. But above all there is an ingenious instrument, known as the *Concordia*, established for the first twenty-five Psalms, and proposing for each Psalm verse an equivalent, often tracked down with ingenuity, from another book of the Bible, establishing that 'concord of the Scriptures' which is the hallmark of Lefèvre's hermeneutics.

The same presentation, inspired by the same pedagogical aims, was to be used by Lefèvre for the rest of his biblical work, the commentaries on the Pauline epistles in

1512, where the degree of theological commitment is more clear-cut, and the commentaries on the Gospels in 1521. In all, Lefèvre employed the same structure, both typographical and pedagogical. Visually, it appeared by way of a parallel presentation of the text of the Vulgate and a new translation, a commentary by groups of verses and an *Examinatio nonnullorum circa litteram*, picking up the difficult points and making ample use of Greek characters.

## THE *LECTIO DIVINA* OF THE HUMANISTS

I have chosen Lefèvre d'Etaples as an example because he represented a decisive stage in the manner of printing the sacred text, and because of the high level of consideration he gave to it. His biblical works were conceived with studious reading or pious recitation in mind, and constituted something of a return to *lectio divina*. In his editions the biblical text of the Vulgate, if it is not entirely *sine glossa*, remains central and complete, replicated by another more ancient or more recent version.

Parallel versions of texts were much appreciated at the time, as the phenomenon of polyglot Bibles shows. One example, much admired by Lefèvre and somewhat deprecated by Erasmus, was the octuple Psalter (DM1411) that the Dominican Agostino Giustiniani, a future professor of Hebrew at the Collège des Lecteurs Royaux in Paris, published in Genoa in 1516, the same year as Erasmus's *Novum Instrumentum* (DM6096). Like the *Complutensis* (DM1412), these biblical texts are accompanied by concordances and various tables which make it possible to read from diverse points of view.

And yet it is the pious reading that prevails: this intention is made clear in the *Quincuplex Psalterium*, because what is at stake is an interpretation that will provide sustenance for the monks of Saint-Germain-des-Prés. But the aim is quite as pedagogical as it is hermeneutical. It is the same preoccupation that will later incite Lefèvre to translate the Bible into French. For this work, he chose to translate from the Vulgate rather than from the original languages on account of the clergy, who were accustomed to Jerome's version and felt more at home with it. 'Simple clerks confering and reading verse by verse will understand more easily what they are reading in the Latin.'[7] It is also the Latin Psalter that Lefèvre explicated to his royal pupils at the court of Francis I.

For Lefèvre the constant desire to explain, rather than to comment on, each word and each verse remained uppermost. He was able to achieve this due, first of all, to the skill of his printers, Henri Estienne in Paris and later Simon de Colines at Meaux. This allowed him to combine initiation (the word chosen for the volume on the Gospels: *commentarii initiatorii*) with piety (the watchword of the time) in the widest sense of the term.

Thus at this period in the circle of Lefèvre and his followers in Paris and in Meaux, the educational goal is still present but culminating in the *pietas* of the humanists. An example of liturgical initiation is to be found among the works of Lefèvre's disciple, Clichtove, with his *Elucidatorium ecclesiasticum* (Paris, Henri Estienne, 1516; IA IX, 112). Here we have a vision in which Scripture is read and ruminated upon, and this is taken up repeatedly in volumes that become more and more easy to handle as cheaper production encourages wider distribution and more private ownership. As far as the

Bible is concerned, printing led to a deepening of the life of faith and charity, but with methods specific to the *studia humanitatis*.

A similar analysis could be made in the case of Erasmus, who also developed an educational project culminating in *pietas*, but it is true that his approach was already more 'critical'. In his *Methodus*, Erasmus proposed a close examination of the context: 'let him consider the origin of what is said, by whom it is said, to whom it is said, when, on what occasion, in what words, what precedes it, what follows'.[8] This approach was already beyond the scope of *lectio divina*.

The humanist enthusiasm for printing the Bible became consolidated in the first twenty years of the sixteenth century, but it was somewhat moderated by the fear that 'poisons might mingle with the remedies' as demonstrated by the bull *Inter sollicitudines* of the Fifth Lateran Council, dated 4 May 1515 on *De arte impressoria*. The Council's view was more positive on the subject than the pontifical documents that preceded (the bulls *Inter multiplices* of Innocent VIII in 1487 and of Alexander VI in 1501). But the Roman Church's position here is also an essentially pedagogical one. The art of printing, which is 'due to divine favour', must edify. The Christian humanists could see no more direct means of taking up this challenge than with the Word of God itself.

## NOTES

1 Anthony Grafton & Lisa Jardine, *From Humanism to the Humanities: Education and the Liberal Arts in Fifteenth and Sixteenth Century Europe* (Cambridge, Mass.: Harvard University Press, 1986), p. xvi : 'the gap becomes, for modern society, the gap between humanism – the zealous faith in an ideal – and the humanities – a *curriculum* training a social élite to fulfil its predetermined role'.

2 *Erasmus Ausgewählte Werke*, ed. by A. & H. Holborn (Munich: Beck, 1933; repr. 1964), p. 33.

3 Jean-Pierre Massaut, *Josse Clichtove, l'Humanisme et la réforme du clergé*, 2 vols (Paris: Les Belles Lettres, 1968), I, p. 237.

4 Guy Bedouelle, *Le 'Quincuplex Psalterium' de Lefèvre d'Etaples: un guide de lecture* (Geneva: Droz, 1979), p. 50.

5 Henri de Lubac, *Exégèse médiévale: les quatre sens de l'Ecriture*, 4 vols (Paris : Aubier, 1964), IV, p. 359.

6 *The Prefatory Epistles of Jacques Lefèvre d'Etaples and Related Texts*, ed. by Eugene F. Rice, Jr (New York: Columbia University Press, 1972), pp. 6-7.

7 Rice, p. 469.

8 Holborn (above, n. 2), p. 64.

# THE PRINTING PRESS AT ALCALÁ DE HENARES

## THE COMPLUTENSIAN POLYGLOT BIBLE

*Julián Martín Abad*
*(Translated by Timothy Graham)*

IT IS WITHOUT DOUBT not widely known among biblical scholars and incunabulists that the story of the famous Valencian Bible of 1478 (B-622), which Konrad Haebler narrated in abundant detail when describing a fragment of it in his *Bibliografía ibérica del siglo XV*,[1] would in 1944 be presented to the reader in the form of a detective novel, in the Valencian idiom of Rafael Tasis, with the simple title *La Biblia valenciana*.[2]

Nor, to be sure, is it well known among scholars specializing in the history of printing in Spain during the sixteenth century that Pedro Ibarra Ruiz, a painter from Elche, worked enthusiastically on a painting called 'Translation and printing of the Complutensian Polyglot Bible (DM1412) under the direction of the great Cardinal Jiménez de Cisneros'.[3] I have tried to track the painting down, but its present whereabouts are not known. However, among Ibarra Ruiz's papers conserved in the Biblioteca Pública Municipal at Elche is the *Memorial* which he wrote to accompany the painting when he exhibited it at a contest organized by the University of Barcelona.[4] This at least is something.

I will not quote the painter's meticulous description in full, but I will briefly outline the moment represented in the painting wherein the Cardinal addressed Antonio de Nebrija, Diego López de Zuñiga and El Pinciano, who occupied the centre of the foreground. Alfonso de Zamora, Pablo Coronel and Alfonso de Alcalá were behind, and still further back, in a third plane, were Juan de Vergara, Demetrio Ducas and Bartolomé de Castro. On the right, between the foreground and the second plane, the copyists were seated around a table. In the same area, a printer's workshop could be made out through a door, 'for', as the painter notes, 'if it is certain that the printing was not carried out in the same place, the author nonetheless thought it a detail worthy of attention'. On the viewer's left were the printer Arnao Guillén de Brocar and other workmen with proofs. At the entrance were intimates of the Cardinal such as Brother Francisco Ruiz, courtiers, pages, and so on. Nor did the painter leave the walls empty. Images and portraits recorded certain of the Cardinal's favourite places and debts of gratitude: there was a picture of Santa Balbina, from which he derived his cardinal's title, and a portrait of Pope Leo X, who lent manuscripts from the Vatican Library for the work of Cisneros's team.

This sixteenth-century painter has handed us on a plate several possible ways to approach my topic, which is the history of printing in Alcalá de Henares (Latin *Complutum*). To pursue all of them would require many pages, and I have only a few at my disposal, so let us salute Arnao Guillén de Brocar, who in the painting had just arrived on the scene, and let us pass through that door opening on to the printer's workshop so that we can become acquainted with this and other workshops of the town.

It is not superfluous to recall two statements by José García Oro, the leading biographer of Cardinal Francisco Jiménez de Cisneros and one of the best historians of the early days of the University of Alcalá de Henares: first his observation that 'The Complutensian book is a reality of modern Spain', and second his comment, full of suggestiveness, that 'printing was one more element of the Cisnerian Academy'.[5] The printing press and the University coexisted in Alcalá, in times both of prosperity and of decadence, like sisters twinned by history. From this point onwards I will dispense with the dithyrambic tone. The image of the Complutensian press that figures in many studies, as in that lost yet remembered painting, is plainly an idealized one, or almost so. The Polyglot Bible takes its place at one moment in the history of Complutensian printing, but it is not that history itself. There are other products of the printing press earlier than, and contemporary with it, with their own *raisons d'être*.

I live at a stone's throw from the place where Arnao Guillén de Brocar set up his workshop, which successively belonged to Miguel de Eguía, Juan de Brocar, Andrés de Angulo and Antón Sánchez de Leyva, and of which the xylographic blocks, showing clear signs of age, could easily be found in workshops active at Alcalá de Henares even beyond the year 1600. I will speak in particular about this one workshop, with a mind to the fact that through the sixteenth century the university town was home to other workshops that gave Alcalá de Henares its particular character as a printing town.[6]

In Spain, the break between the incunable period and the sixteenth century raises issues for the bibliographer. Once the pivotal year of 1500 had been passed, the Iberian book continued to maintain, for some twenty further years, characteristics of the typographic products of the previous century. It should also be added that the origins of Iberian printing history are shrouded in darkness. One must call attention to the wide geographical dispersal of the workshops which, beginning in 1472, were established with great rapidity in twenty-eight different localities. Several of the typically Iberian characteristics in the presentation of books had their roots in the fact that different laws were in effect in the various kingdoms, which were united only in the person of their rulers, and that there was no single capital for the whole peninsula.

There is certainly nothing to make us suspect the presence of a printing press in Henares before 1502, when its typographic history had its beginnings in the workshop, clearly provisional, of the Pole Estanislao Polono, who came from Seville at the invitation of Cardinal Cisneros. This we know thanks to very precise information provided by García de Rueda, a merchant who underwrote the first known Complutensian publication and who, alas, obtained no profit from the venture, or at least not the profit for which he had hoped. Estanislao's stay was brief, for the products of his workshop extend only to the year 1504, when he returned to Seville.

To understand this sequence of events, it is helpful to look at the city of Toledo some years earlier. Liturgical books began to be printed there during the final years of the fifteenth century, by order of the Cardinal; Melchor Gorricio de Novara fulfilled the role of bookseller and publisher, employing the workshop of Pedro Hagenbach. This must have prompted García de Rueda to emulate the Toledo bookseller when Cisneros, no doubt at the request of Queen Isabella, commissioned the translation of the *Vita Christi* of the Carthusian Ludolphus of Saxony. The enterprise proved not to be worthwhile for Rueda, and doubtless this had an effect on the continuation of production in the workshop of Estanislao Polono. The products of the workshop were clearly dependent on circumstance (against the wish of the printer) and were simple commissions. In 1504, the year of the celebrated declaration of the succession of Princess Juana and Prince Philip, Cisneros was living in Toledo. Perhaps the preparatory work for the Polyglot Bible had already begun, for some scholars date its origins to 1502, and it has even been claimed that scholars involved in the project moved in 1504 to Toledo, following their sponsor. The Polish printer left Henares because he could not see any clear future there, now that it seemed that the town could not assure him of further commissions of interest.

For the seven years between 1504 and 1511, Alcalá de Henares had no printer's workshop. Nonetheless, books were not lacking, and perhaps some bookseller whose name has not come down to us had a shop there. Many books acquired from private individuals and from booksellers in Toledo and Salamanca were sent to the young Cisnerian Academy at Alcalá, as is evident from a record in Madrid, Biblioteca Nacional, MS $20056^{47}$, which provides information about expenditure on books commissioned by or acquired for the Cardinal during the period 1497-1509. It is no surprise to find in this account the record of what was acquired, for example: 'the Gospels in Greek; the Gospels in Arabic, parchment, manuscript, which Don A[lej]o Vanegas brought to Burgos in November 1507; the epistles of St Paul in Greek; a Greek word-list; a Hebrew word-list; a Hebrew Bible; a part of the Bible in Hebrew and Chaldean script, parchment, manuscript, brought from Talavera to Burgos in November 1507. ...'[7]

This first experience, along with the summoning of the printer from Seville, reminds us of the invitation received by the two Sevillian workshops active in 1496 from the first Archbishop of Granada, Hernando de Talavera, to work in his city following the Reconquest. On the other hand Cisneros would not at any moment have considered the possibility of leaving Toledo without a shop by taking the one which was then working there (anonymously, but using Hagenbach's materials) to his lordly villa next to Henares. Other reasons led to the return of printing to Alcalá in 1511. I assume that when Cisneros met Nebrija in Salamanca in 1506, he did not fail to ask him for a worthy printer. Likewise, the great humanist would not have hesitated to provide a name: Arnao Guillén de Brocar.[8]

We have little information about this great printer. It is agreed that he was of French origin, that he underwent his apprenticeship in printing shops in Toulouse, and that he was called to Navarre once he had obtained his mastership. He remained in Pamplona until 1501 or early 1502, and his workshop busied itself with printing liturgical books, resolving with elegance the problems involved in the printing of music. Logroño was his next place of residence and activity; here, during the years 1507-8, he consolidated his friendship with Antonio de Nebrija, a friendship perhaps begun in 1503, at the time of the printing of Nebrija's *Introductiones latinae*. At Arnao's workshop in Logroño

Nebrija personally corrected the edition of that work that bears in its colophon the date 31 May 1508. This workshop remained active after the master printer's departure to Henares, where he worked from 1511 until his death late in 1523.[9]

We know the extent to which the recommendation of his name and professional work and his subsequent summons by Cisneros affected Arnao's plans, thanks to two documents: a privilege (already known to scholars for some time), granted by Ferdinand the Catholic at Madrid on 7 January 1511, for the printing of various works at his expense; and a tax certification of these works, dated at Burgos on 24 October 1511, although it is uncertain whether some of the works assessed for tax ever saw the light of day. It is unnecessary to analyse these documents here, given Pedro M. Cátedra's recent meticulous and masterful study. This study also provides information about another group of privileges that shed light on the printer's friendly business relations with Nebrija and with other workshops in Burgos, Salamanca, Saragossa and Seville. The contents of the privilege and the text of other privileges are summarized in a document issued at Valladolid on 4 July 1523. This allowed Arnao to oppose the (almost successful) attempt by Nebrija's sons Sancho and Sebastián to enjoy the rich profits of the exclusive rights to print the works of their deceased father.[10] Some time later, Juan Varela of Salamanca and Jacobo Cromberger from Seville were to attempt to limit the monopoly of Miguel de Eguía following the death of his father-in-law, an attempt in which they partly succeeded.[11] Printing has always been a business, although some historians persist in casting a blind eye on basic economic issues by concentrating on the printers who, we are told, were the individuals responsible for disseminating cultural and ideological currents that produced great changes in Europe. I believe that we should never underestimate the importance of economic factors in the world of printing.

If we return to the workshop of Arnao at Pamplona, which had its beginnings around 1490, we may add up the editions of the works of Nebrija from 15 December 1490 until 1546, the last year of Miguel de Eguía's printing activity in Estella. The high percentage that these editions constitute within the total production of the Pamplona and Alcalá workshops is striking. It is therefore no surprise that when in 1548 Miguel de Eguía's eldest son Jerónimo – who caused the printer no little trouble and expense in his efforts to secure his future, to the extent that Miguel saw himself obliged to disfavour him in his will – opposed his stepmother, the printer's second wife Lucía de Rosas y Verio, in claiming the goods that had belonged to his mother María de Brocar, he observed that one of the mainstays of the fortune was the direct consequence of the exclusive right to print the 'Artes de Gramática del Antonio' for a period of eleven years. In addition to this essential source of income, Jerónimo was also to indicate the significant income derived from the enjoyment, for a period of six years, of the privilege of printing bulls. The activity begun by Arnao as printer of the Bull of Crusade in the Jeronymite monastery of Our Lady of Prado in Valladolid and the Dominican house of St Peter Martyr in Toledo continued until 23 August 1527, when Miguel de Eguía and his brothers-in-law Juan and Pedro de Brocar renounced the privilege in favour of Lázaro Salvaggio, a Genoese merchant based in Toledo.

Although Miguel de Eguía and María de Brocar were married in 1518, we can gather clearly from the above-mentioned document that the profits obtained by Arnao, both from the production of the Complutensian Bible and from printing the magnificent liturgical books that issued from his workshop in Alcalá, remained outside any possible legal claim. We are thereby deprived of information of enormous potential interest. Also beyond any legal claim was the important series of Erasmus editions for which Miguel de Eguía was responsible. It was certainly not Eguía's sole concern to bring to a barbarous Spain the fruits of humanist erudition, as one can read between the lines on many occasions. It was his practice, before launching an edition, to take advice from the professors at the University of Alcalá, and he would calculate his possible sales in advance. The Erasmus editions demonstrate his own good instincts and those of the ones who advised him to undertake this publishing venture. However, in spite of his apparent interest in Erasmus, Eguía was equally capable of publishing a work attacking the Dutchman if he might make money from it.

Brocar and Eguía reflect the specialization that is characteristic of the Spanish printing shops of the sixteenth century, which were always directly linked to their environment, and likewise their limitations in relation to the European book-markets. The Complutensian Bible itself was not a success in terms of the book trade. It is a significant fact that, while the sale price for the six-volume ensemble was six-and-a-half gold *ducados*, on 4 November 1523 Hernando Colón succeeded in buying a set for only three *ducados* in Alcalá itself. I will mention here another curious detail highlighted by Clive Griffin, the distinguished historian of the Crombergers of Seville: 'Cromberger and Eguía exchanged books because the output of their presses was different and an agreement would not be to the disadvantage of either. It is a nice irony that Eguía is here seen arranging to sell books from a press which was well known for printing just the sort of editions he had so roundly condemned in the very year he signed this contract.'[12] He here alludes to a dedication from Eguía to Archbishop Fonseca in 1525, in which the printer attacks 'common and even obscene verses' and books that he calls 'of lesser worth'.

Despite what has been said, the workshop is of the highest interest for the history of printing in Spain during the fifteenth and sixteenth centuries. The participants in the story developed their activities in a good number of different cities: Pamplona, Logroño, Alcalá de Henares, Valladolid, Toledo, Burgos, Estella, Segovia and Sigüenza. It is not that they were travelling printers. Rather, the different workshops acted on occasions as genuine subsidiaries of a principal workshop. Moreover, one must acknowledge that we are dealing with a workshop which, at its height – which undoubtedly coincided with the golden age of printing in Alcalá de Henares, spanning the years 1511-33 – was of enormous cultural significance. It was right on hand to serve the Spanish 'pre-Reformation' (the term was coined by Pedro Sainz Rodríguez) in offering texts whose choice was not the printer's own, given that it was the fruit of the direct patronage of Cardinal Cisneros, and that it consisted, during the period of Arnao's activity, of biographical editions, works by the great names of female spirituality, texts of Savonarola and Ramón Llull, a splendid series of choir books, and the hugely successful *Obra de agricultura* by Gabriel Alonso de Herrera. It was in this luxuriant environment that the Polyglot edition of the Bible, which in technical terms was the principal fruit of the workshop, took its place.[13] The era of Miguel de Eguía, on the other hand, saw the emergence of his conscious plan, no doubt carefully calculated for economic reasons among others, to offer a generous selection of texts by Erasmus. From the cultural standpoint there is yet a third element to be acknowledged in the output of the workshop of Arnao Guillén de Brocar and Miguel de Eguía, namely the abundant series of editions of works by Nebrija mentioned above.

This is not the right moment to describe yet again the most distinguished fruit of Arnao's workshop. Nor is it necessary to do so. Perhaps it suffices to point out that without its having been in conception a product particularly attractive to bibliophiles, Arnao's skill as a printer made it so. The Complutensian Bible is valued today not so much for its rarity, for there survive more copies of it than of any other Complutensian edition, despite the limited run of six hundred copies on paper and six on vellum, and despite such misfortunes as the loss of a good number of copies sent by sea to Italy. It can be found in at least 154 libraries throughout the world, in many cases complete in all six volumes, in others with only some of the volumes remaining.[14] No other Complutensian edition is preserved in such a large number of copies. Its survival was the result partly of its bulk, partly because of its beautiful and appropriate mode of presentation. As I have mentioned elsewhere, the fate of the Complutensian Bible is in stark contrast with the disappearance of twelve thousand copies of Juan López de Úbeda's *Enfados a lo divino* that were printed in a single year during the 1570s. On this we have the certain testimony of the author himself, who mentions the workshop of Juan Íñiguez de Lequerica.

We do not have definite information about the timing of, nor even about the people involved in, each of the stages connected with the Polyglot Bible. The sources are few and present difficult problems in regard to their make-up. One should reread the words of Marcel Bataillon in his *Erasmo y España*[15] side by side with the classic study of the Augustinian Mariano Revilla Rico which admittedly now shows signs of age, for his *La Políglota de Alcalá: estudio histórico-critico* appeared in 1917.[16] One should also bear in mind that we still lack a good biography of Antonio de Nebrija, and have to rely on the old and well-known character study published by the Jesuit Félix G. Olmedo in 1942 under the title *Nebrija (1441-1522): debelador de la barbarie, comentarista eclesiástico, pedagogo, poeta.*[17] In recent years, the most important, highly specialized, work, without doubt, has been accomplished in connection with the various texts.[18] At a broader level, little progress has been made since the time of the books mentioned above.[19] From the purely typographical standpoint, I have barely succeeded in making any advance on the notice provided by F. J. Norton in his distinguished catalogue of early sixteenth-century Iberian printed books;[20] I have succeeded only in discovering two copies that on the sheet corresponding to sigs. CC2 and CC5 of the fifth volume present some interesting variants whose existence had been known since 1824, although nobody, not even Norton, had succeeded in locating a copy that would confirm the fact and allow its study.[21] The Complutensian Polyglot Bible surely demands and would be worthy of study in a future symposium devoted to it.

Juan de Brocar should make his appearance in this historical scenario via the account of Álvar Gómez de Castro, the early biographer of the Cardinal, who describes an event that took place in July 1517: 'I know that Juan Brocario, printer of Alcalá and the son of Arnoldo Guillermo Brocario, frequently told his contemporaries that on the very same day on which his father put the finishing touches to the printing of the work, he himself, being only a boy at the time, went elegantly dressed into Jiménez's presence with the last volume of the Bible. Jiménez, overjoyed, looked up to the heavens and exclaimed: "Lord Jesus Christ, I give you thanks that you have brought to its desired completion the work in which I held so much interest." And turning immediately to his entourage, he said: "Truly, although I have already accomplished many hard and difficult undertakings on behalf of the nation, none is as much to my liking, and there is none for which you should congratulate me more effusively than this edition of the Bible, the only one that opens up the sacred sources of our religion – more than necessary in our time – and from which will be drawn theological knowledge much purer than from the streams formed afterwards."'[22]

The best editions of the workshop of Juan de Brocar[23] appeared in the 1540s and in all cases were external commissions, no doubt obtained on the strength of the prestige of the now ancient workshop. I have in mind the splendid 1542 edition of the *Siete Partidas* of Alfonso the Wise, glossed by Alfonso Díaz de Montalvo, behind which there surely must have lain the money of the Medina bookseller Guillermo de Millis, who sent the printer a pair of wood-blocks representing the imperial coat of arms of Charles V, specifically commissioned from the engraver Juan de Vingles. One of these blocks the printer did not return; after the bookseller's name had been erased, it became, thanks to its constant appearance in editions of legal texts, which were abundant in the 1550s, a type of Complutensian 'trademark'. The same year 1542 saw a double commission from the bishop of Calahorra and La Calzada, Antonio Ramírez de Haro; from Juan de Brocar's workshop at Logroño there appeared, in succession, a diocesan missal and breviary. The bishop must have continued to be satisfied with the printer's work when, following his translation to the see of Segovia on 15 December 1543, there appeared a few years later, in August 1548, a *Manuale sacramentorum* published at his commission by 'Ioannes Brocarius typographus in sua officina Segouiensi ...'. This should not surprise us, for it was common practice on the part of the ecclesiastical chapters that commissioned liturgical editions to require the physical presence of the workshop nearby, so that they could efficiently oversee the correction of the text and verify the full execution of the contract in respect of the materials, the rate of work, the type of paper, and other conditions.

We know that Juan de Brocar's wife was Francisca de Angulo, sister of the printer Andrés de Angulo, native of Miranda de Ebro, and that the latter was the most direct heir to the workshop. Let us move ahead to 1572 to become better acquainted with him and with other masters, and in some cases to learn their personal opinion of the ills afflicting the Complutensian workshops. Unfortunately we do not have all the responses occasioned by the royal decree that was issued at Madrid on 12 November 1572 by Philip II. Directed to the *corregidores* of Toledo, Burgos and Medina del Campo, the rectors of the universities of Salamanca and Alcalá de Henares, the regent of Seville, the judge Diego de Zuñiga, *oidor* of the *audiencia* of Granada, and the judge Antonio de Covarrubias, *oidor* of the chancellery of Valladolid, the decree stipulated that a visitation was to be carried out to investigate the technical and economic capabilities of the uncompetitive printing houses of the places in question, and the degree of qualification of their workforces.

In 1968 Juan Martínez Ruiz announced the discovery, in the Archivo Capitular of Granada, of the supporting documentation for the execution of the royal decree in that city, thereby permitting us to visit the workshops of Granada, to speak with the printers, and so to get to know at first hand, or rather *viva voce*, the specific problems of the trade.[24] I mention the Granada case because the great interest of these documents fosters the hope that, sooner or later, someone will stumble upon the supporting documentation for the other visitations, which will then fill up the typobibliographical map of Spain with the names of workers and the addresses of workshops, and with detailed information about fonts, types of works and economic capabilities in the middle of the second half of the sixteenth century. Documentation relating to the visitation of the Complutensian workshops is preserved in the Archivo Histórico Nacional of Madrid, but it is very incomplete.[25]

The close proximity of the court meant that the royal provision of 12 November 1572 came into effect in Alcalá on the 26th of the same month, and that the visitation of the workshops was conducted much sooner than in Granada. Philip II commanded the visitation in order to find out the 'number of printers' and to inform himself about the 'quality of the printing shops that they hold' and 'the concern that exists there about correctors and compositors and other workers; and whether the persons who perform the said offices are capable and sufficient for the purpose; and also the forms (*moldes*) and the kinds of letters that are held there; and what is the reason that there are commonly so many faults and errors in the books printed in them; and what things it would be necessary to provide and remedy so that from henceforth such errors may not occur, and so that printing may be performed with all the good order that is appropriate; and by what means it may come about that the printed books of these kingdoms may be as abundant and of such perfection as are those outside the same kingdoms, and that good paper may be used in them, and that they may be put on sale at suitable prices.'[26] For the prompt fulfilment of the royal order, the University of Alcalá named as visitors of the town's printing presses Antonio de Torres, canon of the church of San Justo, and Álvaro de Mendoza, precentor of the same church, who were to be accompanied by the *alcalde mayor* Judge Ribero, and by the notary public Bernardino del Castillo.

It is a little frustrating to set the highly detailed report of the Granada visitation against the bare record of the fulfilment of the order by the Complutensian canons. For reasons of space I will not reproduce here the full text of these documents, pleasant though they are to read. The conclusion is immediately evident: the problems of the Spanish printing industry were first and foremost economic and commercial.[27]

Whereas the commissioners of the Andalusian city put on record the whereabouts of each workshop, the Complutensian commissioners performed their visitation in a single day, in haste, and without recording locations. On 15 December 1572 there existed four workshops in Alcalá. The first one to be visited was that of Andrés de Angulo, who declared himself the owner of the press and affirmed that he 'held sufficient capital to be able to print any books, both of the Faculty of Theology and of those of Canon and Civil Law and of Medicine, and any other books with text and gloss, just as is done outside these kingdoms, even if it should be necessary to use Greek, Hebrew and Aramaic characters both large and small. And he can likewise print the digest of the laws, and many other books that natives of these kingdoms have written in all the faculties, of the size and quality that should be requested, and also many Missals, as is well known and is demonstrated by the books in which are imprinted his name and that of Juan de Brocal, his brother-in-law and his predecessor at the said press.'[28] He declared himself to be in possession of a sufficient quantity of types, and announced that from these he would provide a sample printing. Unfortunately the sample, which would be of incalculable value for the typographic historian, is not included with the documentation of the visitation; the same lack exists for all those other informants who likewise mentioned providing samples. Andrés had the means to cast type, and he declared that he had money to bring in from outside any types for which he might be requested. He normally worked with four presses and he maintained a total workforce of sixteen.

The good state of his workshop, which can be gathered from his response, no doubt conditioned the rest of his statement. He tells us that the reason for the many errors, 'according to what he understands of his profession, is that it is a wonder if authors bring originals that are well corrected, or with good spelling or suitable punctuation, because there are few who understand such things, even if they are very literate'.[29] He emphasized that 'the correctors are very poor'[30] and suggested that a solution would be to require them to undergo an examination for their office, to be controlled by the University. He mentioned *sotto voce* that presses were going downhill and that they possessed little capital, although this was not so in his own case.

Sebastián Martínez, a clear case of a travelling printer, had at this time been active in Alcalá for ten years. His was the next workshop to be visited. He too declared himself to be the owner of the workshop, but his response demonstrated a very different economic situation. 'He said that he has two presses and that at the present time he uses only one of them, for which he keeps three workers who are necessary to him, a compositor, a beater and a drawer.'[31] Of great interest is his mentioning that without help he would not venture upon books of a length greater than fifty or sixty sheets. His analysis of the situation is much more realistic than that of Andrés and closer to that of the printers at Granada: 'the cause whereby the books that are printed appear with faults and errors in them rests with the correctors. ... And as regards the printing shops in Spain not being as wealthy as those outside her, according to what he understands from having been in some printing shops in France, this results from the books printed in Spain not having outlet and sale in as many places as do those of the printing houses outside these kingdoms, and ... the lack of paper comes from not having it in such abundance, nor of the same quality and as cheaply as is the case in France.'[32] In his opinion, the remedies consisted in preventing the import of books that might compete with those produced in Spain, and in the establishment of sufficient paper mills.

We now come to the workshop of Juan Gracián, who was of French origin, and who was only part-owner of the press, for he shared it with Juan de Villanueva, who had moved to Lérida a few months beforehand. We find ourselves, therefore, in the workshop of Francisco de Cormellas and Pedro de Robles, which had been active since 1563 and which in the years 1565-6 operated in the name of Pedro de Robles and the said Juan de Villanueva. It represented a situation intermediate between those of the two workshops discussed above, and it was doubtless a workshop of a type characteristic of the Complutensian situation in the sixteenth and seventeenth centuries. But let us examine his statement. 'He said that he has two presses, and for them he has four compositors and two drawers and two beaters, making eight persons in all.'[33] Although he declared that he could print any type of book thanks to his fonts, 'as regards printing books at his own expense, he said that henceforward he will not venture to print anything of greater length than fifty or sixty sheets because of the small amount of capital that he holds, but that he would undertake to print any book in Latin, Romance and Greek for which he might be assisted with capital'.[34] He agreed with Sebastián Martínez in opining 'that the reason why books issued in Spain contain errors is the lack of correctors, who are not abundant in Spain because of lack of experience in the same office',[35] to which he added that it would be necessary to pay correctors adequately. 'As regards the reason why the printing houses in Spain are not as wealthy as those outside of her, it is ... because in Spain merchants do not join together in companies ... to have books printed, as happens elsewhere',[36] an observation to which he added the further comment that success would come by preventing the import of books that could be produced in Spain herself. On the question of paper, his opinion was that it was necessary to construct paper mills and to require from those who ran them an adequate selection of the primary material, that is to say, of rags.

Unfortunately, this most interesting set of documents does not include any information about the other workshop that doubtless was visited, that of Juan Íñiguez de Lequerica y Villarreal, and as a result we do not know his personal view of the problems addressed, but it would surely have been not much different from the opinions recorded above.

In the second half of the sixteenth century, as can be gathered from the information obtained in the Complutensian workshops, Spanish printers went on printing only editions that the national market could easily absorb and for which there was no international competition. The Complutensian workshops were no exception to this general rule. In this second phase of the history of printing at Alcalá, I do not believe that there was a single edition of a great work that required an international market. Indeed, when in the course of the sixteenth century we come upon the publication of a major work in Spain, the European diffusion of the work was normally accomplished by reissues outside Spain. Spanish publishing was enclosing itself within its own geographical limits. The general inability of Spanish workshops to produce generous print-runs or to undertake large-scale projects is to be explained by the lack of typographic material and especially of paper, by the limited number of qualified workers, by legislation that was manifestly restrictive, and by the shortage of economic resources.

In the first decades of the sixteenth century it was very rare for a book that was in Spanish and that was destined for sale in Spain to see the light elsewhere. As the century advanced, the percentage of imported books increased, and it is to be noted that around 1540 the production outside Spain of books written in Spanish was comparable to, and even threatened to surpass, domestic production. This situation contributed to the deterioration in the quality of books printed in Spain. It is likely that imports increased to such an extent that, although demand increased, Spanish printers found themselves obliged to compete with one another and, as a result of their efforts to reduce their costs, quality was seriously affected.

We should now recall another event that had taken place some years before the visitation of 1572. Because of the lack of modern bibliographies on some of the centres of production, we still cannot gauge the true impact that Madrid had on the recession of printing and publishing in other cities, probably depending on the types of works that they published. The royal court established itself at Madrid in 1561, and printing had its beginnings there in 1566. It is possible that Seville was one of the cities most affected. Counterfeit editions abounded in Seville: it was a clear consequence of its distance from Madrid that in a certain manner it exercised sole rights over the first editions of best-selling works. I can say with some confidence that in a city like Salamanca, where production was manifestly academic, concentrating especially on the fields of theology and law, there was no negative impact. Did the proximity of the court have any effect on the Complutensian workshops? To begin with, the effect was assuredly positive, since competition between the Madrid booksellers Alonso Gómez and Francisco López the Elder resulted in commissions from the former for the workshop that was successively associated with Francisco de Cormellas, Pedro de Robles and Juan de Villanueva, and from the latter and his brother Juan de Escobedo, for the workshop of Andrés de Angulo. The editions in question were principally of legal texts.

As Cristóbal Pérez Pastor pointed out in his account of the origins of the first printing workshop in Madrid in mid-1566, 'the cause can be explained quite simply on the assumption that the bookseller Alonso Gómez wished to participate in the profits enjoyed by the printers at Alcalá, or to avoid the inconveniences and delays that occurred when works were printed in a different town; possessing the capital to establish a small printing house, he sought out a business partner who would carry out the role of typographer in it and would share in the earnings. He came upon Pierres Cosín, a printer by trade, and the first printing house at Madrid was established in the name of these two as printers, although Alonso Gómez continued to run his bookshop.'[37] From this time onwards, Madrid undoubtedly took work away from the Complutensian workshops, although the negative effect should not be exaggerated.

There is another matter which perhaps holds greater interest: the migration of Complutensian printers to Madrid. Francisco Sánchez, who worked as a compositor in the shop of Andrés de Angulo and previously tried his luck as a bookseller, in 1572 began working in Madrid as a printer; the products of his workshop witness to the scarcity of resources by the feebleness of the types used in them and the wretched quality of the paper. Juan Gracián, active in Alcalá from 1568, made a somewhat inexplicable appearance in Madrid with a 1572 publication. In the absence of supporting documentation, may we not speculate that he perhaps had a plan, immediately abandoned, to create a subsidiary in Madrid? The Fleming Querino Gerardo likewise set up shop in Madrid after a period of activity in Alcalá.

The migration to Madrid was certainly more intense in the case of booksellers. It is sufficient to record the names of Alonso Calleja, Blas de Robles (who stored books in the house of his father Bartolomé de Robles in Alcalá), Pedro del Bosque, Juan López Perete, Francisco Enríquez and Juan de Montoya.

Undoubtedly printing at Alcalá in the seventeenth century, while not showing major differences from the situation obtained by other Spanish cities that had printing houses, was separated by a real gulf from the production of the previous century, in terms both of typographical quality and of the interest of the contents. Nonetheless, it does not merit total scorn, for it presents us with a most important source, hitherto insufficiently tapped, for the study of the everyday life of Alcalá in that century, as a definer of its history and culture not only in broad terms, but also in the pettiest details. During this period the products of the Complutensian printing houses had a markedly local character. Printing shops and University shared together in an unstoppable decline.

If there was a definite continuity in the choice of texts between the products of the first decades of the seventeenth century and those of the second half of the sixteenth, from the 1620s there began that triumph of printed religious oratory that was to continue throughout the following century. Countless personal and institutional feuds arose throughout the seventeenth century, thereby posing difficult problems regarding the attribution of works to the various workshops. Accounts of events abound. No one will be surprised by the overwhelming presence of religious texts in a city dotted with religious houses whose members announced themselves, practically one by one, not only as authors, but also as critics, versifiers working in the style of the Baroque eulogy, and so on. Later on in the century, some of the monasteries disposed of their own printing presses which issued a constant stream of university texts.

I have now strayed too far from the workshop of Arnao Guillén de Brocar, and the journey has been less welcome with every step. I would prefer to retrace my path and to return silently through the open door of the workshop of the Polyglot Bible in the painting of Pedro Ibarra Ruiz, to contemplate anew the delightful scene revealed there.

## NOTES

1 2 vols (The Hague & Leipzig: Nijhoff, 1903-17), I, no. 49, pp. 22-3.

2 Barcelona: Alberti, 1953.

3 'Versión e impresión de la Biblia Políglota complutense, bajo la inmediata dirección del gran Cardenal Jiménez de Cisneros.'

4 I came upon this information in Rafael Navarro Mallebrera & Manuela Andreu Pujalte, *Archivo municipal: catálogo de manuscritos de Pedro Ibarra Ruiz* (Elche: Ed. del Ayuntamiento, 1978), nos 4, 58 and 212. Unfortunately, the reproduction of the painting in the doctoral thesis by Vicenta Pastor Ibáñez, *Historia de la pintura en Elche: pintores ilicitanos nacidos en el siglo XIX* (Madrid: Ed. de la Universidad Complutense, 1988), p. 444, no. 15, is so reduced in scale and so dark that it is impossible to make out the detail, and it is of no help. Its source, a pamphlet entitled *Pedro Ibarra Ruiz*, by Alejandro Ramos Folqués, published by Casino de Elche, I have not succeeded in finding even in Elche itself, despite the efforts of my diligent and generous friends Carmen Gutiérrez and Rafael Navarro.

5 *El cardenal Cisneros: vida y empresas*, 2 vols (Madrid: Biblioteca de Autores Cristianos, 1993), II, pp. 448 and 479: 'El libro complutense es una realidad de la España moderna'; 'la imprenta es una parte más de la Academia cisneriana'. (An earlier version of this chapter on the subject of 'Libros y bibliotecas en Alcalá' appears in his *La Universidad de Alcalá de Henares en la etapa fundacional (1458-1578)* (Santiago de Compostela: [s.n.], 1992), a work that exists in two editions, or maybe two issues, of the same year.)

6 I draw upon information included in my book *La imprenta en Alcalá de Henares (1502-1600)*, 3 vols (Madrid: Arco Libros, 1991). Also relevant are my notes entitled 'Talleres de imprenta complutenses del siglo XVI: ediciones hasta ahora ignotas y ejemplares rarísimos (1-4)', *Puerta de Madrid*, 1381 (7 May 1994), 10; 1386 (7 June 1994), 8; 1390 (9 June 1994), 9; 1392 (23 July 1994), 9. Also the subsequent series, 'Talleres de imprenta complutenses del siglo XVI: hallazgos de ediciones nunca descritas (1-8)': ibid., 1412 (24 December 1994), 9; 1418 (11 February 1995), 9; 1421 (4 March 1995), 10-11; 1424 (25 March 1995), 10-11; 1427 (22 April 1995), 9; 1466 (17 February 1996), 9; 1467 (24 February 1996), 9; 1470 (25 May 1996), 9-10.

7 'los euangelios en griego; los euangelios en Arauigo de pergamino de mano que truxo a burgos don A[lej]o Vanegas por nouiembre de quinientos 7; las epistolas de Sant Pablo en griego; Vocabulario greco; Vocabulario hebreo; biblia ebraica; Vna parte de la biblia de letra hebraica e caldea en pergamino de mano que se truxo de Talauera a Burgos por nouiembre de quinientos 7. ...'

8 See my paper, 'Nebrija en los talleres de Arnao Guillén de Brocar y Miguel de Eguía', in *Actas*

*del Congreso internacional de historiografía lingüística: Nebrija V centenario*, 3 vols, ed. by R. Escavy, J. M. Hernández Terrés & A. Roldán (Murcia: Universidad, 1994), I, pp. 20-30.

9 I myself have stated that his death probably occurred between 17 November and 24 December 1523. However, according to the information in José García Oro, *Los reyes y los libros: la política libraria de la corona en el Siglo de Oro (1475-1598)* (Madrid: Cisneros, 1995), pp. 44-5, the sad event had already occurred before 7 November. A royal warrant granted at Pamplona on that day confirmed upon Arnao's heirs, Miguel de Eguía and the latter's brothers-in-law Juan and Pedro de Brocar, privileges included in a royal document issued in Arnao's favour at Valladolid on 12 September 1522. The documents are in the Archivo General de Simancas, Cámara de Castilla, 255.

10 Pedro M. Cátedra, 'Arnao Guillén de Brocar, impresor de las obras de Nebrija', in *El libro antiguo español*, ed. by María Luisa López-Vidriero & Pedro M. Cátedra (Salamanca: Universidad de Salamanca, 1996), pp. 43-80. The Valladolid document of 4 July 1523 is in the Archivo General de Simancas, Registro General de Sello (julio 1523). As I have already indicated, García Oro, in *Los reyes y los libros*, pp. 42-7, mentions these same privileges confirmed, at the request and in favour of Arnao's heirs, by the Pamplona royal warrant of 7 November 1523 (see n. 9 above).

11 See García Oro, *Los reyes y los libros*, pp. 45-6, commenting on a royal grant given at Valladolid on 26 October 1524. It mentions 'Jacome Alemán' (*sic*), but this is surely an error for 'Jacobo'.

12 Clive Griffin, *The Crombergers of Seville: the History of a Printing and Merchant Dynasty* (Oxford: Clarendon Press, 1988), p. 11.

13 See Pedro Sainz Rodríguez, *La siembra mística del cardenal Cisneros y las reformas en la iglesia* (Madrid: Universidad Pontificia de Salamanca y Fundación Universitaria Española, 1979). See also the more recent analysis in Felipe Fernández-Armesto, 'Cardinal Cisneros as a patron of printing', in *God and Man in Medieval Spain: Essays in Honour of J. R. L. Highfield*, ed. by Derek W. Lomax & David Mackenzie (Warminster: Aris & Phillips, 1989), pp. 149-68.

14 See my *La imprenta en Alcalá de Henares* (above, n. 6, I), no. 20, to which I can now add these further examples: (1) Huesca, Biblioteca Pública, B-3/664-668 (vols I-V); (2) Leuven, Katholieke Universiteit, Faculteit der Godgeleerdheid, P22.04/F° (see *Early Sixteenth Century Printed Books 1501-1540 in the Library of the Leuven Faculty of Theology*, ed. by Frans Gistelick & Maurits Sabbe (Leuven: Bibliotheek Godgeleerdheid, 1994), p. 257, no. 144); (3) Rome, Biblioteca Angelica, A.20.9-11 and A.19.1-3; (4) Salamanca, Biblioteca Universitaria, 3878 and 3882 (vols I and V) (see *El siglo de Fray Luis de León: Salamanca y el Renacimiento*, catalogue of an exhibition at the Colegio de Arzobispo Fonseca, Escuelas Menores, Antigua Universidad, Salamanca, Oct.-Dec. 1991 (Madrid: Ministero de Cultura, Centro Nacional de Exposiciones, etc., 1991), pp. 390-1, where the title-page of vol. I is reproduced); (5) Sigüenza (Guadalajara), Cathedral, 31/35 (vols I-IV and VI, all incomplete); (6) Saragossa, Catedral de La Seo, 24-11/14 (vols II-V) (see Ángel Escobar Chico, *Codices Caesaraugustani graeci: catálogo de los manuscritos griegos de la Biblioteca Capitular de la Seo (Zaragoza)* (Saragossa: Institución Fernando el Católico, 1993), pp. 96-7).

15 *Erasmo y España: estudios sobre la historia espiritual del siglo XVI*, trans. by Antonio Alatorre, 2nd Spanish edn, corrected and augmented (Mexico, Madrid, Buenos Aires: Fondo de Cultura Económico, 1983).

16 (Madrid: Impr. Helénica, 1917).

17 (Madrid: Editora Nacional, 1942).

18 A general overview is provided in *Anejo a la edición facsímile de la Biblia Políglota Complutense* (Valencia: Fundación Bíblica Española y Universidad Complutense de Madrid, 1987). Emilia Fernández considers 'El texto hebreo' (pp. 25-32); Natalio Fernández Marcos,

'El texto griego' (pp. 33-42); Emiliano Martínez Borobio, 'El texto arameo' (pp. 43-51); and Javier Fernández Vallina and Luis Vegas Montaner, 'El texto latino' (pp. 53-60). All these studies include a full bibliography on the manuscripts consulted and the editorial criteria.

19 See the most recent publication of Rosa Helena Chinchilla, 'The *Complutensian Polyglot Bible* (1520) and the political ramifications of biblical translation', in *La traducción en España: ss. XIV-XVI*, ed. by Roxana Recio (León: Universidad de Léon, 1995), pp. 169-90.

20 *A Descriptive Catalogue of Printing in Spain and Portugal 1501-20* (Cambridge: University Press, 1978), no. 27, A, B, C, D, E.

21 My bibliographical notice can be found in my *La imprenta en Alcalá de Henares* (above, n. 6), I, pp. 222-3, no. 28, A, B, C, D, E.

22 Gómez de Castro, *De las hazañas de Francisco Jiménez de Cisneros*, ed. and trans. by José Oroz Meta (Madrid: Fundación Universitaria Española, 1984), pp. 118-19: 'He sabido que Juan Brocario, impresor de Alcalá, hijo de Arnoldo Guillermo Brocario, contó muchas veces a los de su edad, que el mismo día, en que su padre dio la última mano a la impresión de la obra, él, que era muchacho, había ido elegantemente vestido a presencia de Jiménez con el último volumen de la Biblia. Jiménez, muy contento, exclamó mirando al cielo, "Cristo soberano, te doy gracias porque has llevado al término deseado la obra en que yo tenía tanto interés." Y volviéndose al punto hacia los familiares dijo: "A la verdad, aunque hasta el presente he llevado a cabo muchas empresas duras y difíciles por la Nación, nada es tan de mi agrado, por lo que debáis felicitarme con más efusión, que por esta edición de la Biblia, la única, que abre las fuentes sagradas de nuestra Religión, más que necesaria en este momento, y de donde se sacará una ciencia teológica mucho más pura que de los arroyos formados después.'

23 It is always his name that appears as owner of the workshop, but previously, as we have already seen, when the workshop is mentioned under the name of his brother-in-law Miguel de Eguía, the documentation always refers to the latter and to Juan and Pedro de Brocar. At this moment in the history of the workshop, Juan took steps to acquire a certain benefit in his own name and that of Pedro and Petronila de Brocar, 'his juniors'. The mention of Petronila indicates that the number of the known offspring of Arnao must be increased by another daughter (Archivo General de Simancas, Cámara de Castilla, Leg. 246, f. 39).

24 'Visita a las imprentas granadinas de Antonio de Nebrija, Hugo de Mena y René Rabut en el año 1573', *Revista de dialectología y tradiciones populares*, 24 (1968), 1-2, pp. 75-110.

25 Universidades, Leg. 135, Caja 1. It was Ramón González Navarro who discovered these documents. With his permission, I made the first reference to them in my note 'Talleres de imprenta y mercaderes de libros en España', in *Creadores del libro del: Medioevo al Renacimiento: Sala de Exposiciones de la Fundación Central Hispano, 28 de septiembre-20 de noviembre, 1994*, ed. by José María Fernández Catón (Madrid: Dirección General del Libro y Bibliotecas y Fundación Central Hispano, 1994), p. 55.

26 'número de impresores ... calidad de las imprentas que tienen ... el recaudo que en ellas ay de correctores y componedores y otros oficiales. E si las personas que sirven los dichos oficios, son áviles y suficientes para ello, y los moldes y géneros de letras que en ellas ay. E qué es la causa que, en los libros que se imprimen en ellas, ay comunmente tantas faltas y herrores. E qué cossas será necesario proveer y remediar, para que, de aquí adelante, no los aya, y las impresiones se hagan con toda la buena horden que conbiene, y qué medio se podrá tener, para que las imprentas de estos reinos sean tan caudalosas y de tanta perfición, como lo son las que ay fuera de ellos, y para que se gaste en ellas buen papel, y se halle a precios conbenibles.'

27 For a more detailed evaluation, see Jaime Moll Roqueta, 'El impresor y el librero en el Siglo de Oro', in *Mundo del libro antiguo*, ed. by Francisco Asín Remírez de Esparza (Madrid: Editorial Complutense, 1996), pp. 38-9.

28 'tiene cabdal bastante para poder ymprimyr qualesquyer libros ansy de la Facultad de Teología como de Derecho canónico e cibil e Medicina e otros libros qualesquyer con texto y glossa como se traen de fuera de estos reynos aunque para ello sean necesarios caracteres griegos, ebreos y caldeos, grandes y pequeños y que podrá ansy mismo ynprimyr la recapitulación de las leyes y otros muchos libros que naturales destos reynos an compuesto en todas Facultades del tamaño y marca que se le piden y muchos mysales como es notorio y consta de las mysmas ympresiones donde está ynpresso su nombre y de Juan de Brocal su cuñado, antecesor suyo en el dicha enprenta.'

29 'conforme a lo quel entiende de su officio es que los autores por maravilla traen los originales bien corregidos ny con buena ortografía ny de puntuación como conviene porque pocos ay que aunque sean muy letrados entiendan esto.'

30 'ay muy ruines correctores'.

31 'Dixo que tiene dos prensas y que al presente no trabaja más que la una para la qual tiene tres oficiales que son necessarios, que son un componedor e un batidor e un tirador.'

32 'que la caussa por donde los libros que se ynprimen salen con mentiras y herrores estryba en los correctores. ... Y que en lo que toca a no ser las enprentas de España tan cabdalosas como las de fuera de ella va conforme a lo que él tiene entendido por aver estado en algunas enprentas de Françia no tener salida e benta los libros que se ynprimen en España para tantas partes la tienen las enprentas de fuera destos reynos y ... la falta de papel por no averlo en tanta abundancia ny tan bueno ny tan barato como se halla en Françia.'

33 'Dixo que el tiene dos prensas y para ellas tiene quatro componedores y dos tiradores y dos batidores que son por todos ocho personas.'

34 'en lo que toca a ynprimir libros a su costa dixo que no se atreverá a ymprimir ninguno que pase de cincuenta o sesenta pliegos adelante por el poco cabdal que tiene pero que se atrevería a ymprimyr cualquiera libro de latín y de romanze y de griego porque fuese como fuese ayudado con cabdal.'

35 'que la causa de salir los libros en España con herrores es por falta de los correctores los quales no los ay en España en abundancia por falta de esperiencia en el dicho oficio.'

36 'En lo que toca a la caussa por qué no son las enprentas de España tan cabdalosas como las de fuera della es ... porque en España no ay mercaderes que se junten por companyas ... a hazer ymprimir los libros como se usa y se haze fuera.'

37 *Bibliografía madrileña, o descripción de las obras impresas en Madrid (siglo XVI)* (Madrid: Tipografía de los Huérfanos, 1891), p. xxi: 'el motivo se puede explicar sencillamente, suponiendo que el librero Alonso Gómez querría tener parte en las ganancias de los impresores de Alcalá, o evitarse las molestias y tardanzas consiguientes, cuando estos trabajos se hacen en población diferente; y teniendo capital para montar una pequeña imprenta, buscaría un socio industrial que, trabajando en ella como tipógrafo, fuese partícipe en las ganancias. Encontró a Pierres Cosín, de oficio impresor, y se estableció la primera imprenta de Madrid, a nombre de los dos como impresores, aunque continuando Alonso Gómez con su librería.

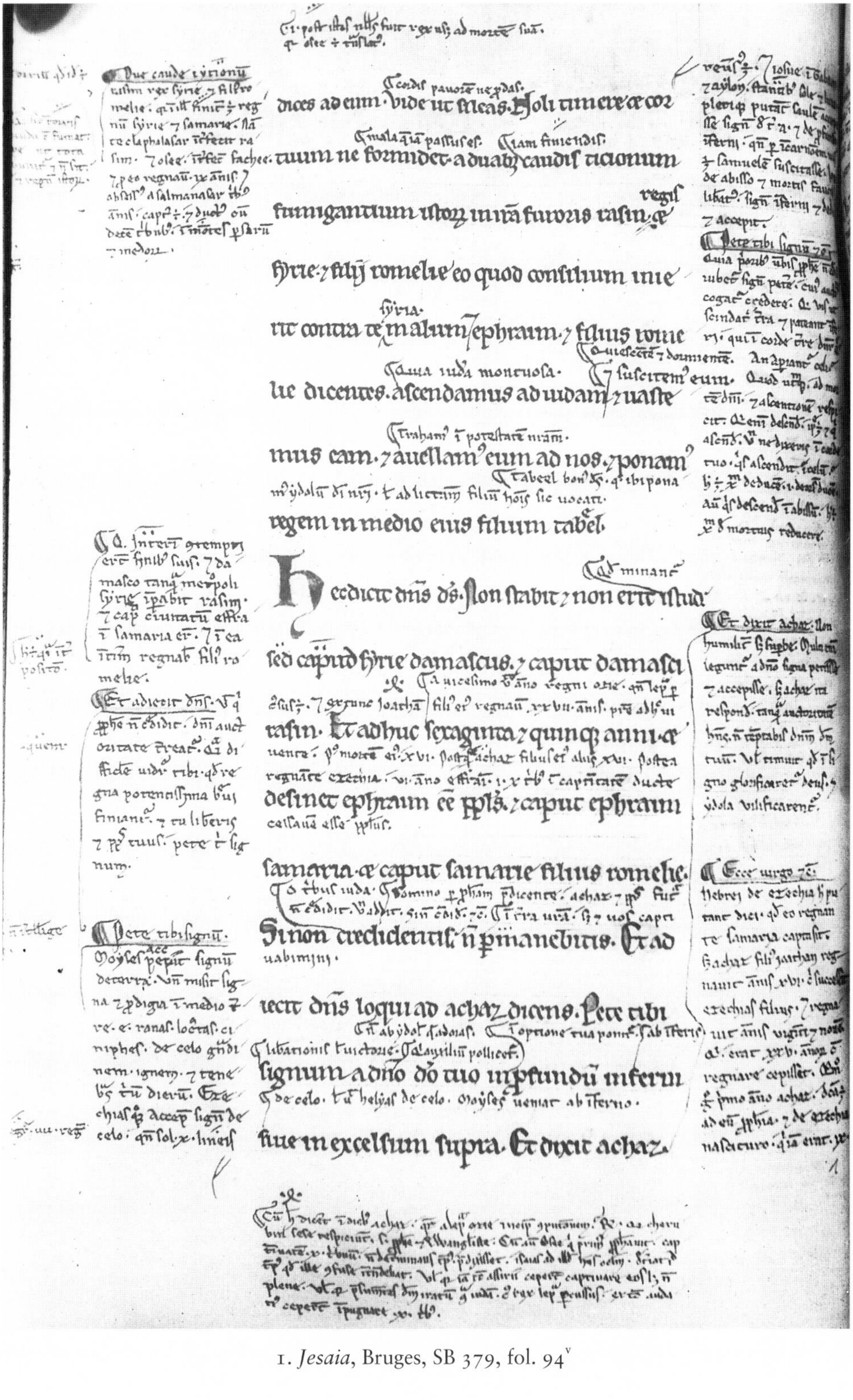

Et post istas nullus fuit rex usque ad mortem suam. [illegible]

Due caude titionum
rasim rex syrie et filius ro
melie. quorum finitum est reg
num syrie et samarie. Na
teglaphalasar interfecit ra
sim. et osee. interfecit facee.
et post eo regnauit. ix annis.
absitus a salmanasar tribus
annis. captus est. et ductus cum
decem tribubus in montes persarum
et medorum.

Vere ad eum. Noli timere. [illegible]

dices ad eum. Vide ut sileas. Noli timere et cor
tuum ne formidet a duabus caudis titionum
fumigantium istorum in ira furoris rasin regis
syrie et filii romelie eo quod consilium inie
rit contra te malum ephraim et filius rome
lie dicentes. ascendamus ad iudam et suscitemus eum et uaste
mus eam et auellamus eum ad nos et ponamus
regem in medio eius filium tabeel.

reus est. Iosue in Gabaon
et aylon. stantibus sole et luna.
plerique putant saulem accepis
se signum de terra. et de profundo
inferni. quando per incantationem
se samuelem suscitasse [illegible]
de abisso et mortis faucibus
liberatus. signum inferni et de [illegible]
et accepit.

Pete tibi signum [illegible]
Quia potentibus ubique propheta non di
iubet signum petere. cui [illegible]
cogatur credere. Vel ut
scindatur terra et pateant in
feri. qui in corde terre [illegible]
dormientem. An appareat celum.
Quod utrumque ad me
te domini. et ascentione [illegible]
cit. Qui enim descendit [illegible]
ascendit. [illegible] ne dixeris in corde
tuo. quis ascendit in celum [illegible]
hoc est christum deducere. id est [illegible]
aut quis descendit in abissum. hoc est
christum a mortuis reducere.

Que inierit contemptus
est finibus suis. et da
masco tamquam metropoli
syrie imperabit rasim.
et caput ciuitatum effraim
in samaria est. et in ea
[illegible] regnabit filius ro
melie.

Et adiecit dominus. [illegible]
propheta non credidit. domini auct
oritate terreat. Quasi di
ficile uideatur tibi quod re
gna potentissima [illegible]
finiantur. et tu liberis
et [illegible] tuus. pete tibi sig
num.

Hec dicit dominus deus. Non stabit et non erit istud.
sed caput syrie damascus et caput damasci
rasin. Et adhuc sexaginta et quinque anni et
desinet ephraim esse populus et caput ephraim
samaria et caput samarie filius romelie.
Si non credideritis non permanebitis. Et ad
iecit dominus loqui ad achaz dicens. Pete tibi
signum a domino deo tuo in profundum inferni
siue in excelsum supra. Et dixit achaz.

Et dixit achaz. Non
humiliter sed superbe [illegible]
[illegible]
et accepisse. Sed achaz [illegible]
respondit [illegible]
[illegible]
[illegible]
[illegible]
ydola uilificarentur.

Ecce uirgo [illegible]
Hebrei de ezechia hoc pu
tant dici. quod eo regnan
te samaria capta sit.
Sed achaz filius ioathan reg
nauit annis xvi. cui successit
ezechias filius. et regna
uit annis uiginti et nouem.
[illegible] erat xxv. annorum cum
regnare cepisset [illegible]
[illegible] primo anno achaz [illegible]
ad eum prophetia. et de ezechia
nasciturum [illegible]

Pete tibi signum.
Moyses petiit signum
de terra. [illegible] misit sig
na et prodigia in medio ter
re et ranas. locustas. ci
niphes. de celo grandi
nem. ignem. et tene
bras [illegible] dierum. Eze
chias [illegible] accepit signum de
celo. quando sol x. lineis

[illegible] de celo. [illegible] helyas de celo. Moyses ueniat ab inferno.

Cum hec diceret ysaias achaz [illegible] orte [illegible] Ad cheru
bin [illegible] respicient. Si prophete et euangeliste [illegible] prophetauit cap
tiuitatem [illegible] non determinans tempus [illegible] ysaias ad illud [illegible]
[illegible] illa [illegible] tendebat. Vel [illegible] rex assiriorum cepit captiuare [illegible] non
plena. Vel [illegible] iudam [illegible] rex [illegible] iuda
non cepere [illegible] pugnare [illegible]

1. *Jesaia*, Bruges, SB 379, fol. 94v

THESSA II

I

AVLVS Quia in prima epla dix quedā de adventu dnī et resurrectione mortuorum. nc aliā scribit in qua significat licet obscure. neq; enim aperte potest de abolitione romani regni. et de antixρo. et de inquietudine quorundā.

ET SIL

UAN.

ET TI

motheus. ecclie thessalonicensi

um. in deo patre nro et dno ie

su xpo. Grā uob et pax. Grās age

re semp debem9 do p uob frs. ita

ut dignum ē. qm supcrescit fi

Quasi. q tenetis tenete. quia bonum. de quo semp debem9 et nūquā soluere possim9 ut ē dignum.

des ura. et abundat caritas

uniuscuiusq; inuicē. ita ut et

nos ipsi in uob gtem in ecctiis

di. p patientia ura et fide in

in omib; psecutionib; uris et

2. *Epistles of Paul*, Laon, BM 108, fol. 165r

DEUTERONOMIUS

110

ibi lex data ē ibi g̃ius s̃ renel scriptus. exodus. numi scriptis ē
et magna pars huius. Inde pedem mouentes anno scdo perue
niunt in cades barne et in spatio illo fecerunt xxi mansiones.
De cades barne miserunt exploratores qui reuertentes nuntiaue
runt terram bonam sed robustos et gygantes homines inuenerunt.
Iterum uolentes redire in terram egipti unde iratus dominus abi
ere retro et lustrauerunt montem seyr per xxxviii annos. ibi mor
tui et prostrati sunt murmurantes. Item In xl anno anno perue
neruntad cades barne unde retro abierunt per desertum et i
illo spatio ix mansiones iterum fecerunt. Undecimo uero dies moy

ses eos antequam ueniret ad cades
barne legem solo uerbo eis re
capitulauit et de cades barne
usque ad campestria moab
et illo spatio xi dierum septo
uoluit commutare. Ecce de pri
mo anno xii de scdo xxi de
xl ix et ita xl ii mansiones.

Rab. Iez. Hec sunt uerba q̃ l
m. et c. Principium deutronomii
in tytulus uidetur totius o
peris quia personam indicat
audi in auctoris et quid fecerit
et locum et tempus. Nomen quoque lib
grecum demonstrat nouum
Deuteronomium namque secunda
lex interpretatur et euangelii legem quia ueteris
per sacramenta spiritualem explan
at. Sicut liber deuteronomii
repeticio ē quatuor librorum
legis. Illi enim proprias con
tinent in se causas. iste repli
cat uniuersa. habet et ipse
propria sacramenta.

Hec sunt uerba que locutus
ē moyses etc. Hec de se tam
quam de alio. de more sacre
scripture dicit. sicut et ubi
erat moyses mitissimus
super omnes homines qui
morabantur in terra. Sic enim
uitat arrogantiam et de
monstrat uitandam. Si
militer et iob de se dicit. Uir
erat in terra hus. et Io. et c. et
iohs. Hic ē discipulus ille
qui testimonium perhibet d. h.

Hec fuit causa huius libri ut ea que
terra fiant breuiter collecta artius
tenerentur in memoria facile et
retinerentur que breuiter dicuntur.

Ec sunt uerba que
(docendo.) (lex.)
locutus est moyses
(Iudaicum populum. cui uniuersaliter lex data est.)
ad omnem israel
(ante baptismum.) (secreti
tate plebis cui dicitur. Relinquetur)
transiordanem in
(uobis domus uestra deserta.)
(ecclesia in qua non ē horror spinarum)
solitudine campe
(i. uitiorum.) (baptismum xpi sanguine rubeum.) (sanctus.)
stri. contra mare rubrum inter pha
(nomina locorum.) (ecclesia. longe lateque
diffusa uel dilatata.) (dealbatio)
ran et tophel et laban.
(ecclesia in baptismo dealbata.)

De se tamquam de alio loquitur
sicut iohs de se ait. Dis
cipulus quem diligebat
ihc. uel sicut sps scs perhibet ei
testimonium. ut nemo
possit dubitare moysen
ista scripsisse.

Quatuor hii montes. qua
tuor euangelia significant.
quibus circumdatur ecclesia.

Insulsitas. ecclesia. n. stul
ta uidetur quia despicit uisi
bilia. cupiens inuisibilia.

Ad. All. Locutus ē in. ad.
o. i. et c. Moyses lex uetus
ē que transiordanem i.
ante baptismum. israeliticum docu
it populum. In iordane enim
figuratur baptismus. in quo bap
tizatus ē xps. In solitudine
campestri. i. insulsitate
carnalis populi. qui fructum
uirtutum non attulit.

Quia generatio praua et peruersa
ablutionem peccatorum in sang
ne xpi credere noluit.

Inter pharan. pharan auc
tus. tophel. insulsitas.

3. *Deuteronomium*, Berlin, Staatsbibliothek Preussischer Kulturbesitz, Theol. lat. fol. 222, fol. 110r

IOB

nunc dicitis persequimur eum: et radicem verbi inveniamus adversus eum. fugite ergo a facie gladii, quoniam ultor iniquitatum gladius est: et scitote esse iudicium. Respondens autem Sophar naamathites dixit: Idcirco cogitationes meae variae succedunt sibi et mens in diversa rapitur. Doctrinam qua me arguis audiam, et spiritus intelligentiae meae respondebit michi. Hoc scio a principio ex quo positus est homo super terram, quod laus impiorum brevis sit et gaudium ypocrite ad instar puncti. Si ascenderit usque in celum superbia eius, et caput eius nubes tetigerit

4. *Job*, Leiden, Bibliotheek der Rijksuniversiteit, Voss. lat. fol. 43, fol. 56[r]

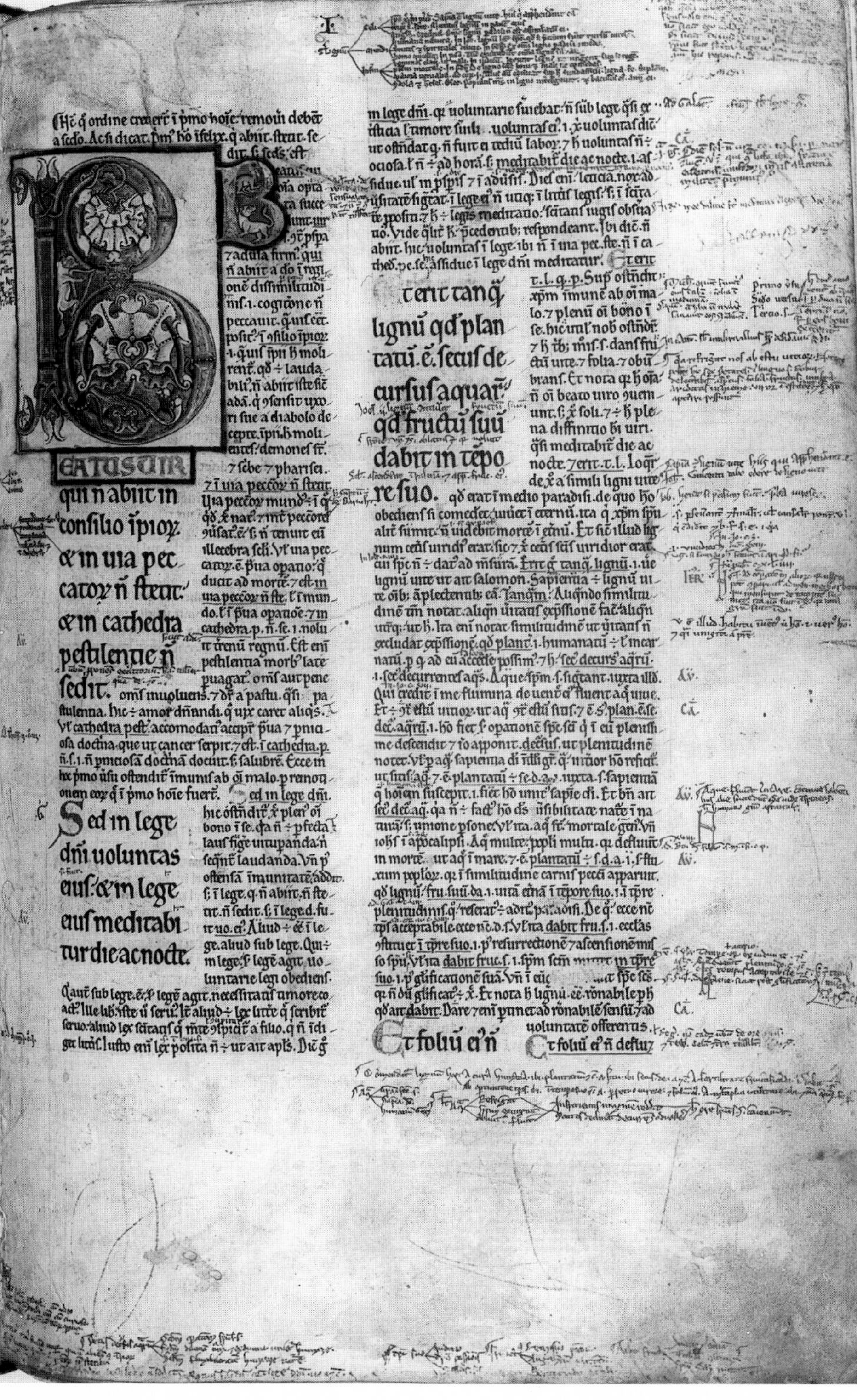

5. *Lombard on Psalms*, Utrecht, Museum Catharijneconvent, BMH h 4, fol. 1r

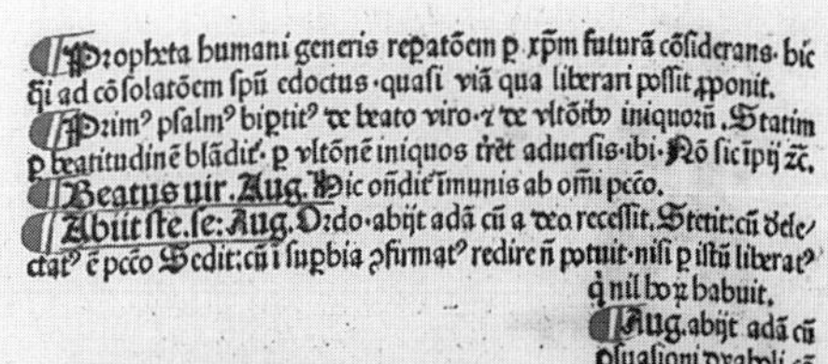

significandos. Primus penitentię in qua et prima psalmorũ quinquagena terminatur scilicet miserere mei de⁹. Secundus iusticię in qua et secunda quinquagena· misericordiam et iudicium cantabo tibi. Tercius status vitę eternę in cuius laudem tercia quinquagena finitur scilicet omnis spiritus laudet dominum.

Aug. Vnus est liber psalmoꝝ nõ quinq; vt in actib⁹ apostolorũ legit· sicuti scriptũ est in libro psalmoꝝ· hiero· tamẽ dicit q̇nq; libros ·id ẽ· quinq; distinctões q̃ fiunt per fiat fiat.

Ordo psalmorum ab ordine hystorię discordat. qr ante peccauit dauid cum vxore vrię· et de penitentia cecinit .mise· mei de⁹ q̃ filius eius cum p sequeret et cecinerit domine quid mult. sed ab esdra ,pphta instinctu diuino· ita ordinati creduntur.

Materia est integer christ⁹ sponsus ⁊ sponsa.

Intentio homies in adam deformatos xpo nouo homini cõformare.

Modus tractandi. Quãdoq; agit d xpo scd̃m q caput ẽ. Aliqñ scd̃m corpus. Aliqñ scd̃m vtrũq;. Scd̃m caput tripliciter· quia vel scd̃m diuinitatẽ· vt tecũ principiũ ⁊c. Aliqñ scd̃m hũanitatem· vt ego dominus ⁊c. Aliquando p trãsumptõnem vt quando vtit voce mẽbroꝝ sicut ibi longe a salute mea ⁊c. Item de ecc̃ia tribus modis. Aliqñ scd̃um pfectos. Aliqñ scd̃m impfectos. Aliqñ scd̃m malos qui sunt in ecc̃ia corpore nõ mente· numero nõ merito· nomie nõ numine.

ʃ Cui succedunt ʃ Contra prospera et omnia optata. aduersa firmus.

**Eatus uir qui non**

† ʃ A deo in regione dissimilitudinis quis impiu hoc molirẽtur· quod laudabilius. ʃ Cogitatione ʃ consensu. ·|· Positus. ʃ vt adã qui vxori consensit a dyabolo decepte.

**abiit in consilio impiorum· et in**

† ʃ In mũdo. ʃ In praua opatione que est via ad morte. ·|· ʃ Quia natus inter peccatores sed nõ tenuit eũ illecebra seculi· i· noluit terrenũ regnũ. ·|· ʃ Opere.

**via peccatorum non stetit: et**

† ʃ Pestilentia ẽ morbus qui fere oẽs inuadit et amore dñandi vix caret aliquis· vel cathe· p· ẽ pniciosa doctrina que vt cancer serpit ʃ docendo. ·|· ʃ Consuetudine.

**in cathedra pestilẽtię nõ sedit.**

† ʃ Quia in volũtate· nõ· sub· quasi ex tristicia vel timore

**Sed in lege domini voluntas**

† ʃ non litteris sed sanctitate ,ppositi.

**eius: et in lege eius meditabitur**

Psalm⁹ iste prim⁹ iõ videt carere titlo: qr de cõmẽdatõe xpi pricipalit loquit ad quem oẽs alij psalmi ptinent; qui loquũtur vel de passione vel de resurrectione· vel de mẽbris ipius· quare videt esse quasi titulus alioꝝ. vel secũdũ hieroni· ne titulus pscriptus libri caput et initiũ videret vel quia iste psalmus est quasi ,plogus et titulus sequẽtis operis· vel quia esdras nõ fuit ausus titulũ ponere· videns in sequẽti dauid in psona xpi hunc psalmuȝ caput libri appellasse.

Hiero. In hoc psalmo loquit ,pphta cõsiderans destructionẽ generis humani q̃ cõtigit p adam· et ex opposito puidens ,pphetico spũ reparatõnem p xpm futurã· et vt cõtraria cõtrarijs curent: vult eum omino reddere oppositũ et dissimilẽ priori adã· qr sicut ille destruxit se ⁊ humanũ genus p supbiã et inobedientiã· eodẽ modo xpus p humilẽ obedientiã suã reduxit quod destructũ fuerat culpa primi pentis ad vitaȝ· et pro hac cõsideratõe ,prumpit in laudẽ illius dicẽs· beat⁹ vir ⁊c. In hoc primo versu notãt tres mortes aĩmę· p tres mortuos a xpo resuscitatos designatę· p filiã archisynagogi resuscitatã i domo pris: designat illa mors· quã p delectatõem et consensum patimur tantũ in interiori. Per filiũ viduę extra portã resuscitatũ exprimitur illa mors quam patitur homo: dũ ducitur in opationẽ per prauã delectatõem ⁊ cõsensum. Per lazarũ iam fętentẽ ⁊ quadriduanũ designat illa quę ,pcedit ex cõsuetudine prauę opatõis· qua phem⁹ nos alijs exemplũ peccandi: ⁊ corrũpim⁹ alios sicut aer corrũpit fetore cadaueris· Rogãtib⁹ discipulis dominũ vt quartũ suscitaret mortuũ: dixisse fertur· dimittite mortuos s·m·s· hi sunt impenitẽtes ⁊ in pcc̃is sepulti.

Propheta humani generis repatõem p xpm futurã cõsiderans· hic hi ad cõsolatõem spũ edoctus· quasi viã qua liberari possit ,pponit.

Prim⁹ psalm⁹ biptit⁹ de beato viro· ⁊ de vltõib⁹ iniquorũ. Statim p beatitudinẽ blãdit· p vltõnẽ iniquos trẽt aduersis· ibi· Nõ sic ipij ⁊c.

Beatus uir. Aug. Hic oñdit imunis ab omi pcc̃o.

Abijt ste. se: Aug. Ordo· abijt adã cũ a deo recessit. Stetit: cũ delectat⁹ ẽ pcc̃o Sedit: cũ i supbia ɔfirmat⁹ redire ñ potuit· nisi p istũ liberat⁹ q nil hoꝝ habuit.

† ʃ ,psperis et aduersis. ʃ vel assidue ʃ Non ad horam. ·|· ʃ ad similitudinẽ· vel homo fiet secundũ opationem spũssancti vel vnitus sapiẽtie. vel insimilitudinẽ carnis peccati. ·|· ʃ vere· similitudinẽ cũ veritatis expressione.

**die ac nocte. Et erit tanquã**

† ʃ Christus viridior ceteris ·|· ʃ p quod ad eũ accedere possumus· ·|· ʃ Secundũ sapientiã

**lignum quod plantatũ est sec**

que homine suscepit· vel secundũ spũmsanctum vel secundũ fluxus populorum. † ʃ vitã eter

**decursus aquarum: quod fructũ**

nã ʃ Ecclesias constituet † ʃ Post resurrectõnẽ et ascensionẽ misso spũ. † tempe plenitudinis nõ est datus spũs· qr nõdum glorificatus est xpũs. ʃ Cũ exaltatus fuero a terra oĩa traham ad me ipsum·

**suum dabit in tempore suo. Et**

† ʃ ·i· verbũ eius nõ erit irritũ cũ celũ et terra transibunt ⁊c. ·|· ʃ Sed ducet ad vitam. ·|· ʃ ·i· fructus et folia· facta· et dicta. ʃ Qr etsi moritetur. tamẽ o·q·f·⁊c· quia et mors eius est salus mũdi.

**folium eius non defluet: et oia**

† ʃ Circa casum ade. ʃ sibi et mẽbris.

**quecunq; faciet prosperabuntur**

ʃ Sed † ʃ Qr nichil horũ poterunt assequi. ·|· ʃ Cas. immobilis firmitas ex repetitõne. † ʃ Cedũt suggestionibus· qr sunt sine humore gratie dei.

**Non sic impij non sic: sed tan**

† ʃ Qui prius conglutinatus in adã ante peccatũ oleo manãte a capite christo· nũc autem arefactus est. ·|· ʃ Ad similitudinẽ. ʃ ·i· Supbia quia inflat et petit alta.

**quã pulvis quez proijcit ventus a**

† ʃ Quia vẽtus ,pijcit. bene dicit eis tolli quod supbi ambiũt· i· vt iudicẽt. quod planius repetit neq; pec· in cõ· ⁊c. ·|· ʃ Non resurgunt in fide a peccatis

**facie terre. Ideo non resurgũt**

Aug. abijt adã cũ psuasioni dyaboli cõsensit. Stetit: dũ pomũ comedit. Sedit dũ se excusauit· mulier quã dedisti michi me seduxit. Ad similitudinẽ exulãtiũ q dũ sunt in via facili reuocant· dũ iaȝ stant: difficili⁹· demũ difficillime· dũ ibi magistri ⁊ dñi effecti sunt.

Remigi. Peccat cogitatõe· actu· et verbis docendo

Cas. Impius in deũ· peccator in se· pestilens in ,pximũ.

In cathedra. Dãs exẽplũ peccãdi.

Cas. Tronus regum· tribunal iudicũ cathedra proprie doctorum.

Cas. q̃si ita aiat. Nos q ecciditis p pmũ adã: pformami huic scdo: qr htũs p mo ɔtrarius.

Sed in lege. Aug. Cas. Hie plenus oĩm bono in se.

Aug. Nõ ẽ laus pfecta fugere vitupãda: nisi sequãtur laudãda.

Quo ordine creuerũt in primo remouentur a secundo.

In lege. Qui ẽ in lege scd̃m legẽ agit. qui sub lege scd̃um legẽ agit. Ille liber· iste seru⁹. Aug. Ambro. Aliud ẽ lex quę scribit seruienti, aliud q̃ mente cõspicit ab eo qui nõ indiget litteris.

Volũtas. Cas. Vt nõ sit tędiũ laboris· nec ociosa· s meditabit sp. Volũtas sensus ẽ sub lege. Ratõis in lege. Diuinitatis supra legẽ

Et erit. Cas. Hic vtilis nobis dãs fructũ vitę· et folia· et obumbrãs.

Beatus uir. Sed in lege. Et erit. Plena diffinitio beati viri. Hec omia nõ omi beato viro. s soli christo cõueniũt.

Tanquã. Cas. Secũdũ similitudinẽ ligni vitę qd est in padiso· vnde obediens homo comederet.

Lignũ. In padiso ẽ lignũ vitę· lignũ ad vitã. Et lignũ scientię boni et mali.

Aquarũ. Aug. Aquę spũssanct⁹ scd̃m illud q̇ crediderit in me flumina de vẽtre ei⁹ fluẽt aquę viuę et ẽ ɔtra ęstus vicõꝝ. Cas. Vel per aquã sapiẽtia dei· qua reficit iterioꝝ hõ· vt sitis aq̃. Aug. Vel mortalę gen⁹ vt iohes· aq̃ multę populi mlti· qr defluũt in mortẽ vt aq̃ in mare.

Dabit. Aug. Dare ptiet ad ratõnalem sensũ· ⁊ ad offerẽtis volũtatẽ

Et folia. Aug. Sicut folia fruct⁹ tegunt· ita verba dñi promissiones suas custodiunt

Et omnia. Aug. quid per singula.

Non sic. Hic de vltõe iniquoꝝ aduersis terret, hoꝝ formido gratiora facit premissa.

A facie terrę. Aug. Stabilitatis eternę· quia vt hec tra nutrit et continet hominem ita illa interiorem.

Ideo non resurgunt. Quia ,pijcit ventus· i· ideo quia dati sunt

6. *Psalms*, Strassburg, Rusch 1480, Utrecht, Museum Catharijneconvent, BMH Warmond i 1263 H, 2 fols, fol. 483v

[illegible]

Obligatio mandati consensu contrahentium consistit. et ideo per nuntium quoque uel per epistulam mandatum suscipi potest. Item siue rogo siue uolo siue mando siue alio quocumque uerbo scripserit mandati actio est. Item mandatum et in diem differri et sub condicione contrahi potest. Mandatum nisi gratuitum nullum est. nam originem ex officio atque amicitia trahit. contrarium ergo est officio merces. interueniente enim pecunia res ad locationem et conductionem potius respicit.

Gaius. l. ii. Mandatum inter nos contrahitur. siue mea gratia tibi tantum mandem. siue aliena tantum. siue mea et aliena. siue mea et tua. siue tua et aliena. quod si tua tantum gratia tibi mandem. superuacuum est mandatum. et ob id nulla ex eo obligatio nascitur. Mea tantum gratia interuenit mandatum ueluti si tibi mandem ut negotia mea geras. uel ut michi fundum emeres. uel ut pro me fideiubeas. Aliena tantum gratia interuenit mandatum ueluti si tibi mandem ut negotia titii geras. uel ut ei fundum emeres. uel ut pro eo fideiubeas. Mea et aliena. ueluti si tibi mandem ut mea et titii negotia geras. uel ut michi et titio fundum emeres. uel ut pro me et titio fideiubeas. [illegible]

[illegible] expediat ei cui creditur. quia liberum est cuique apud se explorare an expediat sibi consilium.

Paul. l. [illegible] Praeterea in causa mandati etiam illud uertitur. ut interdum nec melior causa mandantis fieri possit. interdum melior. deterior uero numquam. et quidem si mandaui tibi ut aliquam michi rem emeres. nec de pretio quicquam statui. tuque emisti. utrimque actio nascitur. quod si pretium statui. tuque pluris emisti. quidam negauerunt te mandati actionem. etiam si paratus esses id quod excedit remittere. namque iniquum est non esse michi cum illo actionem si nolit. illi uero si uelit mecum esse.

Gaius. l. [illegible] Sed Proculus recte eum usque ad pretium statutum acturum existimat quae sententia sane benignior est.

Paul. l. [illegible] Diligenter igitur fines mandati custodiendi sunt. nam qui excessit aliud quid facere uidetur. et si susceptum non impleuerit tenetur. Itaque si mandauero tibi ut domum seianam. c. emeres tuque titianam emeris. longe maioris [illegible] [illegible] [illegible]

[illegible]

7. *Digestum Vetus*, *c.* 1200, Leiden, Bibliotheek der Rijksuniversiteit, BPL 6 C, fol. 156v

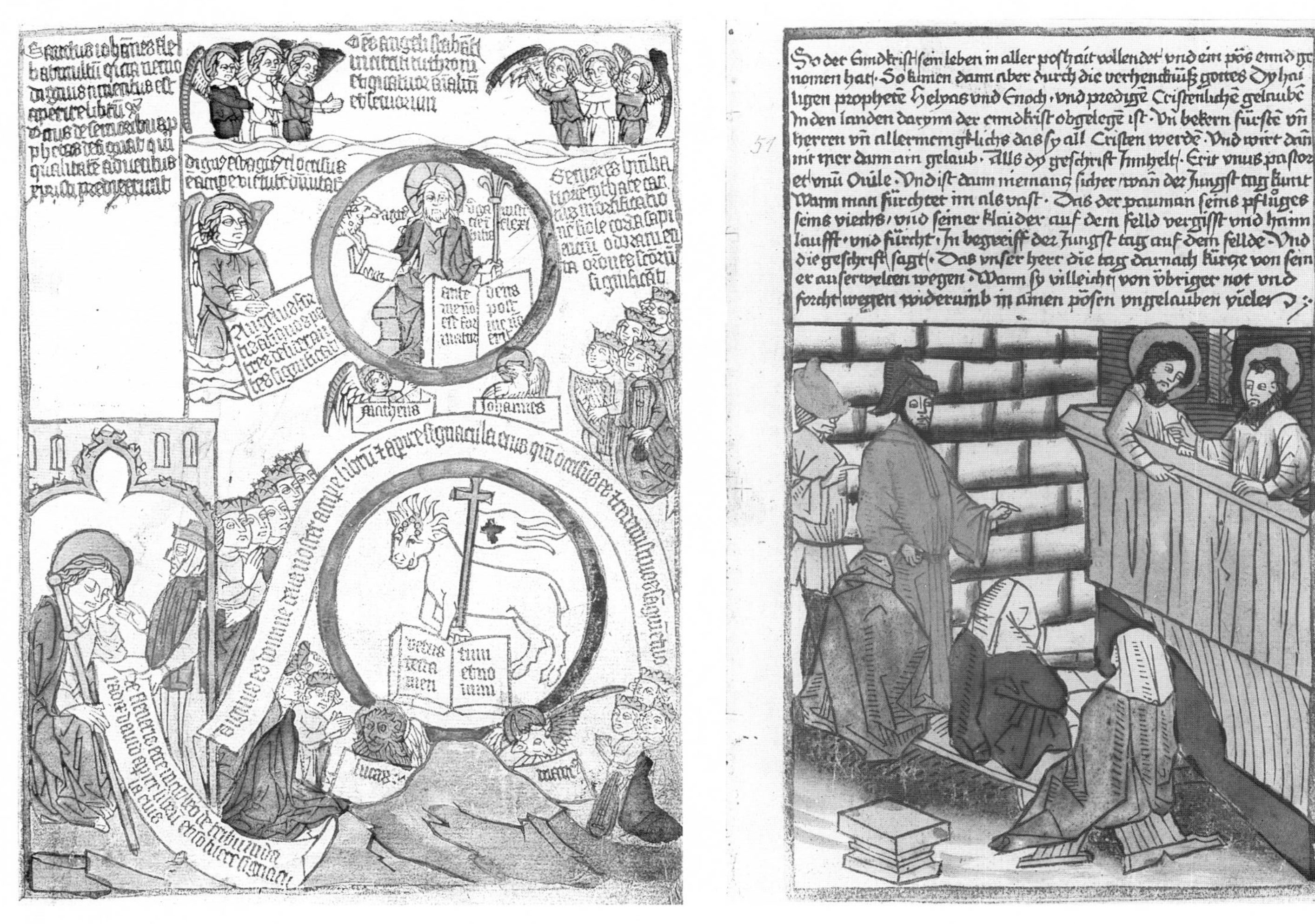


8. *Apocalypse*, John Rylands Library, 3103, plate v

9. *Antichrist und die fünfzehn Zeichen vor dem Jüngsten Gericht*, Bayerische Staatsbibliothek, Xyl, 1, Abb. 51

10. *Biblia pauperum*, Heidelberg, Universtätsbibliothek, Cod.Pal.Germ., 438, fol. 128r

11. *Biblia pauperum*, British Library, IC 45a, fol. v

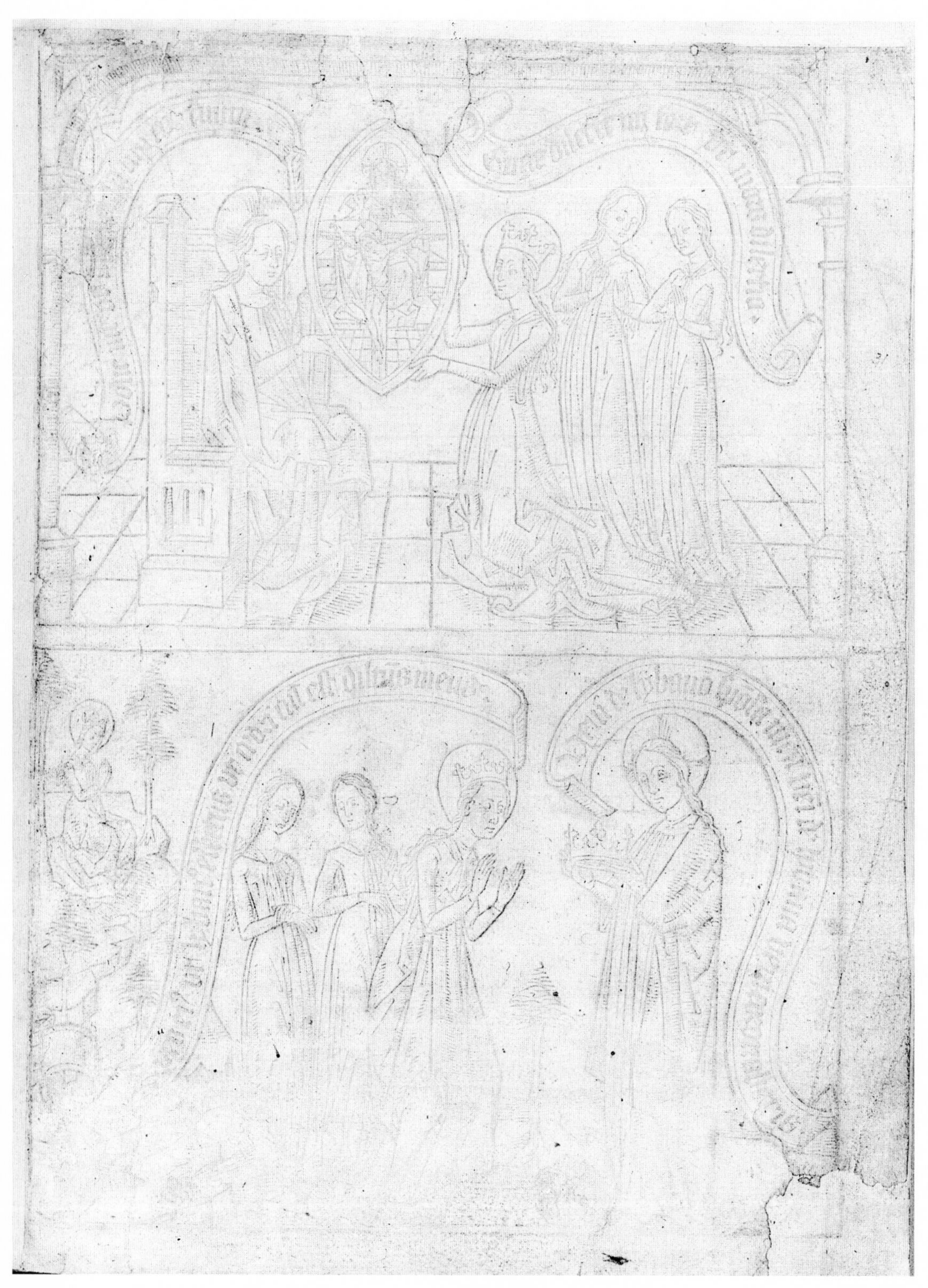

12. *Canticum canticorum*, British Library, IB 46, fol. 16[r]

13. *Historia David*, Innsbruck, Universtitätsbibliothek, 104 H 18/Stück 3, plate 9

14. *Ars memorandi quatuor evangelias*, Innsbruck, Universtitätsbibliothek, 104 H 18/Stück 2 ff.

15. Extract of Matthew, Scriptorium, VK Ms. 792, fols $2^{v}$-$3^{r}$

dum que ponit beatus Iheronimus in septimo capitulo primi prologi biblie ubi dicit quod materia quilibet librorum sit tractaturus

Incipit Registrum secundum ordinem librorum et continet in se in quo folio quilibet liber incipit et quot capitula quilibet liber habet
Genesis folio quarto et habet capitula l.
Exodus fo. xxi. ca. xl.
Leuiticus fo. xxxvij. ca. xxvij.
Numeri fo. xlvi. ca. xxxvi.
Deutronomy fo. lxi. ca. xxxiiij.
Josue fo. lxxiiij. ca. xxiiij.
Judicum fo. lxxxiii. ca. xxi.
Ruth fo. xcij. ca. iiij.
Primus regum fo. xciiij. ca. xxxi.
Regum secundus fo. cvii. ca. xxiiij.
Regum tercius fo. cxvij. ca. xxij.
Regum quartus fo. cxxix. ca. xxv.
Paralipomenon primus fo. clx. ca. xxix.
Paralipomenon secundus fo. cli. ca. xxxvi.
Oratio manasse fo. clxiiij. ca. i.
Esdre primus fo. clxv. ca. x.
Esdre secundus et neemias fo. clxviij. ca. xiij.
Esdre tercius fo. clxxiiij. ca. ix.
Esdre quartus fo. clxxix. ca. xvi.
Thobias fo. clxxxix. ca. xiiij.
Judith fo. cxciij. ca. xvi.
Hester fo. cxcviij. ca. xvi.
Job fo. cciij. ca. xxxxij.
Psalterium fo. ccxiij. ps. clxxi.

Sequitur registrum super secunda parte

Prouerbiorum fo. i. ca. xxxiij.
Parabole salomonis fo. vij. ca. vij.
Ecclesiastes fo. ix. ca. xij.
Cantica canticorum fo. xj. ca. viij.
Sapientie fo. xiij. ca. xix.
Ecclesiasticus fo. xix. ca. l.
Oratio ihesu filii sydrach fo. xxxiiij.
Oratio salomonis fo. xxxiiij.
Ysaie fo. xxxiiij. ca. lxvi.
Iheremias fo. lij. ca. lij.
Trenorum fo. lxxij. ca. iiij.
Oratio iheremie fo. lxxiiij.
Baruch fo. lxxiiij. ca. vi.
Ezechiel fo. lxxvij. ca. xlviij.
Daniel fo. xcvi. ca. xiiij.

Oseas fo. ciiij. ca. xiiij.
Johelis fo. cvi. ca. iij.
Amos fo. cvij. ca. ix.
Abdias fo. cx. ca. i.
Jonas fo. cx. ca. iiij.
Micheas fo. cxi. ca. vij.
Naum fo. cxiij. ca. iij.
Abacuc fo. cxiij. ca. iij.
Sophonias fo. cxiiij. ca. iij.
Aggeus fo. cxv. ca. ij.
Zacharias fo. cxvi. ca. xiiij.
Malachias fo. cxix. ca. iiij.
Machabeorum primus fo. cxx. ca. xvi.
Machabeorum secundus fo. cxxxij. ca. xv.
Matheus euangelista fo. cxl. ca. xxviij.
Marcus fo. cliiij. ca. xv.
Lucas fo. clxij. ca. xxiiij.
Johannes fo. clxxviij. ca. xxi.
Epistola pauli ad romanos fo. cxc. ca. xvi.
Epistola ad corinthios prima fo. cxcvi. ca. xvi.
Epistola ad corinthios secunda fo. ccci. ca. xiij.
Epistola ad gallatas fo. ccv. ca. vi.
Epistola ad ephesios fo. ccvi. ca. vi.
Epistola ad philippenses fo. ccviij. ca. iiij.
Epistola ad colosenses fo. ccix. ca. iiij.
Epistola ad Thessalonicenses prima fo. ccxi. c. v.
Epistola ad Thessalonicenses secunda fo. ccxij. ca. iij.
Epistola Thimotheum prima fo. ccxij. ca. vi.
Epistola ad thimotheum secunda fo. ccxiiij. ca. iiij.
Epistola ad thitum fo. ccxv. ca. iij.
Epistola ad philemonem fo. ccxv. ca. i.
Epistola ad hebreos fo. ccxvi. ca. xiij.
Actus apostolorum fo. ccxx. ca. xxviij.
Epistola iacobi fo. ccxxxiiij. ca. v.
Epistola petri prima fo. ccxxxv. ca. v.
Epistola petri secunda fo. ccxxxvi. ca. iij.
Epistola iohannis prima fo. ccxxxvij. ca. v.
Epistola iohannis secunda fo. ccxxxix. ca. i.
Epistola iohannis tercia fo. ccxxxix. ca. i.
Epistola Jude fo. ccxxxix. ca. i.
Appocalipsis fo. ccxl. ca. xxij. etc.

Laus deo

16. Richel Bible, Basel, 1477, Scriptorium, VK Inc. 765, fol. 526[r]

Incipit tabula canonum ut patet in primo prologo mathei qui sic incipit Beatissimo pape damaso.

Sciendum etiam ne quem ignarum ex similitudine numerorum error inuoluat. quod sicut in subnotatione canonum distinctorum in canone quolibet tres euangeliste bis vel ter vel quater aut etiam amplius eundem numerum per ordinem habuerunt adnotatum. Et quartus econtrario discrepans. quod id quod tres illi in eo loco semel dixerint. quartus totiens in corpore voluminis sui ponat. Quotiens diuisi numeri in eius canone positi sunt. ostendunt predictorum numerorum continuatas similitudines. Item si in vno quolibet eorum aut etiam duobus ibidem in canone numerus. bis. ter. aut eo amplius reperiatur in ordine collocatus et disparis inueniatur in ceteris dubium non erit quod id quod illius illorum ve rationes numerus. bis. ter. repetitum ab hiis in volumine semel dictum sit. Alteri vero eorum totiens in vno atque eodem sensu loquantur. Quotiens pretulerint in numerorum adnotatione distantiam. Hoc et in omnium ix canonum collatione seruabitur. ceterum in decimo quoniam propria singulorum tantummodo continentur non potest contra id comparatio esse quod solutum est. Incipit canon primus in quo quatuor.

| Matheus | Marcus | Lucas | Johannes |
|---|---|---|---|
| viij | ij | vij | x |
| xi | iiij | x | vi |
| xi | iiij | x | xij |
| xi | iiij | x | xiiij |
| xi | iiij | x | xxviij |
| xiij | v | xiij | xv |
| xiiij | v | xiij | xv |
| xxiij | xxvii | xvij | xlvi |
| xxiij | xxvij | xxxiiij | xlvi |
| xxiij | xxvij | xlv | xlvi |
| lxx | xx | xxxvij | xxxviij |
| lxxxvij | cxxxix | ccl | cxli |
| xcviij | xcvi | cxvi | cxx |
| xcviij | xcvi | cxvi | cxi |
| xcviij | xcvi | cxvi | xl |
| xcviij | xcvi | cxvi | cxliiij |
| xcviij | xcvi | cxvi | cxxix |
| xcviij | xcvi | cxvi | cxxxi |
| cxxxiij | xxxvij | lxxvij | cix |
| cxlij | l | xix | lix |
| cxlij | lj | xxi | xxxv |
| cxlvij | lxiiij | xciij | xlix |

| Matheus | Marcus | Lucas | Johannes |
|---|---|---|---|
| clxvj | lxxxij | xciij | lxxiiij |
| clxvj | lxxxij | xciiij | xvij |
| ccix | cxix | ccxxxiiij | c |
| ccxj | cxxj | ccxxxviij | xxj |
| ccxx | cxxij | ccxxxix | lxxxv |
| ccxx | cxxix | ccxlij | lxxxviij |
| ccxx | cxxij | cclxj | lxxvij |
| ccxliiij | cxxxix | ccl | cxlvj |
| ccxliiij | cxxxix | ccl | cxlj |
| cclxxiiij | clvj | cclx | xx |
| cclxxiiij | clvj | cclx | xlviij |
| cclxxiiij | clvj | cclx | xcvj |
| cclxxvj | clvj | lxxiiij | xcviij |
| cclxxx | clxij | cclxix | cxxij |
| cclxxxiiij | clxv | cclxvj | lv |
| cclxxxiiij | clxv | cclxvj | lxiij |
| cclxxxiiij | clxv | cclxvj | lxv |
| cclxxxiiij | clxv | cclxvj | lxvij |
| cclxxxix | clxx | cclxxv | cxxvj |
| ccxcj | clxxij | cclxxix | clvj |
| ccxciiij | clxxv | cclxxxj | clxj |
| ccxcv | clxxvj | cclxxxij | lvij |
| ccxcv | clxxvj | cclxxxij | xlij |
| ccc | clxxxj | cclxxxv | clviij |
| ccc | clxxxj | cclxxxv | lxxix |
| cccij | clxxxiij | cclxxxvij | clx |
| ccciiij | clxxxiiij | cclxxxix | clxx |
| cccvj | clxxxvij | ccxc | clxij |
| cccvj | clxxxvij | ccxc | clxxiiij |
| cccx | cxcj | ccxcvij | lxix |
| cccxiij | cxciiij | ccxciiij | clxxij |
| cccxiiij | cxcv | ccxcj | clxviij |
| cccxiiij | cxcv | ccxcj | clxvj |
| cccxv | cxcvj | ccxcij | clxxv |
| cccxviij | cxcix | ccc | clxxvj |
| cccxx | cc | cccij | clxxviij |
| cccxxv | cciiij | cccx | clxxxiiij |
| cccxxvj | ccv | cccxj | clxxxviij |
| cccxxvj | ccv | cccxiij | cxciiij |
| cccxxviij | ccvj | cccxiiij | cxcvj |
| cccxxxj | ccix | cccxv | cxcvij |
| cccxxxij | ccx | cccxviij | cxcvij |
| cccxxxiiij | ccxij | cccxxj | ccj |
| cccxxxv | ccxiiij | cccxxiiij | cxcviij |
| cccxxxvj | ccxv | cccxvij | cxcviij |
| cccxxxvj | ccxv | cccxix | cxcviij |
| cccxliij | ccxxij | cccxxix | cciiij |
| cccxlviij | ccxxvij | cccxxxij | ccvj |
| cccxlix | ccxxviij | cccxxxiij | ccviij |
| ccclij | ccxxxj | cccxxxvj | ccix |
| ccclij | ccxxxj | cccxxxvj | ccxj |

17. Richel Bibel, Basel, 1475, British Library, IC 37158, p. 459

is þt hous be not worþi:
ȝoure pees schal turne
aȝein to ȝou. & who
euere resseyueþ not
ȝou. neþer heeriþ ȝoure
wordis: go ȝe fro þt
hous or citee. & schake
of þe dust of ȝoure
feet. treuli I sei to ȝou
it schal be more suf-
frable to þe lond of
men of sodom & of
gomor in þe dai of
iuggement: þan to
þilke citee. lo I sen-
de ȝou as scheep in
þe myddil of wol-
ues. þerfore be ȝe sli-
ȝ as serpentis: & sym-
ple as dowues. but
be ȝe war of men.
for þei schulen take
ȝou in counceils: &
þei schulen bete ȝou
in her synagogis.
& to meiris or presi-
dentis & to kyngis:
ȝe schulen be lad for
me: in witnessynge
to hem & to þe he-
þen men. but whanne
þei take ȝou:

nyle ȝe þinke how
or what þing ȝe
schulen speke for
it schal be ȝouun to
ȝou in þt hour: wh[illegible]
ȝe schulen speke for
it ben not ȝe þt spe-
ken: but þe spirit
of ȝoure fadir þat
spekiþ in ȝou. & þe
broþer schal take þe
broþer in to deþ. &
þe fadir þe sone. &
sones schulen rise
aȝens fadir & mod[illegible]
& schulen turmente h[illegible]
bi deþ. & ȝe schulen
be in hate to alle
men for my name
but he þt schal d[illegible]
le stille in to þe ee[illegible]
de: schal be saaf.
And whanne þei
pursuen ȝou in þis ci-
tee: flee ȝe in to anoþ[illegible]
treuli I seie to ȝou
ȝee schulen not ee[illegible]
de þe citees of Is[illegible]
to fore þt mannys
sone come. þe disci-
ple is not aboue
þe maistir: ne þe

seruaunt aboue his
lord. it is inowȝ
to þe disciple: þt he
be as his maistir. &
to þe seruaunt: as
his lord. if þei han
clepid þe husbonde
man belsabub: how
myche more his
houshold meyne. þer-
fore drede ȝe not hem.
for no þing is hid:
þt schal not be sche-
wid. & no þing is þriuy
þt schal not be wist.
þt þing þt I sey to
ȝou in derknessis: sei
ȝe in þe liȝt. & þerfo-
re preche ȝe on housis:
þt þing þt ȝe heere
in eere. & nyle ȝe dre-
de hem þt sleen þe
bodi: for þei mowen
not slee þe soule.
but raþer drede ȝe hym
þt mai lese boþe
soule & bodi in to hel-
le. wheþer two spa-
rowis ben not seeld
for an halpeny: and
oon of hem schal not
falle on þe erþe wiþ-

oute ȝoure fadir.
& alle þe heeris of
ȝoure heed ben noum-
brid. þerfore nyle ȝe
drede: ȝe ben bettere
þan many spa-
rowis. þerfore euery
man þt schal know-
leche me bifore men:
I schal knowleche
him bifore my fadir
þt is in heuenes.
but he þt schal de-
nye me bifore men:
& I schal denye him
bifore my fadir þt
is in heuenes. nyle
ȝe deeme: þt I cam
to sende pees in to
erþe. I cam not to
sende pees: but swerd
for I cam to departe
a man aȝens his
fadir: & þe douȝter
aȝens hir modir.
& þe sones wijf a-
ȝens þe hosbondis
modir. & þe enemy-
es of a man: ben
homli wiþ him. he þt
loueþ fadir or mo-
dir moore þan me:

18. Wycliffite Bible, Scriptorium, VK Ms. 638, fols 17v-18r

MA THEVS

cubitū vnū· Et de vestimentis quid so
liciti estis?/Considerate lilia agri quō
crescūt· Non laborāt neq3 nent· Dico
aūt vob: qm̄ nec salomon in omni glia
sua coopert9 est sicut vnu3 ex istis· Si
em̄ fenum agri quod hodie est et cras
in clibanū mittiť deus sic vestit: quāto
magis vos minime fidei? Nolite ergo so-
licite esse dicentes q̄d manducabim9:
aut q̄d bibem9 aut q̄ operiemur· Hec
em̄ omnia gentes inq̄rūt· Scit em̄ p̄r
vester q2 his omnib9 indigetis·/Que-
rite ergo p̄mū regnu3 dei et iusticiam
eius: et hec omnia adijcienť vob· Nolite ergo soliciti esse i crastinū· Crastin9
em̄ dies solicit9 erit sibiip̄i Suffic̄ diei
malicia sua·

CA· VII

N/Olite iudicare et non iu-
dicabimini: nolite od̄enare
et non odemnabimi:/ in quo
em̄ iudicō iudicaueritis iu-
dicabimi: et in qua mensura mensi fue
ritis remetieť vob·/Quid aūt vides fe
stucam in oculo fratris tui: et trabē in
oculo tuo nō vides? Aut q̄uo dicis frī
tuo frater sine· eijciam festucā de ocl'o
tuo: et ecce trabs est in ocl'o tuo? Ypo
crita eijce p̄mum trabē de ocl'o tuo: et
tunc videb eijcere festuca3 de ocl'o frīs
tui/ Nolite dare sanctum canib9· neq3
mittatis margaritas vestras an̄ porcos
ne forte oculcent eas pedib9 suis: et con
uersi dirumpāt vos·/ Petite et dabiť
vob: q̄rite et inuenietis: pulsate et ape
rietur vob Omnis em̄ qui petit accipit:
et q̄ querit inuenit: et pulsanti aperieť
Aut q̄s est ex vob homo quē si petierit
fili9 suus panem: nunq̄d lapidē porrig3
ei? Aut si piscem petierit: nunq̄d serpen
tem porriget ei? Si ergo vos cum sitis
mali nostis bona data dare filijs vestris
quāto mag̃ pater vester q̄ in cel' est da
bit bona petentib9 se?/ Omnia ergo q̄
cunq3 vultis ut faciāt vob homines: et
vos facite ill'· hec est eni3 lex et p̄phete
/Intrate p angustā portā: q2 lata por
ta et spaciosa via est que ducit ad per
ditōnem: et multi sunt q̄ intrant p ea3
Quam angusta porta et arta via est q̄
ducit ad vitam: et pauci sunt q̄ inueni

unt eam· Attendite a falsis p̄phetis q̄
veniūt ad vos in vestimentis ouiū:/ in-
trinsecus sunt lupi rapaces A fructib9
eo2 ognoscetis eos· Nunq̄d colligūt
de spinis vuas: aut de tribul' ficus/ Sic
omnis arbor bona fruct9 bonos facit·
mala aūt arbor malos fruct9 facit· Nō
potest aūt arbor mala bonos fruct9 facere: neq3 arbor bona malos fruct9 fa-
cere·/ Omnis arbor que non facit fructum bonū excideť: et in ignē mittetur
/Igiť ex fructib9 eo2 cognoscetis eos
/Non omnis q̄ dic̄ michi dn̄e dn̄e intra
bit in regnū celo2: sed qui facit volun
tatem patris mei qui in cel' est: ip̄e in-
trabit in regnū celo2· Multi dicēt m̄
in illa die dn̄e dn̄e nonne in nomīe tuo
p̄phetauim9 et in nomine tuo d̄monia
eiecim9· et in tuo nomine virtutes mł
tas fecim9: et tunc ofitebor ill' q2 nunq̄
noui eos·/ Discedite a me oēs qui ope
ramini iniquitatē· Omnis ergo q̄ audit verba mea hec· et facit ea· assimila
bitur viro sapienti q̄ edificauit domu3
suam sup petra3: et descendit pluuia et
venerūt flumina· et flauerūt venti et ir
ruerunt in domū illam: et non cecidit·
Fundata em̄ erat supra petrā/ Et oīs
qui audit verba mea hec· et non fac̄ ea·
silis erit viro stulto qui edificauit domum suam supra harenā: et descendit
pluuia et venerūt flumina et flauerūt
venti et irruerūt in domū illam· et ceci
dit: et fuit ruina eius magna/ Et fcm
est cum osummasset ihesus verba hec:
āmirabanť turbe sup doctria ei9· Erat
em̄ docens eos sicut potestatem habēs
et non sicut scribe eo2 et phatisei·

CA· VIII·

C/Um aūt descendiss3 de mon
te· secute sunt eu3 turbe mł
te:/ et ecce leprosus veniens
adorabat eum dicēs· Dn̄e
si vis potes me mundare Et extendens
manum ihesus: tetigit eum dicēs· Vo
lo mundare· Et ofestim mundata ē le-
pra eius· Et ait illi ihesus·/ Vide nemi
dixeris: sed vade ōnde te sacerdoti et of
fer munus tuum quod p̄cepit moyses
in testimoniū illis· Cum aūt introisset

19. Richel Bible Basel, 1477, Scriptorium, VK Inc. 765, fol. 153r

[illegible]

20. Blasius Bible, Scriptorium, VK Ms. 648, fol. 247v[9]

21. Codex Wernigerodensis, Scriptorium, VK Ms. 799, fols $45^{v}$-$46^{r}$

NVMERI. Fo.50.

sacerdotis erit aqua amara deficere faciens. ℂEt adiurabit eam sacerdos, & dicet ad mulierem. Si non coiuit uir tecũ, & si nõ declinasti ad immunditiam sub uiro tuo, munda esto ab aqua amara deficere faciente hac. ℂEtsi declinasti sub uiro tuo, & polluta es, & dedit uir in te coitũ suũ præter uirũ tuũ. ℂEt adiurabit eam sacerdos adiuratione maledictionis, & dicet sacerdos ad mulierẽ. Det dominus te in maledictionem, & adiurationem in medio populi tui, cum dederit dominus fœmur tuum cadẽs, & uterũ tuum crepãtem. ℂEt ueniat aqua deficere faciẽs hæc in interiora tua, ut crepare faciat uterũ & cadere faciat fœmur. Et dicet mulier: Amẽ Amen. ℂEt scribet maledictiones has sacerdos in libro, & delebit cum aqua amara, & potum dabit mulieri aquam amaram deficere facientem, & ingredietur in eã aqua deficere faciens amara. ℂEt capiet sacerdos è manu mulieris oblationem Zelotypiarũ, & eleuabit oblationem coram domino, & offeret eam super altare. ℂEt capiet pugillum sacerdos de oblatione cum memoria eius, & suffire faciet super altare, & postea potũ dabit mulieri aquam. ℂEt potum dabit aquã. Et erit, si polluta fuerit, & præuaricata fuerit præuaricationẽ in uirum suum, ingredietur in eam aqua deficere faciens amara, & crepabit uterus ei⁹, & cadet fœmur eius, & erit mulier in maledictionẽ in medio populi sui. ℂEt si nõ fuit polluta mulier, sed munda est, innocens erit, & seminabitur semine. ℂHæc est lex Zelotypiarum cum diuerterit mulier sub uiro suo, & polluta fuerit. ℂVel si super uirum trãsierit spiritus Zelotypiæ, & Zelatus fuerit uxorem suam, & stare fecerit mulierem coram domino. Et fecerit ei sacerdos secũdum omnem legem hanc. ℂEt innocẽs erit uir ab iniquitate, & mulier ipsa portabit pœnam iniquitatis suæ.

Capitulum. 6.

ET locutus est dominus ad Mosch dicendo. ℂLoquere ad filios Israel, & dices ad eos. Vir uel mulier cum separauerit se uouẽdo uotũ Nazarei, ut separet se dño. ℂA uino, & sechar separabit se. Acetũ uini, & acetũ sechar nõ bibet, & oẽ madefactũ uuis, nõ bibet, & uuas recẽtes, & siccas nõ comedet. ℂOmnibus diebus nazareatus sui ab omni qđ fit è uite uini, ab acinis usq; ad corticẽ nõ comedet. ℂOmnibus diebus uoti nazareatus sui, nouacula nõ transibit super caput eius. donec compleantur dies quibus nazareum se fecit domino. Sanctus erit. Crescere faciat comã capilli capitis sui. ℂOmnibus diebus quibus se nazareum fecit domino ad animam mortui non ueniet. ℂSuper patre suo, & super matre sua, super fratre suo, & super sorore sua, non polluet se cũ mortui fuerint, quia nazareatus dei sui est sup caput eius. ℂOmnibus diebus nazareatus sui sanctus erit domino. ℂEt si mortuus fuerit mortu⁹ iuxta eum fortuito mox, & polluerit caput nazareatus sui, radet caput suum in die purificationis suæ, die septima radet illud. ℂEt die octaua afferet duos turtures, uel duos filios columbæ ad sacerdotem, ad ostium tabernaculi ecclesiæ. ℂEt faciet sacerdos unũ pro peccato & alterũ in holocaustũ. & expiationẽ faciet sup eũ de eo qđ peccauit sup animã & sanctificabit caput suũ die illa. ℂEt separabit dño dies nazareat⁹ sui, & afferet agnũ anniculum pro delicto, & dies primi cadẽt, qm pollut⁹ fuit nazareatus ei⁹. ℂEt hæc est lex nazarei. In die qua completi fuerint dies nazareat⁹ ei⁹ adducet seipsum ad ostium tabernaculi ecclẽiæ. ℂEt offerre faciet oblationẽ suã dño. Agnũ anniculũ pfectũ unũ in holocaustũ, & agnam unã anniculã, pfectã pro pctõ, & arietẽ unũ pfectũ p pacificis. ℂEt canistrũ ifermẽtatorũ simulæ, placẽtas mixtas oleo, & lagana ifermẽtatorũ uncta oleo, & oblationẽ eorũ, & libamina eorũ. ℂEt offeret sacerdos corã dño, & faciet hostiã p pctõ illi⁹, & holocaustũ illi⁹. ℂEt arietẽ faciet sacrificiũ pacificorũ dño i canistro ifermẽtatorũ. Et faciet sacerdos oblatonẽ ei⁹, & libamẽ ei⁹. ℂEt radet nazare⁹ ad ostiũ tabernaculi ecclẽiæ caput nazareat⁹ sui, & capiet cæsariẽ capitis nazareat⁹ sui, & ponet super ignem qui est subter sacrificiũ pacificorũ. ℂEt capiet sacerdos brachiũ coctũ ab ariete, & placẽtã ifermẽtatã unã è canistro, & laganũ infermẽtatũ unũ. & ponet sup uolas nazarei, postq̃ rasus fuerit nazareat⁹ ei⁹. ℂEt eleuabit ea sacerdos eleuationẽ corã dño, sanctitas ẽ sacerdotis, cũ pectore eleuatõis, & arm⁹ eleuatiõis, & postea bibat nazare⁹ uinũ. ℂHæc est lex nazarei q uouerit oblationẽ suã dño p nazareatu suo, præter id qđ attinget manus eius secũdum uotũ suũ, qđ uouerit sic faciet secũdum legẽ nazareatus sui. ℂEt locutus est domin⁹ ad Mosch dicẽdo. ℂLoquere ad Aharõn, & ad filios ei⁹ dicẽdo. Sic benedicetis filijs Israel dicendo eis. ℂBenedicat dominus, & custodiat te. ℂLucere faciat dominus faciem suam super te, & misereatur tui. ℂEleuet dominus faciem suam

G ij

22. Santes Pagnini Bible, Scriptorium, VK 708, fol. 50r

# Adam. I

ra in genere suo. & vidit Deus quòd esset bonũ. ¶26 Et ait, Faciamus hominem ad‖imaginem & similitudinem nostrã, & præsit piscibus maris, & volatilibus cæli, & bestiis, vniuersæque terræ, omnique reptili quod mouetur in terra. ¶27 ‖Et creauit Deus hominẽ ad imaginem & similitudinem suam, ad imaginem Dei creauit illum, ‖masculum & fœminam creauit eos. ¶28 Benedixitque illis Deus, & ait, ‖Crescite, & multiplicamini, & replete terrã, & subiicite eam, & dominamini piscibus maris, & volatilibus cæli, & vniuersis animãtibus quæ mouentur super terram. ¶29 Dixitque Deus, Ecce dedi vobis omnem herbã afferentem semen super terrã, & vniuersa ligna quæ habent in semetipsis sementẽ generis sui, ‖ vt sint vobis in escam, ¶30 Et cunctis animantibus terræ, omnique volucri cæli, & vniuersis quæ mouentur in terra, & in quibus est anima viuens, vt habeant ad vescendum. & factũ est ita. ¶31 ‖Viditque Deus cũcta quæ fecerat: & erant valde bona. & factum est vespere & mane dies sextus.

C A P. I I.

3 Benedicitur sabbathum. 4 Repetitio præcedentium. 10 Quatuor flumina paradisi. 21 Creatur Heua. 24 Institutio matrimonii.

IGitur perfecti sunt cæli & terra, & omnis ornatus eorũ. ¶2 Compleuitque Deus die septimo opus suum quod fecerat: & ‖requieuit die septimo ab vniuerso opere quod patrarat. ¶3 Et benedixit diei septimo, & sanctificauit illum: quia in ipso cessauerat ab omni

i.5.a.1, & 9.a. 6, 1. cor. 11. b. 7. coloss. 3. b. 10.
D
Sap. 2. d. 23. eccli 17. a. 1
Eccl. 17. a. 1, 6. matth. 19. a. 4, i. 8. c. 17, & 9. a. 1.
i. 9. a. 3.
Gen. 6. 9
Exod. 31. d. 17 eccli 39. c. 21 marc 7. d. 37.
A
Exod. 20. b. 11, & 31. d. 17. deut. 5. b. 14. hebr. 4. b. 4.

23. Estienne 1555 Bible, Newberry Library, Case C23 .48555, fol. 1r

24. Bible with tabs, Latin Bible, Fischer or Amerbach, Basel, 1492-4. Scriptorium, VK 659

25. Bible with *chasses*, Latin Bible, Fischer or Amerbach, Basel, 1492-4. Scriptorium, VK 659

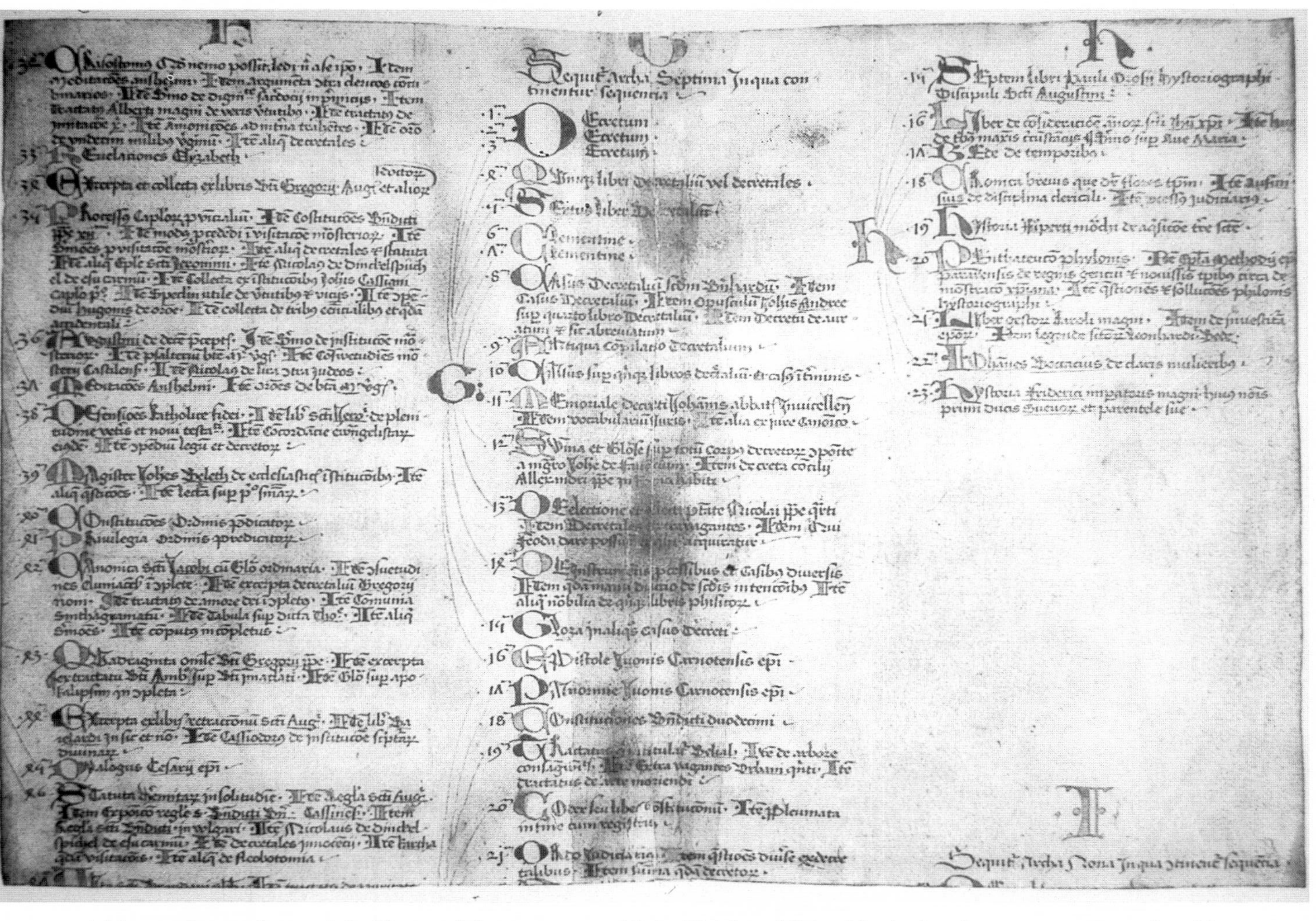

26. Manuscript catalogue of the library of the monastery of Saint Ulrich and Saint Afra in Augsburg, *c.* 1474, reproduced in *Mittelalterliche Bibliothekskatologe Deutschlands und der Schweiz*, 3 (1932), no. 17a

אשרי האיש אשר לא הלך בעצה א׳
רשעים ובדרך חטאים לא
עמד ובמושב לצים לא יש
ישב: כי אם בתורת ײ חפצו ובתורתו יהגה יומם ול
לילה: והיה כעץ שתול על פלגי מים אשר פריו יתן
בעתו ועלהו לא יבול וכל אשר יעשה יצליח: לא כן
הרשעים כי אם כמוץ אשר תדפנו רוח: על כן לא
יקומו רשעים במשפט וחטאים בעדת צדיקים: כי
יודע ײ דרך צדיקים ודרך רשעים תאבד:
למה רגשו גוים ולאמים יהגו ריק: יתיצבו ב׳
מלכי ארץ ורוזנים נוסדו יחד על ײ ועל
משיחו: ננתקה את מוסרותימו ונשליכה ממנו עב׳
עבותימו: יושב בשמים ישחק ײ ילעג למו: אז ידבר
אלימו באפו ובחרונו יבהלמו: ואני נסכתי מלכי
על ציון הר קדשו: אספרה אל חוק ײ אמר אלי ב
בני אתה אני היום ילדתיך: שאל ממני ואתנה ג
נחלתך ואחוזתך אפסי ארץ: תרועם בשבט ברזל
ככלי יוצר תנפצם: ועתה מלכים השכילו הוסרו ש
שופטי ארץ: עבדו את ײ ביראה וגילו ברעדה:

27. Hebrew Psalter in sixteens (first state, with vocalization added by hand), Biblioteca Palatina, Parma, Stampato De Rossi 123

אשרי האיש אשר לא הלך בעצת רשעים וב
ובדרך חטאים לא עמד ובמושב לצים לא ישב: כי
אם בתורת ײ חפצו ובתורתו יהגה יומם ולילה: וה
והיה כעץ שתול על פלגי מים אשר פריו יתן בעתו
ועלהו לא יבול וכל אשר יעשה יצליח: לא כן הר
הרשעים כי אם כמוץ אשר תדפנו רוח: על כן לא
יקומו רשעים במשפט וחטאים בעדת צדיקים: כי
יודע ײ דרך צדיקים ודרך רשעים תאבד:
למה רגשו גוים ולאמים יהגו ריק: יתיצבו מ׳
מלכי ארץ ורוזנים נוסדו יחד על ײ ועל מ׳
משיחו: ננתקה את מוסרותימו ונשליכה מ
ממנו עבותימו: יושב בשמים ישחק אדני ילעג למ
למו: אז ידבר אלימו באפו ובחרונו יבהלמו: ואני
נסכתי מלכי על ציון הר קדשי: אספרה אל חק ײ
אמר אלי בני אתה אני היום ילדתיך: שאל ממני
ואתנה גוים נחלתך ואחוזתך אפסי ארץ: תרעם ב׳
בשבט ברזל ככלי יוצר תנפצם: ועתה מלכים הש
השכילו הוסרו שופטי ארץ: עבדו את ײ ביראה

28. Hebrew Psalter in sixteens (second state), British Library, C.50.a.22

אשרי האיש אשר לא הלך בעצת רשעים ובדרך חטאים לא עמד ובמשב לצים

לא ישב : **אשרי האיש** מלת אשרי הוא לעולם בלשון רבים
זה הטעם כי לא יאשרו האדם בטובה
אחת שתמצא בו או בהצלחה אחת שתזדמן לו אלא הטובות רבות שימצאו בו יאשרו על ו אשריו וכ
וכלל דוד בזה המזמור תורת האדם ומה שראוי לו לעשות בזה העולם והגמול והטוב לצדיקים והעונש
לרשעים והוא מזמור נכבד מאוד לפיכך החל ספרו בו : ואמר אשר לא הלך בעצת רשעים ספר תח׳
תחילה הדרך הרע כמו שאמר גם כן סור מרע ועשה טוב כי מתחילה ילמד האדם מנעוריו דרך תאות
העולם הזה לאכול ולשתות ולשמוח ובהם הוא גדל ׳ כמו שאמר כי יצר לב האדם רע מנעוריו וכשי׳
וכשיעמוד אדם על דעתו ויוחל להכיר הטוב והרע הזהירו שיסור מדרך הרשעים ולא ילך בעצתם וה
והרשעים הם החביבים לקנות ממון והאוה לבם בעולם הזה ולא יבחנו בין הטוב והרע ויגזלו ויגנבו רי
ויהרגו בעבור הממון מרוב חרדתם כי ענין הרשע הוא החרדה כמו והוא ישקיט ומי ירשיע ובכל א
אשר יפנה ירשיע ולא ימלט רשע את בעליו אל תרשע הרבה ׳ ומפני זה כסך הלך עם רשעים ומסך
עמהם העיצה כי הם יושבים ויועצים בני אדם לשמוע אליהם ומראים להם פני דרך עיצה כי היא טובה
לאכול ולכנוס ולשמוח וברוב ישגה האדם בזה כי היושר בעיניו הטובה הנראה לו לעיניו ולא יביט ל
לאחריתם ׳ ואמר ובדרך חטאים לא עמד כי החטא יעשה אתו האדם בהיותו במקומו שקט במעשה
ובדבור ובלב ופירוש ובדרך אינו דרך ההליכה אלא המנהג ועסק האדם ומעשהו כמו והודעתו להם
את הדרך ויאחז צדיק דרכו מעשות דרכיך והרומות להם ׳ ופי׳ לא עמד לא נתעכב ולא השתדל עמהם
ולא עמד בחבורתם כדי שלא ילמוד ממעשיהם ׳ ואמר ובמשב לצים לא ישב והלצים הם הערומים
ברעה לרעה ומתגאים ומדברים דעות על בני אדם ונותנים דופי ומום בבני אדם ומגלים סוד זה לזה
והענין הזה לאנשים בטלים יושבי קרנות ומפני זה אמר ובמושב לצים לא ישב והנה בשלשה אלה כ
כל הכונות האדם או הולך או עומד או יושב והשכיבה בכלל ישיבה ועוד כי השכיבה לישן ברוב ובו
ובעוד האדם ישן לא יעשה לא טוב ולא רע וכאמרו אשרי האיש אשר ויום׳ הרי הזהירו שלא יע
יעשה כמעשיהם ועל זה מאשר האדם שנמנע מדרכם ומה שפירשו בו רבותינו ז״ל הוא מה שאמרו וכי
מאחר שלא הלך היאך עמד ומאחר שלא עמד היאך ישב אלא לומר לך שאם הלך סופו לעמוד ואם ע
עמד סופו לישב ואם ישב סופו ללוץ ואם לץ עליו הכתוב אומר ולמה לבך תשא :

כי אם בתורת יהוה חפצו ובתורתו יהגה יומם ולילה

**כי אם בתורת** אמר אם כי סר מדרך הרע ולא עשה טוב הנה לא השלים מעשיהו ולא יאמרו
עליו אשריו וכו׳ אמר סור מרע ועשה טוב ואעפ׳ שאמרו רז״ל ישב אדם
ולא עשה עבירה נותנין לו שכר כעושה מצוה הם גם כי פירשו והוא שבא דבר עבירה לידו וניצל מ
ממנה שנא׳ סור מרע ועשה טוב סור מרע על מנת לעשות טוב וכן הוא אומר אף לא פעלו עולה בד
בדרכיו הלכו והם חשבו מי שכבש יצרו למעשה כאילו עשה מצוה כיון שבא לידי עבירה אעפי שלא
פעלו עולה צריך שילכו בדרכיו ויעשו מעשה טוב ׳ וכן אמר אשרי האיש אשר לא הלך אלא מה
יעשה בתורת ה׳ חפצו ובכלל החפץ הלמוד והמעשה כמו עשות חפציך ולא יכשר המעשה מבלי הל
הלמוד ׳ ובתורתו כפל ובתורתו כמנהג הלשון כמו נח נ׳ פעמים במקום אחד וה׳ ישראל במקום אחד וא
ואחרים זולתם כי כן דרך לשון עברי ואמרו כי הוא דרך צחות ורז״ל דרשו בתחילה נקראת תורת ה׳
ולבסוף שהתחזק בה ללמוד נעשת תורתו ונקראת על שמו ופי׳ יהגה יהגה בלבו כמו הגיון לבי לפניך
כי כבר זכר התלמוד והמעשה ועתה זכר כוונת לבו ומחשבתו שיהיה היום והלילה מחשבתו על התורה
ועל המצות ולמי שמצוה עליהם בכל מעשה אשר יעשה כמו שאמר וכל מעשיך יהיו לשם שמים .

29. North-Italian Hebrew Folio Psalter, 1477 (with commentary of David Kimhi on leaf 2[a]), British Library, C.50.c.2

and nat excuseth synne. And
therfore the lawe saith that euery wycked custome shulde be do
away.

Here endith the firste p̄cepte.
and begynneth the secounde
precept. The firste chapter

Diues. I pray the en
fourme me nowe i yͤ
secoūde cmaūdmēt.
Pauper. What
doute haste thou therin Diues.
In the secounde maundemente
god byddeth that we shulde nat
take his name ī veyne For who
so dothe shal be gilty & nat passe
vnpunysshed Pauper. In thre
maners goddes name is taken ī
veyne. That is by mysliuyng.
by mys speche/ & by mysheringe
Firste by mysliuyng/ for whan
man or woman is cristned. thē
he forsaketh the feende and alle
his werkes and his lordshyppe.
Whan his god fader and his god
moder aunswere for him sayng.
Abrenuncio. that is to say I for
sake And there he knyttyth him
to criste. & makith couenaunte
with him to be his true seruaūte
withouten ende And there he ta
kethe the name of Cryste vpon
him and bicometh cristen For al
cristen people is named aft cryst
and he is oure principal godfa-
der For cristen cūmyth of criste.
and so alle cristen people bere yͤ
name of criste vpon theim. And
so in asmoche as we been cleppyd
cristē and goddes peple. in that
we bere the name of god vpon.
vs. And therfore sayth the pro-
phete/ Tu in nobis es dn̄e et no-
mē sanctū tuum inuocatum est
super nos: ne derelinquas nos do
mine deus n̄r. Jeremye xiiii. c.
Lorde sayth he thou arte amon/
ges vs/ as a lorde amonges his
seruantes/ and thyn holy name
is cleppyd vpon vs/ lord our god
forsake vs nat But if it be so. þ
we lyue natt after oure name/ þ
we haue taken of cryste ne lyue
nat as cristen men ne as goddes
seruauntes/ but forsake hym &
turne ayen to the feende and lyue nat as cristen folke/ but as ie
wys sarsyn or paynym or elles
worse. than take we goddes na
me in veyne. for our name and
oure lyf accordeth nat.
And as seynt poule sayth/ Wycked cristen folke with their wyc
ked dedys and their wycked ly-
uyng forsake god And therfore
alle wyckid lyuers and namely
ypocrites that bere the name of
holynesse and of cristes seruaun
tes. & wͭ þ they be yͤ feendes seruā
tes/ they take goddes name in



30. *Dives and Pauper*, Scriptorium, VK Inc. 100, fol. b1r

dide he. I slepte: þat is I res
tede me first in synful lif
& in slouþnesse: and I am roked
in my synne longe tyme þt
inne. and syþþen I roos. fro de
þe to lyue: fro ydelnesse to ern
se þt is ens in goddes seruise. &
þis nozt bi my self. bute for
my lord tok me to penaunce
and enspired myn herte for
to hate synne: & þerfore:
Non timebo milia. I schal
nozt drede þousendes of folk
comyng aboute me. þis lord
make me saf my god. þis
þousend of folk. ben alle þe de
ueles of helle & here tempta
ciouns & alle vices þat comeþ
aboute men to deceyue hem
& departe hem fro god. Bute
alle þese þay him nozt drede:
wham god haþ uptake. & þat
bit be so þis lord. þat is ma
ke me þise parfytly in to þi
lune & make me saf my god.
for þi lune saueþ fro drede of
alle þing. Quoniam tu percussisti
omnes. for þou hast smyten
alle contraryinge to me wiþ
oute enchesoun þe teeþ of syn
fulle þou hast al to broken.
þou schalt saue me & þou
schalt smyte þe deuel & al
le his lymes in dampnacioun
wiþ oute enchesoun he seiþ. for
no man haþ enchesoun to nuye
a riztful man. þat nuyeþ no
man. þerfore no man may
ben excused þt harmeþ a guod
man in word or dede: for alle

are holde to helpe him in his
nede & to lune his guodnes
se. þe teeþ of synfulle are þe
malicious gnawynges of bak
biteres & þe deceyuable wor
des of flatereres. þat crist schal
al to breke in here deeþ. for þan
þei schulle nozt cunne seye
yuel azenes riztfulle men. ne
guod of yuel men. whom now
þei flatereþ for awe: or for fauor.
bute þanne þei schulle lese
þe teeþ & brenne for hem in
þe feer of helle. Domini est
salus. of þe lord is hele &
on þi folk þi blessing. whoso[illegible]
þat is seyd & hopeþ in crist and
nozt in zoure self. for hele only
is of him. & he wole nozt sa
ue bute his lueres. and lord
on þi folk. þat is on echon of
vs be þi blessinge þt may brin
ge vs to þi lune. & so to end
les lif in heuene.
Cum inuocarem. when
I clepede here me god
of my riztfulnesse. in tribu
lacioun þou madest brod to me.
þe voys of riztfulle men.
when I incald. þat is inward
ly clepede Ihu crist in to my
soule to zyue me more gre
god zyuere & wyrkere of
my riztfulnesse here me. þt
is he zaf me my zernynge
þat was in profyt of my soul
le. & in wexing in his lune.
nozt in erþely þing. þis he
spekeþ to men tellynge. þat
god haþ herd him. and how he

31. The Rolle Psalter, British Library, Arundel Ms. 158, fol. 15v

than snowe. Therfore the prophete addeth to the same
verse. Lauabis me et super niuē dealbabor.
Lorde thou shalte wasshe me and I shall be made more
whyte than snowe. No creature may expresse how Joy
full the synner is whan he knoweth and vnderstondeth
hymselfe to be delyuered from the grete burden and he=
uynesse of synne/whan he seeth and perceyueth that he
is delyuered vtterly and brought out of the daunger of
so many and grete perylles that he was in whyles he cō=
tynued in synne/whan also he perceyueth the clerenes of
his soule and remembreth the tranquyllyte and peas of
his conscyence. Audit tunc quid loquatur in=
tra se dn̄s/qm̄ loquetur pacē in seruos suos
et in eos qui conuertuntur ad cor. Then he per
ceyueth well in his herte what our lorde wyll shewe in
hym by inspyracyon/what shall he shewe/euerlastynge
peas to come vpon his seruauntes/vpon them that be
sorowfull and do penaūce for theyr synnes/whiche peas
is so Joyfull and confortable and causeth so grete Joye &
gladnes that the prophete remembrynge it seeth. Au=
ditui meo dabis gaudium et leticiaz. Lorde
thou shalte gyue to myn herynge inwardly Joye & glad
nesse. If the peas of this tyme be so gretely to be desyred
to the inwarde herynge of our soule/what Joye trowe
we shal be at that tyme whan the peas euerlastynge shal
be offred to vs/whan the kynge of eternall peas shal saye
vnto all true penytent persones. Uenite benedicti
patris mei percipite regnū quod vobis pa=
ratum est a constitutione mundi. Come to me
ye blessyd chylderne of my fader/take the euerlastynge

32. John Fisher's *Sermons on the Psalms*, Scriptorium, VK 116 (de Worde, 1508), fol. 60v

Vulgata, hodierna

PSALTERIVM GALLICVM. I

Eatus vir qui nō abijt in cōsilio ipiorum/et in via peccatorum non stetit:& in cathedra pestilētie non sedit.

2 Sed in lege domini volūtas eius:et in lege ei⁹ meditabit̄ die ac nocte.

3 Et erit tanq̄ lignū quod plantatū est secus decursus aquarū :quod fructū suū dabit in tēpore suo.

4 Et foliū eius nō defluet: et omnia quecunq; faciet prosperabuntur.

5 Non sic impij nō sic: sed tanq̄ puluis quem proiicit ventus a facie terre.

6 Ideo nō resurgunt impij ī iudicio:neq; peccatores in concilio iustorum.

7 Qm̄ nouit dn̄s viā iustorū:et iter ipiorū peribit.

ROMANVM. I

Eatus vir qui nō abijt in cōsilio ipiorum/et in via peccatorum non stetit:et in cathedra pestilētie non sedit.

Sed in lege dn̄i fuit volūtas eius:et in lege ei⁹ meditabit̄ die ac nocte.

Et erit tāq̄ lignū:qd̄ plātatū est sec⁹ decurs⁹ aq̄rū:

Quod fructū suū dabit: in tēpore suo.

Et foliū eius nō decidet: et omnia quecunq; fecerit prosperabūtur.

Non sic impij nō sic:sed tanq̄ puluis quē proijcit ventus a facie terre.

Ideo nō resurgunt impij in iudicio: neq; peccatores in concilio iustorum.

Qm̄ nouit dn̄s viā iustorū:et iter ipiorū peribit.

HEBRAICVM. I

Eatus vir qui nō abiit in cōsilio ipiorum/et in via peccatorum non stetit: in cathedra derisorū non sedit.

Sed in lege domini volūtas eius:et in lege ei⁹ meditabit̄ die ac nocte.

Et erit tanq̄ lignū transplātatum : iuxta riuulos aquarum.

Quod fructū suū dabit ī tēpore suo/et foliū ei⁹ nō defluet:et omne quod fecerit prosperabitur.

Non sic impij: sed tanq̄ puluis quē proiicit vent⁹.

Propterea nō resurgunt ipij ī iudicio:neq; pctōres in cōgregatione iustorū.

Qm̄ nouit dn̄s viā iustorū:et via ipiorū peribit.

TITVLVS nullus. Psalm⁹ de Christo dn̄o. Est eni q habet clauē Dauid:& q claudit et nemo aperit/ apit et nemo claudit. Propheta ī spiritu loquit̄. Beatus vir: describit̄ Christ⁹. Impij:gētes/idololatre/ dei contēptores/peccatores/trāsgressores diuine legis et nature. cathedra pestilētie:pōtificū/scribarum et pharisеorū iudiciaria potestas/qua corrupti abutebātur. lex dn̄i:lex mosaica non passibiliter sed spiritualiter intellecta/et euāgelica. die ac nocte:iugiter/indesinēter. id Christo propriū est. lignū: lignū vite. decurrētes aque:quatuor paradisi flumina Geon/Phison/Tigris/Eufrates: quatuor riuis decurrētis sāguinis(Christo pendēte in ligno)respondētia. fructus:redēptio generis humani. Tēpus: tēpus passionis. Antichristus ex opposito diffinitur. et impij et peccatores per appropinquationē ad eū:vt pij et iusti per appropinquationē ad Christū. nō resurgūt:nō iustificātur/nō imutātur. Iusti: pij qui legē iplent. Ideo si Christus resurrexit ad vite imortalitatē:& pij ī die iudicij in cetu iustorū & sanctorū ad vitā resurgēt. Antichristus vero et ipij:nō resurgēt ad vitā/sed ad mortē secundā/que est tormentū indeficiens. et nō in cōgregatione iustorū:sed in cōsortio demonū iniustorū/ & dānatorū. Apoc. 3

1 EXPOSITIO CONTINVA. Propheta in spiritu loquit̄. Beatus vir qui nō abiit in cōsilio ipiorū/ et in via peccatorū nō stetit:et in cathedra pestilētie nō sedit. Hic vir beatus diffinitur:eū virū beatū esse et certā vite eterne salutē manere/q sentētijs nō adhesit cōtēptorū dei/q viā trāsgressorū latā nō intrauit:qui iudiciaria potestate pōtificū/scribarū/pharisеorū et aliorū pestilētiū iudicū deniq; hominesq; nō verentiū nō est abusus. 2 Sed ī lege dn̄i volūtas eius:et in lege ei⁹ meditabit̄ die ac nocte. beatus ille vir:qui nō modo priuato nec publico pctō peccauit/qui nō solū a malo abstinuit/sed mēs eius 3 tota in ipletione legis diuine versa est:et in cōtēplatione ei⁹ sine itermissione. Et erit tanq̄ lignū qd

b i

33. Quincuplex Psalterium, Estienne, Paris, 1509, Scriptorium, VK 737, fol. b1[r]

VII

34. Minuscule 234 (Codex Haunensis), Copenhagen, fol. 131v

35. Minuscule 234 (Codex Haunensis), Copenhagen, fol. 137v

36. Complutensian Polygot, Alcala: Arnald Guillen do Broca: 1514-17 (1522), Scriptorium, VK 399, fols KKii,v (Comma Johanneum)

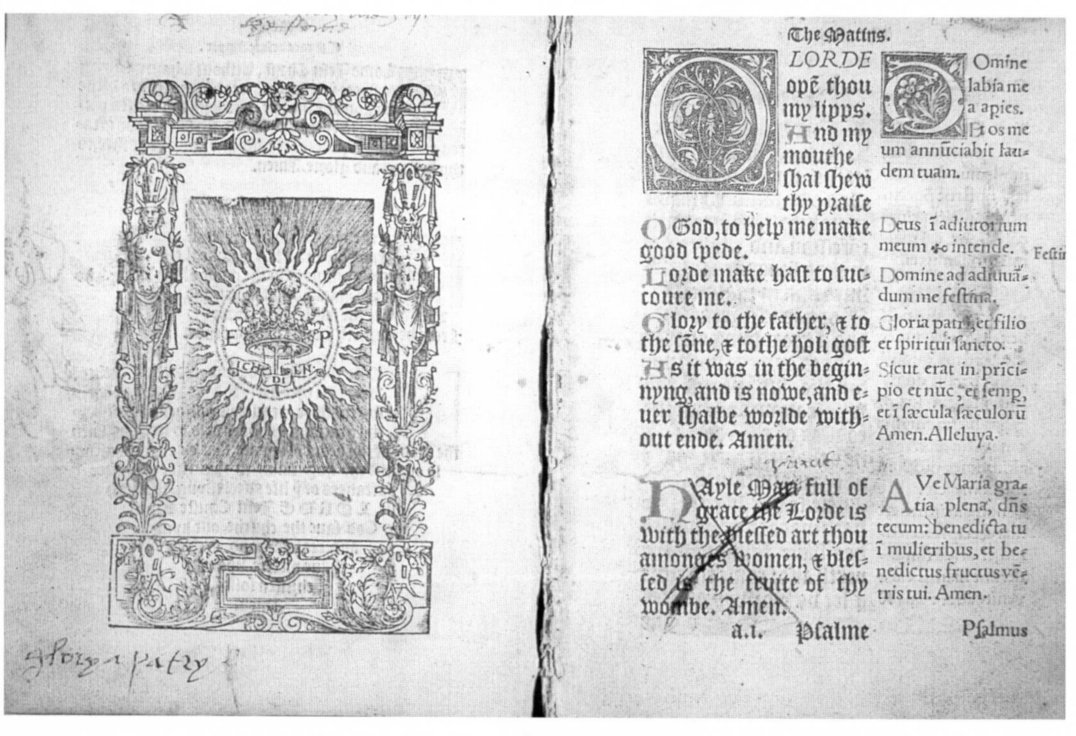


37. Primer, in English and Latin, with modifications by a Protestant user, Grafton, 1545, Huntington Library, RB 62311-2

Boke of remembrance. Malachi. Sunne of righteousnes. 366

9 Ye are cursed with a curse: for ye haue spoyled me, euen this whole nation.

10 Bring ye al the tythes into the storehouse that there may be meat in mine House, & proue me now herewith, saith the Lord of hostes, if I wil not open the windowes of heauen vnto you, and powre you out a blessing k without measure.

11 And I wil rebuke the l deuourer for your sakes, and he shal not destroy the fruite of your grounde, neither shal your vine be baren in the fielde, saith the Lord of hostes.

12 And al nations shal cal you blessed: for ye shalbe a pleasant land, saith the Lord of hostes.

13 Your wordes haue bene stoute m against me, saith the Lord: yet ye say, What haue we spoken against thee?

14 Ye haue said, *It is* in vaine to serue God: & what profite is it that we haue kept his commandement, & that we walked humbly before the Lord of hostes?

15 Therefore we count the proud blessed: euen they that worke wickednes, are set vp, and they that tempt God, yea, they are o deliuered.

16 p Then spake they that feared the Lord, euery one to his neighbour, and the Lord hearkened and heard it, and a q booke of remembrance was written before him for thē that feared the Lord, & that thought vpon his Name.

17 And they shal be to me, saith the Lord of hostes, in that r day that I shal do *this*, for a flocke, and I wil s spare them, as a man spareth his owne sonne that serueth him.

18 Then shal you returne, and discerne betwene the righteous and wicked, betwene him that serueth God, and him that serueth him not.

CHAP. IIII.

*The day of the Lord, before the which Eliah should come.*

1 FOr behold, the day commeth that shal a burne as an ouen, and al the proude, yea, and al that do wickedly, shal be stubble, and the day that commeth, shall burne them vp, saith the Lord of hostes, and shal leaue them, neither roote nor branche.

2 But vnto you that feare my Name, shall the b sunne of righteousnes arise, & health *shalbe* vnder his winges, and ye shal c go forth, and grow vp as fat calues.

3 And ye shal treade downe the wicked: for they shalbe dust vnder the soles of your feete in the day that I shal do *this*, saith the Lord of hostes.

4 d Remember the law of Moses my seruant, which I commanded vnto him in Horeb for al Israel with the statutes and iudgements.

5 Beholde, I wil send you e Eliah the Prophet before the comming of the great & f fearful day of the Lord.

6 And he shal g turne the heart of the fathers to the children, and the heart of the children to their fathers, lest I come h and smite the earth with cursing.

a He prophesieth of Gods iudgements against the wicked, who would not receiue Christ, when as God should send him for the restauration of his Church. b Meaning, Christ, who with his winges or beames of his grace should lighten, and comfort his Church, Ephe. 5.14 and he is called the sunne of righteousnes, because in him selfe he hath al perfection, and also the iustice of the Father dwelleth in him: whereby he regenerateth vs into righteousnes, clenseth vs from the filth of this worlde, and reformeth vs to the image of God. c Ye shalbe set at libertie and increase in the ioye of the Spirite, 2. Cor. 3.17. d Because the time was come that the Iewes should be destitute of Prophets vntil the time of Christ, because they should with more feruent mindes desire his comming, the Prophet exhorteth thē to exercise thē selues diligently in studying § Law of Moses in the meane season, whereby they might continue in the true religion and also be armed against al tentations. e This Christ expoundeth of Iohn Baptist, Matth. 11.13. who both for his zeale, and restoring of religion is aptly compared to Eliah. f Which as it is true for the wicked, so doeth it waken the godlie and cal them to repentance. g He sheweth wherein Iohns office shoulde stand: in the turning of men to God and ioyning the father and children in one vnitie of faith: so that the father shal turne to the religion of his sonne which is conuerted to Christ, and the sonne shal imbrace the faith of the true fathers, Abraham, Ishak and Iaakob. h The second point of his office was to denounce Gods iudgements against them that would not receiue Christ.

... turned to God in that great and vniuersal corruption, and also that this might be an example of Gods mercies to al penitent sinners. q When I shal restore my Church according to my promise, they shalbe as mine owne proper goods. r That is, forgiue their sinnes, and gouerne them with my Spirite.

38. Geneva Bible, Barker, 1576, Huntington Library, RB 17666

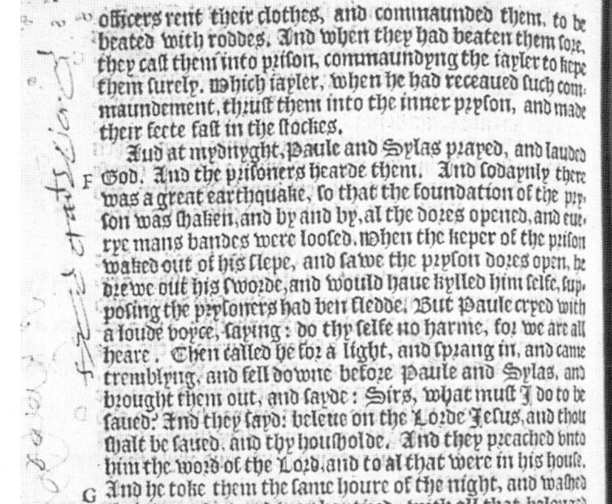

Cap.16. The Actes

officers rent their clothes, and commaunded them to be beaten with roddes. And when they had beaten them sore, they cast them into prison, commaundyng the iayler to kepe them surely. Which iayler, when he had receaued such commaundement, thrust them into the inner pryson, and made their feete fast in the stockes.

And at mydnyght, Paule and Sylas prayed, and lauded God. And the prisoners hearde them. And sodaynly there was a great earthquake, so that the foundation of the pryson was shaken, and by and by, al the dores opened, and euery mans bandes were loosed. When the keper of the prison waked out of his slepe, and sawe the pryson dores open, he drewe out his sworde, and would haue kylled him selfe, supposing the prysoners had ben fledde. But Paule cryed with a loude voyce, saying: do thy selfe no harme, for we are all heare. Then called he for a light, and sprang in, and came tremblyng, and fell downe before Paule and Sylas, and brought them out, and sayde: Sirs, what must I do to be saued? And they sayd: beleue on the Lorde Iesus, and thou shalt be saued, and thy housholde. And they preached vnto him the word of the Lord, and to all that were in his house. And he toke them the same houre of the night, and wasshed their woundes, and was baptized, with all that belonged vnto him straightway. When he had brought them into his house, he set meate before them, and ioyed, that he with all his housholde, beleued on God.

And when it was day, the officers sent the ministers, saying: let those men go. The keper of the prison tolde this saying to Paule: the officers haue sent worde to loose you. Nowe therfore get you hence, and go in peace. Then sayde Paule vnto them: they haue beaten vs openly vncondemned, for al that we are Romaynes, and haue cast vs into prison: and nowe would they send vs away priuyly? Nay not so, but let them come them selues and fet vs out. When the ministers tolde these wordes vnto the officers, they feared, when they heard that they were Romaynes, and came and besought them, and brought them out, and desired them to depart out of the citie. And they went out of the prison, and entred

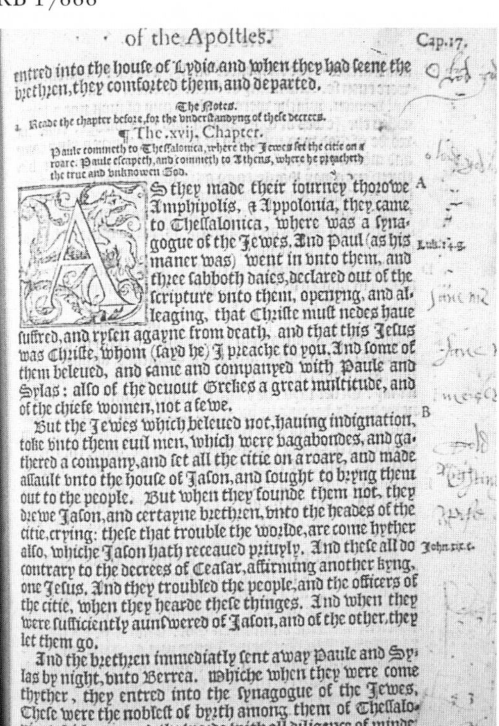

of the Apostles. Cap.17.

entred into the house of Lydia, and when they had seene the brethren, they comforted them, and departed.

The Notes.

1 Reade the chapter before, for the vnderstandyng of these decrees.

¶ The .xvij. Chapter.

Paule commeth to Thessalonica, where the Iewes set the citie on a roare. Paule escapeth, and commeth to Athens, where he preacheth the true and vnknowen God.

AS they made their iourney thorowe Amphipolis, & Appolonia, they came to Thessalonica, where was a synagogue of the Iewes. And Paul (as his maner was) went in vnto them, and three sabboth daies, declared out of the scripture vnto them, openyng, and alleaging, that Christe must nedes haue suffred, and rysen agayne from death, and that this Iesus was Christe, whom (sayd he) I preache to you. And some of them beleued, and came and companyed with Paule and Sylas: also of the deuout Grekes a great multitude, and of the chiefe women, not a fewe.

But the Iewes which beleued not, hauing indignation, toke vnto them euil men, which were vagabondes, and gathered a company, and set all the citie on a roare, and made assault vnto the house of Iason, and sought to bryng them out to the people. But when they founde them not, they drewe Iason, and certayne brethren, vnto the heades of the citie, crying: these that trouble the worlde, are come hyther also, whiche Iason hath receaued priuyly. And these all do contrary to the decrees of Ceasar, affirming another kyng, one Iesus. And they troubled the people, and the officers of the citie, when they hearde these thinges. And when they were sufficiently aunswered of Iason, and of the other, they let them go.

And the brethren immediatly sent away Paule and Sylas by night, vnto Berrea. Whiche when they were come thyther, they entred into the synagogue of the Iewes. These were the noblest of byrth among them of Thessalonia, which receaued the worde with all diligence of minde, and

41. Heavily used 1553 Tyndale New Testament, Huntington Library, RB 32153

39. Velvet Binding, front cover, Huntington Library, James R. Page Collection, no. 70F

40. Velvet Binding, rear cover (courtesy of the Huntington Library)

# EASTER DAIE

92

O steale hym awaye, & saye vnto the people, he is risen frome the deade. & the laste erroure shalbe worse then the fiste. Pilate saide vnto them: ye haue a watche, go youre waye make it as sure as you can. So they wente & made the Sepulchre sure withe ye watche men, & sealed the stone

## EASTER DAY

At mornyng praier in stede of the Psalme, O come let vs &c theis anthemes following shalbe songe or saide

CHRISTE risinge agayne frome the deade nowe dieth not. Deathe from hensforthe hathe no power vpon hym, for in that he dyed, he died but once to put awaye synne, but in that he lyueth, he lyueth vnto God. And so likewise, accompte youre selues deade vnto synne, but lyuynge vnto God in Christe Jesus oure lorde.

CHRISTE is risen agayne, ye firste fruictes of them yt slepe, for seynge yt by man Came death, by man also cometh the resurrection of the deade, for as by Adam all men do dye, so by Christe all men shalbe restored to life.

ALMIGHTY God wc throughe thy

Collecte.

42. Manuscript copy of the Psalter and the Book of Common Prayer from 1560/2 with decorative initial modelled after contemporary woodcut initials, Huntington Library, James R. Page Collection, no. 354

# S. BARTHOLOMEW.

knowe that the prynces of the nations haue domynion ouer them, and they yt are greate men exercise auctoritie ouer the. it shall not be so emonge you. But whosoeuer wilbe greate emonge you, lett hym be youre mynyster, & whosoeuer wilbe cheife emonge you, let hym be youre seruaunte. Euen as the sonne of man came not to be mynystred vnto, but to mynyster, and to geue his life a redemption for many.

## S. BARTHOLOMEW.

ALMYGHTY and euerlastinge God: wc hast geuen grace to thyne Apostle Bartholomewe, truly to beleue and preache thy worde: graunte we beseche the vnto thy churche, bothe to loue that he beleued, and to preache that he taughte, throughe Christe oure lorde

Collect

BY the handes of the Apostells, were many signes & wonders shewed emonge the people, and they were all togethier in Salomons porche. And of other durst no man ioyne hym selfe to them: neuerthelesse the people magnyfied them. The nombre of them that beleued in the lorde bothe of men and women grewe more & more, insomoche that

Epistle Act. 5

43. Pasted manuscript miniature from Huntington Library, James R. Page Collection, no. 354

COMMENTARIUS IN EZECHIELEM. CAP. XLVIII. 375

nominibus tribuum Israel, portæ tres a Septemtrione, porta Ruben una, porta Juda una, porta Levi una. 32. Et ad plagam Orientalem, quingentos & quattuor millia: & portæ tres, porta Joseph una, porta Benjamin una, porta Dan una, 33. Et ad plagam Meridianam, quingentos & quattuor millia metieris: & portæ tres, porta Simeonis una, porta Issachar una, porta Zabulon una. 34. Et ad plagam Occidentalem, quingentos & quattuor millia, & portæ eorum tres, porta Gad una, porta Aser una, porta Nephthali una. 35. Per circuitum, decem & octo millia: & nomen civitatis ex illa die, Dominus ibidem.

℣. 1. HÆc nomina tribuum, Metonymia, q. d. Hæc sunt nomina & hi termini portionum, seu possessionum singulis tribubus assignatarum: *a finibus Aquilonis*, id est, ad latus Aquilonare (a) terræ sanctæ: ex quo latere collocabantur septem tribus, inchoando longitudinem singularum a *plaga Orientali* (b) versus *mare*, id est, versus Occidentem. Ita Vatablus & Hebræi. Prima sors, proxima finibus Aquilonaribus, dabitur tribui *Dan*; ut a templo & a meditullio terræ sit remotissima.

℣. 2. *Super*; hebraice, *al*, id est, juxta (c) *terminum Dan*, extensum ab Oriente versus Occidentem, erit sors *Aser*.

℣. 3. Et juxta sortem *Aser* sors *Nephthali*; dein *Manasse*, *Ephraim*, *Ruben*, *Juda*.

℣. 8. Juxta *terminum Juda*, extensum simili modo versus Occidentem, *erunt primitiæ*, id est, portiones illæ terræ, quas primo loco & ante omnia segregandas esse sacerdotibus, & Levitis & civibus Jerosolymitanis supra (d) dixi, nempe *viginti quinque millia* cubitorum ab Aquilone versus Meridiem: & totidem millia cubitorum ab Oriente versus Occidentem: ut ex tribus illis partibus confletur perfectum quadratum: *sicut* fere habent *singulæ partes* tribuum prædictarum.

℣. 12. *Primitiæ*, id est, prima pars *primitiarum terræ* in tres jam dictas versu præcedenti portiones dissectarum, cedet sacerdotibus *filiis Sadoc* (e), eritque *sanctum sanctorum*) id est, sanctissimus locus, propter *sanctuarium*, seu templum in eo erigendum. Secunda pars primæ contingua & suppar

℣. 13. *Levitis* cedet. Et sicut primæ partis, ita & hujus *omnis*, seu utriusque lateris *longitudo* erit *viginti & quinque millium* cubitorum: & utriusque transversi lateris *latitudo* erit *decem millium*.

℣. 14. Ex utroque hoc Sacerdotum & Levitarum spatio, quia totum Deo sacrum erat, licet ædibus etiam pro habitatione laicorum, multis locis infessum & elocatum; tamen nihil poterat divendi laicis, vel cum locis alibi positis commutari, vel ad alios dominos transferri: sicut poterat

℣. 15. Ex spatio *quinque* aliorum *millium*, quæ *in latitudine supererant* ad perfectum quadratum 25000. cubitorum conflandum, de quo v. 8. & serviebant usibus primariorum civium, & *profana* erant, id est, *laica*, ut Symmachus & Theodotion vertunt. Porro civitatis hujus

℣. 16. *Hæ mensuræ* erant. Versus omnes quatuor plagas extendetur murus, & intra muros primariorum civium habitatio ad quattuor millia & quingentos cubitos: eritque urbis plane quadratæ ambitus octodecim millium cubitorum. Cumque latitudo spatii, quod urbi condendæ designabatur v. 15. esset quinque millium cubitorum, supererant adhuc 500. cubiti ad illud explendum, qui hic

℣. 17. *Suburbanis* (f) *civitatis* deputantur, nempe *ducenta, quinquaginta* utrimque.

℣. 18. *Quod reliquum fuit* ex 25000. cubitorum *in longitudine ejusdem* spatii, *secundum primitias sanctuarii*, hebraice, *juxta oblationem sanctam*; id est, juxta spatium sacerdotum Deo consecratum, quod longum erat 25000. cubitos: omne, inquam, illud spatium, *decem millium versus Orientem, & decem millium versus Occidentem*, adiacens spatio sacerdotum (hoc enim sibi vult istud, *erunt sicut primitiæ sanctuarii*; pro quo hebraice est, *juxta oblationem sanctam*, ut supra) serviet pro habitatione promiscui vulgi, item pro vineis & hortis, ex quorum proventu vel elocatione aletur *qui serviunt civitati*) magistratus, prætores, consiliarii, aliique ministri publici, omne genus, qui ex omnibus tribubus desumi poterunt.

℣. 20. *Omnes primitiæ*, id est, omnia hæc tria spatia, Sacerdotum, Levitarum & civium, primo loco decerpta ex tota terra sancta, (quæ continent simul *viginti quinque millia* cubitorum *in quadrum*,) non deserviant aliorum usibus, quam ministrorum sanctuarii seu templi, & civitatis seu civium.

℣. 21. *Quod reliquum* spatii *fuerit* a tribus illis portionibus usque ad Jordanem versus Orientem, & *usque ad* mare Mediterraneum versus Occidentem: *principis erit*) ut ipse utrimque ambiat, sepiat, muniat ac defendat Sacerdotes, Levitas ac cives suos.

℣. 23. *Reliquis* quinque *tribus* versus plagam Australem sua cuique spatia admetitur Angelus, extensa in longum ab Oriente in Occidentem. Proximum templo spatium obvenit tribui *Benjamin*. Huic vicinus erat *Simeon*: deinde *Issachar*: illi *Zabulon*: ultimo loco *Gad*, cujus

℣. 28. *Finis*, seu terminus, *Australis* erit idem qui totius terræ sanctæ, puta *Thamar*, *Cades & mare* Mediterraneum, ut supra (g) dixi.

℣. 31. Ex sequentibus describit duodecim portas civitatis Jerosolymæ; ternas ex quolibet latere, inscriptas nominibus duodecim tribuum Israel, forte quia ab illis extractæ, juxta ea quæ recenset Nehemias 2. Esdræ 3.

Notat Alcazar, portam *Ephraim*, quæ eadem est cum porta *Joseph*, ab Ezechiele poni ad *Orientem*, cum in veteri Jerosolyma fuerit ad *Septemtrionem*, teste Adrichomio, Villalpando & aliis. Simili modo permutat Ezechiel sortes *Judæ & Beniamin*, multarumque aliarum tribuum. Nam Josue 18. v. 5. tribus *Juda* constituitur ad *Austrum*, *Beniamin* v. 12. ad *Aquilonem*: hic vero prorsus contrario modo. Idem deprehendens in tribubus *Issachar*, *Zabulon*, *Gad*, &c. ut significetur, per Christum multa innovanda in Ecclesia, & primos fore novissimos, & novissimos primos: humiles exaltandos, elatos humiliandos.

℣. 35. *Nomen* quoque *civitatis ex illa die*, seu ex illo tempore quo restaurata fuerit, etiam innovabitur: nam pro Jerosolyma, id est, *visione pacis*, vocabitur *Adonai samma*, id est, *Dominus ibidem*) Quod typice & valde exiguo tempore convenit terrenæ Jerosolymæ: sed proprie & complete convenit Ecclesiæ Christi. Immo de hac sola hæc intelligunt S. Hieronymus, Dionysius, Lyranus, Vatablus, Hugo, Maldonatus, Pintus, immo etiam Thalmudistæ aliique Rabbini recentiores, quos citat Adrianus Finus. In hac distincti ordines Ecclesiasticorum, laicorum, & principum politicorum. In quadro est posita, quia pulcherrima simul ac firmissima, ut nec portæ inferi prævalituræ illi sint umquam. A singulis lateribus tres habet portas, quibus undique ex quatuor mundi plagis patet omnibus in eam ingressus. Hic, si uspiam, *Emmanuel*, id est, *nobiscum* (h) *Deus*; & Christus ejus, ipsomet promittente (i), *Ecce ego vobiscum sum omnibus diebus, usque ad consummationem sæculi*. Anagogico sensu perfectissime hæc omnia conveniunt Ecclesiæ in cælis triumphanti, cui idcirco S. Joannes Apostolus in Apocalypsi sua pene iisdem verbis omnia applicat. Et de illa absque dubio etiam Ezechielem intelligendam affirmat Rabbi Salomon, & plures alii Rabbini.

(a) Ezech. 47. v. 15.
(b) Ib. v. 18.
(d) Ezech. 45. v. 1.
(f) Ezech. 45. v. 2.
(g) Ezech. 47. v. 19.
אדני שמה
Adr. Fin. l. 1. Flagelli Judæorum cap. 8.
עמנואל
(h) Isaiæ 7. v. 14.
(i) Matt. 28. v. 20.
Apoc. 21. v. 10. &c.

D A

44. In universam sacram sripturam commentarius, Jacobus Tirinus, Antwerp, 1760, vol. II, p. 375, Newberry Library BS485 T6 1760

# THE PROBLEM OF THE MANUSCRIPT BASIS FOR THE EARLIEST PRINTED EDITIONS OF THE GREEK NEW TESTAMENT

*Michael Welte*

THE FIRST TWO PRINTED EDITIONS of the Greek New Testament appear in 1514, in the fifth of six folio volumes of the Complutensian Polyglot Bible (DM1412), produced under the patronage and at the expense of Cardinal Ximenez, and in 1516, with the Editio Princeps of Erasmus, prince of humanists (DM6096). These two editions represent the already mature fruits of the intellectual process opened by humanism. From the point of view of cultural history, modern times began with letterpress printing and a philological-critical analysis of texts. With regard to the biblical texts, new scholarship was based on a thorough knowledge of Hebrew, Greek, and Latin.

The Catholic Church after Ximenez and Erasmus – that is, the Catholic Church following the Council of Trent (1545-63) – discovered the value of the original texts of the Bible: 'before the Second Vatican Council the German Catholic bishops ... resolved to make a new translation of the Bible out of the original tongues for the use of the Church in order to enable a better possibility to have access to the word of God'.[1] An educational revolution marked the end of the Middle Ages – the original Greek had come to be printed in parallel with the Latin text in both of the earliest publications, and the Latin text itself was improved by Erasmus on the basis of the Greek.

The motivation for the work on the text of the Bible both for Erasmus and Ximenez was the basic humanist idea of returning to the sources in order to come as close to the original words of the biblical authors as possible. In the dedication to Pope Leo X, printed at the beginning of the first volume of the Complutensian Polyglot Bible, the editors say: 'We are impelled by many reasons to print the original text of holy Scripture. First, since no version can translate faithfully all the force and naturalness of the original, especially when it treats of the language in which God himself has spoken ... When in addition to this the Latin manuscripts of the Bible very frequently disagree among themselves, then there is sufficient ground to feel that they are corrupted by the ignorance and negligence of copyists, and that we must go back, as St Jerome ... and other ecclesiastical authors warn us to do, to the fountains of holy Scripture to correct the books of the Old Testament according to the Hebrew text, and those of the New Testament according to the Greek text. So that, then, those who love the holy Scriptures, not content with the waters of little streams, can quench their thirst in the same sources where issued the living waters that spring forth for eternal life, thus we have commanded to be printed the original texts of both Testaments jointly with its most principal and authorized versions.'[2] In the Preface to the Reader they further say: 'We have obtained especially to serve by their labour and study the most enlightened linguists, and we have taken for the archetype of our edition the most ancient and correct manuscripts. Our intention in undertaking this work has been to reanimate and cause to flourish anew biblical studies which up to now have been as though dead.'[3]

The editors (Antonio de Lebrixa, Demetrius Ducas and Lopez de Zunniga), as we know by contemporary sources,[4] were competent scholars of biblical languages. Their New Testament preface informs the reader that 'ordinary copies were not the archetypes for this impression, but very ancient and correct ones and of such antiquity, that it would be utterly wrong not to use their authority, which the supreme pontiff Leo X, our most holy father in Christ and Lord, desiring to favour this undertaking, sent from the apostolical library to the most reverend Lord, the Cardinal of Spain, by whose authority and commandment we have had this work printed.'[5] Of the large number of Greek New Testament manuscripts in the Biblioteca Apostolica Vaticana (224 text manuscripts and 119 lectionary manuscripts), no manuscript has been identified as having been consulted by the editors of the Complutensian New Testament up to now. Indeed, no Greek New Testament manuscript has ever been determined to have been the exemplar for the project. And yet one could fill a whole book with all that has been written about the importance of the Complutensian New Testament in the last 250 years. A recent Spanish introduction to the history of the Bible concedes: 'No es posible determinar con exactitud cuáles fueron los manuscritos que se utilizaron para realizar esta edición. Se sabe que algunos (antiquissima et emendatissima) fueron enviados de Roma expresamente. Los editores corrigieron en ocasiones el texto griego a partir del texto latino de la Vulgata. Tal es el caso del llamado comma johanneum (1 Jn 5, 7-8).'[6] That is, 'It is not possible to identify precisely which manuscripts were used for this edition. It is known that some ("antiquissima et emendatissima") were sent from Rome expressly for the purpose. The editors occasionally corrected the Greek text by reference to the Latin text of the Vulgate. Such was the case with the so-called "Comma Johanneum" (1 John 5: 7-8).'[7] This summary of the Complutensian Polyglot is not only inadequate but wrong in some respects and I will refer to it as the starting-point for my arguments.

First, a word must be said about the arrangement of the Complutensian New Testament. The colophon at the end of the biblical text mentions the date of publication as follows: 'Anno Domini Millesimo quingentesimo decimo quarto. Mensis ianuarij die decimo.' Two years later the colophon of the Erasmus edition was put at the end of the annotations which were added to the New Testament text: 'Mense Februario. Anno 1516.' As mentioned before, both editions have in common the original Greek text parallel to the Latin text. Small reference letters in the Complutensis denote corresponding Greek and Latin words. A space in the text, in consequence of an omitted word or otherwise, is filled up by special signs. The Complutensian Latin text represents more or less the conventional Vulgate text, the Erasmus Latin column represents his own revised Latin translation.

In nearly all Greek manuscripts the Book of Acts is placed after the Gospels, followed by the Catholic Letters, the Letters of Paul and the Book of Revelation. Erasmus follows the order found in the western translations, testified by the Canon Muratori, later used in most Vulgate editions as well. The Complutensis follows the order of a few Greek (Codex Sinaiticus among them) and Latin manuscripts: the Letters of Paul are placed after the Book of Acts, followed by the Catholic Letters and then Revelation. This order was used by Jerome, as well as in the Gutenberg Bible and in the German Bible translations before Luther, all based on the Vulgate. The Erasmus Edition provides annotations to the Vulgate text, the Complutensian New Testament includes a Greek grammar, followed by a Greek glossary with Latin equivalents. The preface at the beginning of the volume is addressed to the reader first in Greek and then in the Latin language. Certain additions are made based on Greek and Latin traditions: the epistle of Eusebius to Karpian about the correspondence of the Gospels, the prefaces of Jerome to all New Testament books and the υποθεσεις of Euthalius to all New Testament letters.

I return to the summary by Trebolle Barrera mentioned above. His first statement is true. In spite of every effort made in the last 250 years there is, up to now, no reliable identification of any manuscript used by the Complutensian editors in preparing their Greek New Testament. Nevertheless Franz Delitzsch, a hundred years ago, thought himself to have been successful. He was convinced,'dass wir, wenn nicht alle Zeichen trügen, diesen jetzt in Kopenhagen befindlichen Codex für einen in Alcala gewesenen und dem Bibelwerk zu Grunde gelegten erkennen müssen' ('if I'm not completely mistaken there is one manuscript now conserved in Kopenhagen that has to have been used in Alcalá in editing the Complutensian New Testament').[8] He is unfortunately mistaken. In the comparison of a series of manuscripts in different passages with the Complutensis, I have found that agreements and deviations balanced each other in most cases. Delitzsch's top candidate is the Codex Haunensis, Minuscule 234, dated 1278, containing the text of the New Testament apart from the Revelation, written by Theodorus Hagiopetrites, who worked as it is supposed in the Thessaloniki area between 1277/78 and 1307/08. Delitzsch's evidence is derived from the following three passages from the Letter to the Hebrews.

On fol. 131ᵛ (Hebrews 7.3; Pl. 34) of the Haunensis, which is written in two columns, there is, above the right column, the τιτλος (heading) of a υποδιαιρεσις (subdivided section) in accordance with the Euthalian divisions: εν ω οτι και του αβρααμ προετιμηθη. In the manuscripts there is usually a special sign in the margin at the point of the passage referring to this Euthalian κεφαλαιον (section), repeated before the τιτλος. Here you find the reference sign in the space between both columns placed too soon in the text: Hebrews 7.3. It should be found at Hebrews 7.6. The Complutensian editors misunterstood τιτλος as a supplement to the text and added it to Hebrews 7.3: μενει ιερευς εις το διηνεκες] add. εν ω οτι και του αβρααμ προετιμηθη (he [Melchizedek] continues a priest forever – taking precedence over Abraham). On this evidence, we see that a part of an Euthalian κεφαλαιον crept into the Complutensian text. Delitzsch claims: 'Eine Handschrift mit deren Vorgang sich diese Irrung entschuldidgen liesse, existirt nicht' ('There is no other manuscript with the same occurrence to verify it'). But there is at least one manuscript with the same occurrence, or better yet, the same mistake, because in this manuscript the same κεφαλαιον is found, not only assigned likewise to Hebrews 7.3 but even closer to the passage, in the margin next to it. It is minuscule 390, a Vatican manuscript of the Ottoboniani, a somewhat earlier collection. In both Minuscule 234 and 390, I have found a series of agreements with the text of the Complutensis.

In both cases in Minuscule 234 (Hebrews 9.8 and Hebrews 12.13) a word is spelled incorrectly and makes no sense at all (see Pl. 35). The first is πεφανωσθαι, which Delitzsch calls 'ein unerhörtes Wort' ('a tremendous word') and claims: 'kein Codex als allein der Haunensis enthält dieses monstrum' ('no other manuscript – Codex Haunensis alone contains this monster'). The word, which spelled correctly is πεφανερωσθαι (to be opened), is most certainly a slip but not at all unique to the the Haunensis. I found the same in minuscule 390. Delitzsch then continues: 'Theodorus hatte, als er dieses Stück des Hebräerbriefes schrieb, keine gute Stunde. Denn gleich im folgenden Verse (Hebrews 9.9) schreibt er: εις τον καιρον τον εστηκοτα für ενεστηκοτα' ('For Theodorus it was not a big moment writing this passage of the Hebrews. Just in the following verse he writes: εις ... εστηκοτα instead of ενεστηκοτα' – for the present age.') The copyist of minuscule 390 wrote τον ενεστηκοτα correctly at the same place. The word gets into Complutensis through this means, albeit with an alternate reading: instead of τον it is τουτον ενεστηκοτα. In Hebrews 12: 13 a similar error occurs. In both manuscripts 234 and 390, as well as in the Complutensis, there is τραχιας instead of the correct τροχιας. τροχιας means 'paths', τραχιας is not a Greek word.[9]

A collation of manuscripts 234 and 390 to the Complutensis reveals many such small agreements throughout, which are typical for a Greek text that does not depend on the Vulgate. Indeed, Delitzsch even found six additional manuscripts besides the Haunensis which were copied by Theodor Hagiopetrites. Since that time, we have discovered twice as many more. Beyond the three cited passages, minuscule 390 harmonizes with minuscule 234 in a number of other passages, and as such may be associated with Theodorus Hagiopetrites. The number of witnesses against Delitzsch's circumstantial evidence increases.

I return to the statement by Barrera. Expressing his opinion on the Complutensian Greek text, Barrera asserts: 'The editors occasionally corrected the Greek text on the basis of Latin Vulgate', taking up the old reproach that Ximenez had corrected the Greek text on the basis of the Vulgate. But Ximenez searched for the *veritas graeca*, expressing it in unmistakable terms. Barrera's statement, based on 'some passages', is an exaggeration. In general there is, as far as I see it, only one passage in which Ximenes corrected the Greek with the Vulgate: the so-called Comma Johanneum, a trinitarian addition in the last chapter of the First Letter of John (5.7) (see Pl. 36): οτι τρεις εισιν οι μαρτυρουντες] εν τω ουρανω, ο πατηρ, ο λογος και το αγιον πνευμα, και οι τρεις εις το εν εισιν. (For there are three who bear witness in heaven, the Father, the Word and the Holy Ghost; and these three are one.) In only four cases the editors of the Complutensis addressed textual problems in annotations. The note to the Comma Johanneum is one of those cases. By these cases alone, we learn something about their textual work.

Bruce M. Metzger in his Commentary, which is the best of all commentaries on the Greek New Testament, discusses the Comma Johanneum in detail: 'The passage is absent from every known Greek manuscript except eight, and these contain the passage in what appears to be a translation from a late recension of the Latin Vulgate. Four of the eight manuscripts contain the passage as a variant reading written in the margin as a later addition to the manuscript.'[10] The eight manuscripts are the minuscules 61, 88[vr], 221[vr], 429[vr], 636[vr], 918, 2318, 2473.

Why was this passage not quoted by the Greek Church Fathers? It would have been a primary text in the Trinitarian controversies. But indeed, the passage is absent from the manuscripts of all ancient versions. Nevertheless, the inclusion of the Comma Johanneum is not the point. The matter in question is an omission after it, where the earthly witnesses are spoken about: και τρεις εισιν οι μαρτυρουντες επι γης, το πνευμα και το υδωρ και το αιμα (and there are three that bear witness in earth, the spirit and the water and the blood) followed by a passage which is testified by the Greek manuscripts omitting the trinitarian addition, that is, in all except eight: και οι τρεις (το πνευμα και το υδωρ και το αιμα) εις το εν εισιν (and these three – the spirit and the water and the blood – agree in one). Omitting the latter passage here is the real issue, and not the inclusion of the Comma Johanneum. The annotations only give reasons for the passage after it: *hoc in veris exemplaribus non habetur. sed dicitur esse appositum ab hereticis arrianis ad pervertendum intellectum sanum auctoritatis premisse de unitate essentie trium personarum.* Jerry H. Bentley, who has shed new light on the editing of the Complutensian New Testament in his study of 1980,[11] was nevertheless incorrect in proposing that the editors included the Comma Johanneum because they assumed '... the Vulgate to be more accurate than their Greek manuscripts, they translated the comma from Latin into Greek, citing then the text of the Comma Johanneum. Bentley fails to mention the passage following.

A second, but slightly different, argument involves the annotation at Matthew 6.13. The text reads: '*In exemplaribus grecorum post hec verba orationis dominice, videlicet, Sed libera nos a malo, statim sequitur*: οτι σου εστιν η βασιλεια και η δυναμις και η δοξα εις τους αιωνας' ('For thine is the kingdom, and the power, and the glory, for ever.') After that the editors give reason for the omission of this expansion at the close of the Lord's prayer which they had found in other Greek manuscripts: '*magis credibile videtur quod ista verba non sint de integritate orationis dominice, sed quod vicio aliquorum scriptorum fuerunt hic inserta, nam videntes, quod publice dicerent in missa, crediderunt esse de textu.*' The editors realized that receiving an expansion of the text means to receive a later adaption to liturgical use, in this case, closing the Lord's prayer by these words.

Both annotations to the First Letter of Paul to the Corinthians are also examples of textual decisions by the editors in the face of a split tradition in the Greek text. At chapter 13.3 they say: '*In aliis exemplaribus grecis habetur* καυχησομαι.' This alternate reading is cited on the witness of Jerome: 'καυχησομαι, *id est* glorier, *ut ait beatus Hieronymus super epistola ad galatas capit. 5. Vide ibi.*' The editors realized the necessity of noting this. And indeed: up to this day there is the dispute, whether Paul has written εαν παραδω το σωμα μου ινα καυθησομαι or ινα καυχησομαι (if I deliver my body to be burned or in order to boast) – important, of course, for the exegesis.

The annotation to I Corinthians 15.51 starts as well with the premise that there is an alternate reading to the edited Greek text: '*Alia littera graeca habet* παντες μεν ουν κοιμηθησομεθα, αλλ ου παντες αλλαγησομεθα' and goes on: '*id est: omnes quidem igitur dormiemus, sed non omnes immutabimur*' ('We shall all therefore sleep, but we shall not all be transformed'). The agreement of the Greek text and its Latin translation is to be found only here in the margin. In the edition, there is a considerable difference between the original text and its translation. In the Greek column the editors say: 'παντες μεν ου κοιμηθησομεθα, παντες δε αλλαγησομθα' ('We shall not all sleep, but we shall all be transformed') and in the Latin: 'omnes quidem resurgemus, sed non omnes immutabimur' ('We shall all rise, but we shall not all be transformed'). On the evidence of these four annotations, Bentley made a hasty judgement: 'all four notes betray a deep respect for the Vulgate: in no case did the editors tailor the Vulgate to fit the Greek text ... they declined to employ their talents except in the service of traditional Latin orthodoxy'.[12] Did he read the sources carefully enough? He is not right, for instance, in his commentary to the latter annotation, claiming: the editors 'only cited an alternate reading in the Greek text reported by Jerome'. No, they neither say 'ut ait' nor 'ut dicit beatus Hieronymus'. They only say: 'Vide de hoc in epistola ad Miner[v]ium & Alexandrum de resurrectione carnis.' At the end of his explications to this passage Jerome says: 'hoc, quod in Latinis codicibus legitur: omnes quidem resurgemus, non omnes autem inmutabimur, in Graecis voluminibus non haberi, sed vel: omnes dormiemus, non omnes autem inmutabimur vel: non omnes dormiemus, omnes autem inmutabimur (that which can be read in Latin manuscripts: 'We shall all rise, but we shall not all be transformed' can't be in Greek manuscripts, but rather: 'We shall all sleep, but we shall not all be transformed' or: 'We shall not all sleep, but we shall all be transformed').[13] By this we are informed in detail about the difference both within the Greek manuscript tradition as well as between the original Greek and its Latin translation.

Although Jerome presents a number of alternate readings to this passage in his letter, there is not one which corresponds exactly with the wording of the Complutensian annotation. The editors could have used the one or the other in order to adapt the Greek to the Vulgate, but they did not. They put the younger text in the margin and left the Vulgate untouched in its column, for *veritas graeca*, not *veritas vulgata*, was the goal. In both columns of the Complutensian New Testament there is material enough to prove the editors' claim. For now it appears that there are several manuscripts very close to the Greek text of the Complutensis, and the editors of the Complutensis remained true to the Greek manuscripts they used.

On the whole the Complutensian New Testament represents the Majority Text as it is known and as such has influenced subsequent editions of the Greek New Testament as well as the translations of its original text into modern European languages. As a result of extensive collations in the Institute for New Testament Textual Research, certain uniquely Greek readings may be identified, in spite of the fact that such readings are found in some manuscripts representing a different text. In other words, the search continues for the manuscript exemplars for the Complutensian Polyglot New Testament.

## NOTES

1 'An die Leser dieser Ausgabe,' *Einheitsübersetzung der Heiligen Schrift, Neues Testament* (Stuttgart: Katholische Bibelanstalt, 1979).

2 Cited by the translation of Basil Hall, in *Studies in Church History* v, ed. by G. J. Cuming (Leiden, 1969), p. 126.

3 ibid.

4 Juan de Vallejo, *Memorial de la vida de fray Francisco Jimenez de Cisneros*, ed. by Antonio

de la Torre y del Cerro (Madrid: Bailly-Bailliere, 1913); Alvar Gómez de Castro, *De rebus gestis a Francisco Ximenio Cisnerio, archiepiscopo toletano, libri octo* (Alcalá: Andream de Angulo, 1569); Mariano Revilla Rico, *La Poliglota de Alcalá* (Madrid, Imp. Helénica: 1917).

5 Cited by the translation of James P. R. Lyell, *Cardinal Ximenes* (London: Grafton, 1917), p. 39. The orignal text says: 'Illud lectorem non lateat, non quevis exemplaria impressioni huic archetypa fuisse, sed antiquissima emendatissimaque, ac tante praeterea vetustatis, ut fidem eis abrogare nefas videatur. Que sanctissimus in christo pater et dominus noster, Leo decimus pontifex maximus huic instituto favere cupiens ex apostolica bibliotheca educta misit ad Reverendissimum dominum Cardinalem hispanie.'

6 Julio Trebolle Barrera, *La Biblia judía y la Biblia cristiana: introducción a la historia de la Biblia* (Madrid: Trotta, 1993), p. 353.

7 Translated by Timothy Graham.

8 Franz Delitzsch, *Fortgesetzte Studien zur Entstehungsgeschichte der Compluten-sischen Polyglotte* (Leipzig: Alexander Edelmann, 1886), p. 41.

9 See ibid., pp. 41f.

10 See Bruce Metzger, *A Textual Commentary on the Greek New Testament* (Stuttgart: Deutsche Bibelgesellschaft, 2nd edn, 1994).

11 Jerry H. Bentley, 'New Light on the Editing of the Complutensian New Testament', in *Bibliothèque d'Humanisme et Renaissance, Travaux et Documents* XLII (Geneva: 1980).

12 Jerry H. Bentley, *Humanists and Holy Writ* (Princeton, N.J.: University Press, 1983), pp. 95-7.

13 Epistula119, in 'Sancti Hieronymi Epistulae', recensuit Isidorus Hilberg, *Corpus Sanctorum Ecclesiasticorum Latinorum* LV, pt II (Leipzig: 1912), p. 469.

# 'THE BOOK THUS PUT IN EVERY VULGAR HAND'

## IMPRESSIONS OF READERS IN EARLY ENGLISH PRINTED BIBLES

*William H. Sherman*

'These Bibles have been used.' – S. L. Greenslade[1]

ONE OF THE MOST GENERAL PROCESSES which these papers have set out to explore is how the Bible emerges from the manuscript tradition and, under the influence of the twin forces of printing and Protestantism, becomes a layman's book. To gain a fuller appreciation of this trajectory, we need to pursue the Book beyond the limits imposed by traditional bibliographical study and examine (to borrow John Dryden's decidedly ambivalent formulation) 'the Book thus put in every vulgar hand';[2] to look not only at its production by translators, editors and printers, and its circulation by distributors and booksellers, but at its reception and use by readers. For obvious reasons (involving a complex set of devotional, ecclesiastical and economic factors), attending to these later stages in what has been called 'the communication circuit'[3] is especially relevant to the study of Scriptural texts. Within the English context, these factors became more sharply defined, and more hotly debated, as they interacted in the chain of events and editions leading up to the Authorized Version of 1611. At the risk of moving away, not only from this volume's focus on *incunabula* but also from the beauty of the Biblical texts and the erudition of their humanist editors, I will offer some introductory comments on what the growing number of readers did with the growing number of religious texts that made their way into their hands.[4]

Early bibles are both historical and religious relics, and often they are seen – literally and figuratively – behind glass. It is easy to lose sight of the spaces and hands through which they have passed, from the moment of their inception to their arrival in their current resting places. But like all books, bibles, the transcendence of their texts notwithstanding, are physical objects created, circulated and used by particular people. And while religious texts moulded the lives of Renaissance readers, structuring their routines, guiding their beliefs and behaviours, readers, for their part, did not hesitate to leave their own marks on religious books (including bibles).

The individual volumes that come down to us are full of the signs (and scars) of their human contact. This evidence is difficult to recover and even more difficult to interpret; but, as Roger Stoddard explained in his useful catalogue *Marks in Books*, 'When we handle books sensitively, observing them closely so as to learn as much as we can from them, we discover a thousand little mysteries. ... In and around, beneath and across them we may find traces ... that could teach us a lot if we could make them out.'[5] In the course of a comprehensive survey of early English printed books at the Huntington Library I encountered a wide range of evidence for the use of biblical, liturgical and theological texts; and these traces provide an instructive, and sometimes amusing, perspective on the 'Bible as Book'.[6]

This survey focuses on the most common and immediate category of readers' marks: manuscript notes (or 'marginalia'). Manuscript annotations are not, however, the only form of evidence for the interaction of texts and readers; and before I turn to them I want to touch briefly on some of the other techniques involved in reading, digesting and personalizing the written Word. One practice that was particularly common in the Renaissance was the use of commonplace books for entering notable passages according to a set of pre-conceived topics. When readers were told to 'mark' some feature of the biblical text, as they often were in prefaces to vernacular bibles (especially in the set of instructions entitled, 'Howe to take profite by reading of the holy Scriptures', which was issued in many editions of the Geneva Bible[7]), this marking could actually involve pen and paper. The period's most explicit set of instructions on how to construct a commonplace book can be found not in a humanist pedagogical treatise but in Edward Vaughan's guide to Bible study, published in 1594 and entitled, *Ten Introductions: How to read, and in reading how to vnderstand; and in vnderstanding how to bear in mind all the bookes, chapters, and verses contained in the holie Bible*.[8]

There were also devices within the text, such as epistles 'To the Reader' and commentaries which attempted to assist and influence readers and their interpretations. Especially important were the printed marginalia that increasingly surrounded the vernacular text. In 1538, Miles Coverdale wrote to Thomas Cromwell seeking permission to include annotations in the 'Great Bible'. 'Pitie it were,' he explained, 'that the darck places of the text (upon the which I have allwaye set a hande) shulde so passe undeclared.' Tyndale, who made pioneering use of marginalia in his 1534 New Testament, informed his readers that, 'I have in many places set lyght in the margent to understonde the text by.' And the Geneva Bible, one of the more aggressively annotated of the English Bibles, 'endevored ... to explicat all suche [dark or hard] places', to profit not only people 'already advanced in the knollage of the Scriptures, but also the simple and unlearned ...'.[9]

But as Evelyn Tribble and William Slights have shown, this practice of casting light on the dark places of the text was double-edged, and the authorities were never entirely comfortable with it.[10] In practice marginalia served one of two functions, each of which was potentially dangerous. Many annotations offered interpretations of obscure passages, and – instead of leaving these mysteries to the mediation of a carefully directed priesthood – these notes served to advance one doctrinal position over others and even gave some interpretative licence to the reader. The other form of annotation – linguistic glosses on source-words or textual variants – could claim to be more neutral; but these too created a contested space on the edges of the text, and revealed to readers a multiplicity or indeterminacy in the transmission of God's Word. As the preface to the King James Bible acknowledged, 'Some peradventure would have no varietie of sences to be set in the margine, lest the authoritie of the Scriptures ... by that shew of uncertaintie, should somewhat be shaken.'[11]

While these practices have been well studied, manuscript marginalia remain a relatively untapped resource, and constitute a veritable archive of the way particular books were read and their role in the intellectual, spiritual and social lives of their readers. I have now covered almost all of the Huntington Library's English Short Title Catalogue holdings, i.e. most of those texts printed between 1475 and 1640, looking for any roughly contemporary traces left by readers (especially any manuscript markings in any part of the book, produced – insofar as they could be dated – within about fifty years of the date of publication). Before describing the variety of marginalia turned up by the survey, it is worth pausing to share a few preliminary statistics. Statistics are, of course, crude tools to bring to the study of artifacts as complex as texts, but they can at least draw attention to some general patterns and identify some questions to be studied with more sophisticated methods.

Perhaps the most striking figure is the crudest of all – the overall frequency of marginalia. For the entire period, just over 20 per cent of the volumes contain significant marginalia; and that figure does not include notes of ownership or underlinings and other non-verbal notes. When we take those traces into account, and also consider how much marginalia has disappeared over the last four centuries, this is a striking, and for some, a staggering figure.[12] These numbers suggest that the practice of writing in books during the Renaissance was remarkably widespread. While we might expect bibles and other religious books to be exempt from such treatment (and this expectation is something I will return to) the overall frequency of marginalia in bibles and prayer books turns out to be almost identical to that of the whole collection: just over one in five. And when we turn to other religious texts such as sermons or theological treatises, the number more than doubles: in the polemics which flooded from the presses in the wake of the Reformation the proportion with manuscript notes is well over half.

Breaking down the statistics by decade also reveals an important trend. While the average number of annotated books for the incunable period is high (between 60 per cent and 70 per cent), the numbers do not fall away as drastically in the sixteenth century as one might expect, and for a decade as late as the 1590s, 52 per cent of the volumes still contain manuscript marginalia. Slights, mentioned above, and others have found that the amount of printed annotation increased over this period: as books freed themselves from the visual and organizational models of the manuscript tradition, 'the exploitation of the margins [i.e. by authors and printers] continue[d] to grow'.[13] Since many of these printed notes provided the kinds of apparatus for which earlier readers had relied on manuscript annotations, scholars have assumed that manuscript marginalia decreased proportionally. In an important essay on 'Incunable Description and its Implication for the Analysis of 15th-Century Reading Habits', Paul Saenger and Michael Heinlen argue that in the first few decades of printing, books still contain enough in the way of illuminations, rubrications and annotations that they deserve to be catalogued as if they were manuscripts. They go on to suggest that this situation changed rapidly, arguing that

> The printer's provision of all the aids that previously had been added [by hand] ... effected the final step in the transformation of reading. In antiquity reading had implied an active role in the reception of the text. ... Throughout the Middle Ages readers, even long after a book had been confected, felt free to clarify its meaning through the addition of...marginalia. Under the influence of printing, reading became increasingly an activity of the passive reception of a text that was inherently clear and unambiguous.[14]

Saenger and Heinlen imply that this transformation was largely complete by the second decade of the sixteenth century. Whether or not readers ever became quite so passive, or printers ever delivered texts that were 'inherently clear and unambiguous', neither of these were the case 50, 100 or even 150 years after the invention of printing. The evidence left in sixteenth-century English books suggests that readers actively added to texts (again, sometimes long after they had been confected, and not always in ways that clarified or beautified the text) on a scale that was comparable to the incunable period. Printers did not provide anything like clear or uniform texts, nor could they provide everything that every reader needed in order to make sense of the text. In other words, Saenger and Heinlen's primary argument could be extended; that at least as late as 1600 books still contain enough copy-specific attributes to justify copy-specific cataloguing.

These quantitative figures do not begin to do justice to the qualities of marks in books, to their varied purposes and techniques. The undifferentiated statistics hide an extraordinary range of traces, filling every available space. What kinds of marks, then, did Renaissance readers make in their Bibles?

'Making one's mark' can simply refer to the signing of a document. Signatures and notes about family histories were, predictably, the most common inscriptions in Renaissance bibles, and were one of the principal ways of not only signalling that the Scriptures had become private property but of personalizing and domesticating the text. It is sometimes possible to follow the births, marriages, and deaths of particular families for decades and even centuries in the blank spaces of their bibles – a practice which continues to the present day.[15]

Marginalia in the period's bibles also offer direct evidence of the ways in which the Reformation left its traces on books as much as on bodies and buildings. In England, some pre-Reformation bibles and prayer-books remained in circulation after the break with Rome (when most of them were destroyed); but readers often censored their copies by scratching out newly offensive terms like 'Pope' or 'Virgin Mary' or by crossing out sections that were no longer endorsed. In a 1545 Primer at the Huntington (STC 16040) the Hail Mary has been crossed out and the word 'Vacat' written in (Pl. 37).[16]

Most marginalia, however, was concerned less with censoring than with clarifying and digesting the text, making it easier to read and use for particular purposes. While there are no cases at the Huntington as elaborate as some of the bibles at the British Library, in which learned commentaries in a number of hands completely surround the printed text, there are a number of heavily annotated bibles and dozens with sparser marginalia. One 1582 New Testament at the Huntington has been covered with notes on the paste-downs, in the index, and on the colophon in which passages are copied out under such headings as 'Against astrologers'.[17] In the text itself we find the full range of annotational techniques – including brackets, underlinings, cross-references and summaries.[18]

Very often the notes and underlinings simply serve to highlight passages, but it can be interesting to see which sections particular readers are interested in. Especially in cases such as a 1574 Bishops' Bible, where the reader has only annotated passages in the Apocrypha (in fact, almost exclusively the Book of Esdras), and systematically picked out verses on angels, prophesies, signs and tokens.[19]

Some readers clearly had access to more than one Bible and were fully aware of what the Authorized Version called 'the varietie of sences'. It is not unusual to find variant versions, or alternative translations, copied out in the margins.[20] Readers regularly made the corrections identified in the lists of 'faults escaped in the printing', and also did not hesitate to enter their own emendations when it was clear that the printer had garbled the text. In a 1580 translation of Calvin's commentaries on the First Epistle of St John, the text seems to have been badly mangled: among the reader's corrections are the substitution of 'the fault of our flesh' for 'the fault of our faith'.[21] Throughout the history of the printed English Bible, compositors' slips have had serious theological consequences.

The Huntington's printed bibles (even those from the late sixteenth century and beyond) contain a surprising amount of illumination, rubrication and coloured ruling and underlining. It is often very crudely executed; and in some cases it defaces more than beautifies the text (as in one 1540 Coverdale Bible, in which a reader has re-copied some of the woodcuts, making grotesque modifications[22]). Others contain artistry similar to that found in a 1576 Geneva Bible, where the engravings have been beautifully and brightly coloured by an unidentified artist (Pl. 38).[23]

A related practice is the decorative packaging of books: in late Tudor and Stuart England there was something of a vogue for putting bibles in embroidered bindings.[24] They are especially plentiful in smaller format Psalters; and, indeed, the Huntington has a fine collection of these, including one tiny 32mo book of Psalms with a delicate needlework binding featuring cartouches with King David playing the harp.[25] It is less common to find them in larger formats; and of this variety the Huntington has a little known treasure. A large folio Bible from 1616 has an elaborate velvet binding with embroidered portraits of Moses and Aaron (representing the Old Testament) on the front cover, and the crucifixion (representing the New Testament) on the back (see Pl. 39 and 40).[26] It is worth noting in passing that the function of these bindings is more than merely decorative. They are one of the places where we can see the persistence of religious pictures after Protestant scripturalism and iconoclasm have taken root in England, largely supplanting the image with the word and effectively banishing illustrations from the texts of bibles and prayer books.[27]

Perhaps the most pervasive indication of readers' access to and assimilation of the Bible is the extent to which it figures in their marginalia in other books. The frequent cases, found especially in printed sermons, where a reader notes the precise reference for an unidentified scriptural passage, suggest how thoroughly familiar many lay readers had become with the Bible (to the point where they could cite, as the phrase goes, 'chapter and verse').

It should be clear, then, that the margins of early bibles contain sources of edification that have been overlooked. But we should not underestimate the difficulty of accessing marginalia and of interpreting the motives and mentalities that lay behind them: they are often as ambiguous and mysterious as the 'dark places' in the text itself which the printed annotations were designed to illuminate. Do we have, for instance, a reliable sense of what constituted pious reading or use of Bibles in the fifteenth or sixteenth centuries? Some readers were not only crude in their comments but quite rough with their Bibles: in a case like the 1553 Tyndale New Testament at the Huntington which has its pages covered to the point of damage with penmanship exercises and doodles but also with extremely devout observations, can we comfortably say that this Bible was being abused (Pl. 41)?[28] Perhaps such rough treatment was an inevitable by-product of putting Bibles into 'every vulgar hand': Dryden's satire on Bible reading laments that 'The tender page with horny fists was galled.'[29] And while Greenslade noted that to 'place every book of Scripture in the hands of children' was 'an instruction of the fourth-century apostolic constitution',[30] even in an age before the invention of the crayon they had to know that children would do with the bibles that were thrust into their hands what they tend to do with every other book – namely use it for entering their signatures, for practising their penmanship, and above all for colouring (in the Huntington's bibles engraved coats of arms proved especially popular).[31] In one other sense, Bibles were bound to be consumed more actively and more literally than other texts, after they entered household economies. The Book of Revelation (10:8-10) contains a passage in which the angel instructs John to 'take the book and eat it up'; and not every reader read this metaphorically. (In an interesting essay on 'books as totems', David Cressy cites reports of people eating bibles for their curative powers as late as the nineteenth century.[32]) I would suggest that we have a long way to go in understanding the 'book etiquette' (to borrow Saenger and Heinlen's useful term) of Renaissance readers: clearly they did not share the modern attitude which 'views the printed page as sacrosanct and consequently all handwritten additions to the printed page as ... detrimental ....'[33]

Finally, while it is remarkable how quickly after the advent of printing bibles made their way into the hands and under the pens of laymen and women, we should be wary of seeing this as a smooth and uni-directional movement. We should not forget, first, the ambivalent attitudes of the authorities toward lay reading of the Bible: as late as 1543 King Henry VIII prohibited women, husbandmen and labourers from reading the Bible. As David Kastan has explained, early efforts 'to prevent interpretive debate was obviously destined to fail, and by 1543, the Act for the Advancement of True Religion would pointedly seek to restrict access to the Bible itself, forbidding it to all subjects "of the lower sort".'[34] And, second, while new sectors of the population gained access to the Bible in this transitional period, the readers themselves often drew on traditional techniques and attitudes. Looked at from the users' perspective, there are significant continuities of manuscript traditions and devotional practices associated with what Eamon Duffy has aptly called 'traditional religion',[35] and it is not surprising that older practices proved persistent in accommodating the new religion and the new media that were used to propagate it.

A graphic example – indeed, almost an emblem – of these mixed mentalities and complex motives is another unusual book from the James R. Page Collection at the Huntington Library. It is neither a Bible nor a printed book, but it captures the way in which traditional features of devotional texts were retained (or, in this case, literally recycled) in the newly authoritative liturgical books. Between 1560 and 1562 an as yet unidentified scribe carefully copied out the entire Book of Common Prayer and Psalter into an octavo volume of some 500 pages.[36] While the text does not seem to be altered in any way, the entire manuscript is decorated in surprising ways, making it a mixed-media devotional text like those popular in pre-Reformation contexts.[37] The layout, and in places the lettering, follow the appearance of the printed page. And the major initials are elaborately ornamented in two contrasting styles. About half of them have been done by hand and are modelled on woodcut initials, comparable but not identical to those used throughout the printed text (see Pl. 42). The other half have been plundered from five different late medieval manuscripts and pasted into appropriate spaces in the text (see Pl. 43).

Looking at readers' marks in general, then, what is most striking is the diverse uses to which books – including the Book – could be put. Perhaps King Henry VIII was right to be worried: once you put the Bible into the hands of lay men, women and children you could not ultimately control what they would do with it. And in this way, while the Bible penetrated the homes of individual readers, playing a more intimate role in their lives and even their language, it may have lost some of its monolithic integrity and authority. What seems clear is that well after the transitional period of incunabula – indeed, up to a century after the printed book had 'left the cradle' – both print culture and Protestant culture were still experiencing birth pangs.[38]

## NOTES

1 'Epilogue' to *The Cambridge History of the Bible* (Cambridge: University Press, 1963), III, p. 479. Greenslade's contributions to *The Cambridge History*, along with Elizabeth Eisenstein's classic chapter on 'The Scriptural Tradition Recast', in *The Printing Press as an Agent of Change* (Cambridge: University Press, 1979), provide invaluable introductions to the translation and printing of the Bible in the Reformation.

2 John Dryden, *Religio Laici, or A Layman's Faith* (London: Jacob Tonson, 1682), line 400.

3 Robert Darnton, 'What Is the History of Books?', *Daedalus*, 111:3 (Summer 1982), 65-83.

4 For a very recent attempt to place the earliest Christian texts in this sort of context, see Harry Y. Gamble, *Readers in the Early Church: a History of Early Christian Texts* (New Haven & London: Yale University Press, 1995). Gamble addresses 'questions about the production, circulation, and use of books in the ancient church, that are almost never raised by historians of the canon' (p. ix).

5 *Marks in Books, Shown and Explained* (Cambridge & Mass.: Harvard University Press, 1985).

6 I am grateful to the Huntington Library for its generous support of this project. The research awards committee provided two short-term Mellon Foundation Fellowships, and the librarians (especially Curator of Rare Books Alan Jutzi) have enabled me to access large numbers of rare books, shown an interest in what I found in them, and provided the illustrations that accompany this essay.

7 This synoptic table is signed by 'T. Grashop.' and appears in the editions of 1579, 1580, 1581, 1586, 1587, 1592, 1599, 1607 and 1616. One indication that it was itself 'marked' in both senses of the term (attended to and modified) is a Huntington Library copy of the 1575 Bishops' Bible (shelf-mark RB 294479-80). Among the four pages of manuscript notes bound in at the beginning of the text is a version of this table – which the reader has condensed into 4 (from its original 7) points.

8 (London: Adam Islip, 1594). The treatment of commonplace books forms the tenth and final 'introduction,' and is prefaced with the remarkable passage, 'The conclusion of all acts and studies do consist of three parts; to weet, Reading, Noting, and Exercise. To the end you may make perfect use of your Reading, I have thought good to compose this order for your Noting; then (Gods spirit assisting) your Exercise will be easie' (sig.K4v).

9 These passages can all be found in *Records of the English Bible: The Documents Relating to the Translation and Publication of the Bible in English, 1525-1611*, ed. by Alfred W. Pollard (London: Oxford University Press, 1911). For sample pages of these editions, as well as an excellent potted account of the history of the Bible, see the John Rylands Library's *Catalogue*

*of an Exhibition Illustrating the History of the Transmission of the Bible* (Manchester: University Press, 1935).

10 William W. E. Slights, '"Marginall Notes that spoile the Text": Scriptural Annotation in the English Renaissance,' *Huntington Library Quarterly*, 55 (1992), 254-78; Evelyn B. Tribble, *Margins and Marginality: the Printed Page in Early Modern England* (Charlottesville: University of Virginia Press, 1993), especially ch.1.

11 Pollard, *Records of the English Bible*, p. 373.

12 In fact, there are strong indications that the Huntington's books are unusually clean, and that a similar survey of comparable collections, such as that of the Folger Shakespeare Library, would turn up an even higher proportion.

13 William W. E. Slights, 'The Edifying Margins of Renaissance English Books', *Renaissance Quarterly*, 42 (1989), 687.

14 Paul Saenger & Michael Heinlen, 'Incunable Description and Its Implication for the Analysis of Fifteenth-Century Reading Habits', in *Printing the Written Word: the Social History of Books, circa 1450-1520*, ed. by Sandra L. Hindman (Ithaca, N.Y.: Cornell University Press, 1991), pp. 253-4.

15 We should be wary, I think, of attributing any special significance to this practice. Families also used other types of books to record their histories – for instance, a Huntington copy of Jacques Guillemeau's *Child-Birth, or the Happy Deliverie of Women* (1612) contains notices of births to the 'Holles' family in the 1620s [RB 87312]. The reason why more family histories are found in bibles than in any other text may simply be due to the fact that families were more likely to possess a Bible than any other text.

16 RB 62311-2. This book can actually be associated with the royal household: among the manuscript notes bound in at the front of the volume are such memoranda as 'Item payd to Thomas Luffington for haye for the kinge – v$^{s}$ and iiij$^{d}$.'

17 Fly-leaves were often filled with references and citations, with commentaries on points of particular interest to the reader, glossaries of difficult or useful words, and chronological tables of biblical history.The best examples I have seen are at the British Library. A 1546 Latin Bible (shelf-mark C.51.i.6) has an orderly table in two columns headed 'Index temporis praecipuarum & notatum dignarum historiarum et veteris et novi testamenti'. It runs from Anno Mundi 1 to *c.* 2400 (the time of Joshua). Another table, added to the end of the index in a 1540 Estienne Bible (C.23.e.1) runs from 130 (Adam) to 3954 (Christ).

18 RB 96514.

19 RB 292510.

20 A 1634 Psalter (RB 47877) is a particularly interesting example. A variant version of Psalm 2 is inscribed, in which line 3 is changed from 'Why did the Iewish people muse' to 'Why did the foolish people muse'.

21 RB 228144.

22 RB 96523.

23 RB 17666, fol. 366$^{r}$.

24 For a good overview see Giles Barber, *Textile and Embroidered Bindings* (Oxford: Bodleian Library, 1971).

25 Huntington Library, James R. Page Collection, No. 200.

26 Huntington Library, James R. Page Collection, No. 70F.

27 On English iconoclasm see the work of Margaret Aston, and the chapter on 'The Cultural Revolution' in Patrick Collinson's *The Birthpangs of Protestant England* (London: Macmillan, 1988). For a ground-breaking study of the interweaving of visual and verbal culture in the century after the Reformation see Tessa Watt, *Cheap Print and Popular Piety, 1550-1640* (Cambridge: University Press, 1991).

28 RB 32153.

29 *Religio Laici* (above, n. 2), line 404.
30 Greenslade (above, n. 1), 'Epilogue', pp. 490-1.
31 For a broad perspective on children and Bibles see Ruth B. Bottigheimer's *The Bible for Children, From the Age of Gutenberg to the Present* (New Haven: Yale University Press, 1996).
32 'Books as Totems in 17th-Century England and New England', *Journal of Library History*, 21 (1986), 92-106; 99.
33 Saenger & Heinlen (above, n. 14), pp. 253-4.
34 David Scott Kastan, '"The Noyse of the New Bible": Reform and Reaction in Henrician England', in *Religion and Culture in Renaissance England*, ed. by Claire McEachern & Debora Shuger (Cambridge: University Press, 1997).
35 For an indispensable analysis of 'traditional religion' in this transitional period see Eamon Duffy's *The Stripping of the Altars: Traditional Religion in England, 1400-1580* (New Haven & London: Yale University Press, 1992).
36 James R. Page Collection, no. 354.
37 Mary C. Erler, 'Pasted-In Embellishments in English Manuscripts and Printed Books c.1480-1533', *The Library*, 6th Series, XIV:3 (September 1992), 185-206.

# THE RE-EVALUATION OF THE PATRISTIC EXEGETICAL TRADITION IN THE SIXTEENTH CENTURY

*David Steinmetz*

IT IS IMPORTANT to remember that the Reformation, insofar as it was a religious and theological event, had the character of a civil war.[1] It began as an internal controversy within Latin Christendom between Catholic insiders. Many of the would-be reformers had gone to the same schools as their traditionalist opponents, heard lectures on the same texts (often by the same teachers), participated in same required ordinary and quodlibetal disputations over many of the same themes, and mastered the same glosses. Not infrequently, reformers and defenders of the status quo knew each other from chapter or college or diocesan meetings. All the first generation of Protestant reformers and most of the second had been baptized and educated as Catholics. Their criticisms of the Catholic Church and its theology were based on their experience and not merely on their reading. John Calvin, for example, is savage in his attacks on the Catholic practice of offering prayers for the dead as he saw it done in the cathedral at Noyon. Indeed, he is so critical that one might be tempted to forget that a good portion of his education at Paris, Orléans and Bourges was supported by funds collected from exactly this source. Furthermore, the fundamental introduction of most early Protestants to biblical studies, whether by representatives of the Old Learning or the New, had taken place under Catholic auspices.

This fact complicates any attempt by historians to characterize biblical studies in the sixteenth century. It is not the case that there was a unified Catholic approach to biblical studies in the sixteenth century dominated by traditional Catholic biblical scholars, deeply suspicious of humanism (a plodding *via exegetica antiqua*), that was challenged by a unified Protestant approach, inspired by humanism and promoted by newly-hatched Protestant dissenters (an innovative *via exegetica moderna*). Nor did Catholics and Protestants disagree in predictable ways over the exegesis of biblical texts (aside, of course, from a few texts on which they had principled and irreconcilable disagreements).[2] One could, for example, predict with a fair degree of accuracy how Catholic and Protestant interpreters would explain Romans 4 concerning Abraham's justification by faith, but one could not predict with equal accuracy how Catholic and Protestant biblical scholars would understand Romans 7 with its agonized cry for deliverance.[3] Was Paul speaking in this text of life under the law or under grace? Important medieval authorities like Peter Lombard, Nicholas of Lyra and Denis the Carthusian (though not Thomas Aquinas) thought that Paul was referring to life under the law. The vast majority of biblical scholars in the sixteenth century disagreed. On this text Catholics like Domingo de Soto, Girolamo Cardinal Seripando and Ambrosius Catherinus Politus joined Protestants like Huldrych Zwingli, Johannes Oecolampadius and John Calvin, not only in rejecting the dominant late medieval exegetical tradition, but also in opposing the views of such prominent contemporaries as the Catholic prelate Jacopo Cardinal Sadoleto and the radical Protestants Bernardino Ochino and Fausto Sozzini.[4]

I would like to examine some aspects of the renewal of biblical studies in the sixteenth century, focusing on the re-evaluation of the Christian exegetical tradition stemming mainly from the early Christian fathers.[5] Interest in the biblical exegesis of the Fathers was, of course, nothing new in the sixteenth century. Medieval preoccupation with both the Bible and the Fathers was reflected not only in liturgy, prayer, sermons, polity and doctrine, but also in theological education. From the thirteenth century to the sixteenth the principal task of a scholastic master at Paris (and the many universities modelled on it) was to lecture on the literal sense of the Bible as interpreted or glossed by the Fathers.[6] A teacher of *sacra pagina* was required to master both the Latin biblical text and the standard glosses on it. The glosses were drawn from traditional authorities, principally from the writings and biblical exegesis of the Fathers. When Peter Lombard assembled his four books of *Sentences*, a work that became the standard text for lectures on dogmatic theology until roughly the middle of the sixteenth century, he drew heavily on citations of the Fathers from the glossed Bible.[7]

Knowledge of one or another of the biblical languages was much less important to scholastic theologians than knowledge of the glosses, though some Christian commentators like Nicholas of Lyra and Paul of Burgos read Hebrew and even consulted rabbinical literature. Interest in biblical languages was first fostered in a programmatic way by humanist scholars in the fifteenth and sixteenth centuries. These scholars stressed the importance of a knowledge of Hebrew and Greek for the proper understanding of Scripture. Unlike Hugh of Saint-Cher and Denis the Carthusian, two standard medieval commentators on the biblical text, humanist theologians aspired to be *homines trilingui*, masters of Latin, Greek and Hebrew.[8] In this respect the great majority of early reformers from Martin Luther and Hans Denck to John Calvin and Peter Martyr Vermigli embraced the humanist ideal. Even commentators like Thomas de Vio Cardinal Cajetan, who knew no Hebrew, sought the help of Hebrew linguists in the preparation of his commentaries on the Old Testament.[9]

Substantial as the differences were between scholastics and humanists, it is important not to exaggerate them. It was certainly possible to be both a humanist and a scholastic, to love Hebrew philology and to allegorize the biblical text.[10] Indeed, it was no contradiction in terms to say that John Smith edited or translated Greek texts and that he presided at quodlibetal disputations. Even Martin Luther, who made if not the first, assuredly the most successful, translation of the Bible into German, presided at university disputations until he was an old man.[11] Furthermore, not everything written by scholastic doctors was itself scholastic in nature. When university lecturers wrote hymns, prayers, sermons or commentaries, they wrote as hymnists, liturgists, preachers and exegetes, not as scholastics in the strict sense of the term.[12] Anyone who compares the lectures of Thomas Aquinas on Romans with his essay on grace in the *Summa Theologiae* can see the difference immediately.[13]

It is important as well not to romanticize the very real advantages brought to

Christian biblical study by the reintroduction of a knowledge of the biblical languages. After all, for more than a thousand years the authoritative biblical text in the West had been its Latin translation. Doctrinal formulations echoed its wording and not the wording of the original Greek and Hebrew. An appeal to older Greek and Hebrew originals had the often undesired result for traditional theologians of destabilizing the Latin biblical text and subverting the dogmatic formulations that rested on them.[14] When the Council of Trent (1545-63) and the later Roman Catechism appealed to the Vulgate Latin translation as authoritative rather than the original Greek and Hebrew texts, they had clearly in mind the subversive character of the New Learning. In elegant Renaissance Latin the *Roman Catechism* rejected one of the fundamental assumptions of Renaissance learning; namely, that an original text is always to be preferred to its translation.

It was not clear to everyone, moreover, that desirable scholarly canons were equally satisfying theological norms.[15] Why, wondered some Catholic authors, should theologians prefer the ambiguous Hebrew (ambiguous even to the rabbis) to the reasonably clear Latin? When Erasmus complained that the Latin text of the Vulgate in fact was riddled with problems, his critic, Edward Lee, responded by asking whether there were any problems in the Greek. If, as it appeared from the arguments of the humanists, the Church had in no case – Latin, Hebrew or Greek – a text that was free from difficulties, why, inquired uneasy conservatives, should anyone feel compelled to change?

Still more troubling was the unargued assumption that transformed the mandate to return to the sources from a philological first principle into a theological axiom. The question was not easily answered as to when the dogmatic principle was established, at what council, and by whom, that the Holy Spirit could inspire original authors but never providentially guide their translators? Perhaps the humanists had been misled by their own rhetoric concerning the purity of the fountain (the original sources) and the lesser purity of the river (later manuscripts and translations). What if the relationship between texts and translations were more accurately described as the relationship between raw materials and finished product?[16] After all, the Hebrew Bible had never been the scriptures of the Latin West, which had read Moses first in Greek and then in Latin. For more than a millennium, western Christians had heard, read and pondered the gospel in Latin. In spite of what some more recent scholars regarded as an unfortunate linguistic handicap, the largely Hebrew- and Greekless Catholic Church believed it had been led into all truth by the Holy Spirit.[17] If the gates of hell could not prevail against such a Church, it seemed unlikely it could be overturned by an aorist verb or a waw-consecutive. Indeed, the maturity of the Latin Vulgate, composed in tranquility and tested for centuries in the medieval Catholic Church, might even represent an advance over the ambiguity and limitations of the often rough and ready Greek and Hebrew originals. It was, at least, a thinkable thought.[18]

Protestants, on the whole, were not sympathetic to this line of reasoning. Since they were engaged in a programmatic destabilizing of aspects of Catholic tradition, they were not alarmed by the subversive potential of the original Greek and Hebrew texts, and were optimistic that the only traditions called in question by such a scholarly procedure were traditions that were doubtful on theological grounds as well. They conceded that it was possible to master the New Learning without acquiring the theological profundity that had characterized the Old. One might learn to read Greek and Hebrew and yet be preoccupied with incidental information about the biblical text or lost in grammatical trivialities. Luther even warned against the easy assumption on the part of some of his contemporaries that biblical interpretation was a discipline solely for grammarians and rhetoricians. One could, after all, be deficient in one's knowledge of biblical languages, as Augustine, Bernard and Aquinas undoubtedly were, and yet engage the biblical text at a profound level of theological insight. Luther was only too painfully aware how much he owed to his Hebrew- and Greekless predecessor at Wittenberg, John Staupitz.[19]

Nevertheless, the humanists changed the theological situation at the end of the Middle Ages by providing reliably edited editions of the complete, or at least more nearly complete, works of patristic writers. Many of these Fathers had formerly been read by medieval theologians in anthologies such as the *Milleloquium divi Augustini* or as standard glosses on the Bible or canon law. One could now read the homilies of Chrysostom on John, both in the Greek original and in Latin translation. It became possible for sixteenth-century theologians, as it had not been for their predecessors in the thirteenth, to test the traditional interpretations of Scripture reflected in the glosses against the interpretations found in the more complete writings of the Fathers themselves.

Among the proponents of the New Learning, the enduring Christian impulse to reform the present by embracing the past stimulated a fresh return to the sources. Scholars were urged to move from the unsatisfactory and unsatisfying collections of anthologized quotations to the study of the complete writings of the Fathers themselves. In a way which had not been possible for Duns Scotus or John Capreolus, theologians could now hear directly the unmediated and uninterrupted voices of the generations of Christian saints and teachers who had lived in close, or at least in closer, proximity to the apostolic age. The new editions of early Christian writings offered theologians in the sixteenth century fresh and exciting sources for the validation and criticism of existing teaching and practices. When the great controversy broke out between Protestant and Catholic (and, later, between Protestant and Protestant), all parties appealed to the Fathers to support their own position and to subvert the positions of their opponents. Since the charge of theological innovation was tantamount to a charge of heresy, each group was eager to show that it was more ancient than its rivals.

Of course, it was precisely the great controversy that stimulated theologians and scholars to to reprint old anthologies of the Fathers like the *Milleloquium* and to compose new ones. By the year 1566 more than eighty anthologies of patristic writings had been assembled by Catholics and Protestants alike, books that frequently enjoyed multiple printings. Some of the anthologies were intended either as commentaries on Scripture or as convenient summaries of the teaching of one particular writer worth anthologizing. But a great many were composed as handbooks for use in theological controversies. Philip Melanchthon, for example, compiled an anthology on eucharistic theology. Other anthologies were devoted to the doctrine of justification by faith alone, a doctrine that had proved more diffcult to support from the Fathers than early Protestants had anticipated. Justification was an important theme in anthologies by such Protestant editors as Robert Barnes, Anton Corvinus, Erasmus Sarcerius, Guy de Brès and Andreas Musculus.[20]

Whatever the slogan *sola scriptura* may have meant to later generations of Protestants, it did not accurately describe the situation in the early Reformation. Early Protestants did not intend to read and interpret Scripture without reference to the Fathers. They were convinced that they had recaptured the ancient gospel no longer obscured by the innovations of the late medieval Church. Not unnaturally, they expected to find in the Fathers insights into that ancient gospel that would clarify, support and enrich their own. If the teaching of Scripture as early Protestants understood it clashed with the teaching of a Father and no reconciliation seemed possible, the teaching of the Father might be declared by them inadequate, confused or simply false.[21] Scripture was always to be preferred to the teaching of any human writer, however venerable and holy. But the hope and expectation of early Protestants was that the general drift of the Fathers (or, at the very least, of the sounder Fathers) was in the direction of Protestant teaching and against what they regarded as the doctrinal deviations from ancient truth promoted by the late medieval Church. They read the Fathers in the cheerful confidence that they were reading the writings of natural and wise allies, members of the same family who professed the same faith, against the modern innovations defended by Rome that masqueraded as ancient tradition. Not unsurprisingly, their opponents embraced a different vision.

If indeed the early Protestants were eager to find ancient authorities that would support their wide-ranging critique of medieval Catholic traditions, they were attempting, if one may cite the maxim of Harnack, to overcome history with history – or, more accurately, tradition with tradition. In their view, many of the customs and ideas they had been taught as children in traditionally Catholic homes failed the threefold test of catholicity proposed by Vincent of Lérins. What they had been taught were customs and ideas that should have been (but clearly had *not* been) taught everywhere, always, and by all (*ubique, semper, ab omnibus*) throughout the history of the Catholic Church.[22] Judged by this stringent standard, such western medieval traditions as papal monarchy, the immaculate conception of Mary, and the doctrine of transubstantiation were put in some doubt. By the same token the early Fathers could be cited to support the doctrines of the Trinity, the two natures of Christ, the priority of prevenient grace, and the real presence of Christ in the eucharist. Although no doctrine could be affirmed or denied that was not, in the judgement of early Protestants, supported or undermined by explicit biblical teaching, the Fathers provided an important secondary validation of their proposed critique of tradition by tradition.

Theologians and scholars in the sixteenth century longed for a consensus that perpetually eluded them. Early Protestants in particular cherished the hope that good exegesis would drive out bad theology and that learned and godly men, immersing themselves in the study of the Bible, would consent in the same truth. But good exegesis produced, as Catholic critics warned it might, competing theologies. While all Christians agreed about some things and many Christians agreed about many things, few Christians agreed about all things. Even the search for a *consensus Patrum* fell short of its intended end, as the Fathers themselves were enlisted by opposing parties in the often bitter controversies between Protestant and Catholic, Lutheran and Reformed, Reformed and Anabaptist, Lutheran and Lutheran, and Anglican and Puritan. By the middle of the century Christians appealed to a Catholic, a Lutheran and a Calvinist Augustine. Even some Anabaptists agreed with Julian of Eclanum and rejected Augustine as an unreformed Manichean.

By the same token Catholic theologians realized that the Protestant appeal to the Fathers could not be answered by a merely formal appeal to an unbroken Catholic tradition. Commonplaces from the Fathers that might have served theologians well in the thirteenth century lacked convincing power in the sixteenth and sounded hollow to a newly sophisticated generation of theologians, Catholic as well as Protestant. Not only did Protestant exegesis have to be answered painstakingly by Catholic biblical scholars, as John Eck and Cardinal Cajetan had concluded in the 1520s, but so, too, did Protestant use of the writings of the Fathers. By the end of the century Catholic study of the Fathers had outstripped that of the Protestants as it developed sophisticated tools which the Protestants used and attempted to emulate.[23]

In a recent review in the *Journal of Theological Studies* John Milbank suggested that the unglossed Bible was a product of humanism, printing and Protestantism.[24] Although I understand his point, the observation is, of course, incorrect, since the unglossed Bible always had a role to play in liturgy and prayer, and the standard manuscript Bibles of the thirteenth century were normally unannotated, a format which was replicated in many incunable editions. Protestants did actively promulgate vernacular Bibles, translated from Greek and Hebrew originals and made available through the new printing technology for purchase at reasonable prices by all who could afford them. Lay people could own and read the unglossed (or, perhaps, only minimally glossed) Bible in their native tongue.

However, it would be a serious mistake to conclude from this fact that Protestants commended the uninterpreted Bible to the laity, whose untutored musings on the text were taken with the seriousness previously accorded to the judgements of theologians and the decisions of bishops. Protestants left the printed glosses out of the biblical text, but attempted to place a theologically learned glossator in every parish. The pastor was expected to do from the pulpit on a somewhat more elementary level what the medieval lecturer had done from the university lectern; namely, expound the biblical text in the light of the best secondary authorities – catechism, creed, the ancient Fathers and a generous selection of widely respected later teachers (including, for the Protestants, *recentiores* like Luther and Melanchthon). This reconception of the pastoral office more on the model of the mendicant friar than on the model of the parish priest was essential for Protestants to serve a Church they regarded as both Mother and school. In this connection it was no accident that later Puritans built churches in the New World that looked more like schoolhouses than sacred space for the celebration of religious mysteries, or that a welcome compliment in Puritan circles was to congratulate the pastor for a sermon that had been well studied.

If we ask whether sixteenth-century exegesis was representative of the Old Learning or the New, whether it was backward-looking or innovative, whether we see in it the last vestiges of the Middle Ages or the first glimmerings of the modern world, the only possible answer is yes. In its own dynamic and inimitable way sixteenth-century exegesis was a lively and never completely settled combination of all of the above.

## NOTES

1 I argue this case in 'Der intellektuelle Reiz der Reformation', in *Rechtfertigung und Erfahrung*, ed. by M. Beintker, E. Maurer, H. Stoevesandt & H. Ulrich (Gütersloh: Christian Kaiser, 1995), pp. 43-58.

2 Karlfried Froehlich reminds us of the difficulty of predicting medieval exegesis as well. See his article, 'The Significance of Medieval Biblical Interpretation', *Lutheran Quarterly*, 9.2 (Summer 1995), 139-50.

3 The question of whether Abraham was justified by faith alone was already under discussion in the Middle Ages as the exegesis of Romans 4 by Denis the Carthusian clearly demonstrates. Although the thief on the cross was justified *sola fide*, his case was regarded by medieval theologians as clearly exceptional. See the exegesis of Romans 4 by Denis the Carthusian, *In Omnes Beati Pauli Epistolas Commentaria* (Cologne: Peter Quentel, 1545).

4 For a discussion of the sixteenth-century debate on Romans 7, see David C. Steinmetz, *Calvin in Context* (New York: Oxford University Press, 1995), pp. 110-21.

5 Glosses from early and high medieval sources also play a role in the late medieval exegetical tradition like Lanfranc in Hugh of Saint-Cher and Thomas Aquinas in Nicholas of Lyra, but the principal sources for glosses in the later middle ages are the writings of the Fathers.

6 The most helpful treatment of this subject I have found is in an as yet unpublished essay by John Van Engen, Director of the Medieval Studies Institute at Notre Dame, entitled, 'Studying Scripture in the Early University'. See also William Courtenay, 'The Bible in the Fourteenth Century: Some Observations', *Church History*, 54 (1985), 176-87.

7 This fact is clearly evident from the notes and apparatus of Ignatius Brady in the critical edition of Lombard's *Sentences*, 'Magistri Petri Lonbardi Sententiae in IV Libris Distinctae', *Spicilegium Bonaventurianum*, 5 (Grottoferrata, 1981).

8 Erasmus himself knew almost no Hebrew and relied on Johannes Oecolampadius for help with this language. See 'New Testament Scholarship: Annotations on Romans', ed. by Robert D. Sider, *Collected Works of Erasmus 56* (Toronto: University of Toronto Press, 1994), p. xvii, n. 2.

9 See, for example, Cajetan's frequent references to the original Hebrew text in his exegesis of the story of the binding of Isaac in Genesis 22. Thomas de Vio Cardinal Cajetan, *In Quinque Libros Mosis iuxta Sensum Literalem Commentarii: Et Primum in Genesin, Opera Omnia quotquot in Sacrae Scripturae Expositionem Reperiuntur*, vol. 1 (Lyon: Jacob & Peter Prost, 1539), pp. 91-3.

10 A rather nice example of this phenomenon is provided by Peter Artopoeus in his *Aphorismoi de Prima Rerum Origine* (Basel: Heinrich Peter, 1546).

11 An excellent overview of German translations is offered by Heimo Reinitzer, *Biblia Deutsch: Luthers Bibelübersetzung und ihre Tradition* (Wolfenbüttel: Herzog August Bibliothek, 1983).

12 Perhaps I should qualify this judgement by observing that our definition of scholasticism is frequently too restrictive. When scholastic theologians lectured on the literal sense of the Bible, they were not taking a holiday from the scholastic program, but fulfilling it. Lectures on the glossed Bible that proceed from the first verse of the first chapter to the last verse of the last chapter are just as scholastic as *quaestiones*, *distinctiones* and *disputationes*.

13 See, for example, my article 'Calvin among the Thomists', in *Biblical Hermeneutics in Historical Perspective*, ed. by Mark S. Burrows & Paul Rorem (Grand Rapids, Mich.: Eerdmans, 1991), pp. 198-214, and reprinted in *Calvin in Context*.

14 Erasmus provides excellent examples of such subversion in his discussions of Romans 5:12 and 9:5. See Sider (above, n. 8), pp. 139-51, 242-52.

15 The criticisms by Edward Lee of the work of Erasmus and his defence of the Vulgate may

be taken as an example of a reasoned theological response to the New Learning by a conservative Catholic. See Cecilia Asso, 'La Teologia e la Grammatica: la Controversia tra Erasmo', ed. by Edward Lee, *Studi e Testi per la Storia Religiosa del Cinquecento* 4 (Florence: Leo S. Olschki Editore, 1993).

16 G. R. Evans refers to this notion as the principle of Scripture's progress to perfection and cites the 1515 letter of Maarten Dorp to Erasmus, in which she argues that Hebrew and Greek were preparatory to the authoritative Latin text: see *Problems of Authority in the Reformation Debates* (Cambridge: University Press, 1992), pp. 46-7.

17 Erasmus claimed that one could not be a theologian without a knowledge of Greek, an assertion which, if taken seriously, swept away the work of such figures as Anselm, Abelard, Bonaventure, Scotus, Thomas Aquinas and Ockham. He did not extend that claim to a knowledge of Hebrew.

18 The new zeal for Hebrew learning was thus not reflected in the text of post-Trent Catholic printed Bibles, but rather the discipline was relegated to the marginal notes (see Pl. 44).

19 On this point see my 'Luther and Staupitz: an Essay in the Intellectual Origins of the Protestant Reformation', *Duke University Monographs in Medieval and Renaissance Studies* 4 (Durham, NC: Duke University Press, 1980).

20 See especially the essays by A. N. S. Lane, 'Early Printed Patristic Anthologies to 1566: a Progress Report', in *Studia Patristica*, 18.4, ed. by Elizabeth A. Livingstone (Kalamazoo, Mich.: Cistercian Publications, 1990), pp. 365-170 and 'Justification in Sixteenth-Century Patristic Anthologies', in *Auctoritas Patrum: Contributions on the Reception of the Church Fathers in the 15th and 16th Century*, ed. by Leif Grane, Alfred Schindler & Markus Wriedt (Mainz: Philipp von Zabern, 1994), pp. 69-95.

21 The Lutheran theologian, Aegidius Hunnius, thought that Calvin was altogether too free in his criticisms of Patristic exegetical tradition. He composed a treatise, *Calvinus Iudaizans*, sharply critical of Calvin, which was answered by the Reformed theologian, David Pareus, in *Calvinus Orthodoxus*. See my essay on this controversy, 'The Judaizing Calvin', in the forthcoming volume, *Die Patristik in der Bibelexegese des 16. Jahrhunderts*, published later in 1996 by the Herzog August Bibliothek in Wolfenbüttel, Germany.

22 This a point forcefully made by Calvin in his public letter to Cardinal Jacopo Sadoleto. For a discussion of this letter and the issues it addresses see my essay 'Luther and Calvin on Church and Tradition', *Michigan Germanic Studies*, 10.1-2 (Spring/Fall 1984), pp. 98-111.

23 For an excellent brief treatment of the use of the Fathers in the sixteenth century, see the article by Irena Backus, 'Patristics', in *The Oxford Encyclopedia of the Reformation*, vol. 3, ed. by Hans J. Hillerbrand (New York: Oxford University Press, 1996), pp. 223-7.

24 *Journal of Theological Studies*, 46.2 (October 1993): 666-70.

# BIBLIOGRAPHY


Adams, Herbert M., *Catalogue of Books Printed on the Continent of Europe, 1501-1600, in Cambridge Libraries* (Cambridge: University Press, 1967).

Albino, Diana, 'La Divisione in capitoli nelle opere degli antichi', *Annali della Facoltà di lettere e filosofia (Università di Napoli,* 10 (1962-3).

Alexander, J. J. G. & M. T. Gibson, eds, *Medieval Learning and Literature: Essays Presented to Richard William Hunt* (Oxford: Clarendon Press, 1976).

Andrieu, Michel, *Les* Ordines *romani du haut moyen âge*, 5 vols, Spicilegium sacrum Lovaniense 11, 23-4, 28-9 (Louvain: Université catholique de Louvain, 1931-61).

*Anejo a la edición facsímile de la Biblia Políglota Complutense* (Valencia: Fundación Bíblica Española y Universidad Complutense de Madrid, 1987).

Artopoeus, Peter, *Aphorismoi de Prima Rerum Origine* (Basel: Heinrich Peter, 1546).

Aston, Margaret, *Lollards and Reformers: Images and Literacy in Late Medieval Religion* (London: Hambledon Press, 1984).

Aurner, N. S., *Caxton: Mirror of Fifteenth-Century Letters* (New York: Russell, 1965).

Baptist-Hlawatsch, Gabriele, *Der katechetische Werk Ulrich von Pottenstein* (Tübingen: Niemeyer, 1980).

Baras, Elisabeth, Jean Irigoin & Jean Vezin, *La Reliure Médiévale: Trois conférences d'initiation* (Paris: Presses de l'Ecole Normale Supérieure, 1978).

Barber, Giles, *Textile and Embroidered Bindings* (Oxford: Bodleian Library, 1971).

Barker, Nicolas, ed., *A Potencie of Life: Books in Society* (London: The British Library, 1993).

Barns, J. W. B. & G. D. Kilpatrick, 'A New Psalm Fragment', *Proceedings of the British Academy*, 43 (1957).

Bataillon, Marcel, *Erasmo y España: estudios sobre la historia espiritual del siglo XVI*, trans. by Antonio Alatorre, 2nd Spanish edn, corrected and augmented, 2nd repr. (Mexico, Madrid, Buenos Aires: Fondo de Cultura Económico, 1983).

Baurmeister, Ursula, *Catalogue des incunables (CIBN)*, vol. I, fasc. 1 (Paris: Bibliothèque nationale, 1992).

Baurmeister, Ursula, *Livrets xylographiques et collectionneurs* (Paris: Bibliothèque nationale, 1991).

Bayerer, Wolfgang G., *Die Handschriften des ehem. Fraterherrenstift Sankt Markus zu Butzbach* (Wiesbaden: Otto Harrassowitz, 1980).

Bedouelle, Guy, *Le 'Quincuplex Psalterium' de Lefèvre d'Etaples: un guide de lecture* (Geneva: Droz, 1979).

Beintker, Michael, E. Maurer, H. Stoevesandt & H. Ulrich, eds, *Rechtfertigung und Erfahrung,* (Gütersloh: Christian Kaiser/Gütersloher Verlagshaus, 1995).

Beit-Arié, Malachi, *Hebrew Manuscripts of East and West: Towards a Comparative Codicology* (London: The British Library, 1992).

Bennett, H. S., *English Books and Readers: 1475-1557* (Cambridge: University Press, 1952).

Bentley, Jerry H., *Humanists and Holy Writ: New Testament Scholarship in the Renaissance* (Princeton, N.J.: Princeton University Press 1983).

# Bibliography


Bentley, Jerry H., 'New Light on the Editing of the Complutensian New Testament', *Bibliothèque d'Humanisme et Renaissance, Travaux et Documents* XLII (Geneva: 1980).

Berger, Samuel, 'Un ancien texte latin des Actes des Apôtres retrouvé dans un manuscrit provenant de Perpignan', *Notices et extraits des manuscrits de la Bibliothèque Nationale et autres bibliothèques*, 35, pt 1 (1895).

Berger, Samuel, *La Bible française au XVIe siècle: Etude sur les origines de la critique biblique* (Paris, 1879).

Berns, Jörg Jochen & Wolfgang Neuber, eds, *Ars memorativa: Zur kulturgeschichtlichen Bedeutung der Gedächtniskunst 1400-1750*, Frühe Neuzeit 15 (Tübingen: Max Niemeyer Verlag, 1993).

Bing, Gertrud, 'The Apocalypse Block-Books and their Manuscript Models', *Journal of the Warburg and Courtauld Institutes*, 5 (1942).

*Blockbücher des Mittelalters: Bilderfolgen als Lektüre*, ed. by the Gutenberg-Gesellschaft and Gutenberg-Museum (Mainz: Gutenberg-Gesellschaft, 1991).

Bonnard, Jean, *Les Traductions de la Bible en vers français du moyen âge* (Paris: Imprimerie Nationale, 1884).

Bottigheimer, Ruth B., *The Bible for Children, From the Age of Gutenberg to the Present* (New Haven & London: Yale University Press, 1996).

Bouvet, Francis, ed., '*Le Cantique des cantiques: Canticum canticorum. Historia seu providentia Beatae Mariae Virginis ex Cantico canticorum*', Les Chefs d'oeuvre de la xylographie 1.1 (Paris: Éditions de Minuit, 1961).

Bozzolo, Carla & Ezio Ornato, *Pour une histoire du livre manuscrit au Moyen Age: Trois essais de codicologie quantitative* (Paris: Editions du Centre National de la Recherche Scientifique, 1983).

Brown, Michelle P., *A Guide to Western Historical Scripts from Antiquity to 1600* (London: The British Library, 1990).

Brown, Michelle P., *Understanding Illuminated Manuscripts: Guide to Technical Terms* (Malibu: The J. Paul Getty Museum & London: The British Library, 1994).

Bullen, George, ed., *Caxton Celebration, 1877: Catalogue of the Loan Collection of Antiquities, Curiosities and Appliances connected with the Art of Printing* (London: Elzevir Press, Trench Trübner, 1877).

Burrows, Mark S. & Paul Rorem, *Biblical Hermeneutics in Historical Perspective* (Grand Rapids: Wm. B. Eerdmans, 1991).

Busch, Johannes, *Chronicon Windeshemense und Liber de Reformatione monasteriorum*, ed. by K. Grube (Halle i. Sachsen: Hendel, 1886).

Cajetan, Thomas de Vio, *In Quinque Libros Mosis iuxta Sensum Literalem Commentarii: Et Primum in Genesin, Opera Omnia quotquot in Sacrae Scripturae Expositionem Reperiuntur*, vol. 1 (Lyon: Jacob & Peter Prost, 1539).

Callus, D. A., ed., *Robert Grosseteste Scholar and Bishop* (Oxford: Clarendon Press, 1955).

Campbell, M. F. A. G., *Annales de la typographie néerlandaise au xve siecle* (The Hague: Nijhoff, 1874-84).

Carruthers, Mary, *The Book of Memory: a Study of Memory in Medieval Culture* (Cambridge: University Press, 1990).

Cassien, Monseigneur [Serge Bezobrazov] & Dom Bernard Botte, eds, *La Prière des heures*, Lex orandi 35 (Paris: Les éditions du Cerf, 1963).

*Catalogue of Books Printed in the XVth Century now in the British Museum* (London: British Museum, 1908- ).

Catón, José María Fernández, ed., *Creadores del libro del Medioevo al Renacimiento: Sala de Exposiciones de la Fundación Central Hispano, 28 de septiembre-20 de noviembre, 1994* (Madrid: Dirección General del Libro y Bibliotecas y Fundación Central Hispano, 1994).

# Bibliography

Cattley, S. R. & C. Townsend, eds, *The Acts and Monuments of John Foxe*, 8 vols (London: R. B. Seeley & W. Burnside, 1837-41; repr. New York: AMS Press, 1965).
Chartier, Roger, ed., *The Culture of Print: Power and Uses of Print in Early Modern Europe*, (Princeton, N.J., 1987).
Chico, Ángel Escobar, *Codices Caesaraugustani graeci: catálogo de los manuscritos griegos de la Biblioteca Capitular de la Seo (Zaragoza)* (Saragossa: Institución Fernando el Católico, 1993).
Clemen, Otto, ed., *Canticum Canticorum: Holztafeldruck von c. 1465, mit einer Einleitung*, Zwickauer Facsimiledrucke 4 (Zwickau: Ullmann, 1910).
Collinson, Patrick, *The Birthpangs of Protestant England* (London: Macmillan, 1988).
Cornell, Henrik, *Biblia pauperum* (Stockholm: Thule-tryck, 1925).
Corsten, Severin, Günther Pflug & Friedrich Adolf Schmidt-Künsemüller, eds, *Lexikon des gesamten Buchwesens* (Stuttgart: Anton Hiersemann, 1991).
Courtenay, William, 'The Bible in the Fourteenth Century: Some Observations', *Church History*, 54 (1985).
Cowley, Arthur Ernest, *A Concise Catalogue of the Hebrew Printed Books in the Bodleian Library* (Oxford: Clarendon Press, 1929; repr. Oxford: Clarendon Press, 1971).
Crapulli, Giovanni, ed., *Trasmissione dei Testi a Stampa nel Periodo Moderno*, II (Rome: Edizioni dell'Ateno, 1987).
Cressy, David, 'Books as Totems in 17th-Century England and New England', *Journal of Library History*, 21 (1986).
Cuming, Geoffrey John, ed., *Studies in Church History* v (Leiden, 1969).
Daniell, David, *William Tyndale: a Biography* (New Haven & London: Yale University Press, 1994).
Darlow, T. H. & H. F. Moule, *Historical Catalogue of the Holy Scripture in the Library of the British and Foreign Bible Society* (London: The Bible House, 1903).
Darnton, Robert, 'What Is the History of Books?', *Daedalus*, 111:3 (Summer 1982).
*Das werck der bucher, eine Festschrift für Horst Kliemann zu seinem 60. Geburtstag* (Freiburg/Br 1956).
Davies, Martin, 'Juan de Carvajal and Early Printing: the 42-line Bible and the Sweynheym and Pannartz Aquinas', *The Library*, 6th ser. XVIII: 3 (September, 1996).
Deanesly, Margaret *The Lollard Bible and Other Medieval Biblical Versions* (Cambridge: University Press, 1920; repr. 1966).
Debes, Dietmar, *Leipziger Zimelien, Bücherschätze der Universitätsbibliothek* (Weinheim: VCH, 1989).
de Bruyne, Donatien, *Préfaces de la Bible Latine* (Namur: A. Godenne, 1920).
de Hamel, Christopher, *Glossed Books of the Bible and the Origins of the Paris Booktrade* (Woodbridge, Suffolk; Wolfeboro, New Hampshire: D. S. Brewer, 1987).
de Hamel, Christopher, *A History of Illuminated Manuscripts* 2nd edn (London: Phaidon Press, 1994).
Delisle, Léopold, *Le Cabinet des manuscrits de la Bibliothèque Nationale* (Paris: Imprimerie Nationale, 1868-81).
Delisle, Léopold, *Mélanges de paléographie et de bibliographie* (Paris: Champion, 1880).
Delisle, Léopold, *Notice de douze manuscrits royaux du XIIIe et XIVe siècle* (Paris: Imprimerie Nationale, 1902).
Delitzsch, Franz, *Fortgesetzte Studien zur Entstehungsgeschichte der Compluten-sischen Polyglotte* (Leipzig: Alexander Edelmann, 1886).
de Lubac, Henri, *Exégèse médiévale: les quatre sens de l'Ecriture*, 4 vols (Paris: Aubier, 1964).
Denis the Carthusian, *In Omnes Beati Pauli Epistolas Commentaria* (Cologne: Peter Quentel, 1545).
De-Rossi, Johannes Bernardus, *Annales Hebraeo-typographici seculi XV* (Parma: Ex Regio

Typographeo, 1795; repr. Amsterdam: Philo Press, 1969).

*Die Amerbachkorrespondenz, I Band: Die Briefe aus der Zeit Johann Amerbachs, 1481-1513*, ed., Alfred Hartmann (Basel: Verlag der Universitätsbibliothek, 1942).

*Dizionario biografico degli Italiani* (Rome: Instituto della Enciclopedia Italiana, 1960- ).

Donati, Lamberto & Luigi Michelini Tocci, eds, *Riproduzione del codice palatino latino 143: Canticum Canticorum – Biblia pauperum – Dis ist ein baum indem man lichtlicht des biblisthen hystorien geschicht in gedencken mag – Historia Davidis*, Codices e Vaticanis selecti quam simillime expressi, Series minor 4 (Città del Vaticana: Biblioteca Apostolica Vaticana, 1979).

Duff, Gordon, *Fifteenth Century English Books* (Oxford: University Press, 1917).

Duffy, Eamon, *The Stripping of the Altars: Traditional Religion in England, 1400-1580* (New Haven & London: Yale University Press, 1992).

Ehwald, Rudolf, ed., *Biblia pauperum: Deutsche Ausgabe um 1471* (Weimar: Gesellschaft der Bibliophilen, 1906).

*Einheitsübersetzung der Heiligen Schrift, Neues Testament* (Stuttgart: Katholische Bibelanstalt, 1979).

Eisenstein, Elizabeth, *The Printing Press as an Agent of Change* (Cambridge: University Press, 1979).

Erasmus, Desiderius, *Annotationes in Epistolam ad Romanos*, ed. by Robert D. Sider (Toronto: University of Toronto Press, 1994).

Erler, Mary C., 'Pasted-In Embellishments in English Manuscripts and Printed Books c.1480-1533', *The Library*, 6th Series, XIV:3 (September 1992).

Escavy, R., J. M. Hernández Terrés & A. Roldán, eds, *Actas del Congreso internacional de historiografía lingüística: Nebrija V centenario*, 3 vols (Murcia: Universidad, 1994).

Evans, G. R., *Problems of Authority in the Reformation Debates* (Cambridge: University Press, 1992).

Forshall, J. & F. Madden, *The Holy Bible Made from the Latin Vulgate by John Wyclife and his Followers* (Oxford: University Press, 1850).

Froehlich, Karlfried, 'The Significance of Medieval Biblical Interpretation', *Lutheran Quarterly*, 9.2 (Summer 1995).

Froehlich, Karlfried & Margaret T. Gibson, eds, *Biblia Latina cum Glossa Ordinaria: Facsimile Reprint of the Editio Princeps, Adolph Rusch of Strassburg, 1480/81*, 4 vols (Turnhout, Belgium: Brepols, 1992).

Gamble, Harry Y., *Readers in the Early Church: a History of Early Christian Texts* (New Haven & London: Yale University Press, 1995).

Gameson, Richard, ed., *The Early Medieval Bible* (Cambridge: University Press, 1994).

Gamper, Rudolf, *Die Zürcher Stadtchroniken und ihre Ausbreitung in die Ostschweiz: Forschungsgeschichte, Überlieferung, Analyse der Chroniktexte*, Mitteilungen der Antiquarischen Gesellschaft in Zürich 52,2 (Zurich: H. Rohr, 1984).

Gaskell, Philip, *A New Introduction to Bibliography* (first published 1972, repr. with corrections, Oxford: Clarendon Press, 1985).

Gasparri, Françoise, *Le XIIe siècle: Mutations et renouveau en France dans la première moitié du XIIe siècle* (Paris: Le Léopard d'Or, 1994).

Geldner, Ferdinand, 'Amerbachstudien', *Archiv für Geschichte des Buchwesens*, 23 (1982).

Geldner, Ferdinand, *Die deutschen Inkunabeldrucker: ein Handbuch der deutschen Drucker des XV. Jahrhunderts nach Druckorten. Erster Band: Das deutsche Sprachgebiet* (Stuttgart: Anton Hiersemann, 1968).

*Gesamtkatalog der Wiegendrucke* (Leipzig: Hiersemann, 1925-40, repr. 1978; Stuttgart: Hiersemann; Berlin: Akademie-Verlag; New York: Kraus, 1978- ).

Gibson, Margaret, *The Bible in the Latin West*, (Notre Dame: University of Notre Dame, 1993).

# Bibliography

Gibson, Margaret, T. A. Heslop & R. W. Pfaff, eds, *The Eadwine Psalter: Text, Image, and Monastic Culture in Twelfth-Century Canterbury* (London: Modern Humanities Research Association and University Park, Pa.: Pennsylvania State University Press, 1992).

Gilissen, Léon, *La Reliure occidentale antérieure à 1400* (Bibliologia, 1; Turnhout: Brepols, 1983).

Gillet, Louis, *La Cathédrale vivante* (Paris: Flammarion, 1964).

Ginsburg, Christian David, *Intoduction to the Massoretico-Critical Edition of the Hebrew Bible* (London: Trinitarian Bible Society, 1897; repr. with a Prolegomenon by H. M. Orlinsky, New York: Ktav, 1966).

Gistelick, Frans & Maurits Sabbe, eds, *Early Sixteenth Century Printed Books 1501-1540 in the Library of the Leuven Faculty of Theology* (Leuven: Bibliotheek Godgeleerdheid, 1994).

*Glanz alter Buchkunst: mittelalterliche Handschriften der Staatsbibliothek Preußischer Kulturbesitz Berlin* (Wiesbaden: L. Reichert, 1988).

Goff, Frederick R., *Incunabula in American Libraries: a Third Census of Fifteenth-Century Books Recorded in North American Collections*, annotated repr. (Millwood, N.Y.: Kraus, 1973).

Goldschmidt, Lazarus, *The Earliest Editions of the Hebrew Bible: with a Treatise on the Oldest Manuscripts of the Bible by Paul Kahle* (New York: Aldus Book Co., 1950).

Goldstein, David, *Hebrew Incunables in the British Isles: a Preliminary Census* (London: The British Library, *c.* 1985).

Gómez de Castro, Alvar, *De rebus gestis a Francisco Ximenio Cisnerio, archiepiscopo toletano, libri octo* (Alcalá: Andream de Angulo, 1569).

Gómez de Castro, Alvar, *De las hazañas de Francisco Jiménez de Cisneros*, ed. & trans. by José Oroz Meta (Madrid: Fundación Universitaria Española, 1984).

Gould, Karen, 'The Gutenberg Bible at Texas: An Educational Resource', *The Library Chronicle of the University of Texas at Austin*, ns 22 (1983).

Grafton, Anthony & Lisa Jardine, *From Humanism to the Humanities: Education and the Liberal Arts in Fifteenth and Sixteenth Century Europe* (Cambridge, Mass.: Harvard University Press, 1986).

Grane, Leif, Alfred Schindler & Markus Wriedt, eds, *Auctoritas Patrum: Contributions on the Reception of the Church Fathers in the 15th and 16th Century* (Mainz: Philipp von Zabern, 1993).

Graux, Charles, 'Nouvelles recherches sur la stichométrie', *Revue de philologie, de littérature et d'histoire anciennes*, n.s. 2 (1878).

Greenslade, S. L., ed., *The Cambridge History of the Bible*, III (Cambridge: University Press, 1963).

Greitemann, N., *De Windesheimsche Vulgatarevisie in de vijftiende eeuw* (Hilversum: N.v.P. Brand's Uitgeversbedrijf, 1937).

Griffin, Clive, *The Crombergers of Seville: the History of a Printing and Merchant Dynasty* (Oxford: Clarendon Press, 1988).

Griffiths, Jeremy & Derek Pearsall, eds, *Book Production and Publishing in Britain 1375-1475* (Cambridge: University Press, 1989).

Gross-Diaz, Theresa, *The Psalms Commentary of Gilbert of Poitiers: from Lectio Divina to the Lecture Room* (Leiden & New York: E. J. Brill, 1996).

Guarnaschelli, T. M. & E. Valenziani in collaboration with E. Cerulli, eds, *Indice generale degli incunaboli delle biblioteche d'Italia* (Rome: La Libreria dello Stato, 1954- ).

Gumbert, J. P., '"Typography" in the Manuscript Book', *Journal of the Printing Historical Society* 22 (London: Printing Historical Society, 1993).

Haebler, Konrad, *Bibliografía ibérica del siglo XV*, 2 vols (The Hague & Leipzig: Nijhoff, 1903-17).

# Bibliography

Hain, Ludwig, *Repertorium bibliographicum in quo libri omnes ab arte typographica inventa usque ad annum MD. typis expressi ordine alphabetico ... enumerantur* etc. (Paris & Stuttgart: 1826-38; repr. Milan: Görlich, 1948, 1966).

Hamburger, Jeffrey F., *The Rothschild Canticles: Art and Mysticism in Flanders and the Rhineland circa 1300* (New Haven, Conn.: Yale University Press, 1990).

Hellinga, Lotte, 'Three Notes on Printer's Copy: Strassburg, Oxford, Subiaco', *Transactions of the Cambridge Bibliographical Society*, IX: 2 (1987).

Hellinga, Lotte & John Goldfinch, eds, *Bibliography and the Study of 15th-Century Civilisation* (London: The British Library; Wolfeboro, N.H., 1987).

Henry, Avril, ed., *Biblia Pauperum: a Facsimile and Edition* (Aldershot: Scolar Press, 1987).

Herbert, A. S., ed., *Historical Catalogue of Printed Editions of the English Bible, 1525-1961 Revised ... from the Edition of T. H. Darlow and H. F. Moule, 1903* (London: British & Foreign BIble Society; New York: American Bible Society, 1968).

Hilberg, Isidorus, 'Sancti Hieronymi Epistulae', *Corpus Sanctorum Ecclesiasticorum Latinorum* LV (Leipzig: 1912).

Hillerbrand, Hans J., ed., *The Oxford Encyclopedia of the Reformation* (New York: Oxford University Press, 1996).

Hind, Arthur M., *An Introduction to the History of the Woodcut*, 2 vols (London: Constable, 1935; repr. New York: Dover, 1963).

Hindman, Sandra L., ed., *Printing the Written Word: the Social History of Books, circa 1450-1520* (Ithaca, N.Y.: Cornell University Press, 1991).

Hochegger, Rudolf ed., *Liber Regum. Nach dem in der k.k. Universitätsbibliothek zu Innsbruck befindlichen Exemplar* (Leipzig: Otto Harrassowitz, 1892).

Hochegger, Rudolf, *Ueber die Entstehung und Bedeutung der Blockbücher mit besonderer Rücksicht auf den Liber Regum seu Historia Davidis*, Zentralblatt für Bibliothekswesen, Beiheft 7 (Leipzig: Otto Harrassowitz, 1891; repr. Nendeln & Wiesbaden: Kraus Reprint Ltd; Otto Harrassowitz, 1968).

Hodeige, Fritz, ed., *Das werck der Bucher, ein Festschrift für Horst Kliemann zu seinem 60. Geburtstag* (Freiburg/Br: Rombach, 1956).

Holborn, H. & A. Holborn, eds, *Erasmus Ausgewählte Werke* (Munich: Beck, 1933; repr.1964).

Hudson, Anne, *Lollards and their Books* (London: Hambledon Press, 1985).

Hudson, Anne, *The Premature Reformation* (Oxford: Clarendon Press, 1988).

Hudson, Anne & D. Everett, 'The Middle English Prose Psalter of Richard Rolle of Hampole', *Modern Language Review*, 17-18 (1922-3).

Hudson, Anne & H. L. Spencer, 'Old Author, New Work: The Sermons of MS Longleat 4', *Medium Aevum*, 53 (1984).

Hunt, Arnold, Giles Mandlebrote & Alison Shell, eds, *The Book Trade and its Customers: 1450-1900* (Winchester: Hampshire: St Paul's Bibliographies; New Castle, Delaware: Oak Knoll Press, 1997).

Hunt, R. W., 'Manuscripts Containing the Indexing Symbols of Robert Grosseteste', *Bodleian Library Record*, 4 (1953).

Ibáñez, Vicenta Pastor, *Historia de la pintura en Elche: pintores ilicitanos nacidos en el siglo XIX* (Madrid: Ed. de la Universidad Complutense, 1988).

*Index Aureliensis: catalogus librorum sedecimo saeculo impressorum* (Aureliae Aquensis 196, 1962- ).

James, M. R., *The Western Manuscripts in the Library of Trinity College, Cambridge*, 4 vols, vol. 2 (Cambridge: University Press, 1901).

John Rylands Library, *Catalogue of an Exhibition Illustrating the History of the Transmission of the Bible* (Manchester: University Press, 1935).

Kenny, Anthony, *Wyclif* (Oxford: Univeristy Press, 1985).

# Bibliography

Ker, N. R., *Medieval Manuscripts in British Libraries*, 4 vols (Oxford: Clarendon Press, 1969-92).

King, John, *English Reformation Literature: the Tudor Origins of the Protestant Tradition* (Princeton: University Press, 1982).

Kohlschmidt, Werner & Wolfgang Mohr, *Reallexikon de Deutschen Literaturgeschichte* (Berlin: de Gruyter, 1958).

Köllner, Herbert, *Die illuminierten Handschriften der Hessischen Landesbibliothek Fulda* I, (Stuttgart: Hiersemann, 1976).

König, Eberhard, *The 1462 Fust and Schoeffer Bible: an Essay ... with an Original Leaf from the 1462 Bible* (Akron, Oh.: Bruce Ferrini; Evanston, Ill.: Hamill & Barker, 1993).

König, Eberhard, 'Die Illuminierung der Gutenbergbibel', in *Johannes Gutenbergs zweiundvierzigzeilige Bibel ... Kommentarband*, ed. by Wieland Schmidt & F. A. Schmidt-Künsemüller (Munich: Idion, 1979).

König, Eberhard, *Zur Situation der Gutenberg-Forschung: ein Supplement* (Münster: Verlag Bibliotheca Rara, 1995).

König, Eberhard, 'A Leaf from a Gutenberg Bible Illuminated in England', *British Library Journal*, 9 (1983)

König, Eberhard, 'Möglichkeiten kunstgeschichtlicher Beiträge zur Gutenberg-Forschung ...', *Gutenberg-Jahrbuch* (Mainz: Gutenberg-Gesellschaft, 1984).

Kristeller, Paul, ed., *Biblia pauperum: Unicum der Heidelberger Universitätsbibliothek*, Graphische Gesellschaft Veröffentlichung 2 (Berlin: Bruno Cassirer, 1906).

Kristeller, Paul, ed., *Die Apokalypse: Älteste Blockbuchausgabe in Lichtdrucknachbildung* (Berlin: Bruno Cassirer, 1916).

Leclercq, H., 'Canons d'Eusèbe', *Dictionnaire d'archéologie chrétienne et de liturgie* 2 (Paris: Letouzez & Ané, 1910).

Lee, Edward, ed., *Studi e Testi per la Storia Religiosa del Cinquecento*, 4 (Florence: Leo S. Olschki Editore, 1993).

Lehmann, Paul, *Mittelalterliche Bibliothekskataloge Deutschlands und der Schweiz* (1928).

Lehmann-Haupt, Hellmut, *The Göttingen Model Book: a Facsimile Edition and Translations of a Fifteenth-Century Illuminators' Manual* (Columbia, Missouri: University of Missouri Press, 1972).

Lemaire, Claudine, 'La Bible du Gutenberg d'Eton Library, propriété de la comtesse Anne d'Yve de 1811 à 1814', *Gutenberg-Jahrbuch* (Mainz: Gutenberg-Gesellschaft, 1993).

Lemaire, Jacques, *Introduction à la codicologie* (Louvain-la-neuve: Université Catholique de Louvain, 1989).

Leroquais, V., *Les psautiers: manuscrits latins des bibliothèques publiques de France* (Macon: Protat Frères, 1940).

Little, A. G., *Franciscan Papers, Lists, and Documents* (Manchester: University Press, 1943).

Livingstone, Elizabeth A., ed., *Studia Patristica*, 18.4 (Kalamazoo, Mich.: Cistercian Publications, 1990).

Livingstone, Elizabeth A., ed., *Studia Patristica XXVIII, Papers Presented at the Eleventh International Conference on Patristic Studies held in Oxford 1991. Latin Authors (other than Augustine and his Opponents) Nachleben of the Fathers* (Leuven: Peeters, 1993).

Lomax, Derek W. & David Mackenzie, eds, *God and Man in Medieval Spain: Essays in Honour of J. R. L. Highfield* (Warminster: Aris & Phillips, 1989).

Lombard, Peter, 'Magistri Petri Lonbardi Sententiae in IV Libris Distinctae', *Spicilegium Bonaventurianum*, 5 (Grottoferrata, 1981).

López-Vidriero, María Luisa & Pedro M. Cátedra, eds, *El libro antiguo español* (Salamanca: Universidad de Salamanca, 1996).

Lyell, James P. R., *Cardinal Ximenes* (London: Grafton, 1917).

McEachern, Claire & Debora Shuger, eds, *Religion and Culture in Renaissance England* (Cambridge: University Press, 1997).

McLuhan, Marshall, *The Gutenberg Galaxy: the Making of Typographic Man* (Toronto: University of Toronto Press, 1962).

McKerrow, Ronald B., *An Introduction to Bibliography for Literary Students* (first published 1927, repr. with introduction by David McKitterick, Winchester: St Paul's Bibliographies; New Castle, Del.: Oak Knoll, 1994).

Mallebrera, Rafael Navarro & Manuela Andreu Pujalte, *Archivo municipal: catálogo de manuscritos de Pedro Ibarra Ruiz* (Elche: Ed. del Ayuntamiento, 1978).

Mangenot, E., 'Concordances de la Bible', *Dictionnaire de la Bible* 2 (1910).

Mann, Vivian B., Thomas F. Glick & Jerrilynn D. Dodds, eds, *Convivencia: Jews, Muslims and Christians in Medieval Spain* (New York: Braziller 1992).

Manning, Bernard Louis, *The People's Faith in the Time of Wyclif* (2nd edn; Sussex, 1975).

Marsden, Richard, 'Aelfric as Translator: the Old English Prose *Genesis*', *Anglia* (1991).

Marsden, Richard, 'Cain's Face, and Other Problems: the Legacy of the Earliest Bible Translations', *Reformation*, vol. 1 (1996).

Martín Abad, Julián, *La imprenta en Alcalá de Henares (1502-1600)*, 3 vols (Madrid: Arco Libros, 1991).

Martín Abad, Julián, 'Talleres de imprenta complutenses del siglo XVI: ediciones hasta ahora ignotas y ejemplares rarísimos (1-4)', *Puerta de Madrid*, 1381 (7 May 1994); 1386 (7 June 1994); 1390 (9 June 1994); 1392 (23 July 1994).

Martín Abad, Julián, 'Talleres de imprenta complutenses del siglo XVI: hallazgos de ediciones nunca descritas (1-8)', *Puerta de Madrid*, 1412 (24 December 1994); 1418 (11 February 1995); 1421 (4 March 1995); 1424 (25 March 1995); 1427 (22 April 1995); 1466 (17 February 1996); 1467 (24 February 1996); 1470 (25 May 1996).

Martin, Henri-Jean, *The French Book: Religion, Absolutism and Readership* (Baltimore: Johns Hopkins University Press, 1996).

Martin, Henri-Jean & Lucien Febvre, *The Coming of the Book* (London: Verso, 1990; first published as *L'Apparition du Livre*, Paris: Michel, 1958).

Martin, Henri-Jean & J. Vezin, eds, *Mise en page et mise en texte du livre manuscrit* ([Paris]: Editions du Cercle de la Librairie-Promodis, *c.* 1990).

Martz, Louis L. & Richard S. Sylvester, *Thomas More's Private Prayer Book* (New Haven & London: Yale University Press, 1969).

Massaut, Jean-Pierre, *Josse Clichtove, l'Humanisme et la réforme du clergé*, 2 vols (Paris: Les Belles Lettres, 1968).

Meier-Graefe, Julius, ed., *Canticum Canticorum: Editio archetypum anni circiter 1465 imitans*, Marées-Gesellschaft 34 (Munich: Officina 'Ganymedes', 1922).

Metzger, Bruce M. & Michael D. Coogan, eds, *The Oxford Companion to the Bible* (Oxford: University Press, 1993).

Metzger, Bruce M., *A Textual Commentary on the Greek New Testament* (Stuttgart: Deutsche Bibelgesellschaft, 2nd edn, 1994).

Milne, H. J. M. & T. C. Skeat, *Scribes and Correctors of the Codex Sinaiticus* (London: British Museum, 1938).

Mommsen, Theodor, 'Zur lateinischen Stichometrie', *Hermes*, 21 (1885).

Mommsen, Wolfgang J. & Peter Alter, eds, *The Urban Classes, the Nobility and the Reformation* (London: German Historical Institute, 1980), and *Historical Journal*, 25 (1982).

Montecchi, Giorgio, *Il libro nel Rinascimento: Saggi di bibliologia* (Milan: Editrice La Storia, 1994).

Moreau, Brigitte, *Inventaire chronologique des Éditions Parisiennes du XVIe siècle*, III (Paris: Service des travaux historiques de la ville de Paris, 1985).

Morison, Stanley, *German Incunabula in the British Museum* (London: Gollancz, 1928).
Musper, Theodor Heinrich, ed., *Der Antichrist und die fünfzehn Zeichen: Faksimile-Ausgabe des einzigen erhaltenen chiroxylographischen Blockbuches* (Munich: Prestel-Verlag, 1970).
Needham, Paul, 'Aldus Manutius's Paper Stocks: the Evidence of two Uncut Books', *Princeton University Library Chronicle* 55 no. 2 (Princeton, N.J.: Friends of the Princeton University Library, Winter 1994); issued also in: *The Same Purposeful Instinct: Essays in Honor of William H. Scheide*, ed. by William P. Stoneman (Princeton, N.J.: Princeton University Library, 1994).
Needham, Paul, 'The Compositor's Hand in the Gutenberg Bible: a Review of the Todd Thesis', *Papers of the Bibliographical Society of America*, 77 no. 3 (3rd quarter 1983).
Needham, Paul, 'Division of Copy in the Gutenberg Bible: Three Glosses on the Ink Evidence', *Papers of the Bibliographical Society of America*, 79 no. 3 (3rd quarter 1985).
Needham, Paul, 'A Gutenberg Bible used as Printer's Copy by Heinrich Eggestein in Strassburg, *ca.* 1469', *Transactions of the Cambridge Bibliographical Society*, IX: 1 (1986).
Needham, Paul, 'Haec sancta ars: Gutenberg's Invention as a Divine Gift', *Grolier Club Gazette*, 42 (New York: Grolier Club, 1990).
Needham, Paul, 'The Paper Supply of the Gutenberg Bible', *Papers of the Bibliographical Society of America*, 79 no. 3 (3rd quarter 1985).
Needham, Paul, *The Printer and the Pardoner* (Washington, D.C.: Library of Congress, 1986).
Neske, Ingeborg, *Die Handschriften der Stadtbibliothek Nürnberg. Band II: Die lateinischen mittelalterlichen Handschriften. Teil 2: Bibelhandschriften und Liturgica einschliesslich der griechischen Texte* (Wiesbaden: Harrassowitz, 1987).
Nijhoff, Wouter, *L'Art Typographique 1500-1540* (The Hague: Martinus Nijhoff, 1935).
Nordenfalk, Carl, *Die spätantiken Kanontafeln: Kunstgeschichtlichen Studien über die eusebianische Evangelien-Konkordanz in den vier ersten Jahrhunderten ihrer Geschichte* (Göteborg: Isacsons, 1938).
Norman, Don Cleveland, *The 500th Anniversary Pictorial Census of the Gutenberg Bible* (Chicago: Coverdale Press, 1961).
Norton, F. J., *A Descriptive Catalogue of Printing in Spain and Portugal 1501-20* (Cambridge: University Press, 1978).
Oates, J. C. T., *A Catalogue of the Fifteenth-Century Books in the University Library, Cambridge* (Cambridge: University Press, 1954).
Offenberg, A. K. & C. Moed-Van Walraven, *Hebrew Incunabula in Public Collections: a First International Census* (Nieuwkoop: de Graaf, 1990).
Olmedo, Félix G., *Nebrija (1441-1522): debelador de la barbarie, comentarista eclesiástico, pedagogo, poeta* (Madrid: Editora Nacional, 1942).
Oro, José García, *El cardenal Cisneros: vida y empresas*, 2 vols (Madrid: Biblioteca de Autores Cristianos, 1993).
Oro, José García, *Los reyes y los libros: la política libraria de la corona en el Siglo de Oro (1475-1598)* (Madrid: Cisneros, 1995).
Oro, José García, *La Universidad de Alcalá de Henares en la etapa fundacional (1458-1578)* (Santiago de Compostela: [s.n.], 1992).
Ouy, Gilbert, *Le Catalogue de la bibliotheque de Saint-Victor de Paris de Claude de Grandrue* (Paris: Editions du Centre National de la Recherche Scientifique, 1983).
Palmer, Nigel F., ed., *Apokalypse – Ars moriendi – Biblia pauperum – Antichrist – Fabel vom kranken Löwen – Kalendarium und Planetenbücher – Historia David: Die lateinisch-deutschen Blockbücher des Berlin-Breslauer Sammelbandes. Farbmikrofiche-Edition*, Monumenta xylographica et typographics 2 (Munich: Edition Helga Lengenfelder, 1992).
Palmer, Nigel F., 'Junius's blockbooks: Copies of the *Biblia pauperum* and *Canticum canticorum* in the Bodleian Library and Their Place in the History of Printing', *Renaissance Studies*, 9 (1995).

Palmer, Nigel, 'Kapital und Buch', *Frühmittelalterliche Studien* 23 (1989).

Pastor, Cristóbal Pérez, *Bibliografía madrileña, o descripción de las obras impresas en Madrid (siglo XVI)* (Madrid: Tipografía de los Huérfanos, 1891).

Petrucci, Armando, *Writers and Readers in Medieval Italy: Studies in the History of Written Culture* (New Haven & London: Yale University Press, 1995).

Piccard, Gerhard, 'Wasserzeichen Fabeltiere: Greif-Drache-Einhorn', *Findbuch 10 der Wasserzeichenkartei Piccard im Hauptstaatsarchiv Stuttgart. Veröffentlichungen der Staatlichen Archivverwaltung Baden-Württenberg, Sonderreihe* (Stuttgart: Kohlhammer, 1980).

Pilinski, Adam & Gustave Pawlowski, eds, *Ars memorandi reproduit en fac-similé sur l'exemplaire de la Bibliothèque Nationale*, Monuments de la xylographie 3 (Paris: Pilinski et fils, 1883).

Poesch, Jessie Jean, *Antichrist Imagery in Anglo-French Apocalypse Manuscripts* (unpublished doctoral dissertation, University of Pennsylvania, 1966).

Polain, M. Louis, ed., *Catalogue des Livres Imprimées au XVme Siècle des Bibliothèques de Belgique*, (Brussels: La Societé de Belgique, 1932).

Pollak, Michael, 'The Performance of the Wooden Printing Press', *The Library Quarterly*, 42 (1972).

Pollard, Alfred W., ed., *Records of the English Bible: the Documents Relating to the Translation and Publication of the Bible in English, 1525-1611* (London: Oxford University Press, 1911).

Pollard, Alfred W. & G. R. Redgrave, eds, *Short-Title Catalogue of English Books Printed in England, Scotland, and Ireland* (STC), 3 vols, 2nd edn, rev. by Katharine F. Pantzer & Philip R. Rider (London: The Bibliographical Society, 1976-91).

Powitz, Gerhard, *Der Frankfurter Gutenberg-Bibel: ein Beitrag zum Buchwesen des 15. Jahrhunderts* (Frankfurt: Frankfurter Bibliothekschriften, 1990).

Proctor, Robert, *An Index to the Early Printed Books in the British Museum from the Invention of Printing to the Year 1500, with Notes of Those in the Bodleian Library* (London: 1898, repr. London: Hollans Press, 1960).

Quentin, Henri, Dom. *Mémoire sur l'établissement du texte de la Vulgate* (Rome & Paris: Desclée, 1922).

Recio, Roxana, ed., *La traducción en España: ss. XIV-XVI* (León: Universidad de León, 1995).

Reinitzer, Heimo, *Biblia Deutsch: Luthers Bibelübersetzung und ihre Tradition* (Wolfenbüttel: Herzog August Bibliothek, 1983).

Remírez de Esparza, Francisco Asín, ed., *Mundo del libro antiguo* (Madrid: Editorial Complutense, 1996).

Renouard, A. A., *Annales de l'imprimerie des Estienne* (Paris: J. Renouard, 1843).

Rice, Eugene F. Jr, *The Prefatory Epistles of Jacques Lefèvre d'Etaples and Related Texts* (New York: Columbia University Press, 1972).

Riché, Pierre & Guy Lobrichon, eds, *Le Moyen Age et la Bible* (Paris: Beauchesne, 1984).

Rico, Mariano Revilla, *La Políglota de Alcalá: estudio histórico-critico* (Madrid: Impr. Helénica, 1917).

Rischpler, Susanne, '*Biblia Sacra figuris expressa*': *Mnemotechnische Bilderbibeln des 15. Jahrhunderts* (unpublished doctoral dissertation, University of Würzburg, 1995).

Roberts, C. H., *Greek Literary Hands 350 B.C.-A.D. 400* (Oxford: Clarendon Press, 1955).

Rodríguez, Pedro Sainz, *La siembra mística del cardenal Cisneros y las reformas en la iglesia* (Madrid: Universidad Pontificia de Salamanca y Fundación Universitaria Española, 1979).

*Richard Rolle: The English Writings*, ed. by R. S. Allen (New York: Paulist Press, 1988).

Rouse, Richard H. & Mary A. Rouse, *Preachers, Florilegia & Sermons: Studies on the Manipulus Florum of Thomas of Ireland* (Toronto: Pontifical Institute of Mediaeval Studies, 1979).

Rouse, Richard H. & Mary A. Rouse, 'The Verbal Concordance to the Scriptures', *Archivum fratrum praedicatorum*, 44 (1974).

Rück, Peter, ed., *Rationalisierung der Buchherstellung im Mittelalter und in der frühen Neuzeit* (Marburg an der Lahn: Institut für Historische Hilfswissenschaften, 1994).

Ruh, Kurt et al., eds, *Die deutsche Literatur des Mittelalters: Verfasserlexikon*, 2nd rev. ed. (Berlin & New York, 1978).

Ruiz, Juan Martínez, 'Visita a las imprentas granadinas de Antonio de Nebrija, Hugo de Mena y René Rabut en el año 1573', *Revista de dialectología y tradiciones populares*, 24 (1968).

Saenger, Paul, *A Catalogue of the Pre-1500 Manuscript Books at the Newberry Library* (Chicago: University of Chicago Press, 1989).

Saenger, Paul, 'The Impact of the Early Printed Page on the History of Reading', *Bulletin du Bibliophile*, 11 (Paris: Techener, 1996), 237-301.

Saenger, Paul, 'The Implications of Incunable Description for the History of Reading Revisited', *Papers of the Bibliographical Society of America*, 91 (1997).

Saenger, Paul, *Space Between Words: The Origin of Silent Reading* (Stanford: University Press, 1997).

Sauer, Christine, *Studium Lektüre Andacht: zur Handschriftenproduktion im 13. Jahrhundert* (Stuttgart: Württembergische Landesbibliothek, 1996).

Salmon, Pierre, OSB. *Les 'Tituli Psalmorum' des Manuscrits Latins* (Rome: Città del Vaticano: Abbaye Saint-Jérome: Libreria Vaticana, 1959).

Sayle, C. E., *Early English Printed Books in the University Library Cambridge* (Cambridge: University Press, 1900).

Schidmaier, Dieter, ed., *Zur Arbeit mit dem Gesamtkatalog der Wiegendrucke: Vorträge der internationalen Fachtagung vom 26. bis 30. November 1979 in Berlin* (Berlin: Deutsche Staatsbibliothek, 1989).

Schmidt, Charles, *Zur Geschichte der ältesten Bibliotheken und der ersten Buchdrucker zu Strassburg* (Strassburg: C. F. Schmidt's Universitätsbuchhandlung Friedrich Bull, 1882; repr. Graz: Akademische Druck- und Verlagsanstalt, 1971).

Schmidt, Gerhard, *Die Armenbibeln des XIV. Jahrhunderts* (Graz & Cologne: Böhlau, 1959).

Schmidt, Wieland & F. A. Schmidt-Künsemüller, *Johannes Gutenbergs zweiund vierzigzeilige Bibel … Kommentarband* (Munich: Idion, 1979).

Schneider, Heinrich, *Der Text der Gutenbergbibel zu ihrem 500jährigen Jubiläum untersucht* (Bonn: Bonner Biblische Beiträge 1954).

Schreiber, Fred, *The Estiennes* (New York: E. K. Schreiber, 1982).

Schreiber, Wilhelm Ludwig, *Manuel de l'amateur de la gravure sur bois et sur métal au XVe siècle. Tome quatrième contenant un catalogue des livres xylographiques et xylo- chirographiques, indiquant les différences de toutes les éditions existantes* (Leipzig: Otto Harrassowitz, 1902; repr. as id., *Handbuch der Holz- und Metallschnitte des XV. Jahrhundert*, 3rd edn, vol. IX <Manuel IV>, Nendeln & Stuttgart: Kraus Reprint Ltd.; Otto Harrassowitz, 1969).

Schulz, Ernst *Inkunabelsammlungen und ihr wissenschaftlicher Wert: Bemerkungen zur Sammlung Vollbehr* (Munich: Privatdruck, 1927).

Schwenke, Paul, *Johannes Gutenbergs zweiundvierzigzeilige Bibel: Ergänzungsband zur Faksimile-Ausgabe* (Leipzig, 1923).

Scribonius Largus, *Compositiones*, ed. by S. Sconocchia (Leipzig: Teubner, 1983).

Seebohn, Almuth, ed., *Apokalypse – Ars moriendi – Medizinische Traktate – Tugend-und Lasterlehren: Die erbaulich-didaktische Sammelhandschrift London, Wellcome Institute for the History of Medicine, Ms. 49: Farbmikrofiche-Edition*, Codices illuminati medii aevi 39 (Munich: Edition Helga Lengenfelder, 1995).

Sider, Robert D., ed., 'New Testament Scholarship: Annotations on Romans', *Collected Works of Erasmus 56* (Toronto: University of Toronto Press, 1994).

*El siglo de Fray Luis de León: Salamanca y el Renacimiento*, catalogue of an exhibition at the Colegio de Arzobispo Fonseca, Escuelas Menores, Antigua Universidad, Salamanca, Oct.- Dec.

1991 (Madrid: Ministero de Cultura, Centro Nacional de Exposiciones, etc., 1991).
Simmons, Thomas Frederick, *The Lay Folks Mass Book or the Manner of Hearing Mass with Rubrics & Devotions for the People* (EETS, o.s. no. 71; London, 1879).
Slights, William W. E., '"Marginall Notes that spoile the Text": Scriptural Annotation in the English Renaissance', *Huntington Library Quarterly*, 55 (1992).
Slights, William W. E., 'The Edifying Margins of Renaissance English Books', *Renaissance Quarterly*, 42 (1989).
Smalley, Beryl, 'Glossa Ordinaria', *Theologische Realenzyklopädie* XIII (Berlin: de Gruyter, 1984).
Smalley, Beryl, *The Study of the Bible in the Middle Ages*, 3rd rev. edn (Oxford: Basil Blackwell, 1983).
Smith, Margaret M., 'The Typography of Complex Texts: How an Early Printer Eliminated the Scribes' Red', *Typography Papers*, 1 (1996), 75-92.
Steffens, Franz, *Lateinische Paläographie* (Trier, 1909).
Steinmetz, David C., *Calvin in Context* (New York: Oxford University Press, 1995).
Steinmetz, David C., 'Luther and Calvin on Church and Tradition', *Michigan Germanic Studies*, 10.1-2 (Spring/Fall 1984).
Steinmetz, David C., 'Luther and Staupitz: An Essay in the Intellectual Origins of the Protestant Reformation'. *Duke University Monographs in Medieval and Renaissance Studies* 4 (Durham, NC: Duke University Press, 1980).
Stevenson, Allan, 'Watermarks are Twins', *Studies in Bibliography*, 4 (1951-2).
Stock, Brian, *Augustine the Reader: Meditation, Self Knowledge, and the Ethics of interpretation* (Cambridge, Mass.: Harvard University Press, 1996).
Stoddard, Roger, *Marks in Books, Shown and Explained* (Cambridge, Mass.: Harvard University Press, 1985).
Tasis, Rafael, *La Biblia valenciana* (Barcelona: Alberti, 1953).
Thomson, S. Harrison, 'Grosseteste's Topical Concordance of the Bible and the Fathers', *Speculum*, 9 (1934).
Thomson, S. Harrison, *The Writings of Robert Grosseteste Bishop of Lincoln 1235-1253* (Cambridge: University Press, 1940).
Todd, William B., 'The Texas Gutenberg Bible: Procedures Determining the Selection', *Journal of Library History*, 15 (1980).
Trebolle Barrera, Julio C., *La Biblia judía y la Biblia cristiana* (Madrid: Trotta, 1993).
Tribble, Evelyn B., *Margins and Marginality: the Printed Page in Early Modern England* (Charlottesville: University of Virginia Press, 1993).
Turner, Eric G., *Greek Manuscripts of the Ancient World* (Oxford: Clarendon Press, 1971).
Vaassen, Elgin, 'Die Werkstatt der Mainzer Riesenbibel in Würzburg und ihr Umkreis', *Archiv für Geschichte des Buchwesens*, XIII 5-6 (March 1973).
Vallejo, Juan de, *Memorial de la vida de fray Francisco Jimenez de Cisneros*, ed. by Antonio de la Torre y del Cerro (Madrid: Bailly-Bailliere, 1913).
Van Dijk, Stephen J. P., *The Ordinal of the Papal Court from Innocent III to Boniface VIII and Related Documents* (Freibourg, Switz.: University Press, 1975).
Van Dijk, Stephen J. P., *Sources of the Modern Roman Liturgy: the Ordinals by Haymo of Faversham and Related Documents*, 2 vols (Leiden: Brill, 1963).
Van Engen, John, trans., *Devotio Moderna: Basic Writings* (New York: Paulist Press, 1988).
Van Engen, John, 'Studying Scripture in the Early University' (unpublished essay).
Van Eys, W. J., *Bibliographie des Bibles et des Nouveaux Testaments en langue française* (Geneva: H. Kündig, 1901).
Van Kampen, Kimberly, 'The Bible in Print in England Before Tyndale', *Reformation*, vol. II, (1997).

Van Straalen, Samuel, *Catalogue of Hebrew Books in the British Museum, Acquired During the Years 1868-1892* (London: The British Museum, 1894).
Vaughan, Edward, *Ten Introductions: How to read, and in reading how to vnderstand; and in vnderstanding how to bear in mind all the bookes, chapters, and verses contained in the holie Bible* (London: Adam Islip, 1594).
von Hase, Oscar, *Die Koberger: Eine Darstellung des buchhändlerischen Geschäftsbetriebes in der Zeit des Überganges vom Mittelalter zur Neuzeit*, 3rd edn (Amsterdam: Gérard Th. van Heusden, & Wiesbaden: Breitkopf & Härtel, 1967).
Walsh, James E., *A Catalogue of the Fifteenth-Century Printed Books in the Harvard University Library*, 1 (Binghamton, New York: 1991).
Walther, Wilhelm, *Die deutsche Bibelübersetzung des Mittelalters* (Brunswick: 1889-92).
Warner, George F. & Julius P. Gilson, *Catalogue of Western Manuscripts in the Old Royal and King's Collections*, 4 vols (London: British Museum, 1921).
Warner, Sir George, *Descriptive Catalogue of the Library of C. W. Dyson Perrins* (London: Oxford University Press, 1920).
Watson, Nicholas, 'Censorship and Cultural Change in Late Medieval England: Vernacular Theology, the Oxford Translation Debate, and Arundel's Constitutions of 1409', *Speculum*, 70 (1995).
Watt, Tessa, *Cheap Print and Popular Piety, 1550-1640* (Cambridge: University Press, 1991).
Weil, Ernst, ed., *Ars memorativa: Aus der Offizin von Anton Sorg in Augsburg zirka 1490 [...] getreu dem Original neu gedruckt* (Augsburg: Dr B. Filser & Co., 1922).
Weiser, Artur, *The Old Testament: Its Formation and Development* (New York: Association Press, 1961).
Werner, Wilfried, ed., *Die Zehn Gebote – Beicht- und Sündenspiegel – Biblia pauperum – Totentanz – Symbolum apostolicum – Septimania poenalis – Planetenbuch – Fabel vom Kranken Löwen – Dekalog: Farbmikrofiche-Edition der Handschrift und der Blockbücher in dem Cod.Pal.Germ.438 der Universitätsbibliothek Heidelberg*, Monumenta xylographica et typographica 3 (Munich, 1994).
Williams, Daniel, ed., *England in the Fifteenth Century* (Woodbridge, Suffolk, & Wolfeboro, N.H.: Boydell Press, 1987).
Würthwein, Ernst, *The Text of the Old Testament: an Introduction to Kittel-Kahle's Biblia Hebraica* (Oxford: Blackwell, 1957).
Zafren, Herbert C., 'Bible Editions, Bible Study and the Early History of Hebrew Printing', in *Eretz-Israel: Archaeological, Historical and Geographical Studies* (Jerusalem: Israel Exploration Society, 1982).
Zestermann, August Christian Adolph, *Die Unabhängigkeit der deutschen Biblia pauperum von der lateinischen xylographischen Biblia pauperum* (Leipzig: T. O. Weigel, 1866).

# INDEX OF INCUNABLE EDITIONS CITED*

| SHORT TITLE | REFERENCE NO. | CONTRIBUTOR |
|---|---|---|
| Aesop: *Vita et Fabulae*, Pynson, *c.* 1497 | A-118 | Van Kampen |
| Aquinas: *Summa Theologica*, Mentelin, *c.* 1463 | T-208 | Saenger |
| Aquinas: *Summa Theologica*, Schoeffer, 1467 | T-209 | Saenger |
| Aristotle: *Ethica*, Higman & Hopyl, 1497 | A-991 | Bedouelle |
| Augustine: *Divi Augustina in Pauli Epistolas*, Gering & Remboldt, 1499 | A-1277 | Van Kampen |
| ben Ascher, Jacob, *Arba Trim*, Kuzi, 1475 | Heb-47 | Offenberg |
| ben Ascher, Jacob, *Arba Trim*, Nahmias, 1493 | Heb-49 | Offenberg |
| Augustine: *Regula*, Rood & Hunt, *c.* 1483 | (STC 922) | Van Kampen |
| Augustine: *Physics*, Higman, 1492 | F-12 | Bedouelle |
| Bernardus: *Meditations*, de Worde, *c.* 1499 | B-411 | Van Kampen |
| Bib. Lat., Gutenberg, *c.* 1454-5 | B-526 | Saenger<br>Needham |
| Bib. Lat., Gutenberg, *c.* 1458 | B-527 | Saenger<br>Needham |
| Bib. Lat., Fust & Schoeffer, 1462 | B-529 | Saenger<br>Needham |
| Bib. Lat., Eggestein, 1468 | B-531 | Saenger |
| Bib. Lat., Eggestein, *c.* 1468-70 | B-533 | Needham |
| Bib. Lat., Rusch, *c.* 1470 | B-534 | Froehlich |
| Bib. Lat., Sweynheym & Pannartz, 1471 | B-535 | Needham |
| Bib. Lat., Schoeffer, 1472 | B-536 | Needham |
| Bib. Lat., Richel, 1474 | B-537 | Needham |
| Bib. Lat., Richel, 1475 | B-540 | Saenger<br>Needham |
| Bib. Lat., Renner, Heilbronn & Frankfordia, 1475 | B-541 | Needham |
| Bib. Lat., Ferratis, 1475 | B-542 | Needham |
| Bib. Lat., Sensenschmidt & Frisner, 1475 | B-544 | Needham |

* This table also includes the majority of the early sixteenth-century editions cited as well as those blockbooks that have been assigned bibliographic reference numbers. All reference numbers are from Frederick R. Goff, *Incunabula in American Libraries*, Third Census, New York, Kraus International Publications, 1989, except where indicated by parentheses.

# *Index of Incunable Editions Cited*

| | | |
|---|---|---|
| Bib. Lat., Basilea, 1476 | B-549 | Needham |
| Bib. Lat., Gering, Crantz, & Friburger, *c.* 1477 | B-550 | Needham<br>Van Kampen |
| Bib. Lat., Koberger, 1477 | B-552 | Saenger |
| Bib. Lat., Richel, 1477 | B-553 | Saenger<br>Needham |
| Bib. Lat., Koberger, 1478 | B-557 | Saenger<br>Needham |
| Bib. Lat., Fernandez & Palmart, 1478 | B-622 | Abad |
| Bib. Lat., Amerbach, 1479 | B-561 | Saenger<br>Needham |
| Bib. Lat., Winter, 1479 | B-565 | Saenger |
| Bib. Lat., Zainer, 1480 | B-567 | Saenger<br>Needham |
| Bib. Lat., Herbort, 1481 | B-611 | Saenger |
| Bib. Lat., Reinhard & Philippi, 1482 | B-574 | Saenger |
| Bib. Lat., Herbort, 1483 | B-579 | Needham |
| Bib. Lat., Herbort, 1484 | B-580 | Saenger |
| Bib. Lat., Kessler, 1487 | B-585 | Saenger |
| Bib. Lat., Drach, 1489 | B-587 | Saenger |
| Bib. Lat., Froben, 1491 | B-592 | Saenger<br>Needham |
| Bib. Lat., Paganinis, 1492 | B-594 | Saenger<br>Needham |
| Bib. Lat., Froben, 1495 | B-598 | Saenger |
| Bib. Lat., Rusch, 1480 | B-607 | Needham<br>Froehlich<br>Gumbert |
| Bib. Lat., Paganinis, 1495 | B-608 | Needham<br>Froehlich<br>Gumbert |
| Bib. Lat., Froben & Petri, 1497 | B-609 | Saenger<br>Needham |
| Bib. Lat., Amerbach, 1497 | B-610 | Saenger |
| Bib. Lat., Colonia & Jenson, 1481 | B-611 | Needham |
| Bib. Lat., Renner, 1482-3 | B-612 | Saenger |
| Bib. Lat., Koberger, 1485 | B-613 | Gumbert |
| Bib., French, *La bible historiée*, Vérard, *c.* 1498 | B-623 | Van Kampen |
| Bib. Germ., Zainer, *c.* 1476 | B-627 | Saenger |
| Bib. Lat., Sensennschmidt & Frisner, 1476/8 | B-628 | Gumbert |
| Bib. Dutch, van der Meer & Yemantszoen, 1477 | B-648 | Van Kampen |
| Bib., French, *Cy commence la Table*, Le Roy, *c.* 1476 | B-651 | Van Kampen |

# *Index of Incunable Editions Cited*

# Index of Incunable Editions Cited

| | | |
|---|---|---|
| Hanapus: *Exempla*, Gering, 1478/9 | N-105 | Van Kampen |
| Hanapus: *Exempla*, St. Albans, 1481 | N-107 | Van Kampen |
| Jerome: *Epistolae*, Schoeffer, 1470 | H-165 | Saenger |
| Lombard: *Glossa Magistralis Psalterii*, Sensenschmidt and Frisner, 1478 | P-477 | Gumbert |
| Lombard: *Sententiarum*, Kessler, 1486 | P-490 | Saenger |
| de Lyra: *Postilla*, Gering, 1483 | N-123 | Van Kampen |
| de Lyra: *Postilla*, Sweynheym & Pannartz, 1472 | N-131 | Saenger |
| des Moulins: *Biblia Historiale* Buyer, *c.* 1478 | B-651 | Van Kampen |
| Mirk: *Liber Festivalis*, Caxton, 1483 | M-620 | Van Kampen |
| Mollenbecke: *Tabula Directoria*, Koelhof, *c.* 1480 | M-807 | Saenger |
| Nebiim Aharonim (Latter Prophets) Kimhi, Soncino, 1486 | Heb-24 | Offenberg |
| Nider: *Praeceptorium*, Sorg, 1475 | N-199 | Saenger |
| Primer in English, Grafton, 1545 | (STC 16040) | Sherman |
| Psalms (Tehillim), ben Solomon, Ashkenazi, 1487? | Heb-34 | Offenberg |
| Psalterium, Lat., Reyser, 1485 | P-1046 | Saenger |
| Psalterium, Lat., Koberger, 1494 | P-1050 | Saenger |
| Psalterium, Lat.-Fren., Le Rouge, *c.* 1492 | P-1064 | Van Kampen |
| Psalterium, Germ., Ariminensis, *c.* 1474 | P-1066 | Van Kampen |
| Psalterium, Germ., Brandis, 1475 | (Hain 13520) | Van Kampen |
| Psalterium, Germ., Knoblouch, *c.* 1477 | (Hain 13508) | Van Kampen |
| Psalterium, Germ., Zainer?, *c.* 1490 | (Hain 13513) | Van Kampen |
| Psalterium, Germ., Sorg, 1492 | P-1075 | Van Kampen |
| Psalterium, Germ., Dinckmut, 1492 | P-1076 | Van Kampen |
| Psalterium, Germ., Brandis?, 1493 | (Hain 13519) | Van Kampen |
| Psalterium, Lat.-Germ., Ratdolt, 1494 | P-1067 | Saenger<br>Van Kampen |
| Psalterium, Germ., Schönsberger, 1498 | (Hain 13518) | Van Kampen |
| Psalterium, Lat.-Germ, Ratdolt, 1499 | P-1068 | Van Kampen |
| Psalterium, Dutch, van der Meer, 1480 | P-1070 | Van Kampen |
| Psalterium, Fren., Huss & Siber, *c.* 1480 | P-1073 | Van Kampen |
| Psalterium, Germ., Eggestein, *c.* 1475 | P-1074 | Van Kampen |
| Psalterium, Low Germ., Brandis, 1475 | (Hain 13520) | Van Kampen |
| Psalterium, Low Germ., Brandis, 1493 | (Hain 13519) | Van Kampen |
| Psalterium, Germ., Drach, 1504 | (DM 4178) | Van Kampen |
| Psalterium, Germ., Knoblouch, 1508 | (DM 4186) | Van Kampen |
| Psalterium, Low Germ., Bungart, 1509 | (Adams L1252) | Van Kampen |
| Psalterium quincuplex, Estienne, 1509 | (Schreiber 8) | Saenger<br>Bedouelle |

# Index of Incunable Editions Cited

| Edition | Reference | Cited by |
|---|---|---|
| Psalterium quincuplex, Estienne, 1513 | (DM 6095) | Saenger |
| Psalterium, Lat., Bomberg, 1515 | (DM 6095 bis) | Saenger |
| Psalterium, Polyglot (Genoa), Porrus, 1516 | (DM 1411) | Bedouelle |
| Psalterium, Polyglot, Potkin, 1518 | (DM 1413) | Saenger |
| Rampegollis: *Compendium morale*, Monastery of SS. Ulrich & Afra, *c.* 1473 | R-22 | Saenger |
| Rashi, Salomon, *Perush ha-Torah*, Garton, 1475 | Heb-93 | Offenberg |
| Rashi, Salomon, *Perush ha-Torah*, Alkabiz, 1476 | Heb-94 | Offenberg |
| Terence: *Comoediae*, Machlinia, *c.* 1486 | T-111 | Van Kampen |
| Trithemius: *De scriptoribus ecclesiasticis*, Amerbach, 1494 | T-452 | Froehlich |
| Valentia (Thomas Waleys), *Expliciunt super psalterium*, Lettou & Wilcock, 1481 | (STC 19627) | Saenger<br>Van Kampen |
| Virgil: *Eneydos*, Caxton, 1490 | V-199 | Van Kampen |
| Voragine: *Golden Legend*, Caxton, 1483 | J-148 | Van Kampen |

# GENERAL INDEX

# General Index

# General Index